International Handbook of Contemporary Developments in Criminology

International Handbook of Contemporary Developments in Criminology

GENERAL ISSUES AND THE AMERICAS

Edited by ELMER H. JOHNSON

Greenwood Press
Westport, Connecticut • London, England

Library of Congress Cataloging in Publication Data
Main entry under title:

International handbook of contemporary developments in criminology.

Includes bibliographies and index.
Contents: V. 1. General Issues and the Americas—V. 2. Europe, Africa, the Middle East, and Asia.
1. Crime and criminals—Addresses, essays, lectures.
I. Johnson, Elmer Hubert.
HV6028.I53 364 83-1721
ISBN 0-313-21059-4 (set : lib. bdg.) AACR2

Library of Congress Catalog Card Number: 83-1721
ISBN: 0-313-23802-2 (Vol. 1)

First published in 1983

Greenwood Press
A division of Congressional Information Service, Inc.
88 Post Road West
Westport, Connecticut 06881

Printed in the United States of America

10 9 8 7 6 5 4 3 2 1

To Carol Holmes Johnson
My inspiration and partner
for more than four decades

CONTENTS

Figures ix

Tables xi

Preface xiii

Abbreviations xvii

Part I: General Issues

1. CRIMINOLOGY: ITS VARIETY AND PATTERNS THROUGHOUT THE WORLD 5
Elmer H. Johnson

2. INTERNATIONAL ORGANIZATIONS: AN INTRODUCTION 31
Paul Friday

3. INTERNATIONAL SOCIETY FOR CRIMINOLOGY 37
Jean Pinatel

4. THE UNITED NATIONS AND CRIMINOLOGY 63
Gerhard O.W. Mueller

5. CRIMINOLOGY IN DEVELOPING NATIONS—AFRICAN AND ASIAN EXAMPLES 83
William Clifford

6. AN INTERNATIONAL PERSPECTIVE ON WOMEN AND CRIMINOLOGY 99
Nanci Koser Wilson

7. RADICAL CRIMINOLOGY: A RECENT DEVELOPMENT 119
Robert Weiss

Part II: The Americas

8. ARGENTINA 151
Pedro R. David

9. BRAZIL 173
Ayush Morad Amar

10. CANADA 187
Jim Hackler

11. CHILE 209
Marco A. González-Berendique

12. COSTA RICA 233
Jorge A. Montero

13. MEXICO 251
Antonio Sanchez Galindo

14. UNITED STATES OF AMERICA 267
Robert F. Meier

Index 297

About the Contributors 315

FIGURES

4-1	THE WORLD CRIME PICTURE: PROPORTIONS OF TOTAL CRIME ACCORDING TO BROAD CRIME CATEGORIES	71
4-2	CRIME PICTURE FOR DEVELOPING COUNTRIES	71
4-3	CRIME PICTURE FOR DEVELOPED COUNTRIES	72
6-1	A SCHEME FOR UNDERSTANDING THE SOURCES OF INCREASE IN FEMALE CRIME RATES	109

TABLES

3-1	LEADERS OF THE INTERNATIONAL SOCIETY FOR CRIMINOLOGY, 1949-1978	39
3-2	INTERNATIONAL CONFERENCES OF THE INTERNATIONAL SOCIETY FOR CRIMINOLOGY, 1968-1976	46
3-3	RECIPIENTS OF THE DENIS CARROLL PRIZE AND TITLES OF WORKS	47
3-4	WORKS RECOMMENDED BY THE JURY FOR THE DENIS CARROLL PRIZE	47
4-1	MEMBERS OF THE COMMITTEE ON CRIME PREVENTION AND CONTROL	64
6-1	NATIONS WITH UPWARD TRENDS IN FEMALE CRIME ACCORDING TO THREE STUDIES	103
6-2	NATIONS WITH STABLE, DOWNWARD, OR ERRATIC TRENDS IN FEMALE CRIME, ACCORDING TO THREE STUDIES	104
12-1	REPORTED CRIMES IN COSTA RICA, 1974-1979	236
12-2	NUMBER OF CONVICTED PERSONS IN COSTA RICA BY YEAR AND TYPE OF COURT, 1977-1979	238
12-3	NUMBER OF PRISONERS IN COSTA RICA BY JURIDICAL STATUS, 1978-1980	239

PREFACE

Comparative criminology has been handicapped by the insularity of attitudes, sometimes described as ethnocentricity—the tendency to be convinced without careful consideration that the beliefs of one's own ethnic group are superior to those of other groups. "Insularity" conveys a number of interrelated ideas: the isolation of a people from a broader social universe that has crucial impact on their lives; the separation of peoples that denies them the benefits of the joint actions characteristic of social relationships distinctive to human beings; excessively limited perspectives in trying to explain common human experiences; and a provinciality of customs and opinions that ignores promising solutions to those problems encountered in all societies.

The decades since the second World War have been ushered in by a renewal of contacts between peoples which some have heralded as an opportunity to extend the recognition that all of us share the world. Secular "evangelicalism" sometimes seizes on this development to argue that increased contacts are sufficient to impart a "moral purity" to relationships among peoples, but this oversimplistic view ignores the persistence of self-interests that have led to exploitation of one people by another possessing superior power and the tendency of people to cling to ingrained customs. It is necessary to examine the nature of the new contacts and the forces that impel them before we can conclude that they will be of ultimate benefit to all peoples. We must be prepared to find that greater familiarity among peoples will be a mixed blessing.

The caution is supported by the consequences of massive social, economic, and political changes in the decades since World War II. These changes have had the negative effect of increasing the magnitude of the crime problem but have also lent impetus to the development of international criminology. Since crime and reactions to it are symptomatic of broader developments within a given social system, the macro-changes of those decades have underscored the validity of the principle that both crime and criminology are international phenomena.

The economic interdependence and degree of communication among the world's peoples have greatly eroded the insularity of nations and of communities within nations. Both long-established and emergent nations have undertaken programs of economic development that have released the effects of industrialization; some of these societies were previously largely agrarian. Societies with a long history of industrialization are experiencing in new forms increased population mobility, greater scale of social organizations, heightened influence of subcultural divisions within a society, further decline of the viability of informal control institutions, and politicization of social issues.

A noteworthy paradox is found in many nations. In the face of the remarkably great need for public order in highly complex societies, urbanites are less capable of sustaining the moral consensus that traditionally has been seen as the foundation of the social order. Legalization is the process by which selected cultural norms are translated into the abstract language of laws and are made subject to official enforcement. This process is unlikely to capture fully the nuance of those norms, making the administration of legal norms less effective and more visible than informal controls. Yet, the urban paradox, mentioned above, has accelerated the growth of professionalized and bureaucratized systems of criminal justice.

The new possibility of an enriched criminology rests to an important extent on reducing the insularity separating and isolating the criminologists of various nations from one another. With the macro-forces decreasing the insularity of nations, criminologists should be able to take advantage of joint transnational efforts to understand the criminal phenomenon that crosses political boundaries. The provinciality of accepted but unsubstantiated beliefs and excessively narrow explanations can be exposed when criminologists are given greater opportunities to become familiar with the relevant knowledge and research findings of their foreign colleagues.

On several sojourns my search for criminological insights has taken me abroad for intellectually enrichening experiences. Along with many criminologists here and abroad, I have become convinced that transnational investigations are especially promising for disabusing us of the consequences of insularity and giving researchers access to data controlling for different environments. The universality of scientific concepts can be tested to an unprecedented degree. The claims of comparative criminology, however, have been more an expression of hope for the future than a record of tangible and widespread accomplishments.

The years since World War II have underscored the interdependence of nations, the difficulties of socioeconomic development for well-established and emergent nations, and the spread of conditions that contribute to criminality. In upsetting traditional social and cultural systems, these major trends have generated increased crime and new crime patterns that extend beyond national boundaries. These international dimensions are further illustrated by certain patterns found around the world: the apparent rise of crime among females of urbanized-industrialized countries, the overrepresentation of minority and underprivileged persons, the unprecedented recognition of the implications of white-collar offenses, and the growing involvement of the young.

Those considerations motivated me to undertake preparation of the *International Handbook of Contemporary Developments in Criminology*. There is a unique need for a review of the various "criminologies-in-societies." We cannot speak of a single model of criminology because in each country the work, status, and subject matter of the criminologists are determined by the peculiarities of political-legal history, the impact of recent developments, and the general institutional system. Since the patterns of crime, the reactions to crime, and the nature of criminology are creatures of the varying macro-sociocultural systems of nations, it is essential that we expect criminology to occur in a range of models.

Unfortunately, it was not possible for me to visit a great number of nations to experience directly the ideas, work settings, and products of foreign colleagues. As an alternative to such direct experiences, insights may be provided by reports from experts from an array of countries. Readers from many nations would benefit from such a rough equivalent of a sample of the differing versions of criminology.

As for an international conference, there is a need for a scheme to coordinate the reports into a conceptual whole. To that end, each contributor was asked to focus on those elements that characterize criminology as an occupational system. The authors were asked to answer a number of general questions: What is criminology? How are specialists in criminology recruited and educated? How do criminologists see themselves within the division of labor among the disciplines—law, biology, and the social and behavioral sciences—that are relevant to criminology? What are the regularized channels of communication among those persons who see themselves as criminologists? Is criminological research carried out regularly? If so, within what organizational setting is it typically carried out? What are the general parameters of the social, cultural, economic, and political setting within which criminology emerged in your country and is now practiced? What are the dimensions and nature of crime as the subject of criminological study in your country?

The answers make each chapter unique; yet, what also emerges in this book is the awareness of certain similarities that have excited the curiosity of comparative criminologists. In those respects, we are obliged to the contributors who agreed to undertake the assignment and to complete the challenging tasks of preparing their chapters. As editor, I have served as intermediary in assembling a cohort of authors, providing a platform through which each author could present the particular "criminology-in-society" in its own terms. As an additional resource, the authors were asked to prepare representative bibliographies on the criminological literature of the respective nations. Almost all authors compiled bibliographies, many of them annotated.

The decades since World War II have been marked by transnational developments of particular significance for criminology. Part I of the *International Handbook of Contemporary Criminology: General Issues and the Americas* deals specifically with these trends in some of the developing nations, the feminist movement, and radical criminology. Also singled out for special attention are those international organizations devoted to criminological activities on an international plane, especially the United Nations and the International Society for Criminology. The chapters on the two Americas comprise Part II of the volume, although the varieties of "criminology-in-society" are not limited to a particular continent. The chapters on other nations are presented in the *International Handbook of Contemporary Criminology: Europe, Africa, the Middle East, and Asia.*

This handbook represents a major contribution to the literature. The dedicated efforts of the contributors support this claim in a fashion that frees me of the charge of excessive audacity. My primary obligation is to those authors. Scarcely secondary is my obligation to Greenwood Press for originating the idea for a book of this kind.

Many of my fellow criminologists provided an indispensable service in suggesting persons who would be appropriate contributors. The Center for the Study of Crime, Delinquency, and Corrections, Southern Illinois University at Carbondale, has made it possible for me to carry out the time-consuming tasks of editing. A great volume of correspondence and other detailed tasks were accomplished through the support of Jacqueline Goepfert, Sandra Martin, Mary Joiner, and Terry O'Boyle. Dr. Virgil L. Williams and Cyril Robinson served me well in specific professional ways. Marilyn Brownstein, Cynthia Harris, and Arlene Belzer, members of the Greenwood Press staff, generously contributed their respective specialized competencies.

ELMER H. JOHNSON

ABBREVIATIONS

ASC	American Society of Criminology
CORFO	Corporation for the Promotion of Production
FLACSO	Latin American School of Social Sciences
ILANUD	Latin American Institute of the United Nations for the Prevention of Crime and the Treatment of Offenders
ILPES	Instituto Latinamericano de Planificación Económics y Social
INTERPOL	International Criminal Police Organization
ISA	International Sociological Association
ISC	International Society for Criminology
NRC	National Redemption Council
ODEPLAN	Office of National Planning of the Presidency of the Republic
RCMP	Royal Canadian Mounted Police
SDCR	Social Demographic and Criminological Research
SSHRC	Social Service and Humanities Research Council
UNAFEI	United Nations Asia and Far East Institute
UNSDRI	United Nations Social Defense Research Institute
WHO	World Health Organization

I

GENERAL ISSUES

1

CRIMINOLOGY: ITS VARIETY AND PATTERNS THROUGHOUT THE WORLD

Elmer H. Johnson

Before railways were built, most of the young English aristocrats would complete their education by taking the "grand tour" through France, Switzerland, Italy, and Germany. They were supposed to expand their intellectual horizons and cultural appreciation by tracing the historical sources of ideas they had taken for granted and, perhaps, by learning that there were alternatives to their own values and behavior patterns. Collectively, the chapters of this handbook are intended to bring similar benefits to readers by presenting information and interpretations about criminology as it is seen and practiced in a variety of settings around the world.

VICARIOUS "GRAND TOUR" FOR CRIMINOLOGISTS

Inevitably, vicarious experience falls short of direct observation, especially since the readers cannot pose for the authors those questions that would tap issues of special concern to them. A standardized guidebook prepared by a local expert would suit most ordinary tourists, but the criminologist needs more incisive and specialized information. To increase the chances that the chapters collectively would serve this purpose, the authors were asked to organize their treatment of the criminology of their respective country around basic questions. What is criminology? What is the setting for the nation's criminology? What are the noteworthy patterns of crime? What are the characteristics of the nation's criminology as an occupation? How do criminologists associate with one another? How are criminologists recruited and educated? What are the level and direction of research?

Criminology itself is the focus of attention. It is assumed that there are similarities in how criminologists throughout the world perceive their work, in how they go about carrying out the work, and in their hopes of what this work will ultimately accomplish. Yet, there are also differences because criminology is marked by the qualities of the environment within which it operates. The search for these differences is as fascinating as the search for the similarities. In the course of tracing the effects of the similarities and differences in the various environments on the practice of criminology, we also gain insights into the phenomena that influence the differential definitions of crime from among the larger collection of deviant acts and that color the variations in societal responses to criminality.

If it is to exist and persist, criminology must have gained a place and function among the fields of knowledge. Again, the various settings must be taken into account because a particular history of ideas and their management must be considered. We will be concerned with how each nation allocates among the disciplines the functions of the pursuit and dissemination of knowledge. How does criminology as a field of study and as an occupation fit into the particular scheme?

The investigation of criminology in its transnational versions is particularly worthwhile at this time because the end of World War II was a major benchmark in the differing histories of nations. Recent decades have released remarkable changes in social, economic, and political sectors, and, because instability and perceptions of the "crime problem" go hand in hand, criminology is as much a creature of change as its subject matter. There is a logic in our request that the authors concentrate their attention on events since 1945 as an additional means of lending order to the volume as a whole.

Before undertaking the analysis of each of a series of countries, certain facets of the impact of change on the subject matter of criminology will be given special attention. The chapters that immediately follow will deal with the growth of international organizations as vehicles for the accelerated interest in transnational criminology, the expanded activities of the United Nations as an important aspect of that accelerated interest, the special implications of crime and criminology for so-called developing nations, the revised interpretation of crime among women, and the unprecedented level of recognition of the radical perspective.

These chapters highlight the dynamism of variegated criminology in a state of "becoming." Many chapters on developments around the world report opportunities not previously available to criminologists. Other contributors describe a history of frustrations, but, even then, hope is expressed for a better future that will release the potentialities they see in criminology.

CRIMINOLOGY AND THE COMPARATIVE PERSPECTIVE

Durkheim distinguished three applications of the comparative method: "They can include facts borrowed from either a single and unique society, from several societies of the same species, or from several distinct species."[1] The central mission of the *International Handbook of Contemporary Developments in Criminology* is to report on the nature of criminology in each of a sizable number of countries. In this respect, the work is a collection of "single and unique" societies that collectively constitute an inventory of the variations in the conceptions and work of criminologists around the globe. We, the authors, have not undertaken a genuine comparative analysis, but the inventory is a useful resource for such efforts. Some of the raw material is here to stimulate future studies of "several societies of the same species" or of societies "from several distinct species."

The handbook's rationale emphasizes that criminology operates within the contours of sociocultural and political systems varying among nations. This premise is consistent with comparative studies which also stem from the concurrent appearance of similarities and differences in institutionalized behaviors examined from the perspectives of law, sociology, anthropology, history, linguistics, and political science. As a field of study that has a debt to law and the social and behavioral sciences, criminology also has major reasons for undertaking comparative investigations. At the same time, it shares their necessity to overcome formidable obstacles in gaining the benefits of comparative studies, as we shall see.

Those debts are channeled largely through a special interest in social control which, broadly speaking, encompasses all the influences exerted on groups and their members so that all behaviors ideally fit into the general scheme—the social organization—that ideally produces the social order vital to the existence and continuance of society. The most obvious linkage for criminology is probably with the law; certainly, it is dominant in the criminology of most of the nations covered in this book. In countries that make this linkage, social control is seen as a collectivity of mechanisms for placing irresistible pressures on persons to do what their impulses would not instigate, especially when other forms of social control are weak or unavailable.

The law as a process of social control, Black says, may be considered in terms of prescription, mobilization, and disposition;[2] each of the three components is a worthy subject for comparative studies of interest to both criminology and the law. Prescriptions of law define its jurisdiction, the range of conduct subject to its control. Mobilization is the process by which a legal system acquires its cases; this process transforms prescription into reality, and the discrepancy between technical prescription of what the law *could* impose and what administration of justice actually carries out will vary among legal systems. Disposition refers to the official handling of cases, which may involve settlement of a dispute, routine application of a sanction, or dismissal. Here legal systems differ in the style of administration, the range of sanctions and tolerance in evaluating the social significance of the various forms of illegal conduct. Comparative investigations may assess the relative efficacy of various legal systems within the broad span of social control.

The span may also be defined more broadly than that indicated when social control is seen to be limited to the application of force from sources external to the individuals who are being pressed to avoid or abandon deviant behavior. In contrast to this emphasis on coercion as the principal mechanism, another view of social control takes us into the examination of the entire institutional structure and the socialization processes whereby social norms are incorporated into personalities. Conformity, as well as deviance, is subject to examination. Persuasion operates along with direct and indirect coercion. We become interested in the dependence of human beings on the cooperation of others in behavioral relationships that serve both private and social interests. Here also the interests of law and criminology converge, but sociology and psychology are brought more clearly into the picture.

The rationale of the *International Handbook on Contemporary Developments in Criminology* is especially attuned to the latter conception of social control as a bridge between criminology and other specialized fields of study. The chapters place the patterns of crime and reactions to crime within the context of macroanalysis. The history of the given nation's development and the impact of change on its society are central to the analyses of the concerns of criminologists.

THE BENEFITS AND DIFFICULTIES FOR CRIMINOLOGY

There has been a long-standing awareness among criminologists that comparative investigations offer impressive benefits. At the First International Congress on the Prevention of Crime and the Treatment at Geneva in 1955 it was recommended that:

> Comparative, coordinated and interdisciplinary research should be carried out to determine the relative effects of programs in different countries. . . (and) through cooperation between researchers from different countries. . . to develop a highly promising new field of comparative criminology (in order to determine) uniformities and differences in causal influences, in predictive factors, and in results of preventive and treatment programs (and to develop) a true science of criminology.[3]

A number of arguments can be advanced in favor of comparative criminology. Regardless of differences among the versions of criminology found around the world, criminologists share theoretical and practical interests and confront similarities among the patterns of crime and the responses to crime. Presumably, the scholars, researchers, and practitioners of one nation can gain a more reliable and more profound understanding of the issues that concern them by exchanging their experiences and findings with their counterparts in other nations. The accumulation of reliable knowledge can be accelerated by fuller communication and coordinated research at the transnational level. By testing their premises and theories in other sociocultural environments and political orders, criminologists can free themselves of parochial thinking that mistakes notions of cultural superiority for scientific truths.

Comparative studies, Bendix says, make important contributions to answering theoretical questions.[4] In dealing with the problematics of the human condition—for example, the "crime problem"—such studies highlight the contrasts between different human situations and social structures, but they also underscore the necessity to check generalized concepts against empirical evidence. Social and behavioral disciplines advance concepts as though they are universally applicable—examples for criminology are the criminal psychopath, white-collar crime, and gang subculture. Without transcultural comparisons, however, the formulation of concepts will lack necessary testing of their eligibility for being genuine generalizations. Because interrelationships among the parts of society have a space-and-time dimension in their effects on criminality, it is necessary to allow for variations in concepts compatible with differing social structures.

THE SETTINGS FOR INTERNATIONAL CRIMINOLOGY

In this respect, comparative criminology is an exercise in macro-analysis whereby the qualities of a given phenomenon or the purposes and meaning of a given activity are seen to be derived from the broad setting within which they are located. Whether we are concerned about the effects of physical stature (presumably a physiological attribute) on proneness to criminality, when we are concerned about similar effects of intellectual capacity (an attribute charged with "nature *and* nurture"), or when we are concerned about similar effects of subcultural values (an anthropological and sociological consideration)—in these examples of the interdisciplinary span of criminology, macro-analysis raises the level of investigation from a narrow concentration on the particular variables under study to examine the overall setting within which the variables have the hypothesized effects. By placing the investigation within the "big picture," comparative criminology would be in a better position to determine reliably, as Glueck argued, "uniformities and differences in causal influences, in predictive factors and in results of preventive and treatment programs."[5]

The emphasis on macro-analysis represents an effort to bridge two central tendencies that are inherent in the purposes and activities of science. As Mannheim points out, criminology is "both an *idiographic* discipline studying facts, causes and probabilities in individual cases and a *nomothetic* discipline aiming at the discovery of universally valid scientific laws and uniformities or trends."[6] As an idiographic discipline, criminology benefits from intimate interactions between theoreticians and practitioners in the collection of information and narrowing the chances of divergence between abstract conceptualizations and reality. As a nomothetic discipline, criminology converts the collection of facts into generalizations that advance ultimate understanding and free us of the impossible burden of dealing with the almost infinite number of individual events.

"Comparative sociological studies," Bendix says, "represent an attempt to develop concepts and generalizations at a level between what is true of all societies and what is true of one society at one point in time and space."[7] Comparative criminology encompasses perspectives in addition to that of sociology, but his point is relevant because comparative studies, regardless of the particular theoretical orientation, test the limits of principles assumed to be of universal validity. Since criminological phenomena are subject to cultural and structural variations, comparative criminology must seek generalizations that fall between universal propositions (applicable as stated to all situations, times, and places) and propositions that hold true under specified conditions (applicable only to specified situations, times, and places that exhibit those conditions). Unlike the universal effects of the laws of physics and chemistry, certain personality traits (for example, aggressiveness) or socioeconomic and political phenomena (such as modernization) demand research control of a host of other variables before valid testing of their relationship to criminality can become a product of nomothetic criminology. As Przeworski and Teune emphasize, the observations of social reality are relative to particular units.[8]

Crime is one of the classes of social deviance that go with changes in the qualities of the population, the workings of social institutions, the level of economic development, and the rate of urban growth. Because crime in some form is found whenever such changes are coupled with an established social organization that is regarded to be inconsistent with contemporary conditions, similarities exist in how various types of societies experience crime and go about attempting to cope with it. Yet, societies have their own history and characteristics that make for great risk of overgeneralizations when the differences among them are not given serious consideration.

Within a given sociocultural environment, a certain type or types may be noticeably more prevalent. The changes experienced by a society may have produced remarkable trends—either increases or decreases—in rates for particular offenses, and new kinds of crime may have surfaced. The serious methodological weaknesses of official statistics for transnational comparisons have been widely discussed. Inherent in these difficulties is the troublesome question of whether differential rates reflect variations in cultural norms, in the selection of legal norms from the body of cultural norms, in the intensity of law enforcement, or in the actual prevalence of particular forms of criminality.

Analysis of the macro-system of each of the compared societies is essential because the crime rate is affected by sociocultural factors underlying the style and intensity of societal reactions to crime.[9] These factors include cultural homogeneity, demographic variables, public attitudes toward the police and the judiciary, viability of family and neighborhood controls over conduct, degree of traditional emphasis on the duties of the group member as opposed to emphasis on individual rights and privileges, prevalence of the work ethic, and belief in either personalized or abstract justice.

Insufficient recognition of the unique features of each setting has been encouraged by the unexamined premise that the criminology of Western Europe—more recently, with the addition of the criminology of North America as a spinoff—defines *the* rationale and subject matter of international criminology. The premise is not limited to criminology but extends throughout the applications of science to world problems. In considering the complexities of international relationships for cross-cultural communication, Nieuwenhuijze reports a "fundamental confusion prevailing in respect to the real nature of the social units (called all too glibly, nations) which are parties to. . .situations of conflict." He asks: "Do we, notwithstanding all our well-meant attempts at relativization, not continue to assume that the Western pattern is the omnipresent model, at least so far as its fundamental traits are concerned?"[10] The tendency is found in the law, a sphere basic to transnational comparisons of criminological phenomena. David and Brierly report that a century ago the Roman tradition of law was in the preeminent position in international relations. "The English-speaking nations where jurists have been formed according to another tradition," they say, "no longer accept this pre-eminence; the countries of the socialist block reject it, and the 'non-aligned' nations are also demanding that their voices be heard."[11]

Comparative criminologists are prone to treat "modernization" as the major dimension of the events since World War II that have been associated with the rising crime rate in most countries. The term is employed to refer to a totality of social and political changes that go with urbanization, alteration of the occupational structure, social mobility, elaboration of educational institutions, development of representative government, and the emergence of the welfare state. Highly industrialized nations do share the structural features of newly emergent nations and the established countries now experiencing the impact of modernization. Yet, Moore cautions against the assumption of social system theorists that "traditional" forms of social organization will follow the precedent of the long-industrialized nations of Europe.[12]

HOW TO CATEGORIZE ELEMENTS IN ANALYSES?

The attraction of international criminology and the comparative methodology pivot to an important degree on the feasibility of categorizing the micro-elements in such a way that usually unsuspected patterns will emerge. By being made aware of similarities and dissimilarities between the criminology or criminality or control policies of our nation and those of another nation, you and I gain access to the rich benefits of comparative criminology. In the process of grouping the micro-elements, however, it is possible that we will overlook the cautions raised above for striking a balance between idiographic realities and the nomothetic mission of scientific analysis.

The term "transnational comparison" risks error in assuming that the "nation" is a reliable and valid element for comparisons on a worldwide scale. Events since World War II have created political boundaries that violate sociocultural identifications among peoples who historically have been drawn together. Even among nations that are considered well established, there are ethnic and cultural divisions that complicate the maintenance of national unity; recently emergent nations face perhaps even greater difficulties in balancing tribal and national interests.

Capture of the sociocultural and political differences among peoples is even less likely when continents are treated as distinct entities. The amount of materials necessitated the preparation of two volumes, one dealing with the "new world" of North and South America and the other presenting chapters on all the other nations. That arbitrary choice for organizing the material, however, does not imply that a continent is a satisfactory element for any typology of social systems for comparative analyses by criminologists. Since the chapters are presented in alphabetical order by name of the nation-state, the readers are free to group the chapters in a scheme appropriate to the particular purpose.

In correspondence, Gerhard O.W. Mueller has pointed out several classifications of nations employed by the United Nations.[13] First, he groups socioeconomic regions, each one of which is being administered by a "regional commission," as follows:

ECA: Economic Commission for Africa (Addis Ababa).

ECE: Economic Commission for Europe (Geneva), which includes Eastern and Western Europe.

ECLA: Economic Commission for Latin America (Santiago de Chile), which includes the English-speaking countries in the Caribbean.

ECWA: Economic Commission for Western Asia (Beirut, Lebanon).

ESCAP: Economic and Social Commission for Asia and the Pacific (Bangkok, Thailand).[14]

The second grouping of countries is in terms of political affinity, as follows: African countries, Asian countries, Eastern European countries, Latin American countries, Western European, and others (including Canada, the United States, Australia, and New Zealand); the Arab States are generally recognized as a separate entity.

The third grouping of countries is in terms of gross national product, per capita income, and related socioeconomic development factors, as follows:

Developed Countries: Regardless of political system, this category includes the United States, German Democratic Republic, Federal Republic of Germany, Federal Republic of Italy, the Netherlands, and so on.
Developing Countries: This category includes the large bulk of the "Third World" of Africa, Asia, and Latin America.
Least Developed Countries: Here are the countries entitled to special economic assistance, including such countries as Haiti, Nepal, Lesotho, and Swaziland.[15]

The fourth classification scheme groups countries in terms of their market economies, that is, free market economies ("Western" countries), centrally planned economies (socialist countries), and countries with mixed economies. There is a variety of other classification schemes for specific purposes, for example, land-locked countries, island countries, major versus lesser industrial countries, primary versus producing countries, and oil-producing countries.

WHY THE LAG IN COMPARATIVE RESEARCH?

Why has comparative criminology not become more prevalent as a vehicle for applying the principles and methods of science on an international scale? The issue is not that there have been no criminological studies that appear to qualify. Comparative research is not new to criminology; rather, it has been common in all periods. Szabo notes that generally most of the criminological works before 1920 were comparative treatises; "that is, they tried to explain criminality as a natural, universal phenomenon."[16] Actually, Swanson says, all research entails comparisons along a time sequence or among alternatives.[17] "All studies in some sense," Chang agrees, "are of comparative nature."[18]

Nevertheless, comparative criminology has not generated sufficient interest in activities outside the borders of one's own country. Criminologists of the West have been the most active, but too frequently they are only dimly aware that their choice of major issues and their premises are not necessarily relevant to areas outside of Western Europe and North America.

Early studies suffered from deficiencies that made anthropologists disillusioned with the comparative method, as applied in the nineteenth century. At that time, in reconstructing the record of the development of human institutions and societies through anthropology, it was considered valid to link together a series of isolated examples of any type of culture. Examples were taken from very diverse regions and periods of time without regard for the totality of the cultural system from which each was lifted. The selected elements were forced into a prearranged scheme derived from Charles Darwin's principles of evolution.[19]

The lessons for comparative criminology are that the comparative method places heavy demands on research methodology in data collection and analysis, that cultural and social variables must be taken into consideration in transnational comparisons, and that value judgments are endemic to preconceived notions that the course of criminological trends in "advanced" countries are the arbitrary and inevitable precedent for forecasting crime patterns and shaping the orientation of criminology in other countries. The clinical comparative research envisaged by Glueck apparently underestimated these lessons.

Several developments between the two world wars, Szabo believes, undermined the comparative criminology recommended by Glueck.[20] The rise of nationalist or socialist dogmas opposed the universalism and relativism of the comparative method. The commitment of American researchers to social reform and the evaluation of measures for the resocialization of criminals and for crime prevention diverted the resources necessary for comparative studies. The emergence of the interactionist (or labeling) perspective raised the important question of whether either the control institutions or the personal and structural factors were the source of increasing crime rates. Criminology itself became controversial, accused of serving the control institutions in violation of the canons of scientific objectivity.

Previous developments in other fields of comparative research lend support to the argument that increased sophistication and attainments in criminological research within a nation oppose the expansion of transnational criminology. Rokkan[21] notes that nineteenth-century pioneers in statistics, sociology, and anthropology endeavored to establish an internationally and interculturally valid body of knowledge, but they encountered difficulties in observing strict canons of evidence and inference for assuring analytic precision. To win recognition in the academies of their nation, they withdrew from cross-national generalizations in favor of more local inquiries where greater methodological rigor was possible.

CONTINGENCIES OF THE EMERGENCE OF A DISCIPLINE

By experiencing a range of societies in our travels about the globe, you and I can learn more about ourselves and our own people because questions are raised about the ideas and habitual behaviors that we tend to take for granted. We have described this volume as a vehicle for vicarious experiences of this sort for criminologists. As Etzioni and Dubow put it, comparative studies offer answers to such questions as: Who are we? Why are we the way we are? What else could we be?[22] Here the questions are directed toward establishing the identity of criminology. The authors present various models of criminology, differing in qualities but sharing the purpose of defining a field of specialized activities.

"What is the precise meaning of the various terms commonly used to denote scientific research collectivities and intellectual groupings, such terms as discipline, specialty, field, problem area and so on?" Woolgar asks.[23] Addressing scientific research only, he offers a description of such relatively small social groupings, providing a beginning point for our consideration of the field known as criminology.

The intensive investigation required of most scientists tends to make their research activities highly specialized, Woolgar says. Presumably, there are limited sources from which they can draw technical material. Researchers are most likely to communicate with those who are concerned with problems similar to their own. Communication is further constrained when costly components of the research apparatus impel work in close proximity. Then, a scientific collectivity, whatever the term applied to it, is a relatively intensive concentration of interest about a body of established knowledge and a shared set of common problems. There is a boundary that differentiates members from nonmembers and core members from marginal participants.

Certainly, crime attracted the attention of speculative thinkers long before Paul Topinard, a French anthropologist, was credited with coining the word "criminology."[24] However, the creation of a new discipline or specialty is a very different matter. The ideas necessary to create either have usually been available for some time, but only some of the ideas become the intellectual core that attracts disciples as the basis of a new intellectual identity and a new occupational role offering the promise of personal career rewards.[25] From this point, the new discipline is institutionalized through the regularization of relationships among the adherents; the development of a broad organization; the establishment of a communication network; the assured acquisition of resources, distinctive problems, and concerns; and a dependable flow of qualified recruits for continuity of membership.

CHARACTERISTICS OF CRIMINOLOGY AS AN OCCUPATION

We are interested in how criminology stands among the scientific and professional occupations in relative prestige, access to rewards, and gaining resources requisite to its particular activities. It is understandable, first, that any occupational group represents the collective self-interests of its members, and, second, that the boundaries that determine acceptance for membership are set in part to protect and allocate the economic and psychic rewards going with membership in a prestigious reference group. Nevertheless, its standing and functions among occupations ultimately rest on the significance of its unique activities to the macro-system of all occupations.

If criminological research is to be systematic and productive in the long run, there must be continuity in the recruiting, training, and specialized activities of those criminologists who dedicate themselves to this area of research. If there is to be a body of competent policymakers and practitioners, there must be similar continuity in qualifying them as professionals. In these respects, the development of an occupational system is requisite to a cohesive body of criminologists on the international plane.

The characteristics of a nation's criminological occupations tell us much about the position of criminology among the sciences and fields of public service. Is there such a division of labor among occupations that the "criminologist" is a distinct specialist and "criminology" is an autonomous discipline—at least a specialization—or professional field? Whether or not criminology is a discrete discipline, is the work of the criminologist clearly identifiable among the specialties that make up the occupational division of labor in the nation? Does criminological work alone generate a steady flow of income and other incentives for choosing this narrowly defined career? What is the social position of the criminologist within the relevant status-ranking system?

These questions imply that the nature and functions of criminology in any country are dependent on the sociocultural conditions that shaped the legal and educational institutions. As for all occupations, the emergence of criminology as a specialization implies that the economic development of the nation is sufficient to provide a demand for distinctive criminological services and to offer the resources necessary for performing these services. An interesting postulate is that the demand comes from the existence of a serious crime problem—at least a widespread perception of its existence—to induce the nation's decision-makers to seek the distinctive services. The existence of criminology as a distinct occupational field, the relative presence of criminologists, the autonomy or marginal status of criminology, and the institutional locale of the occupational activities—all of these—are symptoms of the host sociocultural and political systems and the nature of the economic development of the nation.

An occupation is any type of activity to which a number of persons give themselves regularly for pay. In the course of specialized training and continuous association, the occupational group develops a subculture of its own and a body of social relations peculiar to and common to its members. When recognized by the society and by themselves as specialists, the members develop their own cultural values. If an occupation repeats and somewhat standardizes its activities, certain attitudes toward recurrent occupational experiences grow out of the concentration on particular values and objects through channeling thinking and doing.

Whatever the conception of their collective nature, criminologists will form a cohesive occupational system to the extent that they share ideological perspectives, identify with one another, and define recurrent situations in a reasonably similar way. In other words, an occupational system functions as a set of reference groups that are relatively homogeneous in technical bases, functions, and jurisdictions over a specific area of work. The social psychological requisites for colleagueship must exist through bonds of reciprocal recognition of one another's right to membership in those occupational groups included under the term "criminologist."[26]

Referring to the hybrid quality of the collection of scholars grappling with the difficulties of formulating theories for criminology, Sellin says: "We are compelled to admit that 'criminology' as traditionally conceived is a bastard science grown out of public preoccupation with a social plague."[27] At the time of his statement, the developments since 1945 were largely in the future. This volume demonstrates that progress has been made, at least in some respects, in raising the worthiness of theoretical generalizations and in establishing a place for the criminologist. Yet, now as then, criminology is colored by the "public preoccupation with a social plague."

This basic linkage places criminology within the subject matter of social control. The significance of criminology among the sciences pivots on the particular conception of social control among the two general alternatives presented above. In its association with the "public preoccupation with a social plague," criminology differs from the natural and physical sciences in its more direct and visible involvement with social values inherent in social control. Even when striving to be *only* a nomothetic science, criminology has particular difficulties in reaching the value-free conclusions that are idealized as the goal of science. Recent decades have brought intensive skepticism whether or not any social and behavioral science—even the natural and physical sciences—is value-free and politically neutral to the degree suggested by the term "pure" science. Through its connection with social control, criminology is especially vulnerable to that critique, but nomothetic validity is more likely when social control is conceived as part of the basic processes whereby individuals become, and act as, members of a human community, rather than the limitation of social control to coercive actions directed against those deviants legally defined as criminals.

When seen as a nomothetic discipline, criminology is committed to the ideology of science which, Merton[28] was early in noting, enjoins its adherents to behave in keeping with certain norms in their work and relationships with one another. The norms are consistent with transnational effort. Under "universalism," it is assumed that natural phenomena are everywhere the same and independent of the characteristics of the individual scientist and his setting. "Communality" refers to the willingness of scientists to communicate findings freely as a contribution to the general advancement of knowledge. "Organized skepticism" entails critical scrutiny of every claim, including one's own, to maximize their validity. "Disinterestedness" refers to the granting of priority to the development of knowledge over receipt of wealth, influence, and fame.

Can there be an ideological connection between the theoretical and applied branches of criminology, and can practitioners be linked transnationally? The possibilities can be advanced through professionalism which also is altruistic. The professionals acquire a fund of theoretical knowledge through prolonged and intensive study. The body of theory prepares them to deal effectively with a range of concrete events and to hold authority over others on the basis of their possession of vital knowledge not universally available. Professional norms regulate behavior and monitor acceptance of neophytes. Training the professionals is a major means of their balancing conformity to organizational norms, obligations to clients, and initiative in decision-making. The professionals' independence of thought is a potential safeguard against ossification of procedures and a likely incentive to getting unfamiliar ideas accepted.

WHAT IS CRIMINOLOGY? INHERENT ISSUES

In the accounts that follow, the authors report differences among nations in the regularization of relationships among criminologists, in the nature and content of the respective communication networks, and in the level of development of an occupational system. Some countries grant steady income and other incentives that attract recruits to criminology as a distinct career field. Demand for services and allocation of resources make for an occupational system for criminologists as criminologists. "What is criminology?" is a meaningful question only when some institutionalization of the field has taken place. Otherwise, the question is largely rhetorical speculation.

The authors make a case for the postulate that we are dealing with *criminologies-in-societies*, rather than any uniform conception of criminology found in all settings. The versions differ in subject matter because of differences among societies in legal systems, selective reactions to various kinds of deviance, and the detailed functions assigned to criminal justice agencies. The favorite explanations for crime mirror an intellectual history that influences the relative emphasis on certain ideas presented by the biological, behavioral, and social sciences. Legal systems also differ according to the cultural histories and qualities of the social structure. The parameters of the given criminology-in-society affect the identity of the criminology among the academic disciplines and among the institutions of control.

The chapters of this book demonstrate the variety of answers given to the question "What is criminology?" as reflections of basic issues. Does "criminology" refer to exclusively research-oriented activities, or does it also include administrative and professional practice within the agencies of criminal justice? Is criminology an autonomous branch of learning or only a meeting place for criminological specialists drawn from various established disciplines? If the latter, what is the relative importance of law, biology and physical anthropology, and the several social and behavioral disciplines?

These issues involve us in considering the different courses that might be followed for the eventual institutionalization of an international criminology. Among the nations covered in this volume, differing points have been reached along the continuum from nonexistence to the creation of a well-established discipline or specialized field. No single course can be reliably predicted as *the* route for greater regulation of uniquely criminological activities.

EXCLUSIVELY RESEARCH OR PARTNERSHIP WITH PRACTICE?

The American Society of Criminology describes itself as consisting "of persons interested in the advancement of criminology, including scholarly, scientific and professional knowledge of the etiology, prevention, control, and treatment of crime and delinquency, the measurement and detection of crime, legislation, and practice of criminal law, the law enforcement, judicial and corrections system." The statement commits the society to a conception of criminology as a field including, as separate but interdependent branches, scientific study and criminological practice. Presumably, the scientific ethic for researchers and theoreticians would be matched for policymakers and practitioners by disinterested and competence-based professionalism cultivated by instruction in criminological practices. Approving the inclusion of "technological" aspects within the scope of criminology, Mannheim says:

> With the growing interest in more scientific methods now shown by many practical penologists it will often be difficult and invidious to distinguish between the scientific and the technological side of criminology, which latter stands much to gain from the closest contact with the practical application of criminal justice.[29]

The statement shows the utilitarian cast of criminology which has lent impetus to its institutionalization in some locales, especially in the United States, but has also aggravated conflict between applied and nomothetic missions. Utilitarian purposes are conveyed in ambitions to make legal institutions more "effective" and to reduce the frequency of certain types of crime. These purposes are accepted by even the theoreticians who undertake research useful to government agencies, prepare instruments that assist the administration of criminal justice, train personnel, and take a hand in framing public policy. Criminological institutes have been established and new ones are being created here and there, with the intention of fusing the potency of science and the advancement of practical goals.

In assessments of the prospects for institutionalizing criminology where it has not been established, one of the themes is that the broad problems and contingencies of socioeconomic development—especially for emergent nations and those whose history only recently produced a strong tendency toward modernization—provide a favorable context for criminology. The theme is expressed again and again in our volume and in the increasingly sophisticated literature of the sociology of science which specializes in investigating the emergence, diffusion, and patterns of scientific research. Predominantly concerned with developments in the physical and natural sciences, the literature presents at least three patterns relevant to the theme.[30]

First, in the years following World War II, the governments and larger industries of many countries recognized that it was important that science and its findings be utilized for their own purposes. Second, previously scientists had had to strive to convince policymakers of the usefulness of their activities. In the 1930s, the sociology of science was frequently devoted to demonstrating that the development of science had always been determined by the needs of the economy and that deliberate harnessing of science to welfare purposes was useful to science and society in general. Third, with the gaining of unprecedented support after World War II, and now in the position of being in a seller's market, the physical and natural scientists became inclined to resist the general optimism that science could solve any practical problem.

The literature of the sociology of science reflects a conviction that the work of scientists is determined largely by conditions internal to the scientific community, rather free of developments in the society at large: the "state of the art," availability of scientific work, organization of scientific work, and so on. Yet, the literature recognizes that the special features of different countries influence the quantity and diffusion of scientific output.

Extrapolating those patterns to the institutionalization of criminology, we might anticipate that, at least in the early phases of the process, academic criminologists would be eager for colleagueship with practitioners and for applied and policy research. Here is the opportunity, as already discussed, that professionalization of policymakers and practitioners would be an ideological connection with the scientific ethic. However, once the acquisition of resources is regular and assured and the criminologist has a secure and reputable status within the academic and scientific communities, the science-oriented criminologists are persuaded that conditions internal to nomothetic criminology essentially determine their work activities and career contingencies. The linkages with practitioners begin to be seen as problematic, and applied research is fraught with the possibility of undermining criminology as a science.[31]

Addressing the natural sciences primarily, Storer[32] contends that applied research tends to be more oriented directly or indirectly to solving "real" problems which, he believes, are usually localized in space and time and are identified by criteria varying from one culture to another. He argues that the concern for immediate issues undermines the potentiality for building a cumulative generalized body of knowledge, and there is a considerably smaller scientific audience for achievements in applied research. The applied researcher depends on nonscientists for research, and the norms of the scientific community are less operative.

If the constraints on scientific criminology were essentially internal to the scientific community, we could argue, as Storer does for the natural sciences, that nomothetic investigation is more likely to transcend national boundaries. The argument has merit because the ideology of nomothetic science is consistent with the free flow of information in the spirit of communality. Nevertheless, the argument exaggerates the insulation of scientists—even those in the physical and natural sciences—from the effects of public policy on the setting of goals and allocation of resources. The premise that basic science is determined largely by its internal environment is a form of technological determinism that overlooks the effects of a wide spectrum of cultural and structural factors shaping the appearance and acceptance of innovation.

The distinctions between "pure" and applied research and between scientific and professional ideologies have been exaggerated. Recent decades have brought into question the claims that "pure" scientists are absolutely value-free and uniquely selfless in abstaining from seeking personal career rewards.[33] The literature on communication patterns among scientists does not bear out the popular image of equal and full participation by all persons eligible to be members of the scientific community. Instead of intensive and extensive ties among all adherents of a discipline, there are a number of relatively small groups of specialists within the field who have difficulties in gaining access to a far-flung audience even among their potential colleagues.[34]

There is another reason to doubt that nomothetic criminology alone is the route for developing a transnational criminology; that is, theoretical criminology has yet to reach the stature of a science that has achieved basic agreement on the essential concepts and postulates. Even in those nations where criminology has progressed far along the route to institutionalization, there is not a cohesive body of theory achieving the level of abstraction, inclusiveness, and sophistication sufficient for translation into a transnational criminology. Theoretical orientations are still too narrow in scope to go beyond capturing the variables of criminal behavior in a particular culture in a particular way.[35] In addition to the absence of any universal explanations for criminality, nomothetic criminology lacks, Friday says, the capacity to export theoretical formulations applicable to the sociocultural characteristics of other societies and tends to reflect the political considerations or personal and societal rationalizations for crime instead of presenting concrete sociological principles. He explains:

> For example, criminality is frequently associated with broken homes or physical conditions in England; to the Swede, alcohol becomes the principal culprit, and in the Soviet Union, mental aberrations dominate as explanations. The result has been that by proceeding from a set premise regarding the etiology of deviant behavior, the conclusions that logically follow may not serve as a scientific interpretation on a universal basis.[36]

AUTONOMY VERSUS MEETING PLACE FOR SPECIALISTS

My collaborators would prefer to accept Wolfgang's definition of the criminologist as: "One whose professional training, occupational role and fiduciary reward are concentrated toward a scientific approach, study and analysis of the phenomena of crime and criminal behavior."[37] Up to this point, his definition is broad enough to include professionals in criminology-related occupations outside the spheres of academia and criminological research. Many authors would include this personnel within their definition of the criminologist. I have indicated that it would be at least premature to exclude those groups from the process of institutionalizing a transnational criminology.

This interpretation is not that of Wolfgang because he moves on to exclude any persons not engaged directly in criminological research. More crucial to this section of my chapter, he calls for a criminology that is an independent discipline:

> We are contending that criminology should be considered as an autonomous, separate discipline of knowledge because it has accumulated its own set of organized data and theoretical conceptualizations that use the scientific method, approach to understanding, and attitude in research. . . . Such a position does not negate the mutual interdependence existing in the contributions to this discipline by a variety of other field specializations.[38]

As we have seen, whether it is a "discipline" or a "specialization," a collectivity of scientists is a reference group bound by common intellectual orientation, by specialization in similar problems, and by a communication network. We should anticipate that such collectivities should aspire to the identity of an independent discipline. Gerontology is a recent illustration of the aspiration. Established disciplines of today—sociology, for example—have such a history. Wolfgang properly notes one of the possible models for a criminology of the future. Many criminologists, including some of the authors of this work, share his view. Furthermore, he is correct that mutual interdependence with other disciplines does not rule out the existence of an independent discipline.

Nevertheless, criminology as a science has yet to accumulate "its own set of organized data and theoretical conceptualizations." Even among those nations with sophisticated activities in criminology, the elements of an autonomous discipline are not present sufficiently to go beyond expressing a hope for the future. The evidence is even stronger when we consider the prospects for a transnational criminology, the issue that is of concern here. Although our chapters document similarities among approaches followed in various nations, international criminology continues to depend on an aggregate of disciplines as it did when Sellin declared:

> The advancement of our knowledge does *not* depend on "criminologists," a title about as meaningful as that of doctor of science or doctor of philosophy, but on sociologists, psychiatrists, psychologists, etc.—"criminologists" by courtesy and, in one sense at least, kings without a country. The advancement of knowledge *does* depend on the degree to which these categories of scientists can formulate and plan more carefully the research projects they undertake; perfect their techniques of investigation and of analysis; and evolve meaningful bodies of theory. If *one* etiological science should ever be possible it will emerge in due time.[39]

His assessment continues to hold today. Internationally, criminology is found within a multiplicity of academic structures and is subject to the conflicting claims of biology (linked with physical anthropology), law, psychology, psychiatry, and sociology. The various definitions of criminology in this book indicate that criminology in most countries is identified more with the law than with any other specific field. Sociology is influential in the United States,[40] Canada, Scandinavia, and Great Britain, but here, too, law is important. Since 1945, the sociological perspective has gained adherents elsewhere, but its utilization is not limited to sociologists.

PROSPECTS FOR INSTITUTIONALIZED INTERACTION

Whether we are considering the prospects for institutionalizing criminology in nations where it has not been firmly established or whether we are considering the prospects for an international criminology, this chapter proposes the concept of an occupational system as a means of framing reliable assessments. The contributors were asked to organize the analyses on the basis of questions derived from that concept.

Glueck has argued, as we have seen, that comparative studies are the means of developing a true science of criminology. Since comparative studies raise serious methodological issues, the existence of a substantial number of sound comparative studies would demonstrate that the principles and methods of science are being utilized internationally in an effective way. Which comes first: sound comparative studies or the "true science of criminology"? Both depend on regularizing the conditions identified in this chapter with the concept of an occupational system for criminology.

One element of an occupational system is a continued and dependable flow of qualified recruits for continuity of membership. The prospects for viable transnational relationships rest on the availability of criminologists capable of and competent to overcome the basic dissimilarities among their respective settings and to take advantage of the similarities that make transnational collaboration mutually meaningful. Without generation of vital resources for research, especially of researchers capable of managing the peculiar problems of comparative analysis, transnational research will not occupy a significant place on the criminological scene.[41]

From what sources do the nation's criminologists come—the law, the social or behavioral sciences, criminology as a specialized occupation, or areas of practical experience? Second is the matter of how the recruits are made more competent. Radzinowicz notes that criminology is taught in various settings.[42] In some countries, criminology is studied in schools of law and is ignored by the faculties of sociology and the social sciences. The reverse is found in some other countries. In another pattern, criminology is included in training courses for personnel who deal directly with offenders. Therefore, the contributors to this handbook were asked to describe the qualities of the persons most likely to become criminologists and to describe how they are educated. Has the nation developed a system for recruiting and training criminologists? If so, is the system institutionalized within the structure of higher education? What are the curricular scheme, organizational structure, and preferences among fields of knowledge? Have criminologists been educated predominantly in foreign universities? If criminologists are trained otherwise—for example, in academies operated by justice agencies—what are the premises and organizations of these training programs?

Criminology is an occupational entity to the degree that specialists identify with one another, are bound to the occupation by career rewards, and enjoy regularized communication as colleagues. "Regularized communication" may be achieved through membership in professional organizations, sharing information on research and other activities, and such short-term devices as specialized seminars. For a given country, are there professional organizations composed of criminologists alone, or do criminologists associate systematically in the course of membership in more generalized organizations? Do institutions of higher education provide seminars and similar settings for interaction? Do patterns of interaction, primarily or secondarily, cross national boundaries?

Transnational criminology is most dependent on free and extensive communication across political boundaries. The media for such communications vary in quality among nations. The sophistication of theories and incisiveness of analysis in books and articles may fall short of the quality justifying communication, and the valid conclusions may be of limited applicability. The need to be competent in foreign languages is a serious barrier; even bilingual competence does not necessarily indicate understanding of foreign concepts and settings. The volume of a worldwide literature—if it is made known and is accessible—poses a problem in itself. As Sellin has noted, the scholar is often compelled to rely on what is published in his own language, encouraging an insular viewpoint.[43]

When conceived as a scientific endeavor, criminology is identified with persistent inquiry and systematic development of theory. When so conceived, criminology is faced with the necessity to overcome serious problems stemming from the elusiveness of its subject matter, the difficulties of carrying out multidisciplinary research, the diversity of methodologies employed, and controversies over the relative merits of pure and applied research. Even under the most favorable circumstances, criminological research is able to marshal resources in skill, finances, and techniques only at a level falling short of the needs for dealing with all worthy questions.

The contributors were asked: Is criminological research—broadly defined—being conducted in your nation? If so, where is the research being conducted—in universities, private institutes, government agencies, and so on? Who are the most prominent theorists and researchers? What is its direction in terms of theoretical orientation and typical problems addressed? What are the level and sources of funding and analytic skills available? What are the variety and quality of available data?

Now that we have considered the orientation of the *International Handbook on Contemporary Developments in Criminology*, we turn to the answers framed by the contributors who are the central figures in the examination of the criminologies-in-societies. The "grand tour" of perspectives and settings around the world now begins.

NOTES

1. Emile Durkheim, *The Rules of Sociological Method* (New York: Free Press, 1938), p. 136.
2. Donald Black, "The Social Organization of Arrest," *Stanford Law Review* 23 (June 1971):1104, 1110.
3. Sheldon Glueck, "Wanted: A Comparative Criminology," in Sheldon and Eleanor Glueck, *Ventures in Criminology: Selected Recent Papers* (Cambridge, Mass.: Harvard University Press, 1964), p. 304.
4. Reinhard Bendix, "Concepts and Generalizations in Comparative Sociological Studies," *American Sociological Review* 28 (August 1963):535-538.
5. Glueck, "Wanted: A Comparative Criminology," p. 304.
6. Hermann Mannheim, *Comparative Criminology* (Boston: Houghton Mifflin Co., 1965), pp. 12-13.
7. Bendix, "Concepts and Generalizations in Comparative Sociological Studies," p. 532.
8. Adam Przeworski and Henry Teune, *The Logic of Comparative Social Inquiry* (New York: Wiley-Interscience, 1970), pp. 8-11.
9. An illustration of attempts to deal with macro-system variables is Sebastian Scheerer,

"The New Dutch and German Drug Laws: Social and Political Conditions for Criminalization and Decriminalization," *Law and Society Review* 12 (Summer 1978):585-606.

10. C.A.O. Van Nieuwenhuijze, *Cross-Cultural Studies* (The Hague: Mouton and Co., 1963), p. 74.

11. Reńe David and John E. C. Brierly, *Major Legal Systems in the World Today* (New York: Free Press, 1968), p. 7.

12. Wilbert E. Moore, *Order and Change: Essays in Comparative Sociology* (New York: John Wiley and Sons, 1967), pp. 21-26.

13. I gratefully acknowledge the cautions raised by Gerhard O.W.Mueller and supplemented by other authors. Furthermore, he suggested reference to the various classifications employed by the United Nations.

14. From *Concise Report in Monitoring of Population Policies*, E/CN.9/338 (New York: United Nations Economic and Social Council, December 22, 1978), Annex II, p. 1.

15. The source of the first three categories is International Monetary Fund, *International Financial Statistics*, various issues.

16. Denis Szabo, "Comparative Criminology," *Journal of Criminal Law and Criminology* 66 (September 1975):336.

17. Guy E. Swanson, "Frameworks for Comparative Research: Structural Anthropology and the Theory of Action, " in Ivan Valier (ed.), *Comparative Methods in Sociology* (Berkeley, Calif.: University of California Press, 1971), pp. 141-144.

18. Dae H. Chang, *Criminology: A Cross-Cultural Perspective*, Vol. 1 (New Delhi: Vikas Publishing House, 1976), p. 8.

19. See Erwin H. Akerknecht, "On the Comparative Method in Anthropology," in Robert F. Spencer (ed.), *Method and Perspective in Anthropology* (Minneapolis, Minn.: University of Minnesota Press, 1954), pp. 117-125.

20. Szabo, "Comparative Criminology," p. 336.

21. Stein Rokkan, "Comparative Cross-National Research: The Context of Current Efforts," in Richard L. Merritt and Stein Rokkan (eds.), *Comparing Nations: The Use of Quantitative Data in Cross National Research* (New Haven, Conn.: Yale University Press, 1966), pp. 3-4.

22. Amitai Etzioni and Fredrick L. Dubow, *Comparative Perspectives: Theories and Methods* (Boston: Little, Brown and Co., 1970), pp. 1-2.

23. S. W. Woolgar, "The Identification and Definition of Scientific Collectivities," in Gerald Lemaine, Roy MacLeon, Michael Mulkay, and Peter Weingart (eds.), *Perspectives on the Emergence of Scientific Disciplines* (The Hague: Mouton, 1976), pp. 233-234; also see David E. Chubin, "The Conceptualization of Scientific Specialties," *Sociological Quarterly* 17 (Autumn 1976):448-476.

24. William A. Bonger, *An Introduction to Criminology*, trans. Emil Van Loo (London: Methuen & Co., 1936), p. 1.

25. Joseph Ben-David and Randall Collins, "Social Factors in the Origin of a New Science: The Case of Psychology," *American Sociological Review* 31 (August 1966): 452.

26. For a more detailed discussion of the implications of these criteria for policymakers and practitioners in criminal justice administration, see Elmer H. Johnson, "Occupational System of Criminology: Its Environment and Problems," *International Annals of Criminology*, Année 1965, no. 1 (1965):77-87.

27. Thorsten Sellin, *Cultural Conflict and Crime* (New York: Social Science Research Council, 1938), pp. 3-4.

28. Robert K. Merton, "Science and Democratic Social Structure," in his *Social Theory and Social Structure*, rev. ed. (New York: Free Press, 1957), pp. 550-561.

29. Mannheim, *Comparative Criminology*, p. 20.

30. The description of the three patterns was taken from Joseph Ben-David, "Introduction," *International Social Science Journal* 2, no. 1 (1970):11-13. His paper introduces a number of articles on the sociology of science.

31. See Edward Sagarin, "The Egghead, the Flatfoot, and the Screw: Some Reflections on the Future of the American Society of Criminology," *Criminology* 18 (November 1980):291-301.

32. Norman W. Storer, "The Internationality of Science and the Nationality of Scientists," *International Social Science Journal* 22, no. 1 (1970):89-90.

33. In the 1960s, the social sciences came under sharp attack in the United States from several constituencies for claiming value-free objectivity, cool neutrality in interest-group conflicts, and the existence of a normative consensus in support of established institutions. In this regard, criminology was a particular target. See Gresham Sykes, "The Rise of Critical Criminology," *Journal of Criminal Law and Criminology* 65 (June 1974): 206-213.

34. The literature on communication among scientists is summarized by Diana Crane, "The Nature of Scientific Communication and Influence," *International Social Science Journal* 22, no. 1 (1970):28-41.

35. Richard R. Bennett, "Constructing Cross-Cultural Theories in Criminology: Application of the Generative Approach," *Criminology* 18 (August 1980):253.

36. Paul C. Friday, "Problems in Comparative Criminology: Comments on the Feasibility and Implications of Research," *International Journal of Criminology and Penology* 1 (May 1973):152.

37. Marvin E. Wolfgang, "Criminology and the Criminologist," *Journal of Criminal Law, Criminology and Police Science* 54 (June 1963):160.

38. Ibid., p. 156.

39. Thorsten Sellin, "The Sociological Study of Criminality," *Journal of Criminal Law and Criminology* 41 (November-December 1950):411.

40. The history of American criminology is intimately related to the struggles of sociology in earlier decades to establish a distinct identity among the social sciences. See Stanton Wheeler, "The Social Sources of Criminology," *Sociological Inquiry* 32 (Spring 1962):139-159; Walter C. Reckless, "American Criminology," *Criminology* 8 (May 1970):4-20; Richard Quinney, *The Problem of Crime* (New York: Dodd, Mead and Co., 1970), pp. 43-100; Gilbert Geis (ed.), *White-Collar Criminal* (New York: Atherton Press, 1968), pp. 1-6; C. Wright Mills, "The Professional Ideology of Social Pathologists," in Mark Lefton, James K. Skipper, Jr., and Charles H. McCaghy (eds.), *Approaches to Deviance* (New York: Appleton-Century-Crofts, 1968), pp. 3-23.

41. Elmer H. Johnson, "Institutionalization of Criminology: A Prerequisite to Comparative Criminology," *International Journal of Comparative and Applied Criminal Justice* 3 (Spring 1979):27-33.

42. Leon Radzinowicz, *In Search of Criminology* (Cambridge, Mass.: Harvard University Press, 1962), p. 177.

43. Sellin, "The Sociological Study of Criminality," p. 406.

BIBLIOGRAPHY

Aubert, Vilhelm. "Researches in the Sociology of Law." In Michael Barkum (ed.). *Law and the Social System*. New York: Lieber-Atherton, 1973. Pp. 50-53.

Aubert distinguishes legal from scientific thinking in several respects. The law is more inclined to the particular than the general and does not seek to establish dramatic connections between means and ends. Truth for the law is normative and nonprobablistic. The legal system sees its responsibilities lying in the past and present, rarely in the future. The formal validity of legal consequences does not inevitably depend upon compliance. A legal decision is an all-or-nothing proposition.

DeVos, George, and Keiichi Mizushima. "Organization and Social Function of Japanese Gangs: Historical Development and Modern Parallels." In R. P. Dore (ed.). *Aspects of Social Change in Modern Japan*. Princeton, N.J.: Princeton University Press, 1967. Pp. 289-325.

As an illustration of the key importance of history and the sociocultural variables to comparative criminology, this paper argues that the nature of criminal groups reflects the social conflicts characteristic of the given society at the time. Professional criminal groups have existed in Japan since the Tokugawa period (1603-1868) when the samurai were often unemployed as protectors of feudal lords. Earlier and contemporary forms of gangs are compared to support the argument.

Hall, Jerome. *Comparative Law and Social Theory*. Baton Rouge, La.: Louisiana State University Press, 1963.

The author summarizes his principal thesis: Comparative law is a composite of social knowledge of positive law, distinguished by the fact that, in its general aspect, it is intermediate between the knowledge of particular laws and legal institutions on the one side and the universal knowledge of them at the other extreme.

Hughes, H. Stuart. *Consciousness and Society: The Reorientation of European Social Thought 1890-1930*. New York: Alfred A. Knopf, 1961.

This survey of the transformation of social thought that shaped the twentieth-century mind includes the revolt against positivism, the critique of Marxism, neo-idealism in history, and the intellectual ferment of the 1920s. As such, the essay provides background for understanding the dramatic changes in criminological thought after 1945 as the surfacing of ideas long developed in societies, rather than representing a sharp break with the past.

Marsh, Robert M. *Comparative Sociology: A Codification of Cross-Societal Analysis*. New York: Harcourt, Brace and World, 1967.

This macro-analytic method would systematize comparative sociology in terms of "societal differentiation" as a state and a process. As a *state*, the term refers to the number of structurally distinct and functionally specialized units in a society. As a *process*, the term is defined as the emergence of more distinct organs to fulfill more distinct functions. The history of comparative sociology, selected studies in several subject matter areas, and methodological problems are reviewed.

Meadows, A. J. *Communication in Science*. London: Butterworths, 1974.
Concentrating on the natural and physical sciences, Meadows documents the notion that rapid and accurate communication is a fundamental requirement of modern science. He assesses the urge to publish, the role of the journal, the acquisition and use of scientific information by researchers, and the diffusion of scientific information.

Merkel, Peter H. *Modern Comparative Politics*. New York: Holt, Rinehart and Winston, 1970.
The political system in an international context is treated—after an analysis of political parties, interest groups and their cleavages, policymaking structures and institutions, the policymaking process, and the judicial process within legal systems.

Merritt, Richard L., and Stein Rokkan. *Comparing Nations: The Use of Quantitative Data in Cross-National Research*. New Haven, Conn.: Yale University Press, 1966.
The papers from an international conference deal with the theoretical context, the availability and quality of national data, methodological and analytical problems, and various concrete actions for implementing data programs for cross-national research.

Newman, Graeme. *Comparative Deviance: Perception and Law in Six Cultures*. New York: Elsevier, 1976.
Using data from India, Indonesia, Iran, Italy (Sardinia), the United States, and Yugoslavia, Newman addresses the relationship between the law and public perceptions of deviance, the possibility of universal values concerning deviance and crime, the organization and structure of public perceptions of deviance, and the relationship between modernization, social change, and perceptions of deviance. He concludes that there is universal agreement concerning the disapproval of a variety of behaviors but considerable cross-cultural variation concerning the appropriateness of the kinds of social controls. He finds that developed and democratic countries have less severe legal sanctions than the public desires; the opposite relationship stands for underdeveloped and more totalitarian countries.

Ormrod, Roger. "The Developing Relations Between the Law and the Social Sciences." *British Journal of Criminology* 4 (April 1964):320-332.
Successful cooperation between these two dissimilar fields depends upon a number of factors: (1) Each must understand the attitudes of the other to common problems. (2) Each must accept the role and frame of reference of the other. (3) A common vocabulary must permit exchange of ideas. (4) Exchange of information, short of acquisition of detailed technical skill in the other specialty, must be sufficient for a common pool of knowledge.

Parsons, Talcott. *Societies: Evolutionary and Comparative Perspectives*. Englewood Cliffs, N.J.: Prentice-Hall, 1966.
From his earlier analytical models of systems and functional problems, Parsons moves to a general evolutionary theory of social change. Four major types are presented: primitive, archaic, historic intermediate empires, and seedbed societies. Particular societies are examined according to the types that are related to structural complexity and overall adaptive capacities.

Radzinowicz, Leon, and Joan King. *The Growth of Crime: The International Experience.* New York: Basic Books, 1977.

In a popular and panoramic treatment, the following topics are broadly sketched: the "relentless upsurge in crime," the "expanding dark figure of crime," ideological perspectives, theoretical approaches, and patterns in various reactions to crime.

Roberts, C. Clifton. *Tangled Justice: Some Reasons for a Change of Policy in Africa.* New York: Negro Universities Press, 1969. Reprint of 1937 edition published by Macmillan and Company, London.

Retired in 1930 from service in the British colonial administration including duties as a judge, Roberts wrote this book in 1935 before the political independence of colonies was a definite prospect. The book illustrates that the barristers of that day were aware of the need for "a judicial system fitted to the mentality and customs of natives" and for major penal reform.

Robertson, Roland, and Laurie Taylor. "Problems in the Comparative Analysis of Deviance: A Survey and a Proposal." In Paul Rock and Mary McIntosh (eds.). *Deviance and Social Control.* London: Tavistock Publications, 1974. Pp. 91-123.

According to the authors, comparative sociologists have not typically been concerned with the comparative analysis of deviance including crime. After presenting specific criticisms, they argue that consideration of cultural and social variables is vital to going beyond ideographic descriptions. They recommend attention to the relationships between the controlled (the deviants) and the controllers (those who sanction).

Robinson, Ronald W. "A Model System for World Crime Statistics." *International Journal of Comparative and Applied Criminal Justice* 2 (Spring-Summer 1978): 61-69.

To circumvent the inadequacies of official statistics for transnational comparisons, Robinson proposes comparisons of major urban centers, substituting behavioral variables for legal definition of crimes, and concentration on *mala in se* offenses.

Roth, Guenther. "Max Weber's Comparative Approach and Historical Typology." In Ivan Vallier (ed.). *Comparative Methods in Sociology: Essays on Trends and Applications.* Berkeley, Calif.: University of California Press, 1971. Pp. 75-93.

Roth assesses Max Weber's use of comparison of models to develop concepts, use of cases within the range of a model, and use of batteries of models to deal with a given case. Weber's critique of evolutionism and the genesis of his typological approach are reviewed.

Roy, Prodipto, and Frederick C. Fliegel. "The Conduct of Collaborative Research in Developing Nations: The Insiders and the Outsiders." *International Social Science Journal* 22, no.3 (1970):505-523.

The practical aspects of conducting social science research in developing countries are discussed: how to obtain sponsorship, selection of professional and supporting staff, seeking and obtaining a suitable base of operation in the host country, and what may be the intellectual products.

Skolnick, Jerome H. "Perspectives on Law and Order." In Sawyer, F. Sylvester, Jr., and Edward Sagarin (eds.). *Politics and Crime*. New York: Praeger Publishers, 1974. Pp. 6-16.
In this illustration of the importance of cultural phenomena to criminology, Skolnick uses the "law and order" issue in this well-directed analysis of American contradictions: the belief in peaceful social progress versus the surfacing of open intergroup conflict; criminological theories assuming social consensus and social pathology versus those stressing criminalization by selfish elites; and America as a land of opportunity and personal freedom versus America as a land of predatory materialism.

Smelser, Neil J. "Alexis De Tocqueville as Comparative Analyst." In Vallier. *Comparative Methods in Sociology: Essays on Trends and Applications*. Pp. 19-47.
The methodology of this influential scholar—whose work is an example of the long history of comparative studies—is evaluated. His comparisons of two nations were based on a partially formulated "model" of the complex interaction of historical forces, which emphasized the *differences* rather than the similarities. His conclusions are weakened by inadequate data.

Sylvester, Sawyer F. "Criminology: Past and Future." *Criminology* 13 (August 1975):223-239.
Prediction of criminology's future is hazardous, Sylvester says, because it is neither cohesive nor well established. He sees a continued movement toward greater rationalism—with modern Western law the model—undermining recognition of custom, and less theoretical interest in individual-oriented etiologies because the objective features of the environment are given precedence. He predicts a large number of highly factual studies and typologies of criminal behavior; granting of priority of assessment of principles over action orientations; and reconsideration of the view that criminology's subject matter is limited to crime.

Warner, R. Stephen. "The Methodology of Marx's Comparative Analysis of Modes of Production." In Vallier. *Comparative Methods in Sociology: Essays on Trends and Applications*. Pp. 49-74.
Warner sets out to analyze Karl Marx's studies comparing capitalist and precapitalist economic formations and especially to make explicit his comparative methodology. The author finds Marx an acute analyst of comparative institutions, with societies examined according to their legal (that is, property), economic (that is, division of labor and exchange), and political institutions.

2

INTERNATIONAL ORGANIZATIONS: AN INTRODUCTION

Paul Friday

International organizations develop over time responding to a common realization that a given issue, topic, or interest can be expanded and developed by the exchange of people and ideas. This is true in criminology where during the latter part of the nineteenth century an emphasis on humanism and increased respect for human rights led to a diminution of corporal punishment and to a search for sanctioning alternatives to capital punishment. National societies oriented toward prison and mental health issues and reform gave birth to the first international conference in 1872 in London.[1]

PRELIMINARY INTERNATIONAL LINKAGES

The orientation of international meetings and the organizations sponsoring them has widened beyond the penitentiaries and convicts. However, the content of those meetings and the purposes of the organizations have been dependent on the theoretical, philosophical, and scientific orientations of the time. The study of crime and criminals, from its initial stages, was oriented toward the unique characteristics of the offender. Each political state had its codified set of norms, and the scientific study of crime tended to compare offenders with nonoffenders from within the same general social environment. For over a century, the study and application of criminology reflected the need for social control by nation-states and the search for an explanation of criminal behavior as a function of individual pathologies or societal deprivations. Within the context of supporting

EDITOR'S NOTE: The next three chapters that follow will treat in detail the International Society for Criminology and the United Nations, two of the major organizations significant to the development of international criminology. These chapters will refer incidentally to similar organizations. Drawing on his contacts with criminologists throughout the world, Dr. Friday provides an introduction to a range of organizations and their diverse perspectives.

the existing social order, meetings addressed policy questions in penal law and corrections.

Despite meetings, there was no world-view or comparative perspective on crime. In fact, it was assumed that comparisons, even if possible, would be irrelevant. Each state was seen to have its own order to preserve, its own method of monitoring behavior, and its own assumptions regarding the etiology of crime.

It is within this context that in 1938 the International Society for Criminology (ISC) was founded with its secretariat in Paris. The ISC has assumed significant international importance, particularly in countries with a Latin-based language and in Eastern Europe. The society's primary contribution at the time was to break the parochial interests of criminology. Bringing persons interested in criminology together from divergent cultural backgrounds, yet with a common interest, was the beginning of efforts to link science with social policy. The primary thrust of the meetings, and the major orientation of the participants, was the social control model for criminology. Concerned with the need to establish contacts between nation-states and the scientific and methodological problems of criminology, the ISC has sponsored numerous conferences and international courses aimed at effectively dealing with the inadequacy or absence of international criminal statistics and other basic comparative data which could ultimately lead to improving or at least containing the problem. Its basic concern has been with scientific methodology, etiology, and evaluation of penal measures. Given the fact that representatives to the ISC have traditionally been governmental officials or academicians with close connections to their ministries of justice, the ISC has tended, until quite recently, to represent a criminology less than critical of traditional policy or theory.

TURNING POINT IN WORLD ORGANIZATIONS

World War II marks a turning point in scientific criminology and in international and regional efforts. Prior to this time most criminology focused on penal law or correctional issues, but after the war the orientation shifted to social science. Sociological and psychological research centered on crime, and the ISC became the primary organization for the dissemination of these new ideas.

Groups tended to organize around disciplinary or theoretical perspectives, including the International Association of Workers with Maladjusted Children, Children's Court Judges, International Federation of Senior Police Officers, and Youth Magistrates. After the war, the International Society for Criminology, the International Society for Social Defense, and the United Nations all sponsored meetings to bring researchers and practitioners together.

The advantages of providing extensive and continuous contact within the criminal justice communities took on a regional dimension in Scandinavia. The Northern Associations of Criminalists published a joint yearbook, and in 1956 the Swedish government proposed to the Nordic Council that cooperation be extended to include purely criminological research.[2] The emphasis on research on issues of common concern for all of the Scandinavian countries led to the development of the Scandinavian Research Council for Criminology in 1962. The council takes the initiative in encouraging and suggesting criminological research but does not grant funds. It arranges meetings within Scandinavia on a wide range of issues relevant to criminology in general. The council has collaborated with other organizations in co-sponsoring meetings including representatives from Socialist Criminology, British Criminology, and the International Sociological Association.

The Scandinavian Research Council and subsequent research from the institutes within the countries represented provided an intellectual thrust that has gone far beyond the geographical boundaries of Scandinavia. While not an international organization in the global sense, the research and theoretical issues generated within the group gave impetus to free criminology from its individualistic and positivistic bonds.

BROADENED CRIMINOLOGICAL PERSPECTIVES

As a result of the Scandinavian efforts and the intellectual growth within the social sciences, the phenomenon of crime and the issues of criminal policy developed a perspective during the 1960s and 1970s that was much in contrast to the social control-oriented and parochial criminology of the previous decades. The concern with policy and official reactions to individual offenders remained but took on a more international aspect and within Europe developed a wider philosophical and political analysis of crime as a social phenomenon.

In 1962, the Council of Europe established the Criminological Research Council which coordinates the collection and distribution of criminological material within Europe. Through its European Committee on Crime Problems, the council disseminates reports of the directors of criminological research institutes and holds conferences, most of which have revolved around technical, statistical, and judicial issues in criminology. Many of the issues discussed by the group were pragmatic in nature. However, during the early 1970s, such themes as "Embodying the Results of Criminological Research in Criminal Policy" and "Perceptions of Deviance and Criminality" became the focal concern of the annual conferences. These themes reflected changes in the professional orientation of a small but ultimately influential new criminology. Much of the criminological thinking at this time was influenced by sociology that was itself challenging the consensus and functionalist orientation of its founders. Given the intense political activism of the 1960s and theoretical developments in deviance theory such as interactionism and labeling, the problem of crime came to be seen within a wider political and social context. Emphasis shifted to a reevaluation and critical analysis of the role and function of law and to an examination of the system and its abuses, instead of simply looking at the offender and the offender's abuses.

Until this time, criminology was oriented within a behavioral paradigm where the primary focus was on the actor and the factors causing him/her to act. One contribution of labeling theory in sociology to criminology was to focus greater attention on the societal reaction to the act and the actor. A definitional paradigm developed, not to explain the act, but to view it in the context of reactions to it. The definitional process was seen to be collective rather than individual.

QUESTIONING THE CRIMINALIZATION PROCESS

In some circles these developments led to a return to the sociological conception of crime as a form of deviance—deviance which, through political processes, had become defined and reacted to as "crime." Crime, seen as an act that takes place in a political, economic, and historical context, thus became subject to a broader political and scientific analysis. New questions regarding the definitional process and procedures of crime control were raised in part as an attempt to fill the gaps in explanation and critique left by traditional criminological perspectives.

Radical or critical criminology emerged out of this context and became formally organized in Europe into the European Group for the Study of Deviance and Social Control. The group was formed in 1973 with an objective to better understand the relevant societal processes and to develop critical theory regarding repressive law and social control.[3] The organization meets annually, offering critical papers designed to theoretically understand both the processes and the motivation of societal and governmental reaction. The European group is interested in developing critical theory which is applicable across national boundaries and is unconstrained by government interests per se. Characteristic of the founding philosophy is not only the emphasis on critical theory but also a commitment to the abolition of repressive legal and social constraints.

While the Council of Europe and the critical criminologists of the European Group represent the spectrum of thought on that continent, the International Sociological Association (ISA) formed a Research Committee for the Sociology of Deviance and Social Control in 1974 to provide an international forum for diverse analysis and orientations. As an international, and not only European, organization, the ISA committee has involved both traditional and radical criminologists on its board and is organized with the goals of encouraging research for crime, deviance, and social control from the sociological perspective. Since the ISA holds no formal ideological position, its Research Committee's primary objectives are to facilitate both research and professional associations within the sociological frame of reference. A strong emphasis has been on fostering indigenous research in developing countries, comparative methodologies, and social structural issues in both etiology and social policy regarding crime, deviance, and social control mechanisms.

The Deviance and Social Control Research Committee of the International Sociological Association sponsors small international symposia generally with a limited theme, but encourages participation from all theoretical perspectives. Conferences with a comparative thrust have been held in France, Ireland, Japan, Sweden, the Netherlands, and Nigeria.

These more recently formed groups join a growing list of organized efforts to effectively study and interpret issues in crime and criminal policy. International groups, in addition to those mentioned, include the International Association of Youth Magistrates, International Commission of Jurists, International Association of Penal Law, International Society of Social Defense, International Chiefs of Police, International Criminal Police Organization (INTERPOL), the International Penal and Penitentiary Foundation, the International Prisoners Aid Association, and the Howard League for Penal Reform.

Organizations tend to emerge within a given political and scientific milieu and to perpetuate themselves long after their initial objectives have been achieved. Until the 1970s, organizations developed in response to specific problems or discipline, but the newer organizations have also demonstrated a rebellion against a purely pragmatic and social control orientation. The newer organizations have had a primary appeal to younger scholars who tend to view the "doing of criminology" as as significant a problem for study as the phenomenon of crime itself.

WHAT ABOUT THE FUTURE?

Science does not always progress at an even rate. Criminology as a science whose roots were clearly in the societal need for social control has had some severe growing pains. Both in terms of theory and in research, there is a general split between those who assume and work within the behavioral or etiological paradigms and those who concentrate on the definitional. Unfortunately, within the field of criminology, theory and research have not tended to develop significantly either in assumptions or theses since the term "criminology" was coined. The multiplicity of purpose and method reflected by the large number of international organizations and regional societies indicates that the discipline has not reached a point of understanding either the phenomenon or itself.

There is a continuous need to provide forums for the dissemination of information, research, and analysis within the limited scope of each group. World congresses per se do not tend to advance science, for it is in the development of collaborative and supplementary research efforts within the confines of smaller groups that the actual work gets done. These smaller and regional groups, as working groups, have an important role to play in developing a line of thinking to the greatest extent possible.

While each organization has a core membership unique to itself, for most that membership overlaps with one or more of the other organizations. In this way, conference participants contribute to and gain from the ultimate synthesis of view which is inevitable when scholars exchange information. In this light, each organization may be seen to contribute to the development of criminological thought in ways that are neither stated nor envisioned in its preamble or constitution. International cooperation and collaboration provide a basis upon which the science of criminology can evolve. Each organization contributes individually and collectively to this end.

NOTES

1. Benedict S. Alper and Jerry F. Boren, *Crime: International Agenda* (Lexington, Mass.: Lexington Books, 1972), p. 4.

2. Johs. Andenaes, "Foreword" in Karl O. Christiansen (ed.), *Scandinavian Studies in Criminology* (Oslo: Universitetsforlaget, 1965), p. 8.

3. Herman Bianchi, Mario Simondi, and Ian Taylor (eds), *Deviance and Control in Europe* (New York: John Wiley and Sons, 1975), pp. xiii-xxiii.

3

INTERNATIONAL SOCIETY FOR CRIMINOLOGY*

Jean Pinatel

While many international organizations are likely to be interested in the study of the criminal phenomenon, this chapter concentrates on only one of them: the International Society for Criminology. Thus, the first part of the discussion is devoted to that organization. The second part concentrates on other international organizations with a greater or lesser interest in the scientific approach to criminal phenomena.

In order to describe the role and the organization of the International Society for Criminology, two complementary points of view, the descriptive and the evaluative, must be adopted.

THE DESCRIPTIVE ASPECT

In December 1934, at the Ministry of Justice in Paris, an international meeting took place during which the idea of a federation of societies of the criminological sciences was given favorable consideration. Benigno Di Tullio was named secretary general of this newly formed organization.[1] It was almost named the International Society of Criminal Prophylaxis, but on July 16, 1937, at Rome the name International Society for Criminology was retained. In October 1938, the first International Congress of Criminology was held in Rome.[2]

*Translated by David L. Gobert, Ph.D., Professor of French, Southern Illinois University at Carbondale.

EDITOR'S NOTE: In this chapter, Pinatel surveys the efforts of many prominent criminologists and organizations to establish the lines of communication essential to genuine international collaboration. The International Society for Criminology, he reports, has mirrored the qualities of criminology itself. The membership has represented the dominant schools that lend the interdisciplinary character to criminology. These ideological differences have called for the intellectual tolerance basic to comparative criminology and the organizational framework conducive to collaboration. As an international platform, the society has sponsored congresses, conferences, courses, and centers for disseminating ideas of transnational importance.

Concurrently with the First International Congress of Criminology, the First Latin American Congress of Criminology was organized in Buenos Aires in 1938. In 1941, the Second Latin American Congress of Criminology took place in Santiago. Then, in 1947 in Rio de Janeiro, the first Pan American Congress of Criminology opened, at which time Benigno Di Tullio proposed, for the first time, the idea of an International Institute of Criminology and where Leonido Ribeiro was instrumental in the decision to hold a Second International Congress of Criminology in Paris. While preparations were being made for this Second International Congress, the Second Pan American Congress of Criminology took place in Mexico in 1949.

In January of the same year, an international meeting preparatory to the Second International Congress was held in Paris. On the occasion of that meeting, the statutes of the society were adopted. Circumstances had prevented their earlier establishment. The seat of the society was transferred from Rome to Paris. Article 1 of the statutes was written as follows:

> There is hereby founded an association known as the International Society for Criminology, whose purposes are those of the International Society for Criminology up to now established in Rome. The association proposes (in coordinating its activity with that of the existing specialized associations) to assure the development of the sciences in their application to the criminal phenomenon. Its future duration is not limited. The association has its headquarters in Paris.

Benigno Di Tullio was named president of the society and was replaced as secretary general by the late Reverend Father Piprot d'Alleaume, secretary general of the Organizational Committee of the Second International Congress.

Honored with consultative status by the United Nations Organization (July 1949), admitted to the status of consultative arrangements by UNESCO (November 1950), and duly recognized by the French government (November 1949)—the International Society for Criminology witnessed its action suspended, out of necessity, until the Second International Congress.

On the occasion of that congress, the General Assembly of the society held two important meetings. On September 16, 1950, the election of twenty-four members of the Directors' Council was held. On September 18, 1950, a resolution was adopted calling for the creation of an International Institute of Criminology.

On November 19, 1950, Denis Carroll was elected president of the society by the Directors' Council in Paris, and I was elected secretary general. Benigno Di Tullio and the Reverend Father Piprot d'Alleaume were named, respectively, honorary president and honorary secretary general of the society.

The composition of the Scientific Commission, provided for by the statutes and made responsible by the General Assembly for planning the International Institute, was determined by the Directors' Council on July 15 and 16, 1951. Etienne De Greeff was to be elected president of the Scientific Commission

TABLE 3-1
LEADERS OF THE INTERNATIONAL SOCIETY FOR CRIMINOLOGY, 1949-1978

Year	President	Head of Scientific Commission	General Secretary
1949	Benigno Di Tullio		Piprot d'Alleaume
1950	Denis Carroll		Jean Pinatel
1951		Etienne De Greeff	
1954		Gregory Zilboorg	
1957	Thorsten Sellin		
1959		Hermann Mannheim	
1962		Sheldon Glueck	
1966		Jean Pinatel	Georges Fully
1967	Trevor Gibbens		
1973	Jean Pinatel	Peter Lejins	John Eryl Hall Williams
1978	Denis Szabo		Jacques Verin

(October 14, 1951). Thereby, the International Society for Criminology was operational.

General Characteristics

The general characteristics of the International Society for Criminology can be determined from an appreciation of the personalities who played a decisive role in its leadership. As seen in Table 3-1, the society can be characterized as international. Its two other principal aspects are multidisciplinarity and doctrinal freedom.

The personalities represented in Table 3-1 came from America (United States 4: Sellin, Zilboorg, Glueck, and Lejins; Canada 1: Szabo) and Europe (France 4: Pinatel, Piprot d'Alleaume, Fully, and Verin; United Kingdom 4: Carroll, Gibbens, Mannheim, and Hall Williams; Belgium 1: De Greeff; Italy 1: Di Tullio). Interestingly, at a time when the scientific literature tends to give less weight to anything that is not written in English, there are practically as many individuals whose working language is French (seven) as there are anglophones.

With regard to the multidisciplinarity of the society, a breakdown shows three groups (putting aside a theologian, Piprot d'Alleaume): six physicians (Di Tullio, Carroll, Gibbens, De Greeff, Zilboorg, and Fully); five jurists (Pinatel, Mannheim, Glueck, Hall Williams, and Verin); and three sociologists (Sellin, Szabo, and Lejins). Certainly, this classification could be elaborated further considering the scientific research of some of the individuals, but the important thing is that among the directors of the society, three fundamental disciplines (medicine, sociology, and law) continue to be encountered. The first team of criminologists was that of Cesare Lombroso, a physician, Enrico Ferri, a sociologist, and Raffaele Garofalo, a jurist.

Finally, there is doctrinal freedom. Among the individuals listed, there are proponents of all the dominant schools of contemporary criminology, of whatever bent they may be—biological, psychoanalytical, psychological, psychiatric, sociological, or eclectic. The specialist in cultural conflict is in the company of the innovator in the area of prediction tables, and of the founders of clinical criminology and of comparative criminology.

Thus, the general characteristics of the International Society for Criminology reflect those of the field of criminology itself.

Statutes

As of November 18, 1950, it was decided to review the statutes of the society in their entirety.[3] A commission was named and actuated by Thorsten Sellin and Jean Graven. The plan they presented was adopted by the General Assembly of the society on September 18, 1955, in London. The statutes and the internal operating paper thus adopted reflect both an essentially democratic spirit and a procedural awkwardness.

The democratic spirit that dominates the statutes and the operating procedures is especially evident in the systematic recourse to voting in the functioning of the society. Thus, the General Assembly elects a Council of Directors, which in turn elects an Executive Committee, Scientific Commission, and new members of the society. In 1950, the society's General Assembly met on the occasion of the congress in Paris, and the Directors' Council was elected in the assembly during the meeting. The authors of the plan opposed this practice because a general assembly, meeting in such circumstances, necessarily reflects the will of a minority of the society's members, those who were present at this event. Sellin and Graven's main concern was to call upon all the members of the society for the election of the Directors' Council. For that reason, they gave their support to the principle of voting by correspondence, which was to take place during the year following the congress. As for the Directors' Council, the Executive Committee, and the Scientific Commission, recourse to voting by correspondence outside their annual meeting also became the required procedure.

The execution of this procedure of voting by correspondence requires much paper work and is rather expensive. But these disadvantages are negligible compared to the advantage of a strictly democratic system of governance.

With respect to the procedural cumbersomeness of the administration of the society, operating procedures have not simplified the already complex provisions of the statutes. They have arranged in minute detail the elections to the Directors' Council and the functioning of the diverse mechanisms of the society. Here again heavy correspondence costs result. Thus, for example, delegates of affiliated associations may attend the meetings of the Directors' Council in a consultative role. This is an excellent provision, but to be carried out, all of the affiliated associations must be notified in time of the date and place of the meetings.

The rigidity and formalism of the statutes and the operating procedures are demonstrated by the fact that they have had to undergo numerous secondary modifications.[4] Amendments to the statutes require (1) a discussion by the General Assembly and (2) an affirmative vote of two-thirds of the members through a referendum held by correspondence! This procedural awkwardness is the result of the society's democratic organization.

Means of Action

The society is proud of being an organization with limited resources. In fact, it is very easy to organize colloquia when there is an adequate budget. But when the budget permits merely the functioning of a permanent secretariat, whose personnel and quarters are provided by the French Ministry of Justice, when the only resources that support it are membership dues and the subsidies of a dozen governments—then one can be assured that if something is still accomplished, it is because there is a strong sense of mission. Two-thirds of the receipts are provided by the dues of approximately five hundred individual members and three hundred collective memberships. This proves the existence of a sure commitment on the part of the membership.

At the organization's central office, the permanent secretariat, managed competently by Ms. Ch. Cambounet, includes only three persons who attend to general direction and administration, finances, and the library. The library, with 3,136 volumes exclusive of journals, constitutes an excellent documentation resource.

In member countries national delegates, appointed by the Directors' Council, serve as intermediaries between the home office and the individual and collective members living in the given country. Through the activities of these national delegates, the numerous accomplishments of the society have been realized.

THE EVALUATIVE ASPECT

To evaluate the activities and accomplishments of the International Society for Criminology, it is necessary to consider the international congresses, the international centers, the international courses, the international conferences, the Denis Carroll Prize, and the *Annals*.

International Congresses

The international congresses of criminology are the successors to the international congresses of criminal anthropology that were held for many years.[5] The First Congress of Criminal Anthropology took place in Rome in 1885. During this congress there were debates about the most appropriate name for the science of crime and the criminal. At this time of Lombrosian euphoria, "criminal anthropology" was the chosen name. Nevertheless, since within the congress a section on biology and a section on sociology were created, it was actually criminology that was emerging under the name "criminal anthropology." After the congress in Rome, the Second Congress of Criminal Anthropology in Paris (1889) marked the appearance of an anti-Lombrosian opposition that became more pronounced in Brussels (1892). Then congresses were held in Geneva (1896), in Amsterdam (1901), in Turin (1906) where Lombroso's scientific jubilee was celebrated, and finally in Cologne (1911).

Following the tradition of the Congresses of Criminal Anthropology, the First International Congress of Criminology was held in Rome on October 3-8, 1938, presided over by the jurist M. d'Amelio. The essential result of this congress is expressed in the wish that "the study of the delinquent personality be formally inserted into the function of justice."[6]

In 1950, the Second International Congress of Criminology was organized and presided over by the eminent lawyer H. Donnedieu de Vabres. As a result of this congress, criminology succeeded in freeing itself from the criminological sciences (biology, psychology, psychiatry, psychoanalysis, and criminal sociology) and in defining itself on the clinical level.[7]

This historical development explains why the Third International Congress of Criminology (London, 1955), presided over by Denis Carroll,[8] was devoted to recidivism, and the fourth, presided over by M. E. Lamers (The Hague, 1960), to mentally abnormal delinquents.[9] These themes had in fact given rise to clinical studies in numerous countries. In the same vein, the Fifth International Congress of Criminology (Montreal, 1965), presided over by the Reverend Father Mailloux, centered on the treatment of delinquents.[10]

With the Sixth International Congress, presided over by J. del Rosal (Madrid, 1970),[11] a change took place. It had as its theme scientific research in criminology considered as a link between theory and practice. Three years later in Belgrade the Seventh International Congress, chaired by M. Milutinovic, took up the theme of the comparison of the broad orientations of contemporary criminology (interactional, clinical, and organizational).[12] Therefore, it was logical that the Eighth International Congress (Lisbon, 1978) did not have a specific theme. It was devoted entirely to research in progress.[13] Sections were constituted, and they showed that the principal concerns of research were criminogenesis, the administration of justice, and the treatment of delinquents and juvenile delinquency. The researchers were only secondarily attracted to history and epistemology, victimology, prevention, and deontology of research.

By abandoning the formula of a specific theme for its international congresses, the International Society for Criminology followed the example of the large international associations in the disciplines of psychology and sociology.

International Centers

The idea of creating an international institute of criminology, first advanced at the congress in Paris (1950), only slowly gained adherents. Sheldon Glueck at the congress at the Hague (1960) and Lloyd Ohlin at the International Course of Criminology at Montreal (1967) made suggestions that ultimately led to the creation of international centers of criminology.

The following principles were established in 1969:

1. An international center is created through an agreement arrived at between the International Society for Criminology, which gives its assistance at the international level, and a local organization which takes responsibility for its technical and financial operation.

2. The local organization must act, through its geographical location and its cultural situation, as a link between different countries.

3. The center is to be specialized in a particular area of criminology, and it is to be autonomous juridically, administratively, and financially.

4. A council of the center—composed of an equal number of representatives of the Scientific Commission of the society and of the concerned local organization and ultimately of persons accepted into membership—defines and supervises its scientific program and its administration and financial operation.

5. The director of the center is named by the council and is responsible to it.

Through application of these principles (adopted on May 25, 1969), the University of Montreal and the International Society for Criminology shortly thereafter jointly created the International Center of Comparative Criminology.[14] Directed by Denis Szabo, this center sponsors numerous activities: technical assistance, exchange of specialists, international symposia, and regional seminars. It also carries out many research projects.

At first, the research of the Montreal center was dominated by an organizational orientation and was devoted to problems of administration of justice, including those related to the police, with particular emphasis on those of a practical nature involving especially Quebec and Canada. A second orientation was added that, on one hand, employed a theoretical synthesis in analyzing intensively contemporary problems (for example, terrorism or public attitudes toward criminality and deviance) and that, on the other hand, employed a geographical approach in assessing patterns of criminality and the reactions to criminality produced around the world.

Among the scientific activities of the International Center for Comparative Criminology, its involvement in clinical criminology must be mentioned. This involvement became apparent with its collaboration with the Institute of Criminal Anthropology of Genoa. Interest in this particular research area motivated the establishment of the International Center of Clinical Criminology on August 27, 1975, jointly by the International Society for Criminology and the University of Genoa. The establishment was made possible by the cooperation engendered between the International Center of Comparative Criminology and the Institute of Criminal Anthropology of Genoa; the resources of the institute are henceforth at the disposal of the International Center of Clinical Criminology. This center, under the direction of G. Canepa, has some interesting research in progress and publishes a bulletin.[15]

International Courses

Whereas the international centers are responsible for their specialized and autonomous activities, the international courses are created directly by the International Society for Criminology.[16] The courses emphasize instruction, whereas the international centers engage essentially in research.

The First International Criminology Course was held in 1952 at the Maison de l'UNESCO in Paris under the direction of Georges Heuyer who then occupied the chair of child neuropsychiatry of the Faculty of Medicine. He should be credited with implementing international courses; all of his authority and persuasive ability were required to convince the Directors' Council to have the first international course held in Paris.

From 1952 to 1961 courses were held in Europe. They took place successively in Paris (1952, G. Heuyer; 1953, J. Pinatel), Stockholm (1953, O. Kinberg), London (1954, D. Carroll and H. Mannheim), Rome (1955, C. Erra, F. Grispigni, and B. Di Tullio), Lausanne (1956, H. Thelin), Vienna (1957, R. Grassberger), Brussels (1958, P. Cornil), Copenhagen (1959, G. Stürup), Freiburg (1960, T. Wurtenberger), and Madrid (1961, J. Del Rosal). Among the directors of the respective courses were some of the most prestigious criminologists of the time. Seven of the eleven courses were devoted to problems of clinical criminology.

From 1962 until 1969, the courses took place both within and outside Europe: Jerusalem (1962, I. Drapkin), Cairo (1963, A. Khalifa), Lyon (1964, M. Colin), Rome (1965, B. Di Tullio and G. Vassali), Abidjan (1966, A. Boni), Montreal (1967, D. Szabo), and Belgrade (1968, M. Milutinovic). During this period, the clinical tendency was maintained while comparative criminology began to emerge.

From 1970 to 1975, all the courses were held outside Europe: Mendoza (1969, Ortega del Campillo), Lagos (1970, T. Asuni), São Paulo (1972 and 1973, A. Amar), Maracaibo (1974, L. Aniyar de Castro), Teheran (1974, E. Pad), and Guayaquil (1975, G. Zavala Baquerizo). These courses reveal that criminology is traversed by different currents; that the clinical tendency is being deemphasized; and that there is special interest in general problems or contemporary problems.

In the period 1976 to 1977, the courses were held at Pau-Bayonne-St. Sebastian (1976, R. Ottenhof and A. Beristain) and Wuppertal (1977, J. Haussling). These courses emphasize, on one hand, juvenile delinquency and, on the other, they are heavily oriented toward scientific research.

In sum, of the twenty-seven courses listed above, sixteen were held in Europe, six in America (Canada and Latin America), three in Africa, and two in Asia. Most were organized around a criminological infrastructure. Some (Abidjan, Mendoza, Lagos, São Paulo, Teheran, and Guayaquil) were implemented completely outside the criminological infrastructure. Some courses led to the realization of international congresses (London, Madrid, Belgrade) and to the creation of an international center (Montreal), of an international society (the Latin American Society of Criminology, Mendoza), and of national institutes (Abidjan,

Teheran, Guayaquil, Saint Sebastian). The international courses have had very positive results.

INTERNATIONAL CONFERENCES

At its meeting in Montreal on August 29, 1965, the Directors' Council referred to the Scientific Commission for its consideration a proposal of the Reverend Father Mailloux, sponsored by the Aquinas Foundation, suggesting the organization of conferences to be held in certain universities. The Scientific Commission established the following guidelines:

1. To proceed so that the conferences would contribute as much as possible in the areas of theoretical principles of criminological research and of practical applications in the field of treatment of delinquents.
2. To choose universities in underdeveloped countries that hold promise for criminology, but this potentiality has not been realized.
3. To choose lecturers of international renown who are experienced in developing contacts between academic and governmental leaders, because criminology touches on university, administrative and juridical areas.

Table 3-2 summarizes the facts on the conferences.

The purpose of the conferences—to spread scientific data into the milieu likely to understand and to put them to practical use—was achieved.

Denis Carroll Prize

When Denis Carroll, president of the society, died in 1956, the Directors' Council decided to create a prize in his honor. The conditions of the prize were approved on February 21, 1958. Article 2, which describes the nature of the prize, was amended in 1969. Comparison of the two descriptions is very informative.

Article 2 (1958 version): The Denis Carroll Prize is awarded at each occasion of the International Congress of Criminology. It recognizes an outstanding scientific work in criminology published in its first edition after the preceding congress.

Article 2 (1969 version): The Denis Carroll Prize aims to call attention to an outstanding scientific work constituting an original contribution to criminology, published in its first edition after the preceding congress. It is awarded on the occasion of each International Congress of Criminology.

The change made in 1969 was intended to give special prominence to jurisprudence, which had been well established, and to give those whose reputation had not been well established an advantage over well-known criminologists.

The prize is given by a jury of nine members, nominated by the Scientific Commission and confirmed by the Directors' Council.

The awardees and the titles of their works are given in Table 3-3. The jury also named the works they deemed worthy of being recommended on scientific grounds (Table 3-4).

TABLE 3-2
INTERNATIONAL CONFERENCES OF THE INTERNATIONAL SOCIETY FOR CRIMINOLOGY, 1968-1976

Year	Country	Lecturer	Lecture Topic
1968	Poland (universities of Warsaw and Cracow)	J. Pinatel	Can Prisons be Transformed into Institutions for Treatment?
1969	Mexico (Autonomous University of Free School of Law, Ibero-American University)	T.C.N. Gibbens	Treatment in an Open Milieu
1970	India	Rev. Father Malloux	
	Bombay		The Judiciary: Treatment of Young Delinquents
	Hyderabad		The Prevention of Juvenile Delinquency
	Madras		The Psychological Treatment of Young Delinquents
	New Delhi		The Development of Reeducational Programs for Young Delinquents
1972	Lebanon	D. Szabo	
	Beyrouth Justice Department		Judiciary Individualization of Sentences and Contribution of Medical-Biological Research
	Beyrouth Justice Department		Role of Criminology in Formation of Personnel Responsible for Administration of Justice
	Beyrouth Faculty of Social Sciences and Law		Contribution of Criminology to Planning of Social Defense Services
1974	Nigeria	P. Lejins	
	Zaria		Significance of Culture in Development of Criminology
	Ibidan		Crime Control Strategy in a Developing Country
	Port Harcourt		Constitutional Rights of Accused and Their Impact on Treatment Methods
	Lagos		Applications of Criminology in Sentencing Process
1976	Hungary Budapest	J.E. Hall Williams	Myths about Crime Prevention and Crime Control
			Myths about Corrections and Reform of Offenders
			Criminologist's Role

TABLE 3-3
RECIPIENTS OF THE DENIS CARROLL PRIZE AND TITLES OF WORKS

Year	Awardee	Title of Work
1960	Ch. Debuyst	Criminals and Living Values
1965	R. Cloward and L. Ohlin	Delinquency and Opportunity
1970	Ph. Robert	Adolescent Gangs
1973	Frances H. Simon	Prediction Methods in Criminology
1978	Th. Mathiesen	Politics of Abolition

TABLE 3-4
WORKS RECOMMENDED BY THE JURY FOR THE DENIS CARROLL PRIZE

Year	Author	Title of Work
1960	R. Andry	Delinquency and Parental Pathology
	M. Wolfgang	Patterns of Criminal Homicide
1965	N. Christie	Young Norwegian Law Violators
	T. Willett	Criminal on the Road
1970	D. Gonin	Group Psychotherapy of Adult Delinquent in a Prison Environment
	D. J. West	Present Conduct and Future Delinquency
1973	J. P. De Waele	Methodology of Programmed Cases in Criminology
	J. Hogarth	Sentencing as a Human Process
1978	T. Bandini and U. Gatti	Juvenile Delinquency
	P. Lascoumes	Prevention and Social Control

The Annals

The International Society of Criminology has been and continues to be committed to publishing a reputable international journal of criminology. Since 1951, a biannual journal has been published. It was first named the *Bulletin of the International Journal of Criminology*, and, after 1962, it was called the *International Annals of Criminology*. This publication contains a section devoted to original theses and articles or communications on a specific theme proposed to members of the society. Included in the journal are national reports, systematic bibliographies of papers in specialized journals, and news items about the field, as well as critical reviews of criminological works, prepared chiefly by Jean Susini.

In 1975, one issue was devoted to a bibliographical index for the period 1951-1974. The index, developed by Ms. B. Merle, librarian of the society, is based on a dual classification: by subject matter and by names of authors. The subject matter classification groups all doctrinal articles under these broad headings:

I. General Criminology: General; International Colloquia; International Congresses; International Courses; History of Criminology; Teaching of Criminology (a) Research, (b) Theories.

II. Biological Criminology.

III. Psychological Criminology: General; Criminal Psychiatry; Criminal Psychology; Psychoanalytic Criminology.

IV. Sociological Criminology.

V. Special Criminology: Crimes and Misdemeanors against Persons; Crimes and Misdemeanors against Goods; Military Crimes and Misdemeanors.

VI. Social Pathology: Alcoholic Criminality; Sexual Criminality; Prostitution and Pandering (proxenetisme); Drug Addicts and Drug Addiction; Timely or Controversial Problems.

VII. Penal Philosophy and Criminal Policy: Penal Philosophy; Criminal Policy; Responsibility; Prevention.

VIII. Penal Sciences and Penitentiaries: Penology; Penitentiary Science (probation, prison, parole).

IX. Clinical Criminology: General; Dangerousness; Methods of Investigation; Methods of Treatment.

X. Judiciary Psychology.

XI. Juvenile Criminology.

XII. Comparative Criminology: General; Countries under Development; Europe; America; Africa; Asia; Oceania.

XIII. Penal Law, Penal Procedure, and International Matters.

XIV. Scientific and Technical Control and Verification.

XV. Most Recent Developments in Criminological Research.

In his status as delegate to the Scientific Commission, F. Canestri was instrumental in initiating a review of the administration of the *International Annals of Criminology*. This review involved the organization of a secretariat for the *Annals* under the direction of J. Susini and the naming of a committee by the

Directors' Council to study the problems of the publication. The committee membership was limited to Hall Williams, Susini, and Philippe Robert. The task of this committee is to examine all of the scientific, administrative, technical, and financial questions that are beginning to appear in light of the present economic situation. During the *Annals'* current transitional period, the committee has been responsible for its publication.

Thus, perseverance and initiative have compensated for the society's paucity of funds.[17]

INTERNATIONAL ORGANIZATIONS INTERESTED IN CRIMINOLOGY

A juridical criterion determines the classification of international organizations; there are both governmental and nongovernmental organizations.

Governmental Organizations

Among these are organizations whose purview is worldwide (the United Nations, the International Labor Organization, UNESCO, and the World Health Organization) and those whose outreach is regional only (Council of Europe).

UNITED NATIONS ORGANIZATION

Inasmuch as a special chapter in this volume is devoted to the United Nations, here it will be sufficient to relate only some of its activities.

1. The International Society for Criminology benefits from consultative status with the United Nations and is in a special category of nongovernmental international organizations. The society has permanent representation at the United Nations' headquarters in New York City.
2. The United Nations encourages the coordination of specialized institutions (International Labor Organization, UNESCO, World Health Organization) with those organizations interested in crime prevention and the treatment of delinquents. To achieve this end, meetings have been organized, first in Geneva and then in New York. A permanent liaison group between nongovernmental organizations was created under its aegis in New York (Alliance of Non-Governmental Organizations on Crime Prevention and Criminal Justice).
3. The world congresses of the United Nations for the prevention of crime and the treatment of delinquents, of course, have criminological dimensions. At first, the United Nations Congresses and the International Congresses of Criminology were held the same year. Finally, it was agreed that the congresses would take place in different years. That is why the Seventh

International Congress of Criminology was held in Belgrade in 1973, three years after the one in Madrid. In that way, the Fifth United Nations Congress could be held in Geneva in 1975 without an International Congress of Criminology taking place at the same time.

4. The United Nations publishes annually the *International Journal of Criminal Policy* which includes articles on criminology.
5. International colloquia were organized by the United Nations in Brussels in 1951 on the topic of medical-psychological and social diagnoses of adult delinquents and in London in 1952 on probation.
6. The International Organization for Drug Control regularly publishes reports with a criminological interest.
7. The United Nations has created regional institutes in Japan for the Far East and in Rome for developing countries. The institute in Rome publishes a series of studies and works useful to criminology.

INTERNATIONAL LABOR ORGANIZATION

The purpose of this specialized arm of the United Nations is to promote and protect the physical, moral, and intellectual well-being of workers. From this perspective, the field of juvenile delinquency and its prevention have always been of interest to the International Labor Organization, especially in regard to its multiple interests in the problems of work and specifically to a professional orientation.

UNESCO

The United Nations Educational, Scientific, and Cultural Organization is also a specialized institution of the United Nations. The International Society for Criminology has benefited from its consultative status with UNESCO since 1950, and in Category B since December 22, 1961, UNESCO's interest in criminology has been manifested in the following ways: (1) UNESCO has facilitated the organization of certain international courses in criminology, specifically those in Paris, Abidjan, and Lagos. (2) It has published studies undertaken by the International Society for Criminology on the teaching of criminology and on documentation and bibliography in criminology.

WORLD HEALTH ORGANIZATION

The International Society for Criminology has had an official relationship with the World Health Organization (WHO) for a number of years. WHO is interested in the psychiatric aspect of crime prevention and in the treatment of delinquents, as well as in their treatment in a more strictly medical sense. A specialized institution of the United Nations, WHO is particularly concerned with the criminological problems relative to alcoholism, drug addiction, mentally abnormal delinquents, and juvenile delinquency generally.

COUNCIL OF EUROPE

Because of its Scientific Council founded in 1963, the Council of Europe plays the role of a European regional institute of criminology. It organizes annual conferences of directors of research institutes and awards scholarships to facilitate the exchange of researchers and practitioners among the different countries.

Publications in criminology are produced by the Council of Europe from research projects, from studies related to research, from proceedings of the directors' conferences, and from specialized colloquia. In addition, there are diverse publications of more irregular nature.

Nongovernmental Organizations

Four groups must be distinguished among the nongovernmental organizations: (1) organizations interested in penology, (2) professional organizations, (3) organizations only occasionally interested in criminology, and (4) other international organizations that do not fall into the preceding categories but merit mention. Only the first three benefit from consultative status with the United Nations.

ORGANIZATIONS CONCERNED WITH PENAL LAW, PENOLOGY, AND CRIMINAL POLICY

There are three large organizations in the realm of penal law, penology, and criminal policy: the International Association of Penal Law, the International Penal and Penitentiary Foundation, and the International Society of Social Defense.

In 1924, the International Association of Penal Law superseded the International Union of Penal Law which had been founded in 1889 by Franz von Liszt, G. A. von Hamel, and A. Prins. It publishes a biannual journal, the *International Journal of Penal Law*, and extends its reach through the Advanced International Institute of Criminal Science of Syracuse which sponsors numerous colloquia and seminars. Dean P. Bouzat has been director of this large association for about thirty years. He was its general secretary before serving as its president.

The International Penal and Penitentiary Foundation is the successor to the International Penal and Penitentiary Commission of Bern,[18] which was an intergovernmental organization responsible for preparing international congresses centered around penitentiary matters and penology. The last congress, the program of which was established by the Bern Commission, was held at The Hague in 1950. After that congress, the United Nations assumed the activities of the International Commission. But its "spiritual legacy" went to the International

Penal and Penitentiary Foundation which organizes international congresses every five years and produces a few publications. Its current president is J. Dupreel, the general secretary of the Ministry of Justice of Belgium.

The International Society of Social Defense was founded on the occasion of the First International Congress of Social Defense in San Remo in 1947 which took place on the initiative of Felippo Gramatica (recently deceased). Until 1955, it published the *International Journal of Social Defense*. At that time the journal was renamed the *Bulletin of the International Society of Social Defense*. It is within this society, which is oriented toward criminal policy, that scholars, practitioners, criminologists, and jurists can compare opinions and collaborate. Its honorary president was Count Gramatica, and its acting president is Marc Ancel, president of the Honorary Chamber of the supreme court of appeals of France.

After productive negotiations, the general secretaries of these three associations, joined by the general secretary of the International Society for Criminology, decided to organize joint international colloquia. Their preparation was entrusted to the Centro Nazionale di Prevenzione a Difesa Sociale of Milan, the "guiding spirit" of which is an important Italian magistrate, Beria Di Argentine. Such colloquia were held in Bellagio in 1963, 1968, 1973, and 1975 on mentally abnormal delinquents, the determination of penal sentencing, decriminalization, and deprivation of freedom. Conferences bringing together the presidents and general secretaries of the four associations are held regularly and make possible the coordination of their respective activities and their cooperation with the United Nations.

PROFESSIONAL ORGANIZATIONS

Some organizations are interested in criminology for professional reasons. Most of these institutions bring together practitioners and are concerned with juvenile delinquency and maladaptation. They are, for example, the International Association of Judges for Juveniles, which has become the International Association of Magistrates for Youth, and the International Union for the Protection of Children. Roundtable discussions are organized regularly among nongovernmental international groups interested in the problems of childhood and adolescence. Thus did the International Society for Criminology participate in a roundtable held in Lausanne in 1970 at which were represented the International Association of Educators of Maladapted Youth and the World Union for the Protection of Children and of Adolescents.

Other organizations have a police function. First among these is the International Criminal Police Organization (INTERPOL) which is well known for its activities in the realm of the "war" against international criminality. In addition, it organizes annual international meetings and publishes monthly the *International Review of Criminal Police*. It also provides for the publication of statistics on international criminality. Besides the International Commission of Criminal Police, the International Federation of High Police Officials must be mentioned.

In regard to penitentiary policy, the Howard League for Penal Reform plays a very important role on the international scene, although its activities are carried out mainly in the United Kingdom. It publishes the *Howard Journal*, offers summer courses, and increases its public contacts through the mass media.

Finally, on the juridical level is the Nordic Association of Criminalists within which all Scandinavian countries participate in congresses and the publication of a journal and an annual. The Scandinavian institutes of criminology have organized a regional coordination of their scientific activities.

ORGANIZATIONS OCCASIONALLY INTERESTED IN CRIMINOLOGY

It is impossible to discuss all of the international organizations that are likely to be occasionally interested in criminology. Such organizations include the Salvation Army, the World Youth Assembly, the International Bureau for the Elimination of White Slavery, the International Conference of Catholic Charities, the International Council of Women, the Institute of Statistics, the Society of Comparative Legislation, the International Catholic Union of Social Services, and the World Mental Health Federation.

OTHER INTERNATIONAL ORGANIZATIONS

The International Academy of Legal and Social Medicine exercises a decisive role in its own field, which sometimes touches on the field of criminology. Similarly, the International Conference of Societies for the Encouragement of Mental Health is interested in criminality in the world. Finally, there is the Council for the Coordination of International Congresses of Medical Sciences which has always shown a great interest in criminology.

CONCLUSIONS

This study confirms the interdisciplinary nature of criminology and suggests the existence of different currents of thought in the realm of doctrine. The interdisciplinary nature of criminology is demonstrated by the relationships which the International Society for Criminology maintains with multiple organizations belonging to related disciplines. The existence of different currents of thought in criminology and in the peripheral sciences is suggested by the variations in the programs of international congresses of criminology and in the great number of organizations of penal law, penology, and criminal policy.

NOTES

1. B. Di Tullio, "La Société internationale de Criminologie" [The International Society of Criminology], *Revue de criminologie et de police technique* (April-June 1949): 75-80.

2. L. Vervaeck, "Le I° Congrès international de Criminologie" [The First International Congress of Criminology], *Revue de droit pénal et de criminologie* (1938):1108-1116.

3. The statutes and the internal operating paper of the society were published, including the revisions made at that time, in Volume 14 (1975) of the *International Annals of Criminology*. It reads thus (Article VI 1 e, the operating paper relative to the Scientific Commission): "The Commission itself names its President and its Secretary for the same term, with the possibility of reelection." Article VI 1 f of the operating paper states: "The General Secretary is ex-officio member of the Commission."

4. These modifications were made on the following dates: December 22, 1960; November 30, 1973; and September 16, 1978.

5. J. Pinatel, "Le III° Congrès international de Criminologie, sa place dans l'histoire de la Criminologie" [The Third International Congress of Criminology, Its Place in the History of Criminology], *Revue internationale de criminologie et de police technique* (1955):83-94.

6. Vervaeck, "The First International Congress of Criminology."

7. L. Ducloux, "Le II° congrès de criminologie" [The Second Congress of Criminology], *Revue internationale de Police Criminelle* (December 1950):362-365; L.G., "II° Congrès international de Criminologie" [The Second International Congress of Criminology], *Revue pénitentiaire et de droit pénal* (October-December 1950):825-829; P. Marabuto, "Le Deuxième Congrès international de Criminologie" [The Second International Congress of Criminology], *La Tribune du Commissaire de Police* 24 (1950):19-28; R. Pettinato, "El secundo Congreso internacional de criminología" [The Second International Congress of Criminology], *Revista penal y penitenciaria* (1950):267-336; G. Sinoir, "Le deuxième Congres international de Criminologie" [The Second International Congress of Criminology], Rééducation (February-March 1951):35-40; "II° Congrès international de Criminologie" [Second International Congress of Criminology], *Revue de droit pénal et de criminologie* (1950-1951):319-326.

8. J. J. Klare, "Apports scientifiques du III° Congrès international de criminologie—Conférence au Colloque international sur les apports scientifiques du III° Congrès international de criminologie—" [Scientific Actions of the Third International Congress of Criminology—Conference on International Discussion on the Scientific Actions of the Third International Congress on Criminology], *Bulletin de la Société internationale*, no. 1 (1956):33-42; R. P. Vernet, "Apports scientifiques du III° Congrès international de criminologie (Communication au Colloque international sur les apports scientifiques du III° Congrès international de criminologie)" [Scientific Actions of the Third International Congress on Criminology—A Communication of the International Discussion of the Scientific Actions of the Third International Congress of Criminology], *Bulletin de la Société international de criminologie*, no. 1 (1956):43-47; "Le troisième Congrès international de criminologie, Londres, 12-18 septembre 1955" (The Third International Congress of Criminology, London, September 12-18, 1955), *Bulletin de la Société internationale de Criminologie*, no. 1 (1956):13-30. In regard to Denis Carroll, see "Vie et oeuvre du Docteur Denis Carroll" [Life and Works of Dr. Denis Carroll], *Bulletin de la Société internationale de Criminologie* (1957):155-238.

9. J. Pinatel, "Les aspects psychopathologiques de la conduite criminelle" [Psychopathological Aspects of Criminal Conduct], *Revue de science criminelle* (1960):688-696; J. M. Van Bemmelin, "Le quatrième congrès international de Criminologie: son but, sa portée, ses résultats" [The Fourth International Congress of Criminology: Its Purposes, Its Span, Its Outcomes], *Bulletin de la Société internationale de Criminologie*, no. 1 (1961):43-52; "Quatrième Congrès international de criminologie" [Fourth International Congress of Criminology], *Bulletin de la Société internationale de Criminologie*, no. 1 (1961):41-64.

10. In regard to the congress in Montreal, see *Annales internationales de Criminologie* 4 (1965):251-312; L. M. Raymondis, "Compte rendu du V° Congrès international de Criminologie" [Report on the Fifth International Congress of Criminology], *Revue pénitentiaire* (1966):63-82. The papers of the congress in Montreal have been published in the *Annales internationales de Criminologie* 8 (1969); L. M. Raymondis, "Conference du R. P. Mailloux au V° Congrès international de Criminologie" [Lecture of R. P. Mailloux at the Fifth International Conference of Criminology], *Annales internationales de Criminologie* 5 (1966):41-46; "Le V° Congrès international de Criminologie, Montréal, 29 août—3 septembre 1965" [The Fifth International Congress of Criminology, Montreal, August 29—September 3, 1965], *Annales internationales de Criminologie* 4 (1965):249-312.

11. On the Sixth International Congress of Criminology in Madrid, September 21-27, 1970, see *Revue de Science criminelle* (1972):698-707.

12. J. Pinatel, "L'unité de la criminologie: Réflexions suscitées par le VII° Congrès international de Criminologie" [The Unity of Criminology: Thoughts Raised by the Seventh International Congress of Criminology], *Revue de Science criminelle* (1974):393-398.

13. J. Pinatel, "Le domaine et les grandes orientations de la criminologie: Réflexions suscitées par le VIII° Congrès de Criminologie" [The Domain and General Orientations of Criminology: Thoughts Raised by the Eighth International Congress on Criminology], *Revue de Science criminelle* (1979):909-916.

14. J. Pinatel, "La Faculté des sciences sociales, économiques et politiques de L'Université de Montréal" [The Faculty in Social Sciences, Economics and Politics of the University of Montreal], *Revue de Science criminelle* (1968):112-119; "L'apport scientifique du Centre international de criminologie comparee" [The Scientific Contributions of the International Center of Comparative Criminology], *Revue de Science criminelle* (1977):872-879.

15. An international center for biological and medical-legal criminology, which was established at the Oscar Freire Institute in São Paulo in 1973, has had an ethereal existence.

16. J. Pinatel, "Un quart de siècle de Cours internationaux de Criminologie" [A Quarter Century of International Courses in Criminology], *Revue de Science criminelle* (1978):141-149.

17. J. Pinatel, "Le vingt-cinquième anniversaire de la création de la Société internationale de Criminologie" [The Twenty-fifth Anniversary of the Establishment of the International Society of Criminology], *Bulletin de la Société internationale de Criminologie* (1959):258-260.

18. In regard to the International Penal and Penitentiary Commission of Berne, see the *Bulletin de la Société général des prisons* (1881):126.

BIBLIOGRAPHY

International Society for Criminology

Fully, G. "Rapport scientifique pour les années 1965-1969" [Secretary General's Report for 1965-1969]. *Annales internationales de Criminologie* 11 (1972):23-44.

Hall Williams, J. F. "Rapport moral pour les années 1973-1977" [Secretary General's Report for 1973-1977]. Mimeo.

Lejins, P. "Rapport scientifique pour les années 1973-1977" [Scientific Report for 1973-1977]. Mimeo.

Pinatel, J. "Rapport moral pour les années 1950-1954" [Secretary General's Report for 1950-1954]. *Bulletin de la Société internationale de Criminologie*, no. 2 (1955):213-231.

———. "Rapport moral pour les années 1955-1959" [Secretary General's Report for 1955-1959]. *Bulletin de la Société internationale de Criminologie*, no. 1 (1961):103-133.

———. "Rapport moral pour les années 1960-1964" [Secretary General's Report for 1960-1964]. *Annales internationales de Criminologie* 4 (1965):474-511.

———. "Rapport moral pour les années 1970-1972" [Secretary General's Report for 1970-1972]. Mimeo.

———. "Rapport scientifique" [Scientific Report]. *Bulletin de la Société internationale de Criminologie*, no. 2 (1955).

———. "Rapport scientifique pour les années 1955-1959" [Scientific Report for 1955-1959]. *Bulletin de la Société internationale de Criminologie*, no. 1 (1961):142-171.

———. "Rapport scientifique pour les années 1960-1964" [Scientific Report for 1960-1964]. *Annales internationales de Criminologie* 4 (1965):512-533.

———. "Rapport scientifique pour les années 1970-1972" [Scientific Report for 1970-1972]. Mimeo.

International Congresses of Criminology

Actes du I° Congrès international de Criminologie [Acts of the First International Congress of Criminology]. Rome: Tipografia della Mantellate, 1939. 5 vols.

Actes du II° Congrès international de Criminologie [Acts of the Second International Congress of Criminology]. Paris: Presses Universitaires de France, 1951, 1952, 1953, 1954, 1955.

Actes du III° Congrès international de Criminologie, Londres, 1955 [Acts of the Third International Congress of Criminology, London, 1955]. London: Dunstan and Co., 1957.

Actes du IV° Congrès international de Criminologie, La Haye, 1960 [Acts of the Fourth International Congress of Criminology, La Haye, 1960]. La Haye: Imprimerie Administrative.

Actes du V° Congrès international de Criminologie, Montreal, 1965 [Acts of the Fifth International Congress of Criminology, Montreal, 1965]. *Annales internationales de Criminologie* 8, No. 2 (1969). Special issue.

Memoria del VI° Congresso international de Criminología [Acts of the Sixth International Congress of Criminology]. Madrid: Instituto de Criminologia de la Universidad de Madrid, Vol. 1, 1973.

VII° Congresso internacional de Criminología, Belgrado, 1973 [Seventh International Congress of Criminology, Belgrade, 1973]. Caracas: Istituto de Ciencias penales y criminólogicas, Facultad central de Venezuela, 1973.

VIII° Congrès International de Criminologie, Lisbonne, 1978 [Eighth International Congress of Criminology, Lisbon, 1978]. In press.

International Center for Comparative Criminology

Fifth International Seminar in Comparative Clinical Criminology: Overview of Ongoing Research in the Basic Sciences in Connection with the Treatment and Rehabilitation of Delinquents. Montreal: International Center of Comparative Criminology, 1978. Mimeo.

Hostage-taking: Problems of Prevention and Control. Montreal: University of Montreal, 1976.

The Impact of Terrorism and Skyjacking on the Operations of the Criminal Justice System. Montreal: University of Montreal, 1976.

La criminalité urbaine et la crise de l'administration de la Justice [Urban Criminality and the Crisis of the Administration of Justice]. Text assembled and presented by D. Szabo. Montreal: Les Presses de l'Université de Montréal, 1973.

La Criminologie clinique: État Actuel et perspectives futures dans le domaine du traitment et de la recherche [Clinical Criminology: Present State and Future Perspectives in the Areas of Treatment and Research]. Under the direction of G. Canepa and D. Szabo. Genoa: Istituto di Antropologia criminale, Universita di Genova, Italie, 1973.

Le coût de l'administration de la justice et de la criminalité [The Cost of Crime and Crime Control]. Ottawa: Ministry of the Solicitor-General, 1974.

Police, Culture et Société [Police, Culture and Society]. Text assembled amd presented by D. Szabo. Montreal: Les Presses de l'Université de Montréal, 1974.

Third International Seminar in Comparative Clinical Criminology: Differential Diagnosis and Prognosis of the State of Dangerousness and Treatment of Juvenile Delinquency. Montreal: International Center of Comparative Criminology, 1976. Mimeo.

International Courses in Criminology

I° Cours international de criminologie: L'examen médico-psychologique et social des délinquants, Paris, 1952 [First International Course in Criminology: The Medico-Psychological and Social Examination of Delinquents, Paris, 1952]. Prepared by Georges Heuyer and Jean Pinatel. Melun: Imprimerie administrative, 1953.

II° Cours international de criminologie: Le problème de l'état dangereux, Paris 1953 [Second International Course in Criminology: The Problem of the Condition of Dangerousness, Paris, 1953]. Prepared by Jean Pinatel. Melun: Imprimerie administrative, 1954.

III° Cours international de criminologie: Samhället och (Société et criminalité), Stockholm, 1953 [Third International Course in Criminology: Society and Criminality, Stockholm, 1953]. Prepared by Olof Kinberg. Stockholm: Norstedts, 1955.

V° Cours international de criminologie: Delitto e Personnalits (Délit et Personnalité) Rome, 1955 [Fifth International Course of Criminology: Offenses and Personality, Rome, 1955]. Milan: Dott A. Giuffrè, 1955.

VII° Cours international de criminologie: La prevention des infractions involontaire, Bruxelles, 1958 [Seventh International Course in Criminology: Prevention of Involuntary Infractions, Brussels, 1958]. Nivelles: Imprimerie pénitentiaire, 1960.

IX° Cours international de criminologie: The Treatment of Criminals, Copenhague 1958 [Ninth International Course in Criminology: The Treatment of Criminals, Copenhagen, 1958]. *Bulletin de la Société internationale de Criminologie*, no. 2 (1960).

X° Cours international de criminologie: Kriminologie und Vollzug der Freiheitsstraft (Criminologie, régime pénitentiaire et pédagogie) [Tenth International Course in Criminology: Criminology, Penitentiary Administration and Education]. Stuttgart: Ferdinand Enke Verlag, 1961.

XI° Cours international de criminologie: Los delinquentes mentalments anormales [Eleventh International Course in Criminology: Mentally Abnormal Delinquency]. Madrid: Artes Gráficas Helénica, 1963.

XII° Cours international de criminologie: Les causes et la prévention du crime dans les pays en voie de développement, Jérusalem, 1963 [Twelfth International Course in Criminology: Causes and Prevention of Crime in Developing Countries, Jerusalem, 1963]. Melun: Imprimerie administrative, 1963; *Proceedings of the 12th International Course in Criminology*. Jerusalem: Publication of the Institute of Criminology, 1963.

XIII° Cours international de criminologie: Le développement économique et les problèmes du comportement social, Le Caire, 1963 [Thirteenth International Course in Criminology: Economic Development and Problems of Social Conduct, Cairo, 1963]. *Annales Internationales de Criminologie* 13 (1964):13-132.

XIV° Cours international de criminologie: L'équipement en criminologie, Lyon, 1964 [Fourteenth International Course in Criminology: The Requisites of Criminology, Lyon, 1964]. Prepared by M. Colin. Paris: Masson et Cie, 1965.

XVI° Cours international de criminologie: La criminalité et sa prévention en Afrique, Abidjan, 1966 [Sixteenth International Course in Criminology: Criminality and Its Prevention in Africa, Abidjan, 1966]. Paris: Librairie générale de droit et de jurisprudence, 1968.

XVII° Cours international de criminologie: Criminologie en action, Montréal, 1967 [Seventeenth International Course in Criminology: Criminology in Action, Montreal, 1967]. Montreal: Les Presses de l'Université de Montréal, 1968.

"XX° International Course in Criminology: Non-institutional Treatment of Offenders." *Annales internationales de Criminologie* 10 (1971).

XXIII° Cours international de criminologie: La Violence, Maracaïbo, 1974 [Twenty-third International Course in Criminology: Violence, Maracaibo, 1974]. Prepared by L. Anivar de C. *Los rostros de la Violencia* [The Faces of Violence]. Maracaibo: Centro de Investigaciones Criminológicas, Universidad del Zulia, 1975.

XXVI° Cours international de criminologie: Delincuencia y inadaptación juvenil [Twenty-sixth International Course in Criminology: Delinquency and Juvenile Maladjustment]. Prepared by A. Beristain and P. Ottenhof. Caja de Ahorros Provicial de Guipuzkoa, 1977.

XXVII° Cours international de Criminologie: Conflits des jeunes avec les Institutions, Wüppertal, 1977 [Twenty-seventh International Course in Criminology: Conflicts of Youth with Institutions, Wüppertal, 1977]. Prepared by J. Häussling.

XXVIII° Cours international de Criminologie: Police, Justice et Communauté, Montréal, 1980 [Twenty-eighth International Course in Criminology: Police, Justice and Community, Montreal, 1980]. Prepared by Mrs. Limoges.

XXIX° Cours international de Criminologie: Le rôle de la Criminologie dans les démocraties nouvelles, Pamelune, 1980 [Twenty-ninth International Course in Criminology: The Role of Criminology in the New Democracies, Pamplona, 1980]. Prepared by Mr. Hualde.

XXX° Cours international de Criminologie: Les nouvelles dimensions du crime: les formes transnationales de la Criminalité, New York, 1981 [Thirtieth International Course in Criminology: New Dimensions in Crime: Transnational Forms of Criminality, New York, 1981]. Prepared by Mr. Stead and Mr. MacNamara.

XXXI° Cours international de Criminologie: Connaître la Criminalité: Le dernier état de la question, Aix-en-Provence, 1981 [Thirty-first International Course in Criminology: Knowledge of Criminality: Latest Developments, Aix-en-Provence, 1981]. Prepared by Mr. Boulan and Mr. Gassin.

International Conferences

Gibbens, T. "Treatment at Liberty." *Annales internationales de Criminologie* 9 (1970): 9-30.

Hall Williams, J. F. "Criminological Myths and Reality." *Annales internationales de Criminologie* 15 (1976):13-44.

Lejins, P. "Crime, Its Prevention and Control in a Developing Country, Nigeria." *Annales internationales de Criminologie* 15 (1970):141-171.

Pinatel, J. "La prison peut-elle être transformée en institution de traitement?" [Can the Prison be Transformed into a Therapeutic Institution?] *Annales internationales de Criminologie* 8 (1969):33-82.

Denis Carroll Prize: Awards and Honorable Mentions

Andry, R. *Delinquency and Parental Pathology*. London: Methuen and Co., Ltd., 1960.

Bandini, T., and U. Gatti. *Delinquenza giovanile* [Juvenile Delinquency]. Milan: Guiffré, 1974.

Christie, N. *Unge Norske Lovovertredere* [Young Norwegian Law Violators]. Oslo: Universitetsforlaget, 1960.

Cloward, R., and L. Ohlin. *Delinquency and Opportunity: A Theory of Delinquent Gangs*. Glencoe, Ill.: Free Press, 1960.

Debuyst, Ch. *Criminels et Valeurs Vecues* [Criminals and Life Values]. Paris: Nauwelaerts, 1960.

De Waele, J. P. *La Méthode des cas programmés en criminologie* [Methodology of Programmed Cases in Criminology]. Brussels: Dessart, 1971.

Gonin, D. *Psychotherapie de groupe du delinquant adulte en milieu pénitentiaire* [Group Psychotherapy of Adult Delinquents in the Prison Environment]. Paris: Masson et Cie, 1967.

Hogarth, J. *Sentencing as a Human Process*. Toronto: University of Toronto Press, 1971.

Lascoumes, P. *Prevention et controle social* [Prevention and Social Control]. Geneva: Medecine et Hygiene, 1977.

Mathiesen, Th. *The Politics of Abolition*. London: Martin Robertson, 1974.

Robert, Ph. *Les bandes d'adolescents* [Juvenile Gangs]. Paris: Les Editions Ouvrières, 1966.

Simon, Fr. *Prediction Methods in Criminology*. London: Home Office, Research Studies, Her Majesty's Stationery Office, 1971.

West, D. J. *Present Conduct and Future Delinquency*. London: Heinemann, 1969.

Willett, T. *Criminal on the Road*. London: Tavistock Publication, 1964.

Wolfgang, M. *Patterns of Criminal Homicide*. Philadelphia: University of Pennsylvania, 1958.

United Nations

Costa, J. L. *Etude comparee sur la delinquance juvenile: Deuxieme partie: Europe* [Comparative Study of Juvenile Delinquency: Second Part: Europe]. New York: Nations Unies, Departement des questions sociales, 1952.

Grunhut, M. *Resultats pratiques et aspects financiers de la probation chez les adultes dans un certain nombre d'Etats* [Practical Results and Financial Aspects of Adult Probation in a Certain Number of Nations]. New York: Nations Unies, Departement des questions sociales, 1954.

La Probation (regime de mise a l'épreuve) et les mesures analogues [Probation, A Regime Put to the Test, and Analogous Measures]. New York: Nations Unies, 1952; Melun: Imprimerie administrative, 1953.

UNESCO

"Elements d'une documentation en criminologie" [Selections from a Documentation in Criminology]. *Rapports et documents de sciences sociales*. Paris: UNESCO, Place Fontenoy, 1963.

Les sciences sociales dans l'enseignement superieur: Criminologie [The University Teaching of Social Sciences: Criminology]. Paris: UNESCO, Place Fontenoy, 1957.

Pinatel, J. "Bibliographie choisie" [Selected Bibliography]. *Revue internationale des sciences sociales* 18, no. 2 (1966):224-243.

World Health Organization

Bovet, L. *Les aspects psychiatriques de la delinquance juvenile* [Psychiatric Aspects of Juvenile Delinquency]. Geneve: Organisation mondiale de la sante, Palais des Nations, 1951.

Council of Europe

Ière Conférence des directeurs d'Instituts de Recherches Criminologiques, La recherche en criminologie [First Conference of Directors of Criminological Research Institutes, Research in Criminology]. Strasbourg: Council of Europe, 1964.

2ème Conférence des directeurs d'Instituts de Recherches Criminologiques, La recherche en criminologie et la recherche sur les prisons [Second Conference of Directors of Criminological Research Institutes, Research in Criminology and Research on Prisons]. Strasbourg: Council of Europe, 1966.

4ème Conférence des directeurs d'Instituts de Recherches Criminologiques, Aspects criminologiques des infractions routières, Vol. 1 [Fourth Conference of Directors of Criminological Research Institutes, Criminological Aspects of Highway Violations]. Strasbourg: Council of Europe, 1967; *L'étude prospective de la criminalité*, Vol. 2 [The Prospective Study of Criminality]. Strasbourg: Council of Europe, 1967.

5ème Conférence des directeurs d'Instituts de Recherches Criminologiques, La Criminalité chez les migrants européens—La Correspondance des typologies des délinquants et des typologies de traitements [Fifth Conference of Directors of Criminological

Research Institutes, The Criminality of European Migrants—The Linkage between Typologies of Delinquents and Typologies of Treatments]. Strasbourg: Council of Europe, 1968.

6ème Conférence des directeurs d'Instituts de Recherches Criminologiques, Le chiffre noir: L'organisation type de la répression pénale dans un Etat modern [Sixth Conference of Directors of Criminological Research Institutes, The Black Figure: The Organizational Type of Penal Repression in a Modern State]. Strasbourg: Council of Europe, 1969.

7ème Conférence des directeurs d'Institute de Recherches Criminologiques, Orientations actuelles de la recherches criminologique [Seventh Conference of Directors of Criminological Research Institutes, Current Orientations of Criminological Research]. Strasbourg: Council of Europe, 1970.

8ème Conférence des directeurs d'Instituts de Recherches Criminologiques, L'Application des resultats de la recherche criminologique à la politique criminelle [Eighth Conference of Directors of Criminological Research Institutes, The Application of the Results of Criminological Research into Political Crime]. Strasbourg: Council of Europe, 1971.

9ème Conférence des directeurs d'Instituts de Recherches Criminologiques, La perception de la déviance et de la criminalité [Ninth Conference of Directors of Criminological Research Institutes, The Perception of Deviance and Criminality]. Strasbourg: Council of Europe, 1972.

10° Conférence des directeurs d'Instituts de Recherches Criminologiques, Réunion sur les aspects méthodologiques de la classification en criminologie [Tenth Conference of Directors of Criminological Research Institutes, Bringing Together the Methodological Aspects of Classification in Criminology]. Strasbourg: Council of Europe, 1973; *La Violence dans la Société* [Violence in Society]. Strasbourg: Council of Europe, 1973.

11° Conférence des directeurs d'Instituts de Recherches Criminologiques, L'importance des stupéfiants par rapport a la criminalité [Eleventh Conference of the Directors of Criminological Research Institutes, The Importance of Drugs in Connection with Criminality]. Strasbourg: Council of Europe, 1975.

12° Conference des directeurs d'Instituts de Recherches Criminologiques, Aspects criminologiques de la delinquance d'affaires [Twelfth Conference of Directors of Criminological Research Institutes, Criminological Aspects of Delinquent Matters]. Strasbourg: Council of Europe, 1978; in a similar view, *Traitment des détenus en détention de longue durée* [Treatment of Detainees in Long-Term Detention]. Strasbourg: Council of Europe, 1977; *Dédommagement des victimes d'infractions pénales* [Compensation of Victims of Penal Infringements of Rights]. Strasbourg: Council of Europe, 1978.

L'efficacité des programmes en cours concernant la prévention de la délinquance juvénile [The Efficacy of Programs Dealing with the Prevention of Juvenile Delinquency]. Strasbourg: Council of Europe, 1963. *Méthodes de traitement courte durée des jeunes délinquants* [Methods of Short-Term Treatment of Young Delinquents]. Strasbourg: Council of Europe, 1967. *L'efficacité des peines et autres mesures de traitement* [The Efficacy of Sanctions and Other Measures of Treatment]. Strasbourg: Council of Europe, 1967. *Etudes relatives à la recherche criminologique*, 11 volumes from 1967 to 1974.

Joint Colloquia at Bellagio

Elaboration de la sentence pénale (Bellagio, 1968) [Elaboration of the Penal Sentence]. Milano: Centro Nazionale di prevenzione e difesa sociale, 1971.

La décriminalisation, Bellagio, 1973 [Decriminalization, Bellagio, 1973]. Milano: Centro Nazionale di prevenzione e difesa sociale, 1975.

Les délinquants anormaux mentaux, Bellagio, 1963 [Mentally Abnormal Delinquents, Bellagio, 1963]. Paris: Editions Cujas, 1963. Text in French and English.

Privation de liberté dans les perspectives de la lutte contre le crime particulièrement à l'égard de ses nouvelles formes, Bellagio, 1975 [Deprivation of Liberty from the Perspective of the Impact Against Crime Particularly in Regard to Its New Forms, Bellagio, 1975]. Milano: Centro Nazionale di Prevenzione e difesa sociale, 1975.

4

THE UNITED NATIONS AND CRIMINOLOGY

Gerhard O.W. Mueller

ORGANIZATIONAL STRUCTURE

Legislative Bodies

The United Nations, as a worldwide intergovernmental organization, can be compared to state or national governments. Foremost among its legislative bodies is the General Assembly at which each of the 152 member states has one vote, and which is seized of all matters provided her by the charter of the United Nations. Three legislative or policymaking bodies of limited membership supplement the legislative structure, namely, the Security Council, the Trusteeship Council, and the Economic and Social Council.

At the next lower rung of the legislative structure are the functional and expert bodies, which obtain their mandates from their parent bodies to whom they report. For example, the Social Development Commission and the Committee on Crime Prevention and Control report to the Economic and Social Council. Whenever the Economic and Social Council or, for that matter, the General Assembly decides to take up any issue dealing with crime prevention and criminal justice (formerly called "Social Defense"), the Committee on Crime Prevention and Control is normally instructed to resolve the matter and bring it before that higher body for disposition.

EDITOR'S NOTE: This world survey of criminology includes the United Nations because it is the most inclusive international body. Gerhard O.W. Mueller is in the best position to explain the organizational context and procedures whereby the United Nations deals, first, with the fundamental transnational issues of which criminality is a symptom and, second, directly with the problems of crime prevention and criminal justice. Even more significantly, he describes the work of the Crime Prevention and Criminal Justice Branch in six vital types of activities: information gathering and analysis; support for policymaking and planning; setting and implementing standards; research and development; technical assistance; and dissemination of information.

TABLE 4-1
MEMBERS OF THE COMMITTEE ON CRIME PREVENTION AND CONTROL

Region	Country	No. of Years
Asia		
Yoshio SUZUKI	Japan	4
Dhavee CHOOSUP	Thailand	2
YIP Yat-Hoong	Malaysia	2
P. R. RAJAGOPAL	India	4
Ramananda P. SINGH	Nepal	2
Saladh El-Din SALHADAR	Syrian Arab Republic	4
Africa		
S. N. BADU	Ghana	2
Albert METZGER	Sierra Leone	2
Tolani ASUNI	Nigeria	2
Mustafa Abdul Majid KARAH	Libyan Arab Jamahiriya	4
Ahmad M. KHALIFA	Egypt	4
Chadly M. A. NEFZAOUI	Tunisia	4
	one open	
Eastern Europe		
Stanislav V. BORODIN	USSR	4
Dušan COTIC	Yugoslavia	4
Josef GODONY	Hungary	2
Western Europe and others		
Francis Joseph MAHONY	Australia	4
John OLDEN	Ireland	4
Giuseppe di GENNARO	Italy	2
Anthony J. E. BRENNAN	United Kingdom	2
Simone Andrée ROZES	France	4
Ronald L. GAINER	USA	2
Latin America		
Jorge Arturo MONTERO	Costa Rica	4
Silvino Julián SORHEGUI MATO	Cuba	4
Miguel SCHWEITZER SPEISKY	Chile	2
Manuel LOPEZ REY Y ARROYO	Bolivia	4
Aura Guerra de VILLALAZ	Panama	2

The committee now has twenty-seven members (see Table 4-1), which is exactly half of the composition of the Economic and Social Council. The members are nominated by the governments of member states and are elected by the Economic and Social Council. The distribution of seats is by region, according to the principle of equitable geographic distribution. The members are experts in the field of crime prevention and criminal justice, spanning the entire range of the field, including scholars, administrators, and policymakers. The committee meets biannually for a two-week period and may be called together for *ad hoc* meetings. Through a 1979 resolution of the Economic and Social Council, the Committee on Crime Prevention and Control no longer needs to report through the Commission for Social Development. It appears that the Committee on Crime Prevention and Control has been made politically co-equal with the commission and therefore reports directly to the Economic and Social Council.

The current terms of reference of the Committee on Crime Prevention and Control are set out in General Assembly Resolution 32/60 and ECOSOC Resolution 1979/19, entitled "Functions and Long-term Program of Work of the Committee on Crime Prevention and Control," which states:

> *The Economic and Social Council,*
>
> *Conscious* that the main responsibility for solving the problems of crime prevention and control lies with national Governments,
>
> *Reaffirming* its duty to promote international co-operation in solving economic, social, cultural and humanitarian problems and the responsibility assumed by it for promoting international co-operation in the area of crime prevention and control,
>
> *Recalling* paragraph 5 of General Assembly resolution 32/60 of 8 December 1977, as well as the other relevant resolutions of the General Assembly and the Economic and Social Council,
>
> *Aware* of the need for and importance of more effective and better co-ordinated arrangements for the work of United Nations bodies dealing with crime prevention and the treatment of offenders,
>
> *Recognizing* the role of the Committee on Crime Prevention and Control in assisting the Economic and Social Council in organizing and co-ordinating activities concerning crime prevention and control in the United Nations system,
>
> 1. *Entrusts* the Committee on Crime Prevention and Control with the following main functions:
>
> (a) Preparation of the United Nations congresses on the prevention of crime and the treatment of offenders with a view to considering and facilitating the introduction of more effective methods and ways of preventing crime and improving the treatment of offenders;
>
> (b) Preparation and submission to the competent United Nations bodies and to those congresses for their approval, of programmes of international co-operation in the field of crime prevention on the basis of principles of sovereign equality of States and noninterference in internal affairs, and other proposals related to the prevention of offences;
>
> (c) Provision of assistance to the Economic and Social Council in the co-ordination of the activities of United Nations bodies in matters concerning crime control and the treatment of offenders, and preparation and submission of findings and recommendations to the Secretary-General and to the appropriate United Nations bodies;
>
> (d) Promotion of exchanges of experience gained by States in the field of crime prevention and the treatment of offenders;
>
> (e) Discussion of major issues of professional interest, as a basis for international co-operation in this field, particularly those related to the prevention and reduction of crime;
>
> 2. *Requests* the Secretary-General to take all necessary measures to ensure the implementation of the present resolution.
>
> *14th plenary meeting*
> *9 May 1979*

This resolution refers to the all-important United Nations congresses on the Prevention of Crime and the Treatment of Offenders, which have been convened quinquennially since 1955 (1955 Geneva, 1960 London, 1965 Stockholm, 1970 Kyoto, and 1975 Geneva). These congresses have grown out of the congresses which prior to World War II had been organized by the International Penal and Penitentiary Commission, most of whose functions were taken over by the United Nations in 1950 (G.A. Resolution 415(V)). The congresses on the Prevention of Crime and the Treatment of Offenders are intergovernmental meetings at which the member states, as represented by their official delegations, agree on policy with respect to matters of crime prevention and criminal justice if votes are taken, as in all other United Nations congresses convened on various subject matters.

Nonmember states are represented, as are other intergovernmental organizations, specialized agencies, and other units of the United Nations Secretariat, as well as the officially recognized liberation organizations, whose number is rapidly dwindling because more and more of them have become the legitimate governments of their newly independent countries. Particularly noteworthy at these congresses is the participation, as observers, of delegations of the large number of nongovernmental organizations with expertise in crime prevention and control which are in consultative status with the Economic and Social Council. Their experience and expertise provide input into the governmental debates.

The most unusual feature of these congresses is the participation of specialists in the field invited by the secretary general to attend in their individual capacity as observers. While the participation of a large number of scholars and practitioners does not turn these intergovernmental meetings into criminological conventions, it does add a considerable scientific and practical touch, depoliticizes these otherwise political meetings, and introduces issues frequently not discussed in purely governmental gatherings. All discussions at these congresses, whether in plenary or in sections, are on the basis of working papers—one for each of the normally five topics—prepared by the secretariat. The resolutions and conclusions of these congresses, contained in the final report, are transmitted to the Committee on Crime Prevention and Control and other functional bodies, for example, the Commission on Narcotic Drugs, the Commission on Transnational Corporations, and the Commission on Human Rights, as well as the Economic and Social Council and the General Assembly.

These conclusions and recommendations may find themselves swiftly transformed into legislation, and they may be utilized for preparing the so-called Medium-Term Plans (five-year planning exercises) and program budgets (two-year planning exercises). An example of swift legislative enactment is the famous Declaration against Torture, drafted by the Fifth United Nations Congress on the Prevention of Crime and the Treatment of Offenders, and only weeks later, unanimously adopted by the General Assembly.

The secretariat for the congresses is composed of the Crime Prevention and Criminal Justice Branch, whose head doubles as executive secretary of the congresses.

Judicial Bodies

The question necessarily arises as to whether the United Nations in its efforts to deal with matters of crime prevention and criminal justice also exercises any judicial authority. The member states have not yet seen fit to delegate any part of their sovereignty with respect to jurisdiction over questions of criminal justice or related issues of human rights in the international body. The International Court of Justice, an organ of the United Nations located at The Hague, the Netherlands, does not exercise criminal jurisdiction. The post-World War II international war crimes tribunals were not organs of the United Nations but of the Allied powers.

While there are various types of standing or *ad hoc* bodies of inquiry into matters connected with criminal justice and with human rights, member states keep affirming "that the main responsibility for solving the problem of crime prevention and control lies with national governments" (ECOSOC Resolution 1979/19, preambular para 1). This means that in the areas of crime prevention and criminal justice, the United Nations may set standards, make demands, educate, sensitize, report, and publicize, but it may not adjudicate.

The closely intertwined issues of the potential establishment of an International Criminal Court, and the drafting of an International Code of Offences against the Peace and Security of Mankind, dating back to proposals of the mid-1950s, have lain dormant for decades but have recently excited renewed interest. Indeed, the question of the International Criminal Code as a prerequisite for the establishment of an International Criminal Court now has priority on the agenda of the General Assembly.

Administration

To complete the analogy to national governmental systems, reference must now be made to the administrative branch of the United Nations, in other words, the secretariat. The work of the organization concerned with crime prevention and criminal justice is divided among various units, whose establishment has been, more or less, a historical accident. Most prominently, inasmuch as matters of crime prevention and criminal justice fall within the jurisdiction of the Committee on Crime Prevention and Control, it is the unit servicing that committee which is entrusted with the main responsibility of executing legislative mandates in that area. This unit is the Crime Prevention and Criminal Justice Branch, Center for Social Development and Humanitarian Affairs, within the Department of International Economic and Social Affairs, previously located in the New York City headquarters but now transferred to Vienna, Austria.

The Committee on Crime Prevention and Control has been entrusted with assisting "the Economic and Social Council in the coordination of the activities of United Nations bodies in matters concerning crime control and the treatment of offenders and preparation and submission of findings and recommendations to the Secretary-General and to the appropriate United Nations bodies." Thus, the committee, and the branch which services it, have in effect become a focal point for the organization's work in this area.

All matters in the area of international criminality, including the already mentioned proposals for the establishment of an International Criminal Court and the adoption of an International Criminal Code, as well as past and future instruments and conventions dealing with terrorism, hostage taking, and related matters, fall within the province of the Office of Legal Affairs, and are reported to the Sixth Committee of the General Assembly as well as to specially created legislative committees. Matters of narcotics control fall within the terms of reference of the Division of Narcotic Drugs and the International Narcotics Control Board. The appropriate functional body is the Commission on Narcotic Drugs.

The recent interest of the United Nations in the conduct of multinational commercial enterprises is exemplified by the establishment of the Commission on Transnational Corporations, which is being serviced by the Center on Transnational Corporations. The commission is particularly concerned with drafting a code of conduct for transnational corporations.

While the Crime Prevention and Criminal Justice Branch deals with many program elements relevant to human rights in criminal justice, several other programs have been assigned to the Division of Human Rights in Geneva which reports to the Commission on Human Rights. Problems of juvenile justice and juvenile delinquency fall within the jurisdiction of a great many units and specialized agencies, including UNESCO and UNICEF but also the Crime Prevention and Criminal Justice Branch and the Social Development Branch.

Indeed, very few units within the secretariat do not have to deal, from time to time, with problems of crime prevention and control, since crime problems are all-pervasive, and the solution of the crime problem requires the orchestration of all governmental agencies and services.

CRIME PREVENTION AND CRIMINAL JUSTICE BRANCH

The Crime Prevention and Criminal Justice Branch performs a variety of broad-ranging tasks. Being a small unit, it can accomplish its tasks only by relying on a whole host of other services and units. Thus, in preparing for its congresses, the substantive staff of the branch is augmented by consultants recruited from all over the world, who prepare research papers that the staff utilizes in preparing the secretariat working paper. For conducting the congresses, the staff swells to about 250 professional and general service officers—including interpreters and translators for six languages (Arabic, Chinese, English, French, Russian, and Spanish)—documents production officers, and a variety of technicians.

The staff only occasionally carries out technical assistance assignments. Frequently, the branch relies on consultants or on technical or regional advisers who work on funds provided by the United Nations Development Program. Until

1974 the branch had several interregional advisers who were almost constantly on missions assisting countries, at their request, with their crime prevention problems. Those posts had been discontinued in the wake of the world's great fiscal crisis, but their reinstatement has now been requested by the Economic and Social Council. Most functions that do not strictly require criminological expertise—whether pertaining to personnel, translation, documents production, or administration of budget—are carried out by other functional units of the secretariat.

To gather information from member states, the secretariat frequently relies on *notes verbales*, accompanied by questionnaires, to member states. It may also rely on direct contacts with the National Correspondents in Crime Prevention and Criminal Justice. These are presidentially appointed experts who serve as direct liaison between member states and the United Nations Secretariat. Each member state may appoint one or several such expert-correspondents, of whom there are currently about five hundred.

Perhaps the greatest aid to the branch in fulfilling its various mandates are the United Nations or United Nations-affiliated institutes for crime prevention. At the hub of the network is the Rome-based United Nations Social Defense Research Institute which conducts international policy research and supplies the branch with research data and information needed to fulfill the branch's legislative mandates. In addition, there are three United Nations or United Nations-affiliated institutes for crime prevention and criminal justice which service their respective regions by training functionaries, conducting research, and providing technical assistance. These institutes are located in Fuchu, Tokyo, Japan, serving the Asian and Pacific region; Cairo, Egypt, serving the region of the Arab States; and San José, Costa Rica, serving the Latin American region. The institute at Fuchu has been outstanding in its training courses, with over one thousand graduates in all countries of the region. In its short life-span, the institute at San José has distinguished itself in its regional and subregional conferences and its research.

As yet, there is no institute specifically serving Africa south of the Sahara, but the Economic and Social Council has requested its establishment. Negotiations have likewise been under way to create similar institutes to service the region of the East European socialist countries and the region of the "West European and other" countries, which includes North America, Australia, and New Zealand.

WORLDWIDE INFORMATION AND ANALYSIS

Data gathering, analysis, and dissemination in a quantified form is an indispensable prerequisite for policy decisions, planning, budgeting, and the provision of technical assistance to member states. At the same time, the limitations of data gathered cross-culturally must be recognized, and not simply as regards developing countries, which for the most part rank crime problems low on the list of national priorities. Cross-cultural hurdles have to be overcome in all cases, and technical concepts frequently have to be reduced to a common denominator. This reduces all quantified reports in crime prevention at the world level to crude dimensions. Yet, that crudeness is not necessarily an obstacle for comparison and for policy implications. It may well be an aid in recognizing common problems. After all, many of the details of technical distinction, especially with respect to elements of crime, have been the outgrowth of litigation and interpretation of little or no consequence to the underlying social and economic issues.

World Crime Survey

The most ambitious of the worldwide information-gathering exercises has been the report of the secretary general to the General Assembly on crime prevention and control (A/32/199), of September 22, 1977, popularly referred to as the world crime survey. Pursuant to an invitation by the General Assembly in 1972, member states informed the secretary general of the situation concerning crime prevention and control in their respective countries and on the measures being taken to deal with the crime problem. This inquiry was conducted by means of a questionnaire, to which an astonishing sixty-seven governments responded—the highest response rate in the field of crime prevention. All but one region responded, the missing one being Africa south of the Sahara. The countries in this area have emerged from colonialism only recently and are still struggling with the task of nation-building and the provision of basic goods and services. The results of the survey can be summarized as follows:

Developed and Developing Countries

For the years 1970-1975, for the world as a whole, 1,311.2 offenses were committed annually for every 100,000 of the population, including intentional homicides and assaults, sex crimes, kidnapping, robbery, theft, fraud, and major narcotics offenses. If we differentiate between crimes against the person and crimes against property, 20 percent of all the world's crimes are against the person, and 72 percent are against property, like theft and fraud, with an unreliable 8 percent accounting for drug offenses (Figure 4-1).

There is a significant difference in crime rates between the developing and the developed countries, as these have been categorized by the United Nations. More than twice as much crime is reported for developed countries as for developing countries, with 787 per 100,000 population counted for developing countries, and 1,835.3 for developed countries. The chances of being victimized seem to be more than twice as high for inhabitants of a developed country, like the United States, as compared to Ecuador, which is a developing country. Some of the differences may be the result of differences in reporting, but even in developing countries law enforcement officials have improved their methods for inventorying reported offenses.

Particularly startling is the difference in the type of criminality in the two types of countries: in developing countries, crimes against the person and crimes against property are nearly evenly split (Figure 4-2), while in developed countries, crimes against property assume the vastly greater role and crimes against the person account for a proportionally smaller share (Figure 4-2).

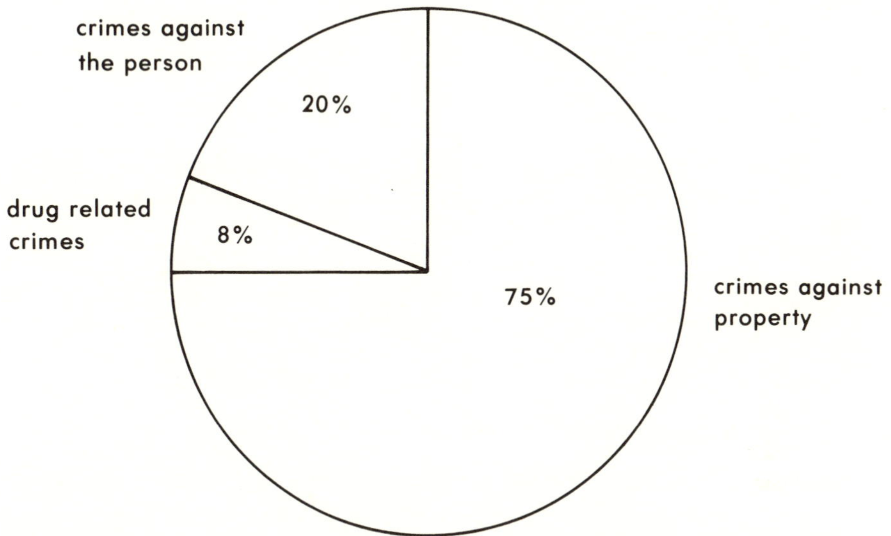

FIGURE 4-1
THE WORLD CRIME PICTURE: PROPORTIONS OF TOTAL CRIME ACCORDING TO BROAD CRIME CATEGORIES

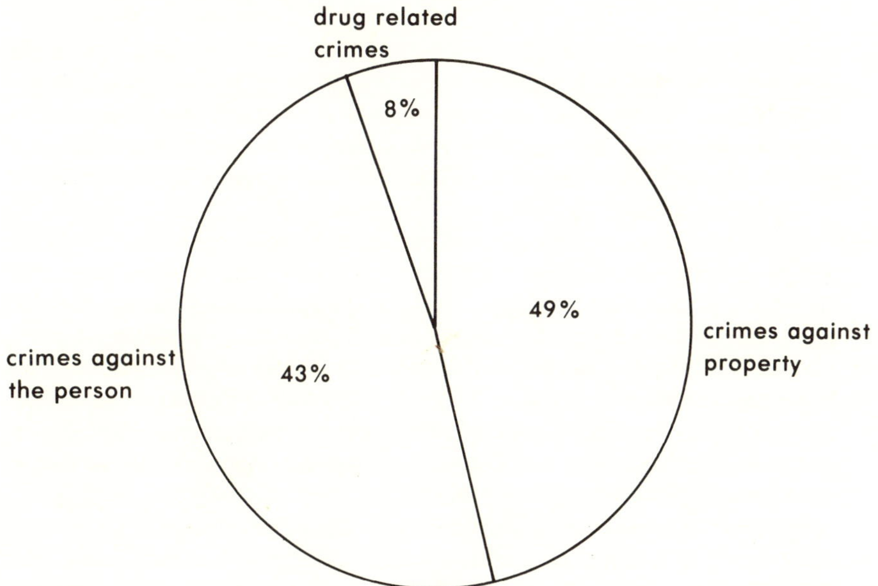

FIGURE 4-2
CRIME PICTURE FOR DEVELOPING COUNTRIES

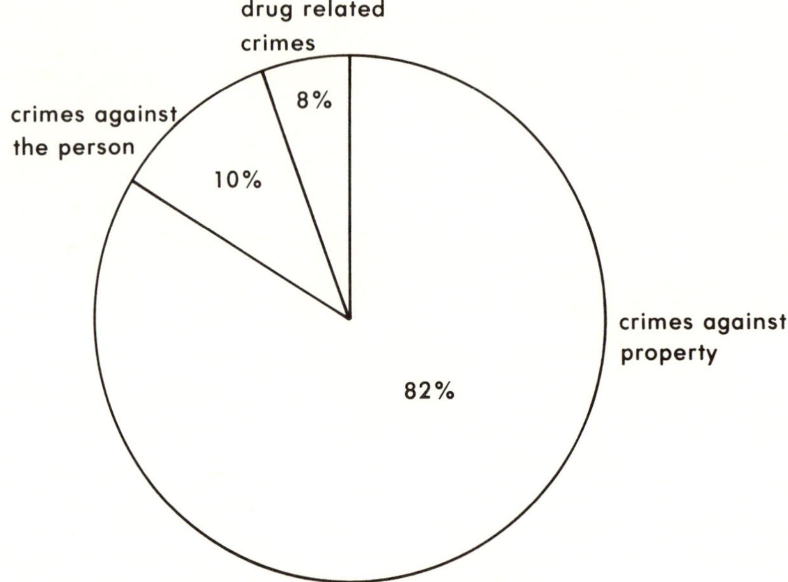

FIGURE 4-3
CRIME PICTURE FOR DEVELOPED COUNTRIES

Proportions of Crime 1970-1975

Does that mean that property criminality increases with increasing wealth? If it does mean that, would it be proper to say that increases in wealth bring about a higher regard for human beings, with a proportionately decreased victimization of the human being itself? Alas, the emphasis is on "proportionately," for there remains the fact that, for the world as a whole, progress in socioeconomic development increases the crime rate as a whole.

Fortunately, there are enough countries to demonstrate that it need not be so: Egypt, Ireland, the Maldives, and Turkey reported a decrease in intentional homicides; Chile, Ecuador, Ireland, Jamaica, Kuwait, Morocco, and Oman a decrease in assaults; Egypt, Ireland, Kuwait, Ecuador, and Singapore a decrease in robbery; Iceland, Morocco, and New Zealand a decrease in both theft and fraud; and Algeria and Ireland a decrease in drug-related offenses and alcohol abuse. The socialist countries of Eastern Europe traditionally have had a lower crime rate than Western European countries, despite increasing industrialization, urbanization, and economic well-being. But good examples can be found in every part of the world. The crime rate of capitalist Japan is extremely low and is dropping, despite enormous advances in industrialization and urbanization. But that is also true for countries of totally different outlook, like traditionalist Saudi Arabia, which is moving from the biblical age to the jet age in a single generation.

If we were to group our reporting countries by regions, we would find some rather interesting common characteristics. In the region comprising the Western European industrialized nations and their overseas cousins (including the United States of America, Canada, Australia, New Zealand, and the Caribbean nations), the crime rates are more than twice as high as those in any other region of the world. But the homicide rate is highest in Latin America, closely followed by that of the Caribbean countries. The Eastern European socialist countries show a low rate of intentional homicides. (Much of their criminality is alcohol-related.) Citizens of Western countries, of which the United States is a part, have a tenfold higher chance of being victimized by a theft or fraud than citizens of other regions of the world.

Of particular interest are the figures regarding female criminality. Female criminality is only about 10 percent as high as male criminality for the world as a whole. The figures are a little lower for developing countries and a little higher for developed countries. But the trends are startling: Female criminality is rising 30 percent faster than male criminality in the developing countries and 50 percent faster in developed countries. It appears, therefore, that as developing countries become more developed, their share of the female crime rate may also increase. This change has considerable implications for policymakers. Since unchecked development seems to be correlated with an increase in criminality, women in developing countries are doubly vulnerable as potential offenders, being a specially developing group in a developing national setting.

The report also permits some tentative conclusions with regard to a comparison of crime and criminal justice data with socioeconomic development indicators. Higher or rising crime rates are correlated with increased migration from rural to urban areas, increased literacy rates, decreasing infant mortality rates, and rising per capita incomes and gross national products. In short, it appears that society pays a price for unbridled economic ambitions and advances. Something valuable appears to get lost in the process of urbanization and industrialization. This conclusion is particularly supported by the experience of the relatively few countries that are apparently bucking the general trend, including Greece and Switzerland, Japan, several of the Arab States, and the socialist countries. All of these countries seem to have preserved (or sometimes replaced or restored) the capacity of indigenous social control organs, including the family, the extended family, and cells and units of living and of production, to deal with and to check deviance. Obviously, these countries are willing to pay a price that is deemed unacceptable elsewhere.

The figures descriptive of the criminal justice system are of equal importance to the researcher and planner. The criminal justice system, consisting of law enforcement agencies, courts, and correctional services, with varying amounts of community participation, involves a complex of installations, physical structures and equipment, related services, and personnel, of which the human element is the most important.

Several other conclusions emerge from the report:

First, crime is increasingly becoming a major world problem: its extent, variety and impact, both nationally and internationally, cannot be underestimated. Second, in view of the seriousness of the problem and of its ramifications and repercussions which extend far beyond national frontiers, international co-operation in relation to crime must be strengthened. Lastly, the United Nations has a primary and unique role to play in this direction, not only in the sharing of common experience and the dissemination of reliable and internationally comparable data, but also in providing advice and technical assistance services to requesting countries in the development and promotion of relevant research and in the elaboration of policy guidelines and planning strategies in specific areas of common concern (A/32/199, para. 7).

The Crime Prevention and Criminal Justice Branch, in collaboration with the United Nations Social Defence Research Institute (Rome), is currently engaged in improving the methodology for worldwide crime surveys, in anticipation of a second major inquiry in 1981.

Correctional Information

In this area, periodic surveys are conducted among member states for reports on three issues: First, the extent to which the United Nations Standard Minimum Rules for the Treatment of Prisoners are implemented; second, the prison population census; and third, surveys on capital punishment.

The first inquiry on the implementation of the Standard Minimum Rules was made in 1967. The result of this inquiry, to which forty-four countries replied, was presented to the Fourth United Nations Congress on the Prevention of Crime and the Treatment of Offenders, held at Kyoto, Japan, August 17 to 26, 1970.

In 1974, the secretary general invited all member states to respond to a new inquiry concerning the implementation of the rules. The 1974 inquiry was structured as a questionnaire which, it was felt, might encourage a broader and more meaningful response than had been elicited from the inquiry made in 1967.

Part I of the questionnaire was intended to provide a general survey of the extent to which the rules had influenced the legislation and administrative regulations of member states or were otherwise embodied in national prison laws, as well as to supply information on measures taken in order to disseminate the rules. Simple "Yes/No" responses were given by checking an appropriate square, but room for amplifying comments was structured into the survey form.

Part II of the questionnaire was designed to provide an assessment of the extent to which the rules were being implemented in practice, rule by rule. To make it possible to evaluate and compare the national reports and yet permit a certain range of choices, the replies to the questions in this part were given under the following five categories: implemented, implemented partially, recognized in principle, not implemented, and not applicable.

The survey revealed "that the Standard Minimum Rules have influenced national legislation or regulations to a very large extent." Thus, the great majority of the responding countries have affirmed that both the prevailing prison laws and the executive regulations have been influenced by the rules. One country expressly reported that parts of its prison regulations are a literal translation of the relevant Standard Minimum Rules.

Several countries pointed out that their prison laws had already been established when the rules were adopted and, consequently, were not influenced by the rules. Even in these cases, however, the rules have been important either in the formulation of executive regulations or in interpreting the prevailing legislation. Furthermore, three countries reported that laws currently in preparation took provisions of the rules into consideration. A few states noted that no specific enactments had been made in response to the rules, as these were already generally reflected and embodied in the existing statutory provisions or in instructions issued to penal establishments.

Considerable effort seems to have been made to disseminate the rules. Only three countries reported that the rules were not translated into the official language of the country, but in all three cases English is widely understood. None of the reporting states, however, indicated whether translations were made into languages used in specific areas of the country.

In their replies, most countries answered that the rules were available in their penal and correctional institutions, but several mentioned that the inmates did not have access to them. With few exceptions, the rules were included in programs for staff training. One country, in which the rules were neither available in institutions nor used in training programs, mentioned that it seemed more important for both the prison personnel and the prisoners to know and have access to the valid national provisions than to *de lege ferenda* recommendations, but conceded that knowledge of the rules was necessary for those who had a role to play in the development of statutory provisions. According to the report on the survey:

> The Standard Minimum Rules obviously have had a significant influence on the laws and regulations of jurisdictions within federated systems. . . . Thirty-six per cent of the responding jurisdictions in the United States reported that the Rules had influenced the prevailing prison law, 42 per cent indicated that they had influenced executive regulations and 60 per cent reported that the guarantees embodied in the prison laws themselves are in conformity with those enunciated in the Rules even if not as a direct result of them. With a few exceptions, the reporting Canadian provinces and territories recognized the impact of the Rules on their legislation, and the two Australian states noted that the Rules had influenced both their prison laws and their executive regulations (A/CONF.56/6, Annex I, paras. 6-10).

The third inquiry on the extent of implementation of the Standard Minimum Rules is currently under way.

As part of this data gathering in the field of corrections, a prisoner census was taken and was published in conjunction with the 1974 inquiry (A/CONF.56/6, Annex II). Among the forty-seven countries responding, the highest prison populations were recorded for the United States, with 189 prisoners per 100,000 population as of December 31, 1972. Comparably high rates of imprisonment are to be found in Colombia (186 per 100,000), El Salvador (175 per 100,000), and Kenya (165 per 100,000). These figures contrast with low figures for Ireland (35 per 100,000), Cyprus (31 per 100,000), Malaysia (25 per 100,000), and the Netherlands (21 per 100,000). Such contrasts in rates of imprisonment raise serious policy questions about the wisdom of using incarceration as a sanction since the use and impact of imprisonment seem unrelated to crime rates and vary widely even among culturally comparable countries. The working paper of the secretariat on "The Treatment of Offenders, in Custody or in the Community, with Special Reference to the Implementation of the Standard Minimum Rules for the Treatment of Prisoners Adopted by the United Nations" (A/CONF.56/6) discusses these implications in some detail.

The secretariat continues to report on the use of capital punishment among states with the "objective. . .of progressively restricting the number of offences for which capital punishment might be imposed with a view to the desirability of abolishing this punishment in all countries" (ECOSOC Resolution 1574 (L)). Earlier reports were disseminated in 1962, 1967, and 1973. The most recent report was that of 1975 (E/56/5 and Add.1, Corr. 1 and 2). In its cautious conclusions, the secretary general urged member states to consider ways to effect the relatively rapid abolition of capital punishment. "Certainly, the experience of abolitionist states indicates that no dire consequences are to be feared following abolition."

A fifth survey on capital punishment was conducted for the Economic and Social Council and for the Sixth United Nations Congress on the Prevention of Crime and the Treatment of Offenders. This report will also contain information on practices and statutory rules that may govern the right of a person sentenced to death to petition for pardon, commutation, or reprieve (G.A. Res. 2857 (XXVI)).

BROAD-BASED POLICY AND PLANNING

After several years of work by the Committee on Crime Prevention and Control and much research by the staff of the branch, the committee issued its report in 1976 entitled "Methods and Ways Likely to Be Most Effective in Preventing Crime and Improving the Treatment of Offenders," the so-called International Plan of Action (E/AC.57/L.7). The report was received by the General Assembly which invited member states to make use of the report in formulating national crime prevention policies and strategies (G.A. Res. 32/58). "It is the aim of this report to draw attention to those areas of crime prevention and control in which recommendations of the United Nations could achieve the greatest possible yield for the largest possible number of States" (E/AC.57/L.7, para. 2).

While the report is strong in identifying the type of criminality likely to be most troublesome to states during the remainder of the twentieth century, it is particularly strong in its emphasis on the establishment of intersectoral planning for purposes of national crime prevention efforts. "The planning of criminal policy, i.e. of the prevention of crime and of the treatment of offenders, should be part of national development planning. In order to achieve this, countries should establish, whenever possible, a body in charge of criminal policy planning, working in close connexion with the agency dealing with national development planning" (E/AC.57/L.7, para. 5). The report then details the role of various components of the criminal justice system in sectoral planning and concludes with a recommendation for the establishment of international standards and guidelines. The subsequent work of the organization has provided further materials for integrated national and international, cross-sectoral and sectoral, planning methods and strategies to deal with crime prevention.[1]

The number of countries making broad-scale use of planning to deal with crime prevention is increasing, as are positive reports about the planning approach to crime prevention and criminal justice.

STANDARD-SETTING AND IMPLEMENTATION

Since its foundation the United Nations had increased its efforts to secure the rights and preserve the dignity of all those who come into contact with the criminal justice system. The Universal Declaration of Human Rights refers to the protection of human rights in criminal justice in its articles 7, 8, 9, 10 and 11. The principles proclaimed in those articles have been set forth, *inter alia*, in the International Covenant on Civil and Political Rights (articles 9, 14 and 15),[2] the Standard Minimum Rules for the Treatment of Prisoners,[3] the draft principles on freedom from arbitrary arrest and detention,[4] the draft principles on equality in the administration of justice,[5] and the Declaration on the Protection of All Persons from Being Subjected to Torture and Other Cruel, Inhuman or Degrading Treatment or Punishment,[6] which has become central to recent efforts towards drafting standards in criminal justice (A/CONF.87/RM.1, para. 69).

There have been significant developments in this regard in recent years. Thus,

in 1976 the Committee on Crime Prevention and Control undertook efforts to strengthen the Standard Minimum Rules for the Treatment of Prisoners, the validity of which has been recognized by most Governments and which have contributed to the improvement of prison conditions in many countries. In pursuance of Economic and Social Council resolution 1993 (LX), paragraph 6, the Committee recommended a new draft rule 95,[7] seeking to assure the applicability of the Rules to all persons arrested or imprisoned with or without charge, and elaborated draft procedures for the effective implementation of the Rules. The revised rule was approved with some changes by the Council in 1977 (ECOSOC Res. 2076 [LXII]).

Finally, the committee recommended the development of new standards to:

(a) Ensure just and effective judicial proceedings, improved selection and training of judges and prosecutors and the establishment of safeguards against the abuse of discretion in sentencing;

(b) Provide minimum rules for the treatment of offenders in the community;
(c) Strengthen inmate grievance procedures by ensuring the prisoners the right to recourse to an independent authority at both the national and international levels;
(d) Facilitate the return of persons convicted of crime abroad to their domicile to serve their sentences; and
(e) Improve the situation of persons detained in police or prison custody before trial (A/CONF.87/RM.1, paras. 73-74).[8]

Perhaps the most encouraging development in this respect has been the elaboration by the Committee on Crime Prevention and Control of the Draft Code of Conduct for Law Enforcement Officials. An intersessional working group of the Thirty-third General Assembly in 1978 reworked the twelve preambular and the first five operative articles of this instrument. The Thirty-fourth General Assembly is expected to complete the work and to adopt the United Nations Code of Conduct for Law Enforcement Officials which, in effect, gives law enforcement the imprimatur of a profession, recognizing the important task which law enforcement officials are performing diligently and with dignity, in compliance with the principles of human rights. The code details the duties of law enforcement officials with respect to the maintenance of the highest standards of human rights, proscribes the use of torture and abusive practices, guards against corruption and other abuses, and protects the confidentiality of information obtained which may be detrimental to persons affected.

With respect to all of these standards, the problem of implementation looms large. The member states have not entrusted the United Nations with the type of enforcement apparatus found at national levels. In this regard, sovereignty in matters of criminal justice continues to be an abiding principle. Consequently, the United Nations can practice only "soft" implementation procedures, which include recommendations for the implementation of United Nations standards by means of national law, wide dissemination, use in training exercises, international reporting mechanisms, and, to some extent, national, regional, and interregional complaint procedures. The types of international implementation procedures have been incorporated in the "Draft Procedures for the Effective Implementation of the Standard Minimum Rules for the Treatment of Prisoners," drafted by the Committee on Crime Prevention and Control and passed by the Social Development Commission, but not yet approved by the Economic and Social Council. This instrument might ultimately serve as an implementation model for all United Nations standards and rules in the area of crime prevention and criminal justice.

The Sixth United Nations Congress on the Prevention of Crime and the Treatment of Offenders, under agenda item V, will devote considerable attention to the growing network of United Nations standards and guidelines, as well as their implementation.

PROBLEM-SOLVING RESEARCH AND DEVELOPMENT

As part of each work program, the Crime Prevention and Criminal Justice Branch has been receiving mandates to deal with crime prevention and criminal justice problems which the Committee on Crime Prevention and Control has identified as particularly troublesome to member states. Thus, the secretariat is currently working on issues related to the prevention and control of violence, including the impact of the mass media on juveniles. Previous projects include the incorporation of crime prevention policies in educational and vocational training and the linking of the rehabilitation of offenders to related social services. Several other such projects have been identified for future work, including the expeditious and equitable handling of criminal cases in the trial and post-trial stages, that may result in the development of standards and guidelines.

Normally, the regular staff of the branch handles these projects as part of the regular budget. Consultants may be engaged, interregional meetings may be conducted (occasionally on extrabudgetary funds), and field work and site visits are frequently undertaken.

PROVIDING TECHNICAL ASSISTANCE

Developing countries are entitled to portions of the overall funds available under the United Nations Development Program. With the increasing awareness of the interrelationship between socioeconomic development and criminality, more and more countries are investing parts of their development funds in projects related to crime prevention and criminal justice. The branch is undertaking all substantive aspects for the development and execution of such projects, although the funding comes from the Development Program and the field staff executing the programs may actually be consultants identified by the branch.

Such technical assistance activities may range from the creation of an entire model for a national criminal justice system (as in the case of Namibia), or a complete analysis of a national crime problem with recommendations for solution (as in Jamaica), to more specific issues such as dealing with a growing problem of juvenile prostitution (Cameroon), the establishment of a metallurgical crime laboratory (Israel), the provision of psychological services in prisons (Hong Kong), or the creation of probation and parole services (Papua-New Guinea).

The previously discussed regional institutes for crime prevention and criminal justice must be seen as an integral part of the technical assistance services, as, indeed, much of the technical assistance for the various regions emanates directly from these institutes.

DISSEMINATION OF INFORMATION

One of the weakest aspects of the work of the United Nations in the field of crime prevention and control is the dissemination of information regarding the work of the organization. As a relatively small unit of an intergovernmental organization, the Crime Prevention and Criminal Justice Branch is not equipped to do much more than to communicate with governments, other intergovernmental organizations (like the Council of Europe or INTERPOL), specialized agencies, and other units of the secretariat.

Collaboration with, or services for, individual scholars or local governments is virtually out of the question, although every effort is made to respond to all inquiries. Cordial and fruitful relations exist with nongovernmental organizations in consultative status with the Economic and Social Council; foremost among them are the International Society for Criminology, the International Association of Penal Law, the International Society of Social Defence, the Howard League, the International Prisoners Aid Association, and Amnesty International. Most of these organizations have formed an alliance of nongovernmental organizations, whose representatives meet on a monthly basis with the head of the branch. These organizations have been of great assistance to the United Nations, through research and publications that have often been specifically designed as aids to the United Nations work program. The congresses of these organizations are also designed to feed directly into the United Nations congresses.

While the regular flow of public documentation in crime prevention and criminal justice is not calculated to reach the public at large, three types of publications are intended for public distribution, namely, the *International Review of Criminal Policy* (of which thirty-four volumes have been published), the Newsletters of the Crime Prevention and Criminal Justice Branch, published biannually, and the Monograph Series, of which two volumes are in print. Each of the institutes has its own publication series. Those of the United Nations Social Defence Research Institute are particularly numerous and useful to the profession.

FINAL COMMENT

The United Nations has a broad commitment and work program in the field which academically is referred to as criminology and in practice as crime prevention and criminal justice. The United Nations' interest is profoundly practical and is geared to helping all nations deal with the prevention of crime in a humane and cost-beneficial manner by avoiding costly mistakes that may have been made elsewhere.

NOTES

1. See especially Instituto Latinoamericano de las Naciones Unidas para la Prevención del Delito y el Tratamiento del Delincuente, "Planificación de la Política Criminal dentro de los Programas de Desarrollo Nacional en Latinoamérica" (San Jose: 1976); Proceedings of the United Nations Interregional Training Course on Crime Prevention Planning (Canberra: 1977); Hardy Wickwar, "The Place of Criminal Justice in Development Planning" (Vol. 1, Monographs of the United Nations Crime Prevention and Criminal Justice Section, New York University Press, 1977).

2. Adopted by General Assembly Resolution 2200 A (XXI), in force since March 23, 1976.

3. First United Nations Congress on the Prevention of Crime and the Treatment of Offenders: Report by the Secretariat (United Nations publication, Sales No. 56.IV.4),

annex I.A. The rules were approved by the Economic and Social Council in Resolution 663 C (XXIV).

4. Study of the Right of Everyone to Be Free from Arbitrary Arrest, Detention and Exile (United Nations publication, Sales No. 65.XIV.2) and "Study of the right of arrested persons to communicate with those whom it is necessary for them to consult in order to ensure their defence or to protect their essential interests" (E/CN.4/996).

5. Study of Equality in the Administration of Justice (United Nations publication, Sales No. E.71.XIV.3). The draft principles were approved by the Sub-Commission on Prevention of Discrimination and Protection of Minorities in its Resolution 3 (XXIII).

6. Adopted by the Fifth United Nations Congress on the Prevention of Crime and the Treatment of Offenders and by the General Assembly in Resolution 3452 (XXX).

7. Report of the Committee on its fourth session (E/CN.5/536), para. 95.

8. Ibid., para. 86.

BIBLIOGRAPHY

Alper, Benedict S., and Jerry F. Borden. *Crime: International Agenda*. Lexington, Mass.: D. C. Heath and Co., 1972.

Australian Institute of Criminology. *Proceedings of the United Nations Interregional Training Course on Crime Prevention Planning*. Canberra, 1977.

Bassiouni, M. Cherif, and Ved P. Verde. *A Treatise on International Criminal Law*. 2 vols. Springfield, Ill.: Charles C Thomas, 1973.

Clifford, William. *Planning Crime Prevention*. Lexington, Mass.: D. C. Heath and Co., 1976.

Clinard, Marshall B., and Daniel J. Abbott. *Crime in Developing Countries: A Comparative Perspective*. New York: John Wiley and Sons, 1973.

López-Rey y Arroyo, Manuel. *Criminologia: Criminalidad y Planificación de la Política Criminal*. Madrid: Aguilar, 1978.

Mueller, Gerhard O.W., and Edward M. Wise. *International Criminal Law*. South Hackensack, N.J., and London: Sweet and Maxwell, Ltd., 1965.

United Nations. "Economic and Social Consequences of Crime: New Challenges for Research and Planning." Working paper prepared by the Secretariat A/CONF.56/7, 1975.

———. *Fifth United Nations Congress on the Prevention of Crime and the Treatment of Offenders*. A/CONF.56/10, 1975.

———. *International Review of Criminal Policy*, No. 34. (Survey volume covering all activities.) Sales No. E.78.IV. 8, 1978.

———. *The United Nations and Human Rights*. New York: 1978, Sales No. E.78.1.18.

Wickwar, Hardy. *The Place of Criminal Justice in Development Planning*. New York: New York University Press, 1977. (Vol. I, Monographs of the United Nations Crime Prevention and Criminal Justice Branch.)

5

CRIMINOLOGY IN DEVELOPING NATIONS—AFRICAN AND ASIAN EXAMPLES

William Clifford

The statement made on August 25, 1980, by the secretary general of the United Nations to the Sixth United Nations Congress on the Prevention of Crime and the Treatment of Offenders held at Caracas in Venezuela, contained the following passage: "Today, we perhaps stand on the threshold of a new perception of the problem of crime in the context of economic and social development."

A PERENNIALLY "NEW" APPROACH

This statement was made nearly fifteen years after the first course for Asian and Far Eastern peoples on "Crime and Economic Development" was held by the United Nations Asia and Far East Institute for the Prevention of Crime and the Treatment of Offenders at Fuchu, near Tokyo, Japan. Then, how could the secretary general think he was still on a threshold? Did it mean that the by now familiar relationship between crime and development had only just percolated to the higher levels of the United Nations and world diplomacy?

Any other explanation is difficult to accept because, in 1968, the entire (No. 25) issue of the United Nations' own *International Review of Criminal Policy*

EDITOR'S NOTE: Emergent and "underdeveloped" nations constitute a new phenomenon since 1945. Their socioeconomic development has particularly illustrated the convergence of criminology and more general socioeconomic planning, the effects of urbanization and industrialization on the incidence and patterning of crime, the association of the institutionalization of criminology with the creation of a full-fledged academy, and the vital importance of previous sociocultural history on the course of such institutionalization. To provide background for the chapters that deal with the criminology of those nations endeavoring to cope with crime in these terms, William Clifford draws on his expertise in criminological policy and research in Africa and Asia. By emphasizing the activities of the United Nations in this respect, his chapter extends our earlier consideration of international collaboration in dealing with the political, economic, and social facets of crime.

was devoted to the theme of the "prevention of delinquency in the context of national development." This issue was in preparation for the second meeting of the United Nations Consultative Group on the Prevention of Crime and the Treatment of Offenders which met in Geneva in August 1968 with the development theme as the first of its three agenda items. In 1973, a world survey of crime was undertaken by the United Nations Secretariat and was presented to the United Nations General Assembly in 1976,[1] showing a clear relationship across the world between the levels of economic and social development and the levels of crime.

So if the United Nations in Caracas was to wake up to the idea that it was really on the threshold of a new approach to crime by treating it within the "new" perspective of economic and social development, it was woefully behind events not only within criminology, but also within its own organization for more than a decade before.

"Development" and "crime" are "venerable bedfellows." The interrelationship between crime and development has been conspicuous and thoroughly predictable whether in connection with the Enclosure Acts, which dispossessed the small holders to develop England in the seventeenth and eighteenth centuries, or with reference to gold rushes in America, South Africa, and Australia in the nineteenth century, or in connection with the drilling for oil, the building of great railroads, or the colonial exploitation of the so-called developing countries. Extend the notion of crime to white-collar or corporate crime, and most of our modern technological inventions, from computers to kidney machines, have lent themselves to illegal or, at least, highly questionable, maneuvers to promote an exploitative monopoly.

DOES DEVELOPMENT INCREASE CRIME?

The developing countries are well aware of this surge of crime in the wake of investment, industrialization, modernization, and urban growth. Not infrequently, they have experienced violent revolutions and widespread dislocation as aid flowed and corruption set in; they are by no means reconciled to the activities of some transnational corporations within their borders. It was within the context of developing country problems that, at the Fifth United Nations Congress on Crime in Geneva, Professor Khaleeg Naqui lectured on economic crime. He defined it as crime that in some way affects incomes, employment, supplies, or distribution. Activities by foreign companies have frequently had profound effects on local economies.

The aftermath of civil war and guerrilla activities has meant bolder and more frequent armed robberies in at least two African countries. In Uganda, before the reign of Idi Amin, crowds in the streets lost confidence in the police and sometimes took the law into their own hands. Crime and politics were interrelated as armies of youthful unemployed became politically active in the towns. Much of the political instability of the developing countries is traceable to crime out of control. Conversely, political instability provided opportunities for crime which were not there previously. Everywhere, in the towns, the traditional social controls have been diluted by mobility and a new opportunism. In developing countries, as elsewhere, success is too often being measured by power and possessions, with little regard to any moral or legal principles of acquisition.

Yet, when all is said and done, it appears that the developing countries have a good deal less crime than the developed ones. Even when allowance is made for differences in recording and for the incomparability of much of the crime in different countries, it is difficult to escape the conclusion that crime has followed development so faithfully that one can almost cite the levels of crime by knowing the levels of development. The only exception to this general rule is Japan.[2]

The Arab League States were said in a Caracas lecture to have recent rises in crime rates corresponding to increases in per capita incomes, and this is probably the situation in most of the so-called development world.[3] The types of crime have changed, of course, with process of development. Older crimes of vengeance and personal attack in defense of honor or property have been overtaken by economic crimes of one kind or another. Property crimes abound, and it seems that economic and social development not only brings crime but specific types of crime as well. Drug offenses are following the development flag, as are corruption, white-collar, and corporate crimes. Crime as a profession is also a relatively new concept for the Third World, except in the more open form of banditry or piracy. The spread of the mass media makes it inevitable that, whatever the type of crime in other parts of the world, it will have an imitative effect. As modern communications and global interdependence expand, crime, like heart disease, follows the affluent and most comfortable conditions.

ELUSIVENESS OF RELIABLE INFORMATION

Yet, developing nations have their share of crime, and, within their borders, crime usually reflects international trends—that is, it generally follows the lines of improvement in economic and social conditions. The difficulty is that it is almost impossible to prove any such statements with hard data.

It is known that statements about crime in developed countries are difficult to prove. Is crime increasing or decreasing? Is it really greater in urban areas? Are minority groups more criminal? When such questions are asked in London, Paris, and New York, the answers differ, and the interpretations of the answers differ even more. Those who use published figures will be reminded of the "dark figure" for unrecorded crime. Those who depend upon case studies or investigations of selected research will find their samples being questioned as unrepresentative and their generalizations cast into doubt. Those who use delinquent and control groups will be challenged on the conclusions they derive from such comparison without knowing the distribution of such factors in the general population.

In developed countries we know a lot about crime, yet we know very little. Imagine, therefore, the situation in countries where there is no regular system of annual reports, or where figures may be far less consistently gathered or reliable. Sometimes the available data are for one area or region only, or there have been political upheavals and older records and files may have been lost or deliberately destroyed. More than that, the older records may have little modern relevance. Consider, for example, the criminal records in Zimbabwe before and after the political settlement. Many of those now in power were on the most "wanted" lists; the older "crimes" of violence, even where people were killed, are most likely to be regarded now as acts of war. In Iran, the records kept during the reign of the Shah and those kept afterwards are probably not comparable. Even when reference is made to crime following development, it could be argued that in some of the developing countries this is not a rise in crime but a reflection of better recording.

A great deal of what is known about crime in developing countries is, therefore, born of experience and of local reports that may not be generalized. The cultural differences within and between developing countries in Asia and Africa are such that they affect the very meaning of crime and, therefore, complicate any attempts at comparison. For many years such problems inhibited the development of criminology. The dearth of reliable data made some of the early studies of crime in developing areas not very respectable in the sophisticated centers of criminological learning in the West.

REASSESSMENT OF CRIMINOLOGY AS A SCIENCE

Then three things happened. First, as the crime problems in the developed areas continued and even ramified despite the amounts spent on the study and control of crime, the idea that criminology as a science might be narrowly conceived or might not be really so sophisticated as had been thought gained currency. A younger generation of researchers was prepared to attack criminology's "sacred cows." A new political mood attacked the system which created offenders and discriminated in the way the system worked. Criminologists of earlier renown now appeared in this interpretation to be not unlike Lombroso: looking for types when they should have been questioning the very basis for distinguishing between criminals and others.

Second, the absurdity of criminologists in countries with more crime sitting in judgment on the value of work in countries with less crime began to permeate the international consciousness. Sometimes the technical machinery for collecting criminological data was not there simply because crime was not regarded as a real problem. Sometimes the psychological or sociological constructs of the West did not apply in developing regions where life-styles and basic problems of survival, both collective and individual, were so very different.

As this new awareness grew, scholars began to regret the fact that law and criminology had so very rarely been among the qualifications or interests of the earlier social anthropologists who had done so much writing on those simpler peoples in developing areas who were now in the turmoil of modernization.

Above all, it was more and more appreciated that the cultural dimensions of crime and its control had more significance than they had previously been accorded. To explain crime and its control, it was as necessary to know as much about the areas of the world that were untroubled with crime as it was to have libraries of publications on the situation in the more developed but crime-ridden areas. If the developing nations had less crime and were likely to get more with modernization and socioeconomic growth, could they not preserve at least some of their advantages by profiting from the mistakes of the developed countries?

Third, the travel explosion of the 1960s and 1970s, as well as schemes for young people to join the Peace Corps or its equivalent organizations of volunteers in other countries, brought the developing areas into sharper focus in the developed areas. They were no longer remote and esoteric but areas of new concern for all those with a conscience and concern for humanity.

So the interest in learning as much as possible about crime in developing countries has mushroomed. Obviously, the criteria for quality in criminological research are the same, whether the work is in developed or developing areas, but there is now a greater openness about accumulating information by methods or techniques that would have had little academic status in earlier years. Even purely descriptive studies are now acceptable as valuable contributions to knowledge in areas where hardly anything is known or recorded about crime. Attempts are being made to establish criminology in the various universities of the developing countries which, until now, have been concentrating on basic faculties. There is a lively appreciation that, in trying to explain human behavior in developed areas, one cannot neglect the social changes taking place in developing areas. To do so would be to lose a great opportunity for a deeper understanding of human nature in varied and contrastable social settings.

GENERALIZATIONS ABOUT CRIME PATTERNS

A few general statements may be made about crime in developing areas on the basis of experience and present knowledge. These are as challengeable, of course, as any statements about crime in developed countries, and they are less general in their application because of the great variety of cultures and political systems in any one developing region. With such reservations it is still generally true that:

1. Developing areas seem to have less crime and are less concerned than are developed countries about crime as a problem. They are more concerned with improving standards of living, avoiding malnutrition, and building a sound basis for development.
2. Family structures, communal loyalties, and social controls are stronger in the developing areas. While urban conditions approximate those in the West, family, communal, and even tribal links have frequently survived to a remarkable extent.

3. There is less difference than is usually thought between local traditional nations of tolerable and intolerable behavior and the legal codes imported from the developed areas.
4. The motiveless, pathological types of offenses that are not unfamiliar in developed countries, especially in the larger cities, are correspondingly rare in developing areas.
5. The developing and, therefore, less atomized societies have a capacity for absorbing the eccentric nondangerous individual—a capacity that seems to contract as neighborliness declines.

Some of these generalizations are functions of size. Crime is obviously no great public issue in a simple, small, relatively static, homogeneous, and competition-free community. It acquires a more serious proportion as the number of people increases, mobility accelerates, and the division of labor subdivides. But not all developing countries are small, and the interest develops around the ways in which some of the integration of smaller societies has survived the onslaught of industrialization, urbanization, and culture contact with the developed nations via the mass media. Of course, this may be due to a simple time lag. Future generations in developing countries may be facing the crime problems now being faced by people in developed countries. The question is whether developing countries can manage to change the rhythm and step of this apparently inexorable march of time. The issue is whether they can act now to improve their prospects of achieving a quality of life less plagued with the social problems accompanying economic growth.

AFRICA: A CRIMINOLOGICAL LABORATORY

The vast expanse of the African continent with its temperate and tropical regions, its deserts and forests, its diverse peoples with hundreds of cultural religions and language variations, and its constantly changing political complexion make it particularly difficult to use as an example of crime in the developing areas of the world. From its Islamic north through the mountains of ancient Christian Ethiopia to the ostracized apartheid lands of the south, the changing reality of Africa makes exceptions to almost any general statement that might be attempted. For the most part there is a lack of data on crime and where it is available it is not easy to interpret.

Yet, Africa cannot be excluded from any attempt to consider crime in developing areas. Its cultural diversity is a challenge to the very meaning of crime; and there have been some modern attempts at socialist change, military dictatorship, and urban control which have great significance for the theories of crime control. Penalties have been made more severe to control crime, different forms of anti-corruption measures have been applied, and youth corps of various kinds have been mobilized to deal with youth unemployment and to deal indirectly with crime arising from youth unemployment. Moreover, there is a fascinating history of Africa which has yet to be written. From the piracy that flourished along the Barbary Coast to the diamond smuggling that still plagues the African interior; from the external slave raids on the east and west coasts and the internal selling of people to traders, to the traffic in women which continues along the borders of the Sahara; from the rural cattle stealing which is traditional to some tribes, to the modern counterfeiting along the West Coast and from witchcraft killings and ritual murders to sophisticated economic, corporate, and sometimes clearly organized crime in the larger urban areas—African crime is full of interest and criminological meaning.

The question is what do we mean by crime in Africa? Professor Eric Paula Kibuka of Makerene University in Kampala has recently argued that:

> The general crime trends prevailing in Africa in so far as they can be related to the socioeconomic situation. . . can be summarized as resulting from the serious situation of poverty and unemployment prevailing in countries in Africa which are typified by a labor surplus.[4]

He calls for more social justice and public participation to prevent crime. Social justice is desirable for its own sake, not only in relation to crime; and no crime prevention anywhere is possible without public involvement. But if countries across the world were to be placed on a scale according to their levels of social justice, it is not unlikely that those that have achieved most in this direction would be among the most crime-ridden. More significantly, Professor Kibuka refers to the serious problem of communication in Africa which so frequently prevents laws from being known and makes it impossible for breaches of such laws to be known, reported, or prosecuted.

Crime in Africa or elsewhere is a composite reflection of history and tradition, modernization and social disruption, foreign influence, government ineptitude, exploitation, and sheer opportunism. Change itself has multiplied the opportunities for crime while at the same time diluting or hampering the traditional or governmental measures for its control. Corruption, illegal forms of trading, prospects for counterfeiting, drug trafficking, smuggling across borders too extensive to be effectively controlled, and exploiting the lack of sophistication of new town dwellers—all of these have added to the problems of crime in Africa.

Of course, much of the crime is the same as that being committed anywhere in the world, but the background to criminal behavior is usually different enough to modify the significance of the act or omission. For example, a study of homicide in Africa about twenty years ago concluded that (using Durkheim's terminology) there was little or no egoistic homicide among the tribes and only a moderate amount of anomic homicide and suicide.[5] Furthermore, stock theft is not a meaningful concept among the Masai in East Africa because the traditional conviction among them is that all cattle really belong to that tribe. According to the morality of most peoples, this is no excuse for stock theft, but anthropologists have found that other pastoral tribes regard the stealing of other tribes' cattle as prestigious rather than wrongful.

This subject has not been properly researched, but informed experience suggests that, in Africa, pathological or motiveless crimes are few and far between. Incest is differently construed where extended family patterns persist and is complicated by the matrilineal, patrilineal, and bilateral lines of descent and degrees of prohibition applied to these various relationships. Wife beating is not regarded as an offense in many societies in Africa where even the women regard it as a mark of concerned affection.[6]

Sometimes the adopted modern legislation does not fit established customary interpretations of the taboo, and there may be retaliatory crimes of vengeance. However, all such variations of belief and practice have to be qualified by urban and rural differences. While there is some carryover of the traditional ties and older values, the urban populations are likely to commit crimes that are more comparable to crimes committed by urban dwellers in other cities across the world than they are to crimes in their own rural areas.

CRIME CONTROL AND CRIME PREVENTION

In terms of formal crime control services and crime prevention structures, the continent of Africa provides examples of all the world's systems of criminal justice. There are countries with patterns of Continental Law, Common Law, Islamic Law, Roman-Dutch Law, and occasionally with modifications consistent with the implementation of communist concepts and policies. As already suggested, these bodies of law are in less conflict with customary ideas of wrongdoing than has usually been supposed. Studies in East Africa by the London University School of Oriental and African Studies, in Zambia by the writer, and by a Belgian researcher in Zaire have found only about six differences between local and imported ideas of conduct that merit a penal sanction. However, the same relevance cannot be claimed for the procedures and institutions that were imported by the developing countries to administer the laws. Indigenous lawyers trained abroad can and do implement the systems, but their foreignness is reflected in their frequent failures to fit their actions to local thinking.

First, the court procedures may be quite difficult for local persons to understand. Traditionally in Africa, a court was a device for reconciliation and for determination of fault and compensation. There were rules and even precedents, but legal thinking was not the same as that developed in the West over a period of two thousand years.

Second, imprisonment was particularly difficult to understand as a punishment, by some people on the edge of subsistence, when it guaranteed shelter and three meals a day. Moreover, it usually left the offended party uncompensated so that it did nothing to settle the dispute and avoid the danger of retaliation.

Third, extra manual labor, execution, and corporal punishment had more direct meaning, but in accordance with policies in the metropolitan countries, the colonial powers sometimes excluded these drastic measures. When independence came, it was significant that Tanzania restored corporal punishment, making it mandatory for some offenses. The death penalty was applied in some other countries, and in order to control armed robberies (after the Biafra conflict which had divided the country), Nigeria had recourse to public executions.

It is equally significant that African scholars in all those countries are assessing the effects of those policies on the incidence and gravity of crime, and sometimes they are pressing for changes. There was local and international revulsion to the excesses of Idi Amin in using arbitrary arrest and execution in Uganda. Similar feelings were aroused when the president of the Central African Republic led a task force of military personnel to the local prison to beat inmates "to teach them a lesson."

EFFECTS OF POLITICAL EVENTS ON CRIME PHENOMENA

Over the past thirty years, South Africa has shown how the criminal justice system can be used repressively. It also has provided an example of how a modern country can be effectively ostracized through organized internal resistance and international action. External military assistance has been used to overthrow regimes in Angola and Mozambique and has been used to support existing regimes in Zaire, Chad, and the Congo. In the countries to the north of the Sahara, guerrilla warfare was used to oust the French. Older border troubles have flared anew between Eritrea and Ethiopia. A war of attrition was waged in and around Zimbabwe until an uneasy settlement was reached, but continuing violence indicates that a normal condition of law and order is yet to be established. Uganda is still in great difficulty after Tanzania intervened to oust Idi Amin. Ghana has had a military coup, and Nigeria to the south is moving from a military regime to an elected civilian administration.

Under these circumstances, it is extremely difficult to collect data on the administration of laws and their breach. The difficulties remain even after situations are normalized. In the midst of the suffering and dislocation of many persons, there are the shrewd and quick-witted individuals able to extract personal profits from these situations. For example, in Uganda, from the perspective of many persons, it was the government that was criminal because the abuses of the "criminal justice system" were rife. Since the early 1970s, there has been little point in speaking of crime and its prevention, considering the general turmoil and strife.

Crime in Africa, therefore, is as related to the political events that provide opportunities for it as crime is related to the state of economic and social underdevelopment. It cannot be separated from a spirit of illegality which sometimes has reached into the highest levels of government. It cannot be separated from massive youth unemployment and the squatters who occupy sections of urban areas. It cannot be separated from the lack of local resources for adequate policing and legal administration. It cannot be considered without appreciation for the vastness of Africa which greatly complicates the establishment of comprehensive government.

For all of these reasons, crime in Africa is a particularly intriguing subject for all who are interested in criminology or in its related disciplines. As indicated above, Africa is a remarkable criminological laboratory. Political upheaval brings cultural and legal values into question, and it opens the way for a fundamental reassessment and restructuring of services previously taken for granted in a certain form. Studies of the crime situation before and after such events would be of great usefulness for comparative criminology. Descriptive studies of police work, involving detailed study of cases being processed as well as determination of better ways of reporting cases before the courts, could be a means of gaining new and fundamental insights. Evaluation of prisons, probation work, and the administration of other penal sanctions would provide a basis for comparative assessment of the sanctioning systems of the developed nations of the West.

The development and elaboration of criminology in Africa itself would be a desirable consequence of increasing recognition of these opportunities for research and improvement of practice. Progress can be perceived in the growing interest of universities in providing courses in criminology, in the interest of the United Nations in a possible Institute for Crime Prevention in Africa, and in the efforts to improve criminal justice services.

ASIA: ECHOES DOWN THE CORRIDORS OF TIME

Asia has been the cradle of civilizations and the mother of the great religions of the world. There was an Indus civilization in India when the Pharoahs were ruling Egypt. At about the time the Israelites were led out of Egypt, the first Chinese dictionary of forty thousand characters was published. When pre-Roman Etruscan power was at its height in the West and Sophocles was writing Greek tragedies, the Indian surgeon Susrata was performing cataract operations, and Confucius was teaching how to govern with morality and kindness. While Britain was being invaded by La Tène, an iron-age people around 250 B.C., the Great Wall of China was being completed and a system of weights and measures was being unified in China. This was also the period of the Code of Manu and of the writing of the Manava Dharmashastra, the most authoritative of Indian law books. Considering crime and its control in the developing nations of Asia is a humbling process because in the background are these echoes down the long corridors of time.

Not surprisingly, therefore, the developing countries of Asia are the ones about which most is known about crime and its control. This is not to say that it is possible to measure crime in the Asian countries precisely or to provide the data vital to any thoroughgoing analysis. There still are problems of political change, economic exploitation, and communications in Asia. The cultural variations are perhaps more numerous than anywhere in the world. There are concentrations of people too, which tend to be more intense than elsewhere. Starvation is a camp follower for most settlements, whether urban or rural, in places such as Bangladesh, India, and Pakistan. Even where population pressures have not been a problem, wars and civil strife have created conditions of starvation and insecurity. Kampuchea and East Timor are just two examples.

At one extreme of the Asian complex are the oil-rich developing nations, with rapidly rising standards of living that coincide with increases of recorded crime. At the other extreme, Japan is a populous, industrialized, and highly developed country that has managed to control its crime and to demonstrate that development and crime are not automatically and inevitably linked. Not surprisingly, the developing countries of Asia are looking to Japan rather than to the Western developed nations for guidance on crime and its control.

It is instructive to compare the articles for Africa and Asia in the No. 35 issue of the United Nations *International Review of Criminal Policy*. Whereas the writer of the article on Africa has to depend upon broad generalizations and material from related work on socioeconomic conditions, the article on Asia (which was prepared by the staff of the United Nations Asia and Far East Institute for the Prevention of Crime and Treatment of Offenders at Fuchu) provides statistics for crime in Malaysia, Singapore, the Philippines, Sri Lanka, India, Hong Kong, and Bangladesh, as well as enough socioeconomic data to support a meaningful interpretation. Augmenting the information about Asia are two publications of the Australian Institute of Criminology which, in the past five years, has been helping Asian countries with crime control problems and has been providing information on the region for the rest of the world.[7]

UNIQUE MEANINGS OF CRIME PHENOMENA

Urbanization and population migration creating city slums, unemployment, especially among young persons, minority problems, and cultural conflicts are among the familiar reasons given for crime as a social problem in many of the developing countries of the region. However, nearly everywhere the traditional social controls are strong, and family loyalties have survived much of the pressure of modernization. There is not the atomization and anomie that are typical of Western cities, although—where huge populations throng the narrow streets of some of the larger conurbations—extreme poverty and starvation may be a daily experience. Here, if crime represents a way to survive, it takes on a different meaning.

Inevitably, the extent and significance of crime differ in Asia from other parts of the world. In Asia is the world-famous "golden triangle" for the production of drugs. Once the Asian countries were merely transit or processing centers for a trade directed at American and European markets, but recently the Asian countries themselves have become troubled with increasing drug abuse. There still are to be found in India the dacoits and the remnants of the "criminal tribes" which developed originally from the caste system. Modern, prosperous, highly populated Hong Kong, wrested by the British from the Chinese in the nineteenth century as the price for China's having resisted Western opium smuggling, now has an efficient correctional service with model facilities for drug addicts. Singapore island was once a haven for pirates, and to this day piracy continues off the coast of Malaysia. Martial law, in its imposition as well as in its more recent relaxation in the Philippines, has had effects upon crime and its control which could be important for understanding crime in that country. While there has been no probation and parole in Thailand and most cases have been dealt with by a fine or imprisonment, the monarchy in Thailand has made constructive use of the amnesty, fairly frequently applied, to clear the prisons.

There are new forces abroad. In India, for example, a new militancy in the junior ranks of the police has led to strikes and even to confrontation between the army and the police. It was never necessary previously to consider the police as a political force, but that may be a changing situation. Since 1960, the police in Indonesia have been a section of the country's armed forces, with equivalence of ranks, but the police force retained its separate identity with its own career structure. In 1976 it had 11,116 men. Offenses committed by the police are dealt with by a separate police tribunal within the general framework of military tribunals and beyond the jurisdiction of other courts.

The *Singapore Sunday Times* for January 8, 1978, carried a report from its Kuala Lumpur correspondent to the effect that a statement had been made by the editor of the National Union of the Teaching Profession's journal *Guru Malaysia* that "assaults on teachers, acts of vandalism, indecent behavior, challenging teachers and headmasters to fight, arson and other juvenile offenses have become common occurrences, particularly in secondary schools." Singapore has enacted a series of statutes that have modified traditionally British rules of evidence, strengthened the police role, and removed some of the protection for the accused which, it was felt, was hampering the maintenance of law and order.

Nepal has had an unusual problem created by the attractiveness of that country to Western bohemian types of people. With the growth of tourism has come a number of such people, attracted by the remoteness of Nepal's geographical position within sight of Mount Everest, the simplicity of its people, and the availability of places to grow drugs. It has had to take special measures to deal with this set of circumstances.

Just as the West is attempting to divert persons from the criminal justice system and to provide as many alternatives as possible to imprisonment, so Asian developing nations are reviewing the value of some of their own informal controls of behavior. Across the whole Indian subcontinent, there are variations of the Panchayats—local government reconciliation bodies. These deal with minor offenses and settle local disputes. Similar bodies exist at local levels in Malaysia, Indonesia, the Philippines, and Sri Lanka. Profiting from Western mistakes in overusing the formal machinery of criminal justice, the Asian countries are using their own informal systems more effectively.

FINAL COMMENT: FUNDAMENTAL DIFFERENCE

While the developing countries in Asia and Africa share a greater concern with survival and economic improvement than with crime as such, there is a difference between the two continents which is more felt than perceived. One is impressed by the cultural heritage of Asia still embodied in the calm philosophy and deep religious commitment. This is a dangerous generalization, but it is difficult to escape the impression. There is a passivity characterizing the Asian approach to social problems which is not so evident in Africa. Yet, every now and then Asian animosities flare into quite vicious intercommunal riots which are relatively unknown in Africa, and, when they are known, the violence is more likely to be tribal than either racial or religious. Events in China, Kampuchea, and Iran have demonstrated that politics has its molding effect in the meaning of crime in Asia, as in Africa, but Asia seems to have an inner resilience born of centuries of change which have seen, along with the rise and fall of civilizations, a great variety of meanings assigned to crime and its control.

NOTES

1. United Nations General Assembly, Thirty-Second Session, Item 77, "Crime Prevention and Control," A/32/199, September 22, 1977.
2. See W. Clifford, *Crime Control in Japan* (Lexington, Mass.: Lexington Books, 1976).
3. Lecture to Sixth United Nations Congress, Caracas, August 1980, by Dr. Mohammed Cheddadi, Secretary General of the Arab Organization of Social Defense.
4. Eric Paula Kibuka, "Crime in African Countries," *International Review of Criminal Policy* (published by the United Nations, New York), no. 35 (1980):19.
5. Paul Bohannan (ed.), *African Homicide and Suicide* (Princeton, N.J.: Princeton University Press, 1960).
6. Kibuka, "Crime in African Countries," p. 14.
7. W. Clifford (ed.), "Innovation in Criminal Justice in Asia and the Pacific" (Canberra: Australian Institute of Criminology, 1979), and compiled by W. Clifford, "Corrections in Asia and the Pacific" (Canberra: Australian Institute of Criminology, 1980).

BIBLIOGRAPHY

Obviously, there is a progressively expanding literature on the socioeconomic and political development of emerging nations. Criminologists are increasingly recognizing that the parameters of nation-building and the effects of modernization are crucial to understanding crime and the reactions to criminality. The literature in English is of lesser range and volume but is of increasing sophistication in regard to Africa and Asia. To supplement references employed in this chapter, a limited number of additional items are offered for readers interested in further study.

Bailey, David H. *The Police and Political Development in India*. Princeton, N.J.: Princeton University Press, 1969.

The history and functions of the police in India are analyzed as reflections of the nation's cultural and political evolution.

Boehringer, G. H. "Alternatives to Prison in East Africa." *International Annals of Criminology* 10, no. 1 (1971):91-147.
Alternatives to prison are considered mainly in the context of Tanzania's building a socialist society, but applications to the rest of East Africa are believed appropriate. The evaluation is in the context of a reform of the judiciary, rediscovery of customary reactions to deviance, and the tendencies toward extra-official reactions to deviants.

Clifford, William. *Crime Control in Japan*. Lexington, Mass.: Lexington Books, 1976.
The relative effectiveness of Japanese police is placed within the context of the integration of law enforcement within the broadly defined control system and the social psychology of the Japanese.

Clifford, William. *An Introduction to African Criminology*. Nairobi: Oxford University Press, 1974.
The elements of criminology as "the science of crime" are established, preliminary to an analysis of crime and the responses to crime in the emergent nations of Africa. "A rather different approach to crime and its prevention is called for," the author says, because the countries are so vast and their populations so very widespread that the expense of providing social services is grossly disproportionate. By making a virtue of their necessity, these countries may give a lead to more "advanced" countries.

Clifford, William. "Science, Culture and Criminal Justice in Asia." *International Journal of Comparative and Applied Criminal Justice* 2 (Winter 1978):191-205.
The author highlights the phenomenon of crime, the development of crime prevention and criminal justice services, and the rise of criminology as a science.

Clinard, Marshall B., and Daniel J. Abbott. *Crime in Developing Countries: A Comparative Perspective*. New York: John Wiley, 1973.
Crime, corrections, and law enforcement are evaluated from the perspective of nation-building and the reorientation of social institutions in the face of urbanization, industrialization, and other forces inherent in modernization.

Cohen, Jerome Alan. "Reflections on the Criminal Process in China." *Journal of Criminal Law and Criminology* 63 (September 1977):323-355.
The history of China's relationship with the Western powers is a prelude to a look at the criminal process in the People's Republic of China. Among his observations, the author reports crime is an important problem, resources available to the criminal process are limited, many minor acts that could be deemed criminal are disposed of "on the spot" by unofficial persons, and the unfettered power of the police and courts enables them to directly mete out "noncriminal" sanctions.

Hermassi, Elbaki. *Leadership and National Development in North Africa*. Berkeley, Calif.: University of California Press, 1972.
This volume is an example of scholarly treatments of the basic issues confronting new nations. In this analysis Morocco, Tunisia, and Algeria were found to differ in their

development strategies because of the stamp of the institutions that shaped national unification, the unique events marking the formation, and the social forces that brought the particular nation to prominence.

Martin, Robert G., Jr., and Rand D. Conger. "A Comparison of Delinquency Trends: Japan and the United States." *Criminology* 18 (May 1980):53-61.
The lower juvenile crime rates for Japan continue to hold even when age differences are controlled. The authors suggest that Japan's pervasive information controls and increasing prosperity account for the difference from the United States.

Npka, Nwokocha K.U. "Armed Robbery in Post-Civil War Nigeria: The Role of the Victim." *Victimology: An International Journal* 1 (Spring 1976):71-83.
The Nigerian Civil War (1967-1970) gave further impetus to a wave of armed robbery. Nine types of victims are discussed, ranging from the guileless to those who seemed to invite victimization.

Odekunle, 'Femi. "Capitalist Economy and the Crime Problem in Nigeria." *Contemporary Crises* 2 (January 1978):89-96.
The author argues that Nigeria presents a situation similar to that of many other developing countries oriented toward a free enterprise economy. A crime problem is found to exist in Nigeria, and the "inequalities of the capitalist system" are supposed to color the definition of crimes in laws, the regularities in the violations of these laws, and the defects of justice administration.

Opolot, James S.E. "Organized Crime in Africa." *International Journal of Comparative and Applied Criminal Justice* 3 (Fall 1979):177-183.
Organized crime in Africa is defined as a criminal conspiracy to make quick money through exploitation of business opportunities, corrupt practices, relative lack of enforcement of the law, or political instability.

Weinberg, S. Kirson. "Urbanization and Male Delinquency in Ghana." *Journal of Research in Crime and Delinquency* 2 (July 1965):85-94.
The correlates of the urbanization process are traced in Ghana to attribute male delinquency to adaptation to urban living by lower class youth alienated from the family and school system.

Wood, Arthur L. "A Socio-Structural Analysis of Murder, Suicide, and Economic Crime in Ceylon." *American Sociological Review* 26 (October 1961):744-753.
The sociocultural system of the nation now known as Sri Lanka is identified as the primary influence in the differential distribution of murder, suicide, and property offenses.

Yanagimot, Masaharu. "Some Features of the Japanese Prison System." *British Journal of Criminology* 10 (July 1970):209-224.
Since World War II, "scientific treatment" methods have been adopted, of which *Naikan* therapy is peculiarly Japanese. The correctional system is centralized under the Ministry of Justice. The rarity of escapes is attributed to the Japanese character.

Monographs available at J. V. Barry Memorial Library, Australian Institute of Criminology:

Biles, David. "Crime Prevention in Developing Areas, Port Moresby, Papua New Guinea, July 7-11, 1975." Canberra: Australian Institute of Criminology, 1975.

Biles, David (ed.). *Crime in Papua New Guinea*. Canberra: Australian Institute of Criminology, 1976.

Boehringer, G. H. "Imperialism, 'Development' and the Underdevelopment of Criminology." *Melanesian Law Journal* 4, no. 2 (1976):211-241.

Clifford, William (ed.). "Corrections in Asia and the Pacific." Proceedings of the First Asian and Pacific Conference of Correctional Administrators, Hong Kong, February 25-29, 1980. Canberra: Australian Institute of Criminology, 1980.

Clifford, William, and S. D. Gokhale (eds.). *Innovations in Criminal Justice in Asia and the Pacific*. Canberra: Australian Institute of Criminology, 1979.

Mackellar, M. L. "Crime in Port Moresby." Thesis, Department of Anthropology and Sociology, University of Papua New Guinea, 1977.

6

AN INTERNATIONAL PERSPECTIVE ON WOMEN AND CRIMINOLOGY

Nanci Koser Wilson

A cross-cultural perspective on criminology is important in and of itself, as the publication of this volume attests. However, in the field of crime committed by women, a cross-cultural perspective is especially warranted as an opportunity to test the controversial hypothesis that women's emancipation leads to a rising female crime rate. The status of women varies from nation to nation, and changes in the relationship between women's status and other variables, including crime, vary similarly.

This chapter argues that the recent impact of female crime on criminology has been felt mostly in the theoretical arena rather than in changes in behavior per se. First, although theoreticians have predicted broad-scale changes in the female contribution to crime, the empirical evidence indicates a gradual evolution. In the legitimate labor market, the expanded involvement of women is predominantly in job areas where they have been traditionally employed. Similarly, the increased criminal activity of women is predominantly in those types of crimes in which they have been traditionally engaged. This theme is explored below, in the discussion of transnational female crime trends.

Second, the impact of female crime on criminology is only part of a broader intellectual movement in the discipline. For the first twenty years after World War II, criminology remained wedded to positivism in seeking the causes of crime within the individual, usually viewed as pathological in some sense. Therapeutic reactions to crime usually followed the medical model. However, since

EDITOR'S NOTE: In delineating the sectors of remarkable change since 1945 in the approaches and subject matter of criminology around the world, this volume could not ignore the relationships between women and the complex phenomena of criminality. Dr. Wilson makes the case that, by previously ignoring this topic in favor of the view that crime is essentially a male enterprise, criminology has lost an impressive opportunity to test its theoretical approaches for explaining criminality in general. By outlining the patterns of female crime rates and by summarizing the literature on this topic, she establishes a foundation for this thought-provoking critique of criminology.

the mid-1960s, there has been a movement away from positivism and toward an emphasis on structural variables. The recognition of status and power as crucial influences in shaping criminality can be seen in criminology's recent openness to such theoretical perspectives as labeling theory and Marxism. The switch to a more structurally oriented criminology has necessitated rethinking, revision, and reconstruction of many theories of criminality. The recognition of female criminality as a legitimate topic of study in itself is an example of the reformulation of traditional approaches. In this sense, the increased visibility of crime among women is an important facet of the special dynamism now being experienced by criminological theory in general. The final section of this chapter explores this theme in detail.

TRENDS IN CRIMES AMONG WOMEN

Much of the data on changing patterns of female crime pertains to the United States, and much of the theoretical writing on the topic also speaks to the American situation. Thus, we begin this review with a discussion of the changing female crime picture in the United States and then move on to a comparison with other nations.

U.S. Patterns

In the United States, arrest rates[1] of women have increased in virtually every crime category since 1960. Arrests of women for violent crimes have nearly tripled, while the increases in arrests for property crimes have been even more substantial. The largest increases are for larceny (arrests rose from 32.35 per 100,000 in 1960 to 230.39 in 1978) and for fraud and embezzlement (from 8.29 to 102.36 per 100,000). Large increases have also occurred in arrests for forgery (the rate per 100,000 has quadrupled), burglary (the rate has increased fivefold), armed robbery, and receiving/possessing stolen property.

However, the rates for many of these crimes were quite low to begin with, so that large increases do not really indicate that women are "catching up" with men, especially when we are simultaneously recording extremely large increases for men. Arrests for violent crime are still only about 11 percent for female adults and 16 percent for female juveniles. It is clear that property crime is the area where males and females are coming closest together in the United States. The percentage of females among juvenile arrests for property crime is approximately 18.6 percent; among adult women the increase is most pronounced—they made up only 16 percent of arrests for property crime in 1960, and in 1978 they made up almost 30 percent of such arrests.

American theorists have argued that the changing role of women is responsible for these increases, although they have disagreed as to the source of these changes. (Some, for example, argue that the feminist movement is not involved.) Increases in property crime have variously been explained by: (1) Increasing opportunity to commit work-related crimes such as fraud and embezzlement[2]; (2) increasing economic needs of women resulting from a high divorce rate and a plunging economy[3]; and (3) a change in the social-psychological makeup of women, such that they are becoming increasingly aggressive and independent.[4]

With few exceptions, theorists have argued that these changes have not affected the rate of violent crime among American women, which, it is maintained, has remained stable.

While the major increases have been in property crime, there are two developments which indicate that, in future years, the female rate of violent crime may also increase substantially.

In the first place, there has been a narrowing of the gap between male and female violent crime rates among juveniles. Because researchers have rarely computed age-specific crime rates by sex, most have not noted this increase; yet, it is quite pronounced.[5] If the age cohort now in the teen years continues the pattern of current adolescent offenses, there should be a narrowing of the male-female gap in violent crime at the adult level as well.

Furthermore, increases in arrests for weapon and drug offenses by women augur increases in the violent crimes of aggravated assault, assault, and homicide. As to weapons offenses, the subculture of violence theorists, among others, argues that violent assault and homicide, in particular, are increased when a subculture condones or encourages the carrying of weapons. The increased arrests of women for illegal carrying and possession of weapons is an indication that they, too, are participating more fully in the subculture of violence, and that their homicide and assault rates may therefore increase.

Increases in arrests for the Federal Bureau of Investigation (FBI) category "drug abuse violations" have also been recorded for women in the past twenty years. The manner of FBI reporting and the nature of the offense itself prevent determination of whether arrests listed as drug abuse are for possession and personal use only or for dealing in drugs. The pattern of drug use is such that many users may also deal; a steady marijuana user may buy a pound and sell all but two or three "lids" to friends and acquaintances to finance the user's supply. Furthermore, the police probably arrest more small-time dealers than large ones. Granted these difficulties, it is certain that female arrests for violations of narcotic drug laws are increasing, an indication that in the future women will be involved in more drug-related assaults and homicides.

Another interesting trend in the U.S. data is the decreasing appeal of prostitution to women who engage in crime to make money. While the arrest rate per 100,000 women has not declined, the number of women arrested for prostitution as a percentage of all women arrested for all "income-productive" crime has declined dramatically. This percentage dropped from 35.99 percent in 1960 to 12.48 percent in 1978.[6] This trend, as we shall see, is also reflected in the international data.

In summary, the changes noted in the United States are mostly in the area of property crime, with some evidence that rates of violent crime committed by women will soon be increasing, perhaps substantially.

Trends in Canada and Britain

In the United Kingdom, there have been absolute increases in the number of females convicted of many property crimes—burglary, robbery, theft, handling stolen goods, and fraud. The highest percentages of female convictions are for theft (20 percent female in 1971) and fraud (15 percent female in 1971). However, there appears to have been *no* increase in the percentage female for these offenses, with women making up a constant 2 to 3 percent of those convicted for such offenses and about 14 percent for all offenses.[7] Simon reports "an increase in the proportion of girls under 17 convicted of violent crimes, but not among females in any other age categories."[8] In addition, in England as in the United States, offenses by prostitutes appear to be on the decline.[9]

In Canada, however, since 1960, changes similar to those in the United States have occurred. There the percent female among those charged with offenses increased from 7 percent in 1960 to 14 percent in 1969.[10]

This very brief review of female crime rates and trends for three culturally similar nations should serve to introduce the reader to what follows. In short, there seems to be no consistency in female crime rates and trends that can be linked to the cultural similarity, socioeconomic similarity, or political similarity of the various nations.

Other International Crime Trends

Outside of North America, very few nations evidence a clearcut trend toward increasing female participation in crime. Table 6-1 lists those countries where increases have occurred. This table is based upon data reported by Simon and Adler[11] which refer to the period 1970 to 1975, by Simon[12] which refer to the period 1963-1970, and by Bowker[13] which refer to 1950-1972. It can be seen that researchers disagree even in the matter of the few countries that are reported to be experiencing an increase in the percentage of women engaging in crime. Some of these differences, but not all, can be explained by the different time periods studied by the respective authors.

Students of female crime also disagree on whether given nations are experiencing downward, stable, or erratic trends in female crime. (See Table 6-2.)

Admittedly, assessment of international female crime trends is complicated by the uncertain quality of data. INTERPOL data (on which most of these conclusions are based) are sketchy, with many countries failing to report consistently. In addition, there are the usual problems with comparability of data across national boundaries; laws, legal systems, and reporting methods vary. Nevertheless, there is no clearly consistent pattern of increase internationally. In those countries with more advanced technologies and relatively greater emancipation of women, there are differences in trends of female participation in criminal activities. In the face of these difficulties, several researchers have attempted to explain the differences in international female crime rates by measuring variables related in some fashion to the concept of change in sex roles.

TABLE 6-1
NATIONS WITH UPWARD TRENDS IN FEMALE CRIME ACCORDING TO THREE STUDIES

Simon & Adler 1970-1975	Simon 1963-1970	Bowker 1950-1972
Argentina		
Australia		Austria
Bahamas		
Bahrain	Burma	Burma
Canada		
Chile		
Ecuador		
El Salvador		
Finland	France	France
Guyana	Germany	
Indonesia		
Italy		
Japan		
Maldives		
Mauritius		
Morocco	Monaco	Morocco
New Zealand	New Zealand	
Norway		Norway
Oman		
Pakistan		
Peru		
Spain		Sweden
United Kingdom		U.K. (England and Wales)
United States of America	Tanzania	
	Thailand	Tunisia

Adler points directly to the issue when she asserts that "data from other nations concur with the American experience that as the social and economic disparity between the sexes decreases, there is a correlative increase in female criminality." She cites Western Europe and Australia as areas with a high degree of a rising female crime rate. She suggests that the female-male crime rate disparities "are most pronounced in countries such as Fiji and Malawi where the social gap between the sexes as yet remains greater."[14]

Simon[15] investigated arrest rates for twenty-four countries for the period 1963-1970. She found little support for a linkage between female crime rates and political ideology, religious/social values, or economic development. "The countries that have the highest female arrest rates for all crimes are a mixed lot of modern and traditional, Western and Eastern, with their economies and technologies more and less developed." She similarly found no evidence of an increas-

TABLE 6-2
NATIONS WITH STABLE, DOWNWARD, OR ERRATIC TRENDS IN FEMALE CRIME, ACCORDING TO THREE STUDIES

Country	Simon 1963-1970	Simon/Adler 1970-1975	Bowker 1950-1972
Algeria		down	
Austria	stable	stable	up
Australia		up	stable
Barbados		stable	
Bruni	stable		
Costa Rica		erratic	
Cyprus	erratic	down	
Denmark	down	erratic	down
Egypt			stable
England and Wales	stable	up	up
Federal Republic of Germany	up	stable	erratic
Fiji	down		
Finland	down	up	stable
Greece		stable	
Guyana		up	stable
Hong Kong	down		
Indonesia		up	down
Iraq		down	
Ireland	down	down	stable
Israel	erratic		
Jamaica		stable	
Japan	erratic	up	erratic
Kenya			stable
Korea	erratic		
Kuwait		erratic	
Luxembourg	down		erratic
Malawi	stable		
Malaysia		erratic	
Netherlands	stable		down
Netherlands-Antilles			down
Norway		up	up
Pakistan			stable
Philippines			down
Poland		erratic	
Portugal	stable		
Qatar		erratic	
San Marino		stable	
Scotland	erratic		erratic
Sweden			up
Switzerland		stable	
Syria		stable	

TABLE 6-2 continued.

Country	Simon 1963-1970	Simon/Adler 1970-1975	Bowker 1950-1972
Trinidad/Tobago		down	
Tunisia	stable		up
Turkey		down	
West Indies	down		
Yugoslavia		erratic	

ing female crime rate, for in fewer than seven of the twenty-four countries studied was there such an increase. She did discover that, while there was little relationship between the amount of female crime and the level of economic development, "the highest female arrest rates for financial and white-collar type offenses occur primarily among the most economically developed and technologically advanced countries" (those countries where women are likely to be represented in the commercial labor market).

Bowker[16] in an ambitious undertaking attempted to measure the effect of three variables—social-education equality, economic equality, and SES (socioeconomic status) development—upon the female crime rate in thirty countries for the years 1950, 1955, 1960, 1965, and 1972. Bowker maintains that the female proportion of murders is "declining rather than increasing worldwide," and that, while women commit a larger proportion of larcenies, these rates are not rising significantly.

When he correlated his three independent variables with the total proportionate female crime rate, and the proportionate female crime rates for murder and major larceny, he found that "an increase in the female contribution to murder statistics was associated with low social/educational equality between the sexes, high male-female economic equality and low socioeconomic development." The relationships with the three independent variables and major larceny were all zero or close to zero. Only one of these variables (SES development) was related to total proportionate female crime. "Modernized nations tended to have an increasing female contribution to the total crime rate." Bowker concluded that he had found little support for Adler's thesis that decreasing social and economic disparity between the sexes resulted in an increasing female crime rate.

In a later piece of research, Bowker assessed the relative influences of four social institutions—education, politics, family, and economy—on proportionate female crime in ninety-two countries for the year 1974. His correlational analysis was constructed

> to constitute a test of three competing theories of female crime, the violence-prone "new female criminal," the theory of economic need, and economic opportunity theory. The

data provided only weak support for the theory of the "new female criminal," but considerably stronger support for both the economic need and economic opportunity theories.[17]

Simon and Sharma[18] conducted a provocative inquiry in which they compared female crime rate changes in Japan, Israel, and the United States. Japan interested them for comparative purposes because it is non-Western and because it has undergone recent rapid industrialization. Israel "is less developed economically but shares with the United States many of the cultural and religious values of Western civilization." These three countries then present intriguing contrasts for a comparative study of trends in female crime.

The typical pattern about which so much has been written emerged in the U.S. data, where, over the 1953-1972 period the overall female crime rate increased as did the female property crime rate. In addition, during this time period, there was an increase in the number of women in the labor force, in the number of female-headed families, and in the number of female single heads of household. Furthermore, there are strong positive correlations between the overall female crime rate, the female crime rates for property, economic, and violent crime, and the three social variables (labor force participation, female-headed families, and single female heads of household).

In Israel during the same time period, there has been a fluctuating overall female property crime rate. There has been *no* increase in the number of women in the labor force. Moreover, the correlations between that variable and the various female crime rates are inverse and erratic, with the exception of a positive correlation between overall female crime rates and labor force participation. In addition, there has been little popular support for a feminist movement in Israel, whereas in the United States, the movement has met with some success.

These two countries, then, fit the case for the argument that as women become increasingly liberated, their crime rates ascend. Japan presents a puzzling contradiction. There we have seen a declining crime rate for both men and women. That this has occurred in the midst of rapid industrialization has long puzzled criminologists. Simon and Sharma[19] report that the proportion of females arrested for violent crime has remained stable in Japan; however, the percentage of all those arrested for property crime who were female rose from 9 to 23 percent in the twenty-year study period. In Japan, there has been no successful women's movement, nor has there been an increase in the female commercial labor force.

This set of circumstances produces a strong negative correlation between female labor force participation and the female crime rate (especially for property crimes) in Japan. Simon and Sharma are at a loss to explain the Japanese pattern, but suggest that perhaps female status indicators are only spuriously related to female crime patterns in the United States.

SOURCES OF CHANGE IN CRIME RATES

In reviewing the international literature on the relationship between women's emancipation and increasing female crime rates, we are left with a mass of contradictory evidence. There appears to be no strong, much less overwhelming, evidence that as women become more nearly equal to men, their crime rates approach parity. Yet, some evidence for this assertion does emerge, especially when the variables are those which are most closely linked theoretically, such as labor force participation and property crime.

No small share of the confusion can be attributed to a failure to define carefully the variables involved. Writers in the area have moved from their first careless statements to more definitive measurements of the dependent variable—crime rates. In the more current literature, specific types of crime are delineated, and researchers are less likely to use misleading statistics such as percentage increase. In terms of the independent variable—women's emancipation—definitional chaos is still the rule.

What does emancipation mean? If it is simply a code word meaning that women will become precisely like men in all aspects, then we come dangerously close to a tautology: women will become like men when they become like men; or another absurdity, women will have crime rates exactly like those of men when they become men.

In point of fact, the term "women's emancipation" is not one independent variable but a cluster of such variables. The term has been used in a variety of ways, with its precise meaning rarely specified. At least three separate variables appear to underlie it. One is a collective phenomenon, the political-social movement called feminism. The second, the consciousness of women, is a social-psychological variable difficult to measure. The third variable is structural, mostly economic in nature, which changes with the material circumstances of women.

In referring to women's emancipation as the feminist movement itself, researchers have faced several difficulties because of implicit assumptions. First, it is taken for granted that the goals of the women's movement directly increase the crime rate, an assumption that has angered many feminists. Second, it is assumed that the movement has already achieved its goals. Another difficulty is the selection of a time frame for the movement; did it begin in 1965 or 1968? Has it ended yet? How long a lag should be allowed to permit reliable evaluation of the interaction of the movement and its possible effects on crime rates?

Steffensmeier[20] has attempted to test directly the relationship between the increasing female crime rate in the United States and the women's movement. He compared female crime rates for two time periods: 1960-1967 and 1968-1975, with the later period posited as that potentially affected by the women's movement.

> Assuming that the women's movement begins in the late 1960s, we found little or no change in the magnitude of increase in female arrest rates relative to male arrest rates before, during and after the initial rise of the women's movement. Female increases occurred uniformly during the 1960 to 1975 time period, suggesting that other forces in society already were providing an impetus for changing patterns of female crime well before the initial rise of the women's movement.[21]

Adler[22] and Simon[23] are exemplary of those who concentrate on the social-psychological variable involved—a change in women's consciousness. Both seem to have assumed that the source *and* the major impact of the women's movement have been ideological. Yet, in all probability, as is the case with many attitudinal changes, the behavior came first and the attitudinal changes later. At the very least, the attitudinal changes are logically separable from both the structural changes and the movement itself. One recent study[24] did attempt to measure the attitudes of female felons toward female emancipation. They found that these (incarcerated) women had traditional attitudes toward the importance of motherhood and the dominance of men. However, on three of seven items the women's scores represented highly nontraditional attitudes toward sex roles and toward women's work roles. But the study did not compare the attitudes of female felons to those of nonimprisoned women of the same social class. Neither did it present longitudinal data. Longitudinal data on the sex-role attitudes of women felons and nonfelons, controlled by social class and perhaps race, would be of great import to the hypothesis that it is changing *attitudes* of women which have contributed to their rising crime rate.

Such researchers as Smart,[25] Weis,[26] and Klein and Kress[27] have emphasized structural factors. Weis, for example, cites both economic and technological changes as crucial.

> Other plausible explanations include the possibility that the increase in certain categories of property offenses reflects a depressed economy and concomitant widespread unemployment. . .or the increase may be related to the changed material conditions of consumption over the past two decades [such as] the ever-increasing reliance on self-service marketing and credit purchasing [making] larceny, forgery and fraud more possible among primary consumers.[28]

The feminist movement, consciousness of women, and structural factors are the most commonly measured variables in the literature on female crime, but it is likely that the real change is in the types of social interactions women have. However, this underlying variable is related in a complex fashion to the other three variables. Let me first describe the nature of this underlying change—in interaction patterns—and then attempt to delineate in what manner it is related to the three other variables. (Figure 6-1 graphically depicts this argument. Reference to this figure is useful in understanding what follows.)

The interaction patterns of women are changing significantly, and these patterns are becoming more similar to those of men. That is to say, women's patterns of interaction are becoming, as the given nations modernize, far less restrictive and narrow than in the past.

"Less narrow and restrictive" refers to three dimensions: (1) women are coming into contact with a wider variety of individuals; (2) this is happening in a wider variety of settings, particularly public settings; and (3) women are engaging in more interactions in the role of an independent agent rather than as the interactionally invisible companion of a male.

In traditional cultures, women are bound to the home and to interactions

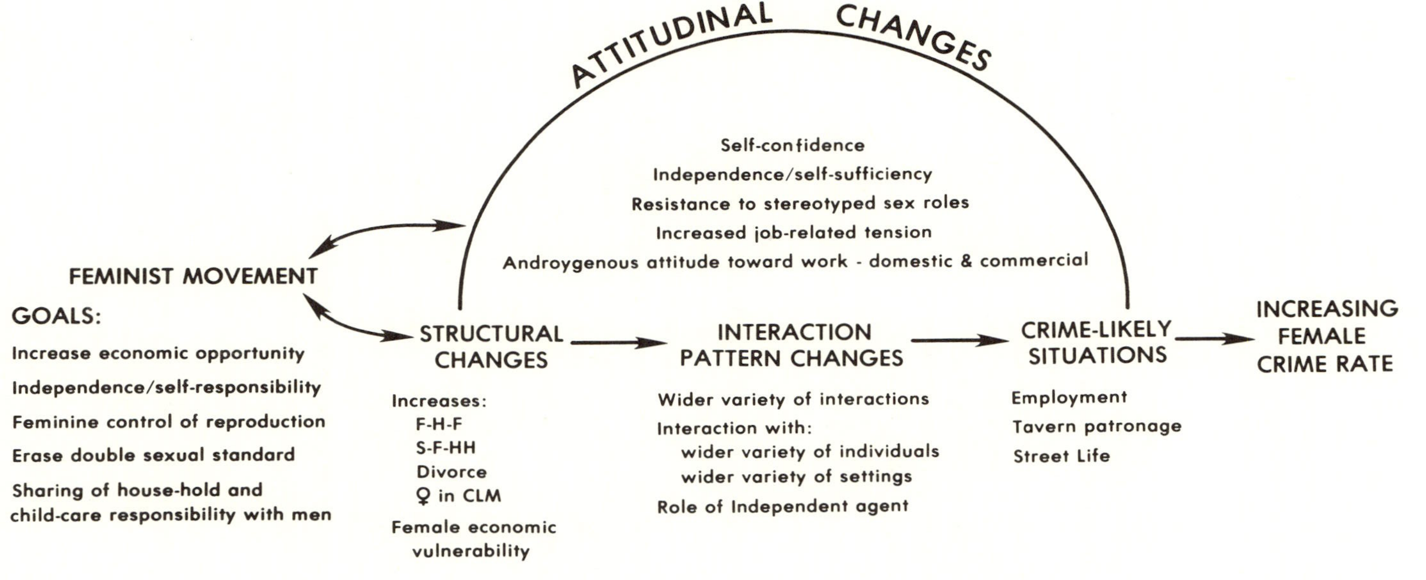

FIGURE 6-1 A SCHEME FOR UNDERSTANDING THE SOURCES OF INCREASE IN FEMALE CRIME RATES

within a very narrow sphere—with a few tradespeople, other child-care agents, and household personnel, such as family members and servants. When women do find themselves in public settings, they are likely to be accompanied by other women or more likely by a man. Very few transactions are carried out by women as independent agents. Rather, their husbands, fathers, or brothers carry out these transactions or aid them in doing so.

As nations modernize, and specifically as women enter the commercial labor market and/or become solely responsible for the financial well-being of their families, they lose this protective shield of masculine aid. They not only leave the home to enter the marketplace as wage-earners; they also enter the economy as purchasers of insurance, repair and maintenance services, and large durable goods such as houses and automobiles, and as sellers of such goods and services. In these transactions, they deal with a much wider variety of individuals than previously, in a wider variety of settings, many of them public, and they engage in a variety of transactions as independent agents.

These changes are occurring very slowly. While there has been a rapid upswing in the number of women entering the marketplace, married women who do so tend to take on two jobs. Because male roles are changing more slowly than female roles, men are still less likely to participate in the life of the household. A married working woman continues to plan meals, to shop for groceries, and to prepare for and clean up after meals. She continues to purchase the family clothes and to do the laundry. Most of all, she continues to be responsible for the children of the family. It is she who deals with the children's teachers and playmates. When the husband does take on some household chores, he is seen as "helping out" his wife rather than contributing a fair share to a mutual enterprise. Thus, the woman is still much more restricted to the home than is the male. Marital responsibilities in the areas of purchasing homes, automobiles, insurance, and other important decisions still rest largely with the male half of a married couple. Divorced women tend to have custody of children and thus are much more likely to be tied to the home than are divorced men.

Thus, even though dramatic changes have occurred in the sexual composition of the commercial work force of many modern nations, changes in the domestic workplace are occurring at a much slower pace. The result is that women are still more tied to the home, are still less mobile than men, and thus, although their interaction patterns are changing in the direction specified, they are doing so slowly.

Slow as it is, however, it is *this change* in interaction patterns which affects the crime rates of women. Because of it, women are increasingly finding themselves in situations where "masculine" behavior, including crime, is a possibility.

As Simon[29] pointed out some years ago, it was impossible for women to have a high rate of embezzlement so long as they were not in a position to embezzle. She predicted that embezzlement rates would increase as women entered the commercial labor market as handlers of other persons' money. As noted in the international surveys reviewed above, the strongest relationship found between any of the suggested independent variables and female crime was that between the number of women in the commercial labor market and their rate of property crime.

In violent crime, traditional patterns persist, changing only very slowly, with a more pronounced increase in the percentage of females among juveniles than among adults. Women are still much less likely than men to kill or assault outside of the home, or to choose a target for violence other than their children, husbands, or lovers. Crime-related violence, such as felony-murder, or assaults arising from armed robberies of illegal drug transactions are still a masculine preserve. For as long as women remain tied to the home, and to limited interactions, this pattern is likely to remain. Their rate of violent crime will increase when they begin to engage in armed robberies and in drug dealing at a commercially successful level, and to appear in significant numbers in taverns, on the street, and in other violence-prone situations without the protection of men. Concomitantly, if men begin to take on more household and child-care responsibilities, their interaction patterns are likely to become more restrictive, thus reducing their opportunities for violent crimes of certain types, but perhaps increasing the rate of child abuse by male offenders.

These changes will come very slowly, and we should expect only moderate increases in the percentage of females among offenders in any given crime category, especially in violent as opposed to property crime. Yet, if women's interaction patterns continue to change in the direction noted, we should predict an eventual increase in total female crime, to the point of parity with male rates at some time in the future. Because changes in interaction patterns are occurring slowly and because we have not directly measured them, we have failed to find a strong and persistent relationship between women's crime rates and changes in the women's situation.

As noted above, the important underlying variable of changing interaction patterns is related to the independent variables that have been proposed by other researchers. One cluster of such variables is large-scale structural changes, particularly those in the economy. Women in modern nations are becoming more vulnerable economically. These nations are experiencing an increase in the number of divorces, in the number of female-headed families, and in the number of single female heads of household. All of these changes are related to the movement of women into the commercial economy and to their increasing likelihood of being solely responsible for a family. These structural changes, in turn, account for the changes in interaction patterns; in fact, they force them.

A major set of social-psychological variables also has been suggested as cogent to increasing female crime rates because, it is argued, women's attitudes are changing. Research has not established whether women's attitudes toward their proper place in the structure and toward the proper behaviors for themselves are changing as a result of the structural changes or are instead a cause of structural changes.

The feminist movement has also been identified as an important variable in the increasing female crime rate, and its presence or absence in various nations has been used as an indicator of changing women's roles. The relationship between the women's movement and the female crime rate is a complex one, which we have yet to unravel. Let me suggest what is occurring.

As a political phenomenon the movement campaigns for *some* of the changes outlined above. As a political platform, the movement promotes equal job opportunity, paid employment outside the home, and equal access to public places such as taverns. It also advocates that women adopt attitudes congruent with independent agent status and with a belief in equality. Thus, the political platform of the feminist movement advocates many of the changes which we have outlined as having occurred, some attitudinal and some structural.

The success of the movement in pushing such changes is not at all evident, however. Many women have entered the commercial labor market, and many women are becoming independently responsible for families. Yet, it is more likely that these changes are a result of a rising divorce rate and a plunging economy than of actions taken by women directly because of the women's movement. For example, most working women are employed in pink-collar jobs. And many working women do not espouse agreement with the women's movement or consider themselves feminists. It is not denied that the goals of the feminist movement are in line with some of the changes that have occurred. What is debatable is the notion that the movement itself caused these changes.

A finding that nations without a feminist movement have increasing crime rates and that countries with a movement have not had enormous increases is therefore not surprising. What are crucial are changes in the interaction patterns of women, in turn brought about by structural changes, and perhaps attitudinal changes. It is entirely possible that all occur without the aid of a political movement, just as it is possible for such a movement to exist, garner widespread support, and yet not have a great impact on crime rates. The successful political movement is several steps removed from the crime phenomenon; first, the intervening variables of attitudinal and structural changes, and then, second, the changes in interaction pattern occur prior in time and in logical sequence to crime participation.

In predicting the future of female crime rates, we should be careful not to concentrate unduly on the female half of the sex equation. What we should probably be predicting is not an increase in the female rate to match the male rate, but instead a convergence of the two rates, which would be brought about in part by a decrease, or at least a slower rate of increase, in the male rates.

A sociological truism is that changes in one role bring about changes in interlocking roles. We should not expect that, as women take on more aspects of the traditional male role, men will be unaffected. Instead, changes in the female role will produce concomitant changes in the male role. As women share more of the financial burdens of establishing a household and rearing a family, men's responsibilities in this arena will decrease. As women do less child care, men's responsibility in child care, *and concomitantly their tendency to be tied down to the house*, will increase. As women become forced by economic circumstances, increasing divorce rates, and so forth, to become more responsible for their own protection, this role for men will dissipate, and even when men do accompany women, they will be less inclined toward protection.

All of these changes should eventually lead to a decrease in the male crime rate, *if* the model we are using to predict and explain increases in the female crime rate is correct. Thus, in the twenty-first century we should see a convergence in crime rates by sex, to the extent that there is convergence of the sex roles in general and especially in domestic and commercial work roles.

On an international plane, convergence in male/female crime rates may be expected in those nations and cultural regions where male/female social and work roles—and therefore *their interaction patterns*—are becoming more similar. In fact, if we were able today to measure accurately the interaction patterns—rather than being forced to make do with dummy variables such as "degree of economic development," "degree of educational equality," and "similarity of divorce laws," which are only tangentially related to this major underlying variable—these differences among nation-states and regions would already be apparent.

IMPACT OF FEMALE CRIME ON CRIMINOLOGY

In the main, this chapter has concentrated on the slow but incremental changes in the rates of participation of women in crime. At least as important has been the impact on criminology itself, as it has given major attention to women as a proper and central topic of study. As Harris has noted, a major failure of criminology has been the exclusion of women as a central focus in theorizing. This exclusion "means that purportedly general theories of criminal deviance are now no more than special theories of male deviance."[30]

This conceptual blindness to fully one-half of the population has two sources. One is the obvious assertion that women play a small part in crime and therefore are less amenable to multivariate research. They are arrested less frequently and make up a much smaller portion of the prison populations that are the subject of much research. The second source of this conceptual blindness is that women do not fit notions of the quintessential criminal.

In their book on homicide, Farrell and Swigert[31] suggest that the criminal justice system stereotypes the criminal as a "normal primitive," a stereotype with overtones of racial and class bias. Similarly, academic criminology holds to a stereotype which can be called the "quintessential criminal." In addition to racial and class biases, this stereotype describes the criminal as a dangerous individual, a successful professional, or an outlaw-rebel. Criminology's preoccupation with these dramatic types of criminals[32] excluded women from consideration as "true" criminals. While the most predominant male offender was a petty thief, an alcohol abuser, or a small-time burglar, criminology was fascinated with the colorful professional thief, whose capacity for efficiency in illegal enterprise was an admirable, and typically male-stereotyped, trait; the rebel, who possessed the audacity to stand apart from others; and the highly dangerous criminal, who seemed inherently masculine. This focus on dramatic and preversely admirable characteristics of the criminal was also a focus on typically "masculine" traits. By contrast, the female criminal seemed not only unimportant in terms of sheer volume, but also dull and uninteresting. Her offenses were petty and mundane, never colorful and exciting. Elliott described her as a "rather pathetic creature, a victim" rather than an offender.[33] In the instances where a case could well have been made for the woman criminal fitting one of these three stereotypes, the chance to do so was ignored for a more "feminine" explanation. For example, the prostitute well fits the image of the professional criminal which Sutherland[34] so aptly described. Yet, instead of seeing the prostitute as a successful professional displaying the usual attitudes of a professional thief toward her occupation and toward straight society, criminology, until recently, pictured her as sexually maladjusted.

While the prevalence of these stereotypes within criminology does not constitute a complete explanation of the short shrift given to female criminality, it does shed some light on the matter. We have ignored the female criminal at least partly because she did not fit our notions of quintessential criminality. She was neither a successful professional, nor a colorful outlaw-rebel, nor a highly dangerous individual.

Now that the comparative insulation of females from crime appears to be dissipating, a fundamental question previously ignored becomes crucial to criminology: What is it about females that insulates them from crime, and what is it about masculinity that creates crime? The question calls attention to explanations for criminality *and* explanations for conformity. By being more specific in defining variables and their relationships—as discussed above—criminologists will learn more about crime among women and, even more significantly, about criminality in general. The opportunity pivots on the capacity of criminologists to reexamine traditional notions about "male" as well as "female" crime.

For example, for many years we have been content to describe patterns of violence rather than to explain the origin of acts of violence. The notion of the subculture of violence has frequently been advanced as an explanation. This theoretical construct has been described as overwhelmingly masculine, to such an extent that Erlanger has suggested that "rather than a subculture of violence [what we may have] is a subculture of masculinity."[35] As more women engage in violent crime, and especially as more scholarly attention is paid to women's part in violence, this explanation increasingly is revealed, as is argued elsewhere,[36] to be a shorthand way of expressing a cluster of variables that underlie the code words "subculture of violence." When these variables are specified, operationalized, and measured, the differential distribution of patterns of violence among cultural groups will make more sense. In this respect, female participation in violence is a pivotal point for a meaningful critique of previously accepted theories, now revealed as overly simplistic.

As a second example, the area of opportunity and learning theory has made little progress beyond Sutherland's suggestion, in 1939, that access to learning structures plays a crucial part in developing a criminal life-style.[37] The most popular explanation of the increase in female criminality has been the notion that women's illegitimate as well as their legitimate opportunities are expanding in the modernizing nations. Yet, since women show very minor increases in such traditionally male crimes as armed robbery and burglary, why are the greater postulated opportunities to commit these crimes not coming to women? Is it because they are still barred from important learning structures? Just what are the skills and attitudes necessary to participation in burglary and armed robbery episodes, and why are women not having access to them? Where would these skills and attitudes be learned? To what reference groups may women not yet have access? Have the answers something to do with their limited, although increasing, interaction patterns? Perhaps these skills and attitudes are transmitted in prison settings, or in casual conversation in the streets or in taverns, where women's participation is still limited.

In asking these questions about women's access to opportunities to learn skills and attitudes appropriate to armed robbery and burglary, it is also asked that formulations of the opportunity structure generally be extended. Where is it that *men* have learned these skills and attitudes? A comparison of male and female interaction patterns promises to shed much light on the opportunity structure.

In extending our formulations for greater understanding of women's participation or nonparticipation in crime, we can gain more similar knowledge about males and about the factors that either insulate them from crime or impel them toward crime. The focus on females in criminology has the effect of forcing reassessment of many widely accepted theories for criminality generally. Some theories will not survive this test, some will require reformulation, and others will gain greater sophistication and empirical thrust. Searching inquiry into crime among women is well merited in its own terms, but beyond the benefits of explaining the unique situation of changing patterns of crime among women, this situation offers a remarkable opportunity to test major theories of criminology in general. In the course of capitalizing on both of these advantages, criminology will rectify its previous isolation of the issues of crime among women from the mainstream of theoretical consideration.

NOTES

1. These data are drawn from the *Uniform Crime Reports* prepared and published annually by the Federal Bureau of Investigation.

2. R. J. Simon, *Women and Crime* (Lexington, Mass.: Lexington Books, 1975).

3. J. G. Weis, "Liberation and Crime: The Invention of the New Female Criminal," *Crime and Social Justice* 6 (Fall-Winter 1976):17-27, and Doris Klein and June Kress, "Any Woman's Blues: A Critical Overview of Women, Crime, and the Criminal Justice System," *Crime and Social Justice* 5 (Spring-Summer 1976):34-49.

4. Freda Adler, *Sisters in Crime: The Rise of the New Female Criminal* (New York: McGraw-Hill, 1975).

5. Nanci K. Wilson, "The Masculinity of Violent Crime—Some Second Thoughts," *Journal of Criminal Justice* 9, no. 2 (1981):111-123.

6. Nanci K. Wilson, "Prostitution, Theft, and Occupational Choice in Crime," *LAE Journal of the American Criminal Justice Association*, 43 (Winter-Spring 1981-1982):7-17.

7. Lee H. Bowker, *Women, Crime and the Criminal Justice System* (Lexington, Mass.: D. C. Heath, 1978).

8. Simon, *Women and Crime*, p. 97.

9. Carol Smart, *Women, Crime and Criminology* (London: Routledge and Kegan Paul, 1977), p. 24, and F. Heidensohn, "The Deviance of Women: A Critique and an Enquiry," *British Journal of Sociology* 19, no. 2 (1968):160-175.

10. Freda Adler, "The Interaction Between Women's Emancipation and Female Criminality: A Cross-Cultural Perspective," *International Journal of Criminology and Penology* 5 (May 1977):104.

11. R. J. Simon and F. Adler, *The Criminology of Deviant Women* (Boston: Houghton Mifflin, 1979), p. 390.

12. Simon, *Women and Crime*.

13. Bowker, *Women, Crime and the Criminal Justice System*.

14. Adler, "Interaction," p. 104.

15. Simon, *Women and Crime*, p. 117.

16. Bowker, *Women, Crime and the Criminal Justice System*, p. 262.

17. Lee H. Bowker, "The Institutional Determinants of International Female Crime," paper presented at the annual meeting of the Society for the Study of Social Problems, New York City, August 1980, p. 19.

18. R. J. Simon and N. Sharma, "Women and Crime: Does the American Experience Generalize?" in Simon and Adler, *Criminology of Deviant Women*.

19. Ibid.

20. Darrell Steffensmeier, "Crime and the Contemporary Women: An Analysis of Changing Levels of Female Property Crime, 1960-75," *Social Forces* 57 (December 1978):566-584.

21. Ibid., p. 578.

22. Adler, *Sisters in Crime*.

23. Simon, *Women and Crime*.

24. R. M. Glick and V. V. Neto, *National Study of Women's Correctional Programs* (Washington, D.C.: NILECJ, 1977).

25. Smart, *Women, Crime and Criminology*.

26. Weis, "Liberation and Crime."

27. Klein and Kress, "Any Woman's Blues."

28. Weis, "Liberation and Crime," p. 25.

29. Simon, *Women and Crime*.

30. A. R. Harris, "Sex and Theories of Deviance: Toward a Functional Theory of Deviant Type-Scripts," *American Sociological Review* 42 (February 1977):3-15.

31. R. Farrell and V. Swigert, *Murder, Inequality and the Law* (Lexington, Mass.: D. C. Heath, 1976).

32. Alexandar Liazos, "The Poverty of the Sociology of Deviance: Nuts, Sluts, and Perverts," *Social Problems* 20 (Summer 1972):103-120.

33. Mabel Elliott, *Crime in Modern Society* (New York: Harper Brothers, 1952), p. 22.

34. E. H. Sutherland, *The Professional Thief* (Chicago: University of Chicago Press, 1937).

35. H. S. Erlanger, "The Empirical Status of the Subculture of Violence Thesis," *Social Problems* 22 (December 1974):280-292.

36. Wilson, "The Masculinity of Violent Crime—Some Second Thoughts."

37. E. H. Sutherland, *Principles of Criminology*, 3d ed. (Philadelphia: J. B. Lippincott, 1939).

BIBLIOGRAPHY

Adler, Freda. "The Interaction between Women's Emancipation and Female Criminality: A Cross-Cultural Perspective." *International Journal of Criminology and Penology* 5 (May 1977):101-112.
Drawing together data from the United States, Japan, England, Canada, New Zealand, Norway, Brazil, India, Poland, Germany, and other countries, Adler seeks to demonstrate that male and female crime rates converge as "females lessen the distance, legitimate and illegitimate, which has separated them from men." Adler contends that it is not the inherent differences between men and women that have traditionally produced lower crime rates among women. The reason, rather, is that "their opportunities have been different." With the increase in women's opportunities will come an increase in their illegitimate behavior.

Adler, F., and R. J. Simon. "Women Offenders: A Cross-Cultural Perspective." In *The Criminology of Deviant Women*. Boston: Houghton-Mifflin, 1979.
In this book, the introductory chapter to a section on cross-cultural crime presents data from the Fifth United Nations Congress on the Prevention of Crime and the Treatment of Offenders in a United Nations survey of female crime rates and trends from 1970 to 1975 in forty-five nations.

Bowker, Lee H. *Women, Crime and the Criminal Justice System*. Lexington, Mass.: D.C. Heath, 1978.
In a chapter on cross-cultural comparisons, the author analyzes the effects of social-educational equality, economic equality, and SES development on the female crime rate for thirty countries from 1950 to 1972. He concludes that modernized nations show increases in female crime.

Simon, R. J. "The British Scene: A Brief Review." In *Women and Crime*. Lexington, Mass.: Lexington Books, 1975.
Simon compares crime rates and prison treatment of women in the United States and Great Britain. He finds that "the British scene has many similarities with the American."

Simon, R. J. "A Comparative Perspective." Appendix to *Women and Crime*. Lexington, Mass.: Lexington Books, 1975.
The author presents comparative data on female arrest rates in major offense categories for about twenty-five countries from the early 1960s to 1970.

Simon, R. J., and N. Sharma. "Women and Crime: Does the American Experience Generalize?" In Adler and Simon, *The Criminology of Deviant Women*.
This work compares trends in female crime rates in Japan, Israel, and the United States. Data are presented on these trends and on their relationship to the following variables:

number of women in the labor force, number of female-headed families, and number of single heads of household.

Smart, Carol. "The Nature of Female Criminality." In Smart, *Women, Crime and Criminology*. London: Routledge and Kegan Paul, 1977. Chapter 1.
This chapter presents data on changing female crime rates in Great Britain and includes a brief comparison with data on the United States.

7

RADICAL CRIMINOLOGY: A RECENT DEVELOPMENT

Robert Weiss

As a distinct movement for fundamental change in criminological theory and practice, radical criminology dates from the mid-1960s, a time of rebellion by university students, workers, and the ghetto poor throughout the Western industrialized world. The state's reactions to this social and political upheaval—including police infiltration, the formation of special tactical units, and *agent provocateur* work—brought into question the consensus model and the notion of political pluralism that have been dominant in the social sciences. Debate within criminology flourished with the birth of radical thought and action.

Radical criminology began a critique of crime control and especially of the academic professions that have been accused of helping support it. A terse definition is difficult, but at the most general level radical criminology holds that criminal law and its administration form part of the state's repressive apparatus, functioning in the interests of the capitalist class. The radical perspective in criminology has not been static and has shown considerable cross-cultural variation in theory and practice. Principal differences concern criminal behavior—its

EDITOR'S NOTE: For those Americans who have been criminologists for several decades, the rather abrupt appearance of radical criminology in the 1960s has been one of the most noteworthy events since 1945. Even among those who found themselves described as "bourgeois criminologists," the radical critique has been beneficial in calling attention to their own long-standing doubts about some of the fundamental assumptions that were not seriously questioned in earlier decades. In this sense, it is significant that the radical critique received serious hearing from audiences other than avowed Marxists.

As a contribution to comparative criminology in a time of unusual intellectual ferment, this volume has the obligation to consider the merits of radical criminology. Dr. Weiss accepted the formidable task of reviewing the history of this recent development, outlining the Marxist concepts that obviously predate the appearance of radical criminology, and subjecting these concepts to a critique that transcends partisanship. In these respects, his presentation provides a background for those chapters that deal with the criminology of nations that have adopted socialism.

meaning and possible role in social change—and the manner in which the state is said to function on behalf of bourgeois interests. For example, is criminal behavior reactionary or can it have radical expressions? Are criminals victims or rebels? Concerning the state, there is debate over whether capitalist interests are served through class-conscious manipulation or by structural imperative. These questions reflect the main currents of Marxist debate, but before discussing the relation between Marxist theory and the development of radical criminology, we will briefly trace the spread of the new criminology throughout the world.

ORIGINS AROUND THE WORLD

In the United States, the principal institutional locale during the movement's early years was the School of Criminology at the University of California at Berkeley, and its earliest proponents and their critics debated in the pages of the school's journal, *Issues in Criminology*. From the journal's establishment in 1965 until its untimely demise ten years later, *Issues* was a major forum for the expression of radical ideas on the topic of crime and crime control.

The Union of Radical Criminologists was formed in the United States in 1972, and among its early collective efforts was the establishment in 1974 of the journal *Crime and Social Justice*, dedicated to developing "a left perspective and practice on crime and social justice." After the politically motivated dissolution of Berkeley's School of Criminology by California's Board of Regents[1] and the demise of *Issues in Criminology* in 1975, *Crime and Social Justice* became the primary journal expression of the ideas of radical criminology in the United States. Later combined with *Issues*, its pages document much of the early history of the movement. Tony Platt's article in the journal's first issue, "Prospects for a Radical Criminology in the U.S.A.," outlined what has become the perspective's main objections to mainstream or "liberal" criminology in the United States.[2]

The radical criminological movement also developed a strong early momentum in Great Britain. The National Deviancy Conference was formed in 1968 by a group of British sociologists and criminologists concerned about providing a forum for interdisciplinary discussion of political and economic processes involved in the definition and control of deviance. Their numerous symposia have brought together radical scholars from such diverse fields as psychiatry, economics, social work, criminology, and community organization. A number of publications have emanated from their proceedings, the first two of which were *Images of Deviance*,[3] edited by Stanley Cohen, and *Politics and Deviance*,[4] edited by Ian Taylor and Lauri Taylor.

In 1973, the first conference of the European Group for the Study of Deviance and Social Control met in Impruneta, Italy, as an effort to overcome the national isolation of radical scholars. Contributors came from Norway, Finland, Sweden, the Netherlands, Great Britain, West Germany, Italy, Austria, and, by special invitation, from Israel, Canada, and the United States. A report on the conference by Drew Humphries highlights the early divergencies and points of convergence of radical criminology within and across cultures.[5] The radical criminological movement now has adherents in Taiwan, South Korea, and in Latin America where many governments exercise massive political repression largely under the guise of "crime control."[6] However, radical criminology's most developed form is in the industrialized West, where there are journals devoted prominently or exclusively to its perspective. Among these journals there are articles on radical criminology in *Contemporary Crises*, *Crime and Social Justice*, and, less frequently, *Marxist Perspectives* and *Social Problems* in the United States; *La question criminale* in Italy; *Kriminologische Journal* in West Germany; and *Déviance et Société* in France. Current centers for radical thought include the Conference for Critical Legal Studies at Madison, Wisconsin, and the Birmingham (England) Center for Cultural Studies.

MAIN CURRENTS IN RADICAL CRIMINOLOGY

Most formulations of radical criminology identify with Marxism, although it is common to preface such efforts with the observation that Marx and Engels had little to say about the matter of crime and its control. This gap is serious because Marx was not an unambivalent theoretician. Marx's thought is genuinely ambiguous on many issues, and attempts at theoretical application to specialized fields of interest have been problematic, especially for criminology. The divergencies within general Marxian theory have not only created variations in interpretation and stirred debate among adherents of the nascent radical criminological perspective, but have also caused some Marxists to deny the very possibility of a Marxist-based criminology.[7] To understand the past developments and future prospects of radical criminology, then, we must review recent controversies in Marxist and New Left social theory.

Among the numerous interpretations and reinterpretations of the thought of Marx, two main currents of Marxian theory have been central in most debates. One current views Marx as a positive "scientist," and the other sees him as a "humanist." These two roles are distinct because they are based on contrasting images of the nature of society and the nature of human action. A scientist, whose model is a structure that functions largely independent of the volition of its members, searches for laws of social determination. The critical philosopher's aim, on the other hand, is to penetrate the ideological notion of a fixed social structure, so as to reveal the hidden rational potential of man. In contrast to scientific Marxism, which sees man as the bearer of social structure, critical or humanistic Marxists see man as the maker of history.

Marx's writings offer evidence for both views. For instance, in the Introduction to *Capital*, Marx refers to "naturalistic laws of capitalistic production. . . working with iron necessity towards inevitable results." Yet, *Capital* is subtitled "A Critique of Political Economy." As Alvin Gouldner observes, a critique is an hermeneutic:

> A critique takes a given belief system, a theory, ideology, indeed science itself—or any cultural "objectification"—as problematic. It seeks to de-reify it, to demystify, to remove its objectivistic false consciousness, to offer an interpretation of it in terms of the everyday life of men living in and constrained by a specific society.[8]

The scientific conception was promoted by Marx's collaborator, Friedrich Engels, and, after him, by Karl Kautsky and the orthodox Marxists of the German Social Democratic party. Among the "scientific" aspects of Marx's work, the theory of an economic determination of history was particularly emphasized and, under Lenin and Stalin, culminated in the official Marxist doctrine of the Soviet Union. According to this doctrine, the economic strictly determines the political and the ideological. Evolution to socialism is inevitable—ensured by dialectical laws of social development. This mechanistic interpretation of Marx was first formulated by Engels in his *Anti-Dühring*. Lenin continued it but added that progress toward socialism could be hastened. In such cases, the working class must be led by a "vanguard party" of intellectuals who will administer from above the transition to communism. During the socialist transition, the means of production will be held by the state in the interest of the proletariat. Such a "scientific" and economistic interpretation of Marx did not go long unchallenged, however.

The humanism of Marx was first given expression by George Lukács, whose *History and Class Consciousness* reemphasized the concept of alienation.[9] Lukács criticized attempts to interpret Marx as a positivist studying immutable laws of social development. To view social reality as governed by naturalistic laws, as science does, is to objectify human relationships, that is, to perceive them as relations between *things*. Marx's critique of political economy entailed revealing the *social* nature and thus historical character of the capitalist productive process. In the process of what Lukács termed *reification*, men come to view their cultural creations as suprahuman, and particular social structures appear natural and inevitable. Demystification of the processes of social structure—that is, revealing capitalist relations as historical and the capitalist system as one governed by human forces—was the *raison d'etre* of *Capital*, according to Lukács.

Many crucial passages of Marx and Engels appear to take an ambiguous stand as to science or critique. Passages concerning social change and the nature of the state are particularly difficult to interpret. In this celebrated passage from *The Eighteenth Brumaire*, Marx observes: "Men make their own history, but they do not make it just as they please; they do not make it under circumstances chosen by themselves, but under circumstances directly encountered, given, and transmitted from the past."[10] Is behavior structurally determined or "voluntaristic"? Concerning the polity, in the controversial and often misquoted passage from the *Communist Manifesto*, Marx and Engels comment: "The executive of the modern state is but a committee for managing the common affairs of the whole bourgeoisie."[11] Is the state a mere instrument of class interest, or is it in some sense autonomous from the manipulation of actors? Other than suggestive phrases, usually in connection with the "base" and "superstructure" metaphor, Marx and Engels did not develop a theory of the state.

Were Marx and Engels equivocal on these questions, or does their thought provide a dialectical reconciliation? So far attempts to bridge the chasm have not been convincing, and a return to Marxist thought would seem to require a choice between the primacy of one or the other—Marx as scientist or as humanist.[12] Theoretical formulations concerning the nature and meaning of criminal behavior, legal creation, and the role of the criminal justice system will differ markedly depending on the version of Marx chosen. Is criminal behavior a voluntary expression or structurally determined? In other words, are criminals "rebels" or "victims"? And is the criminal law a mere instrument of the capitalist class, acting at its behest, or does the state serve the interests of capital as an autonomous but parallel structure? What will be designated as "critical," "materialist," and "structural" versions of radical criminology have developed, each reflecting different answers to those questions.

Radical criminology began largely as "negative critique," a reaction to criminology as a positive science. Traditional criminology, as sociology in general, has viewed itself as a science modeled after the natural sciences, pursuing a value-neutral investigation of empirical reality with the object of formulating general causal laws. Critical criminologists have argued that as a result of this "scientific" attitude criminology has ignored the influence of capitalist economic interests in the formulation and application of the criminal law. Instead, criminology has taken the socioeconomic system for granted and has looked for technical rather than structural solutions to the crime problem. After a background sketch of humanism in Marxist social theory and its influence upon critical criminology, we will note its failure as a critique to provide a revolutionary strategy. Materialist and structuralist versions of radical criminology are developing as scientific Marxist alternatives, but these suffer from economism and determinism. The tension between Marx as a scientist and as a humanist, between structure and process, between determinism and voluntarism, has yet to be resolved. Radical criminology and Marxism await a dialectical resolution.

CRITICAL THEORY AND CRITICAL CRIMINOLOGY

The humanistic interpretation of Marx was taken up in the 1930s by the Frankfurt Institute for Social Research, whose members have become known as the Frankfurt School. Max Horkheimer, Theodor Adorno, Herbert Marcuse, Erich Fromm, and Franz Neumann, among others in the school, sought social explanations for contemporary events that orthodox or scientific Marxism seemed incapable of explaining, such as Stalinism, fascism, monopoly capitalism, and the failure of the working class as agents of revolution. The school's objective, however, was also one of Marx's objectives—to help free man from class domination. The Soviet example, however, contradicted the theory that the political and ideological were determined by the economic base, that eliminating private ownership of the means of production would necessarily and automatically lead to the political and ideological emancipation of all members of society.

Rooted in German (neo-Kantian) idealism, "critical theory" of the Frankfurt School starts from the assumption that "man" is the subject or maker of history. Those forces that dominate and constrain human action are likewise manmade and can be removed through enlightened conduct. The Frankfurt School's critique of traditional theory, then, is of the traditional theory's "mode of cognition" or epistemology, which is derived largely from the natural sciences. In his 1932 article, "Traditional and Critical Theory," Max Horkheimer announced the break of critical theory with that interpretation of science which searches for universal laws of human behavior.

The purpose of critical theory is to substitute a radical philosophical or "negative critique."[13] The terms "alienation," "freedom," and "transcendence" reflect critical theory's emphasis on man as the creator-subject of history, and concepts central to the historical materialism of classical Marxism such as mode of production become secondary in social analysis. The study of political economy is viewed as a philosophical critique rather than a scientific undertaking. This philosophical humanist interpretation of Marx remained the outstanding one in the West through the 1960s and, with the publication in that decade of such works as Erich Fromm's *Marx's Concept of Man*[14] and Herbert Marcuse's *One-Dimensional Man*[15] and *Essay on Liberation*,[16] the perspective became relatively popular reading.

Critical Theory Helps Fuel Social Protest

During the 1960s, every Western European nation experienced enormous social upheaval, including student demonstrations and riots, workers' strikes, and factory takeovers. In Italy, a coalition government was formed, and in a number of major European cities socialist mayors were being elected. In the United States, a decade-long quiescence was shattered by movements involving civil rights, free speech, prison reform, poverty, feminism, and peace in Vietnam. Because of the near vacuum in Marxist theory in the United States at the time (occasioned in part by the decline of the "Old Left" in the aftermath of McCarthyism and as part of the political inertia of the "affluent" 1950s), the humanistic version of Marx found ready acceptance, especially among the student left.

The writings of New Left theorists such as Herbert Marcuse and Erich Fromm, who drew on the early works of Marx, such as *The Economic and Philosophic Manuscripts* (which first appeared in English only in 1959), and the phenomenological and existential writings of the French theorists Maurice Merleau-Ponty and Jean-Paul Sartre, helped fuel rebellious students on campuses throughout the United States as well as Western Europe. While in Europe there emerged a coherent political movement in which workers as well as students took an active part, in the United States radicalism engendered white working-class hostility.

There, with the encouragement of theorists such as Marcuse, the university-based New Left hoped for the creation of a revolutionary front comprising those outside of the productive process. The unemployed and marginally employed, including students and urban ghetto dwellers, would in "late capitalism" combine with the *lumpenproletariat* in replacing the working class as the principal agent of revolutionary social change.

The radical criminology movement emerged as part of that social and political rebellion of the 1960s and early 1970s, and, not surprisingly, early formulations of radical criminology drew theoretical guidance from critical theory of the Frankfurt School. The intellectual style and focal concerns of critical theory are evident in such early works as Richard Quinney's 1973 article, "Crime Control in Capitalist Society,"[17] and in his *Critique of Legal Order*,[18] both of which called for an explicit grounding of criminological analysis in a "critical philosophy." In his *Critique*, Quinney contends:

> It is in a critical philosophy that we are able to break with the ideology of the age. For built into the process of critical thinking is the ability to think negatively. This dialectical form of thought allows us to question current experience. By being able to entertain an alternative, we can better understand what exists. Rather than merely looking for an objective reality, we are concerned with the negation of the established order.[19]

Rejection of the Positivist Paradigm

In its early or "critical" period, radical criminology displayed five fundamental characteristics in common with the New Left and critical theory: (1) overall, the style of "negative critique," (2) a wariness of empiricism, (3) moral commitment and activism on the part of intellectuals, (4) emphasis on a revolutionary potential of the "underclass," including criminals, and (5) belief in volition and a strong faith in rationality.

Centrally, negative critique involves a rejection of epistemological paradigm of positivism upon which the social sciences including criminology developed. According to the positivist perspective, the "science" of criminology represents an objective, value-neutral search for universal laws governing criminal behavior. Ahistorical by assuming an eternal social structure with a fixed system of class relations, criminology in its various traditions—classical, positivist, biological, and Mertonian structural—has functioned as an administrative science, restricted in inquiry to locating the causes of criminal behavior in individual and social pathology and of finding measures to reduce its incidence.

For the most part criminological research, then, has been of the "abstracted empiricist" kind, involving very narrowly conceived problems developed by supposedly disinterested scholars. Platt criticized such a research agenda for failing "to raise general moral and political questions about the nature of society."[20] "Correctionalism" and "reformism"—the focus on adjusting and accommodating individuals and institutions to the prevailing social structure—has been the unquestioned goal of criminological theory and practice. Platt has pointed out that "reformism" is part of the ideology of liberalism, and therefore is "often accompanied by a reliance on technocratic solutions to social problems and a belief that progress will occur through enlightening managers and policy-makers rather than by organizing the oppressed."[21]

Radicals contend that this kind of empiricism tends to reinforce class society when performed under the technocratic ideology of modern social science which holds that its methods and interests are separate. In *Aspects of Sociology*, members of the Frankfurt School observe that when the apparent solutions to a social problem entail not merely the alleviation of specific conditions but structural change, "then interests diverge. That is the real reason why the methods of empirical social science are so readily made to serve manipulative purposes."[22]

A principal difference between critical and traditional theory, according to Max Horkheimer, was whether theory intentionally or inadvertently contributed to the reproduction of capitalist society.[23] The avoidance of theoretical and empirical work because it could contribute to technocratic control became a major concern for critical criminologists as well. Intentional avoidance of concrete social analysis because the results, embodied as social reforms, can be instrumental in the reproduction of capitalist systems of power is reflected in American critical criminology's "strategic anti-correctionalism" and in the "antipathologism" of the British.[24] The idea of "abstentionism" was carried to its extreme in "The Production of a Marxist Criminology," where Richard Quinney suggests in effect that there is little for Marxist criminologists *qua* criminologists to do.[25] If we assume that crime is manifestation solely of class societies, the task of radical scholars should be to help contribute to a revolution and help frame a socialist alternative devoid of criminality.

The Crisis of Critical Criminology

Not surprisingly, critical criminology found itself in the same cul-de-sac as critical theory and the New Left in general. Fundamentally a philosophically based critique of ideology, the Frankfurt School failed to provide a scientifically ascertained political strategy to overthrow capitalism. As Göran Therborn observes, the school's members not only did not "provide Marxism with any instrument to assist in the construction" of a revolutionary strategy, "they denounce all such instruments *simply because they are instruments*."[26] Likewise, critical criminology's "abstentionism" has left radicals without a basis for ascertaining the potential role of "criminal" behavior in social change. Instead of sound analyses of criminal etiology, many critical criminologists have avoided the question or have simply asserted the radical nature of acts of crime and deviance. Thereby, they have left a void in the construction of a revolutionary strategy which must involve determining the revolutionary potential *and* reactionary quality of "criminal behavior." As David Greenberg argues:

The scientific explanation of criminal behavior is then of potential value to radicals as it may suggest ways to redirect energies now invested in individualistic criminal violations toward a more organized, consciously political challenge to the dominant institutions of a capitalist society. This position allows one to seek the elimination of some common forms of lower class crime without embracing liberal meliorism or conservative repression.[27]

Responding to such criticism, Richard Quinney, a leading radical theorist of criminal etiology, has attempted to overcome the "abstentionism" of critical criminology in his *Class, State, and Crime*.[28] This book is the only effort to formulate a comprehensive radical theory of criminal causation, and his typology of criminal behavior under capitalism attempts to take into account crimes committed by persons occupying different levels of the social structure. Generated by class struggle in the development of capitalism, crimes are grouped as to whether they are committed by corporations and state officials in the course of "domination" and "repression," or whether they are committed as acts of "accommodation" or "resistance" to the conditions of capitalism.

Thus, Quinney tries to distinguish between crimes that are reactionary (such as most "street" crimes) and those that have revolutionary potential. For instance, those of *accommodation* include "predatory" crimes, such as burglary and robbery, which are "pursued out of a need to survive in the capitalist system," and "personal" crimes such as rape and murder, which are the result of the "brutalizing conditions of capitalism." Crimes of *resistance*, on the other hand, consciously challenge the social order. Historically, these crimes have been committed largely by those involved in establishing radical political party organizations, and by labor in its struggles against capital—particularly during the 1870 to 1940 effort to unionize in the United States.[29] Thus, crimes of accommodation and resistance may "range from unconscious reactions to exploitation, to conscious acts of survival within the capitalist system, to politically conscious acts of rebellion."[30]

Quinney's typology provides a useful beginning. The categories he designates are not empty, although their relation to one another and to class struggle remains underdeveloped. Crimes of economic "domination" (largely corporate violations such as price fixing and environmental pollution) and the repressive actions of governmental officials committed in the interests of "national security" and "law and order" are well documented. Perhaps more important for a radical criminology is research into crimes of resistance and rebellion. *Albion's Fatal Tree*,[31] *Whigs and Hunters*,[32] and two studies by Eric Hobsbawm, *Primitive Rebels*[33] and *Bandits*,[34] are the most frequently cited attempts to discern political significance in what historians have traditionally defined as "common" criminal behavior.

Hobsbawm claims that banditry is a universal form of peasant protest. Appearing throughout the world relatively unchanged for centuries, banditry reached its peak during the advent of capitalism when peasants and landless laborers were displaced by the new market economy. Fellow peasants look at bandits in their communities not as simple criminals but as "noble robbers," "primitive resistance fighters," and "terror-bringing avengers." While banditry represents a form of social protest against oppression, bandits are only primitive liberation fighters insofar as they lack political organizational capacity, a coherent alternative political ideology, and a revolutionary strategy. Hence, bandits are "prepolitical" phenomena according to the author, reformist rather than revolutionary, and are replaced in time with more sophisticated forms of social protest, including various rural secret societies, millenarian peasant movements, preindustrial urban mobs, labor sects, and early revolutionary labor organizations. In the chapter, "Who Becomes a Bandit?" Hobsbawm discusses the categories from which bandits are most likely to be drawn, and some of the causal mechanisms involved.

There are serious criticisms of Hobsbawm's thesis, some of which bear on discussions concerning the political significance of forms of contemporary criminality. Anton Blok maintains that Hobsbawm exaggerates the degree of class conflict, as "bandits quite often terrorized those from whose very ranks they managed to rise, and thus helped to suppress them."[35] This is not simply an empirical dispute. Logically, bandits who expect to last very long must have connections with established power-holders who protect them and for whom, as the quid pro quo, bandits often act as retainers. So, bandits obstruct national peasant mobilization directly by intimidation and indirectly by providing channels for upward mobility. Similar to *mafia*-like gangs, they undermine class solidarity. Perhaps much the same could be said of contemporary street gangs and forms of organized crime.

While bandits may have been antisocial, eighteenth-century English smugglers, poachers, wreckers, and coastal plunderers were clearly part of a collective effort. According to the authors of *Albion's Fatal Tree*, smuggling and wrecking in particular tended toward crowd activities and sometimes involved entire villages. Villagers did not regard these "social crimes" as genuinely criminal because in precapitalist times they were not defined as such but rather were a legitimate part of local economies. The rural poor people—principally laborers, farmers, and miners—supplemented their meager incomes with poached game, wood, fruit, and the contents of wrecked ships.

With the development of commercial capitalism, however, access to such goods as a customary use-right came to be redefined as theft by the state. *Albion's Fatal Tree*, like Karl Marx's study of laws prohibiting firewood-gathering in the forests of the Rhineland,[36] documents the way in which criminal law acted as a principal instrument in the creation of private property rights. Other forms of resistance included anonymous letters of threat and blackmail. British historian E. P. Thompson examines this form of eighteenth- and nineteenth-century English protest in his chapter, "The Crime of Anonymity." With the spread of literacy, letters threatening arson or bodily injury were sent to government officials to discourage the prosecution of poachers, smugglers, and wreckers. Others sent letters to landowners or gentry, and to employers protesting wages and working conditions. Anonymous handbills protested food prices or called for collective worker action. The penalty for sending such anonymous messages was death.

These studies help debunk the myth of eighteenth-century England as a stable and consensual society. Poor workers and cottagers participated as a community in criminal acts of resistance to the redefinition of rights to game, coal, wood, and the contents of wrecked ships. While this criminality was a social endeavor, the community strongly sanctioned petty or casual theft.[37] These are important indications of criminal behavior as a form of class struggle. At the very same time in history, however, footpads and highwaymen robbed travelers of all classes; ugly urban crowds gathered for hangings, and mobs at other times meted out their own punishments to unfortunates held in stocks; muggers and pickpockets plagued the streets of London; and sailors frequently rioted over the price of whores and liquor.

Although not all crime was predatory or irrational as some conservative and liberal criminologists have suggested, crimes of resistance and rebellion alone do not account historically for the state's police response. The preponderance of arrests and prison commitments in England and the United States, for example, appears to have been for grand larceny and summary offenses.

In discussing the origin of the penitentiary in England, Michael Ignatieff observes that by the mid-nineteenth century vagrants, drunks, prostitutes, the disorderly, petty thieves, and assaulters accounted for 85 percent of arrests and more than one-half of the prison commitments.[38] Likewise, in the United States, research by David Rothman reveals that the early penitentiary was largely populated by Irish laborers and semiskilled workers, sentenced mostly for grand larceny.[39] Petty thieves, drunks, and prostitutes populated the local jails and workhouses. And in the United States today, estimates are that two-thirds of all arrests are for "public order" offenses. While the state may perceive such criminality as "part of a wider pattern of insubordination among the poor,"[40] it clearly represents an "accommodation" rather than conscious resistance to the capitalist social order. Yet, many critical criminologists continue to romanticize crime and deviance by characterizing it as rational and liberating.[41]

Probing the source of many of the problems of critical criminology, Jock Young has criticized the "new deviancy" theorists for creating a "rational Frankenstein constructed out of the inverted conceptual debris of its positivist opponents."[42] As in a number of other points of opposition critical criminologists, rather than working with a radically different conceptual system, have simply inverted traditional criminology. Whereas traditional criminological theory tends toward determinism, critical criminology stresses voluntarism; where the former stresses pathology, the latter substitutes extreme rationality. The state's decision-making is thought to be based on popular consensus in traditional theory, so critical criminologists have argued that it is a simple instrument of the capitalist class. Thus, critical criminology represents more a rebellion within traditional sociology than against it. Failing to extricate themselves from the categories of traditional criminology, many radicals attempt to argue against tradition while at the same time employing tradition's conceptual tools.

In the "Prospects for Radical Criminology" section of the European Group's first conference, Taylor et al. addressed some of the inadequacies of early radical criminology. In response, they suggested moving beyond a criminology based on moral denunciation of class inequities in the administration of justice, and toward the formulation of a positive program for action based on a new theoretical strategy. Just as in *The New Criminology* they called for a "fully social theory of deviance," they now call for a "*fully* materialistic analysis of crime."[43]

DEVELOPING A MATERIALIST CRIMINOLOGY

Submitted originally as a research proposal to the Frankfurt Institute for Social Research in 1931, Georg Rusche's 1933 article, "Arbeitsmarkt und Strafvollzug," set forth many of the principles enunciated by radical criminologists today. He maintained that criminologists have ignored economic theory and have worked with "a more or less static and ahistorical system of class relations."[44] The study of crime and its control is best suited to sociological inquiry, Rusche observed; yet, little research has been conducted which attempts to penetrate the social forces at work. Although sociologists have been concerned with the phenomenon of crime and its control, Rusche says, they have shed little light on the matter:

> For even if the relationship between socioeconomic phenomena and the problems of crime and its control are obvious to sociologists, there is still a long way to go from the naive recognition of this fact to making use of it in a systematic and scientific fashion.

To the embarrassment of radical criminologists, this statement largely holds true today.

In an expanded version of their paper given to the First Conference of the European Group, Taylor et al.[45] criticize previous radical work for failing to go beyond what they term "exposé criminology" and "radical empiricism," by which they mean studies merely demonstrating class duplicity in the operation of the criminal justice system. Studies demonstrating the regular existence of criminal behavior in strata of the ruling class, while criminology and criminal justice focus on the crimes of the working class and the unemployed, are trivial. Radical scholars need to get deeper than such truisms and the indignant responses they invoke. They must go beyond the stage of negative critique to make a positive contribution to scientific theory and practice. In terms of etiology, this new analysis involves searching for the "structural" determinants of criminal behavior at all levels of the social structure: how crimes of the poor and the wealthy alike relate to the process of capital accumulation. Furthermore, investigation of the emergence and development of law and institutions of social control should reveal their material basis in specific social formations during particular historical periods. Marx urged historical specificity, warning against the tendency to view as eternal bourgeois relations of production—private property and the legal system that upholds it—without realizing that "each mode of production produces its specific legal relations."[46] In the words of Taylor et al., radical criminologists must "examine legal norms within the framework of the reproduction of material conditions of social life or the management of capitalist production," so as to reveal the "interconnectedness of criminal activity and legal norm creation with the labour process in a particular society."[47]

There are certain fundamental and interrelated questions, then, that must be addressed in constructing a materialist criminology. First, in any particular social formation, what are the nature and meaning of criminal behavior? Does it represent a "dialectical contradiction"? That is, is crime an inevitable outgrowth of the political economy that at the same time threatens to undermine the social formation? Second, to what extent and in what ways are criminal law and its enforcement in class-based social structures related to the productive and reproductive processes? And why do legal and crime control mechanisms function (directly or indirectly) to maintain class domination? Answering this second set of questions may not be as obvious as it has seemed to many critical criminologists, and involves the formulation of a solid theory of the state. The answers to these questions are obviously crucial to the construction of a Marxian criminology. If criminal behavior is simply a byproduct of capitalist society, and if the law and its enforcement merely reflect class relations but are not in some manner central to their maintenance or change, it is doubtful that the discipline could be of more than a secondary interest to Marxists.

In Steven Spitzer's paper, "Toward a Marxian Theory of Deviance," some propositions are advanced concerning the "production" of deviant and criminal categories and behaviors under capitalism, and a framework for analyzing the nature and scope of "control systems" is established.[48] In a Marxian account, these phenomena should be explicable in terms of the development of the mode of production and the dynamics of the class structure. Spitzer hypothesizes that "problem populations" are generated "either directly through the expression of fundamental contradictions in the capitalist mode of production or indirectly through disturbances in the system of class rule."[49] Either in the form of "social dynamite" or "social junk," they threaten capitalist social relations of production, becoming "generally eligible for management as deviant when they disturb, hinder or call into question" the capitalist mode of production, or its patterns of consumption and distribution. Problem populations have revolutionary potential if they are located "in a position of functional indispensability within the capitalist system."[50]

Criminal Behavior

Spitzer's framework is comprehensive but too abstract. For instance, as long as "problem populations" are largely coincident with the "surplus population," there will be difficulty connecting deviance with class struggle. While there exist reasonable arguments on how the surplus population is generated by the capitalist productive system and how as a "lever" to bring down wages it is integral to capital's functioning, radical criminologists have not shown how its *criminality* relates to "the process of capital accumulation" (Taylor et al.), nor how such crimes could possess revolutionary potential (Spitzer). A claim that criminals *qua* criminals could be revolutionary subjects represents a basic misunderstanding of Marx's ideas, according to many theorists. A turn toward Marx and Engels must consider the basis of their derisive view of criminals, a view that was not simply Victorian prejudice. To the extent that those adjudicated as criminals are drawn from the bottom layers of the "reserve army of the unemployed," they are not in the correct structural location to be principal subjects of progressive social change.

Marx and Engels were interested in the dynamics of social structural *change*, and in their theory the motor of such change was the conflict between just two classes—the producers and the expropriators, generated in this epoch by contradictions within the capitalist economic system. While Marx recognized the existence of other "classes" (strata) which play important roles of alliance during revolutionary confrontations, the worker and the capitalist were the two sides of the fundamental contradiction.[51] In other words, Marx's analysis was of class, not of stratification and its relation to institutions such as criminal justice. This argument represents a serious challenge for a Marxist-based criminology, and it represents one of the grounds for the denial of such a project by Paul Hirst and Stephen Mugford.

Victims as well as the perpetrators of "street" violence and common theft are overwhelmingly the unemployed and working-class poor. Street crime thus serves to debilitate and fragment the working class. In light of this fact, radical criminologists face a challenge to determine the causes of "street" crime with the hope of helping redirect those energies into serious political channels that can help support rather than frustrate a socialist revolution. Yet, contemporary radical theorists of crime causation have failed to provide better arguments concerning "street" criminality than those held by Engels and Willem Bonger.[52] Engels attributed such crime to the material conditions of capitalist society: poverty, poor health, inadequate education, and general demoralization of the working class and the unemployed. But the early twentieth-century Belgian sociologist Willem Bonger, in *Criminality and Economic Conditions*, recognized that poverty alone does not cause crime:

> The potency of economic want as a factor in crime causation is mainly determined by whether or not poverty is experienced as relative deprivation, in a social context (capitalist) wherein people are taught to equate economic advantage with intrinsic superiority and disadvantage with inferiority.[53]

He maintained that the capitalist environment fosters "egoism," and thus a greater capacity in man for crime. And because capitalism is characterized by extreme competition at all levels of the social structure, there is greater uncertainty of existence for both classes.

Taylor et al. reject as "subjectivistic" Bonger's attempt to link individual criminal behavior to the social structure. Their theory denies any pathology: "The task we have set ourselves, and other criminologists, is the attempt to create the kind of society in which facts of human diversity are not subject to the power to criminalize."[54] Their projected "fully social" theory of deviance hopes to be free of any biological, psychological, or other assumptions that suggest limitations on human volition. Yet, their "fully materialist" criminology points to the economic structural determinants of criminal behavior.[55] To have it both ways, they maintain that man's behavior is "both determined and determining."[56] As John Ainlay points out, the authors are here involved in a simple contradiction that they label "dialectical."[57]

Such problems stem from the failure of some theorists to recognize clearly from which version of Marx they are operating and the consequent limitations of one version as opposed to the other. A criminologist's orientation to the early or late Marx has very important implications for criminological theory and practice. As they stand, each version is predicated on different assumptions about the nature of human will and the nature of society. Scientific, materialistic Marxism emphasizes the importance of socioeconomic structures and therefore views people ("agents") as constrained by objective forces, while critical or humanistic Marxism, based on idealism, views humans as rational, purposeful, and potentially capable of removing unnecessary institutional constraints. A radical criminology based on science would view social change basically as a technical problem of determining and predicting structural contradictions, whereas for a criminology based on critique the revolutionary task is one of eliminating "false consciousness" through enlightenment. Whether the two views can be reconciled will depend upon the development of an adequate theory of class consciousness. Until theorists fashion such a "dialectical" resolution, criminologists should choose one perspective or the other and remain consistent in its application.

Materialist Conceptions of the State

The paucity of radical work regarding the causes and significance of criminal behavior raises the question of what the state's crime control agencies actually do for capitalist society per se. This is the deficiency of Quinney's *Critique of Legal Order* which attempts to demonstrate the class character of crime control by examining the class location of top criminal justice personnel. This quasi-theory of the state in the United States concentrates on the interpersonal connections between members of the capitalist ("ruling") class and the state's crime control agencies. Not only are we to assume motivations of conduct, but Quinney's study of the class composition of government agencies does not demonstrate in what ways the state is class selective. Unless we are told in what ways, why, and the social mechanisms by which a state's agencies serve particular class interests, we are not being presented with a genuine theory of the state regarding criminal justice.

Quinney's book on the legal system is an example of the exposé criminology that Taylor, Walton, and Young wish to transcend with their proposed materialist criminology. They wish to go beyond the power subject of critical theory to an analysis of the objective functions of the state system—that is, abandon the attempt to discern motivations of actors and search instead for the logic of structures. According to the British trio, a materialist theorizes that legal norms and institutions of crime control are related to the processes of production and the reproduction of class relations. The most fruitful avenue for such theory and research has been in the examination of the historical relation of penal systems to the labor market. In terms of scope, Georg Rusche and Otto Kirchheimer's *Punishment and Social Structure* (1939, reissued 1967) is the most ambitious of such efforts.[58] A consideration of the book's thesis and the subsequent theoretical controversy surrounding it will serve to illustrate major currents of materialist interpretation and debate on the functions of crime control institutions in general.

The collaborative outgrowth of Rusche's aforementioned research proposal for the Frankfurt School, *Punishment and Social Structure*, examines the history of Western penal systems from the early Middle Ages to the Great Depression. The authors observe three epochs that stand out during which three systems of punishment prevailed. During the early Middle Ages penance and fines prevailed; corporal and capital punishment were predominant during the latter Middle Ages, replaced in the seventeenth century by penal servitude, transportation, and galley slavery.

Wary of the conventional "progress" or "reform" accounts that seek to explain these penal changes as a consequence of the "march of science" or increasing humanitarianism, their theory holds that systems of punishment have significance independent of penal theory. They warn against studying an institution solely by examining its stated purposes. Stripped of their "ideological veils and juristic appearance,"[59] changes in penal policy have correlated with particular stages of social structural development, the authors argue. "Every system of production tends to discover punishments which correspond to its productive relationships."[60]

Penal systems served the economy in a number of ways, responding particularly to the vicissitudes of the labor market. In periods of economic stagnation and consequent unemployment, a harsh system of corporal and capital punishment was introduced as a deterrent to crime. On the other hand, during periods of labor shortage, such as in the mercantile era of the seventeenth century, the penal system directly exploited the labor of convicts. In houses of correction throughout Europe—the Bridewell in London, the rasphouses in Amsterdam and Ghent, the Zuchthaus and Spinnhaus in the German-speaking nations, and the Hôpitaux généraux in France—able-bodied beggars, vagabonds, idlers, prostitutes, and thieves were put to work rasping wood, spinning, and manufacturing pins, silk, and lace. These industries rendered a profit for the authorities and occasionally for private employers.

Rusche and Kirchheimer's analysis, then, suggests that systems of punishment have developed as something more than a response to crime. Penal systems have functioned so as to fill gaps in the labor market, and this culminated in the invention of the factory-like penitentiary during the birth of industrial capitalism. However, just as this penal form was gaining the acceptance of intellectual reformers, its economic basis—the need for manpower—was disappearing. Coincident with the rise of industrial capitalism, with its labor-displacing machinery, was a population boom. The generation of a surplus population, along with the development of machinery, made prison labor uncompetitive with outside industries. Consequently, prison conditions deteriorated and the deterrence function came to the fore. Work became punishment, and methods of torture included the treadwheel or "everlasting staircase," the crank, and rock busting.

Rusche and Kirchheimer's long-neglected book is the most substantial attempt to apply Marxian categories to the study of crime control. Their work is serving as an impetus to those radical criminologists interested in working with basic concepts of the "late" or "scientific" Marx, concepts integral to the theory of historical materialism. Among the most prominent is Italian criminologist Dario Melossi.

In addition to interpretive work and substantive research on the theory of penal evolution formulated by Rusche and Kirchheimer, Melossi has examined the treatment of the penal question implicit in Marx's own works, particularly *Capital*.[61] He directs attention to the value of Marx's method in understanding the functions of state penal policy during the origins of industrial capitalism.[62] This method, however, does not constitute economic determinism as Rusche and Kirchheimer's analysis suggests. After a close biographical and textual study, Melossi contends that Rusche's concept paper and his original two chapters for *Punishment and Social Structure* did not contain the economism that the book as a whole represents. Kirchheimer, Rusche's appointed collaborator *in absentia*, is responsible for the emphasis on direct exploitation as a penal measure under industrial capitalism. While it cannot be well-argued that penal (forced) labor is or was an essential condition for the existence of capitalist accumulation, a trained supply of labor with a disposition to sell itself is a necessary condition. A disciplined supply of laborers could be facilitated by the penal system, and Melossi's work stresses the important deterrent and training functions of state penal policy during the origins of factory manufacture.

The "Free Market" and Labor Discipline

Essential to any mode of production is a tractable labor force. Under the capitalist mode, labor-power takes the form of a commodity—workers must be free to sell their labor-power and have only their labor-power to sell. In his analysis of the so-called primitive accumulation, Marx observed how workers must be stripped of their feudal bonds: "the capitalist system presupposes the complete separation of labourers from all poverty in the means of production by which they can realize their labour."[63] This also means that, unlike slavery or feudalism, in the last instance the worker can only be compelled to work by indirect, economic pressures. In the "free market" economy of laissez-faire capitalism, the worker as a commodity is formally free to withhold or sell labor-power according to the market's supply and demand factors. When demand is high in relation to supply, a worker generally is offered a favorable wage. On the other hand, the employer does not incur an obligation to maintain such wage or even to retain the worker should market conditions change.[64] Moreover, forms of nonproductive subsistence such as relief, theft, or beggary cannot, especially in times of labor shortage, exist for significant numbers as a viable alternative to wage labor. The commodification of land, labor, and money is the minimal condition for the existence of capitalism. The whole process, once forcibly established, must be reproduced on a continually expanding scale.

Just as in the words of Marx, "Nature does not produce on the one side owners of money or commodities, and on the other men possessing nothing but their own labour-power,"[65] so the reproduction of capitalist relations is neither natural nor automatic. Karl Polanyi has forcibly argued that a society based on a totally unregulated economic market is impossible.[66] In his comprehensive study of the origins of machine production in a commercial society, *The Great Transformation*, Polanyi contends that without some interference from outside the market, society would be destroyed—labor, land, and capitalist alike. Such an idea as the "free market" principle is fraught with social contradictions, not the least of which concerns labor: "For the alleged commodity 'labor power' cannot be shoved about, used indiscriminantly, or even be left unused, without affecting the human individual who happens to be the bearer of this particular commodity."[67] What is a "factor" in the productive calculus of the capitalist is life for the worker. Resistance and revolt against the commodity form developed in a myriad of ways: through mendicancy, machine-wrecking, shop floor sabotage, absenteeism, and, most troublesome to capital, labor union organization. In the United States, labor struggled for collective organizational interference in the "free market," and capital responded with spies, blacklists, armed guards, and strikebreakers recruited from the surplus population.[68] Such repressive measures were justified by laissez-faire ideology. Labor combinations were a gross interference in the "free market," where everyone bargains as "free and equal" agents. One's value is determined strictly by the "market principle." At the same time as capital and the state were extolling the virtues of competition, however, industry worked frantically to limit internecine competition, while the state attempted to augment mechanisms of the market in favor of capital.

The principal methods by which the state facilitated the process of capital accumulation and reproduction included the civil and criminal law, the state's "relief" or welfare policies, and the penal system. In England, the process of making land and labor power into commodities involved, originally, "Bills of Enclosure," which facilitated the bloody expropriation of the peasant from the land; the Statute of Labourers, which established a ceiling on wages; and the Draconian vagrancy laws that punished those traveling in search of higher wages as well as mendicants, vagabonds, robbers, and petty thieves.[69]

In the new commercial society where workers, like other elements of production, land, and money, are considered as mere commodities, "conditions of the market" (supply and demand) became the sole determinant for how workers fared, how much wage they received, or whether they would be employed at all. Periodic unemployment, created by downturns of the economic cycle, short-term hiring, and maladjustment caused by rapid change in markets and technology became characteristic features of capitalist society and one of the state's principal concerns.

The manner in which welfare systems since the sixteenth century have expanded and contracted during the depression and prosperity cycles of capitalism, alternately appeasing and deterring the unemployed, is the subject of Piven and Cloward's *Regulating the Poor*.[70] The authors argue that "outdoor relief" expansion was designed to appease the mass of potentially rebellious unemployed during periods of economic depression, while "indoor relief," or confinement in workhouses, was an essential instrument in the regulation of the poor in periods of prosperity. In addition to those who could not be absorbed by nascent industry, there were those who failed or refused to adapt to wage labor and the harsh discipline of the factory. Because economic incentives and punishments— "mechanisms of the market"—were often insufficient to compel many to labor, in times of labor scarcity the state enhanced the market by making its relief an undesirable alternative. Thus, for centuries houses of confinement were an accompaniment to relief programs, and "were repeatedly proclaimed the sole source of aid during times of stability, and for a reason bearing directly on the maintenance of work norms in a market system."[71]

Fear of incarceration in the grim workhouses was meant, then, to give "teeth" to the relief policies encouraging wage labor. For those who would choose beggary, vagabondage, or theft instead, the harsh regimen of the house of correction and, later, the penitentiary awaited them. But even this experience could seem attractive to the utterly impoverished. To act effectively as an incentive to enter the commodity market, English officials soon discovered that conditions of imprisonment as well as those under poor relief had to be "less eligible" than the lot of the lowest paid strata of wage laborers (something that often required considerable imagination). In his examination of the origins of imprisonment under early British capitalism, Russell Hogg observes: "The principle of less-eligibility is the essential mechanism which locked the prison system into the changing class relations and forces of the nineteenth century."[72] In contrast to Rusche and Kirchheimer's economistic labor exploitation thesis, both Hogg and Melossi stress that, while the state's policy made the prison ancillary to the economy, its assistance was indirect. The prison operated outside of the process of production so as to buttress the "laws" of the "free market" economy. This would help explain the nature of prison labor changes during the Industrial Revolution. The thesis of direct labor exploitation appears to hold through the mercantile period, under which workhouses and houses of correction fostered productive labor for the national economy. In some workshops prisoners even received a monetary incentive. Under the new penitentiary system, penal labor becomes futile and debasing because labor cannot be remunerated or even be meaningful if it is to serve as a deterrent.[73]

Punishment and Social Structure is also economistic in that it largely ignores the ideological and political processes involved in shaping penal policy. Penal ideologies appear as direct reflections of economic development, as mechanistic responses to changes in the labor market. Economic determinism is one possible trap involved in a materialist approach. By concentrating on the functional prerequisites of the capitalist system, there is a tendency to ignore the ideological and political as factors.

In his argument for a more adequate sociological explanation, Hogg maintains that there were three ideological streams, "not reducible to pure class terms," involved in shaping eighteenth- and nineteenth-century English penal thought. These were evangelicalism, utilitarianism, and classical political economy. Only after "concrete struggles, alliances and concessions which ultimately cut across and into economic class categories"[74] were these fashioned into a coherent penal ideology. This penal ideology mirrored the general social ideology of liberalism and its central concept of individualism. The penal system was to function in the making of "bourgeois man," "the obedient subject, the individual subjected to habits, rules, orders, an authority that is exercised continually around him and upon him, and which he must allow to function automatically in him," in the words of Michel Foucault who studied the origins of the penitentiary in France.[75]

The reformulation of *Punishment and Social Structure* by Melossi and others has removed much of the mechanistic relation of the economy to penal policy. But economism is implied not only in the specification of how the state is said to serve class interests, but also in why it is said to do so. While Hogg mentions the importance of social, political, and ideological processes, they are not elaborated. Nor are discussions of the "concrete struggles, alliances, and concessions" developed. We are left without a convincing determination of the mechanisms that link economy to the polity.

The pivotal social mechanism cited by Hogg which brought together the three ideological currents was the Prison Discipline Society, and we are told that the "imperatives it laid down became the imperatives of penal reform for the better part of the nineteenth century."[76] This reform group is discussed at length by Michael Ignatieff in *A Just Measure of Pain*, a work that examines the appearance of the penitentiary in England between 1750 and 1850. In his chapter on the ideological origins of the penitentiary, Ignatieff attempts to connect the interests of prison reformers to the new industrial employers by indicating the former's petit bourgeois base.[77] We are to assume motivations of conduct in such an approach.

There are serious problems with such an "instrumentalist" view of the relation of the state to material interests. On the basis of one group of criticisms a new current of radical criminology has emerged, fashioned on the "structural" Marxism of French social theorists Louis Althusser and Nicos Poulantzas.[78] Structuralists maintain that the instrumentalist view of the state as controlled directly or indirectly by members of the capitalist class is merely an inversion of the conventional, or formalist, theory which holds that the state is above the will of particular interests.

While attempting to overcome economism by specifying the social processes that shape ideological commitments, instrumentalists are still working within the framework of pluralism.[79] Rather than staking out new conceptual terrain, they advance counterfactual evidence. This approach is especially evident and problematic in the sociology of law, where radical claims are most open to "simple empirical refutation."[80]

TOWARD STRUCTURAL INTERPRETATION OF THE STATE AND LAW

Structuralists claim that their theory avoids the twin traps of instrumentalism and economism.[81] Their version of materialism rejects the instrumentalist approach and its "problematic of the subject" (early Marx) and "motivations of conduct" (Weber). Although volition and class consciousness play very limited roles in the maintenance and displacement of social structures, structuralists claim not to be espousing a return to the economic determinism of the Second International which reduced the state to the economic "base."

According to Poulantzas, the political and ideological structures are "relatively autonomous" from the economic structure; the economy is determinant only in the "last instance." He maintains that the capitalist class is best served by a state that is above the will of extragovernmental actors. Not only does this avoid the many problems of legitimacy, but also a partially autonomous state is necessary to overcome the narrow, divisive interests of competing factions of the dominant class. The function of the state in this view is to reproduce the capitalist class as a whole by maintaining the social formation and by reproducing the conditions of production.

One possible threat to the social formation is working-class unity. Poulantzas contends that, largely through the institutions of democracy and justice, the state individualizes workers, undermining their political unity and class interest while at the same time representing itself as a universal interest.[82] Isaac Balbus and Piers Beirne, leading proponents of a structuralist approach to the sociology of law, following Pashukanis, have suggested ways in which the legal system undermines the working class while giving the appearance of fairness and neutrality.[83]

According to Balbus and Beirne, the logic of the legal form parallels the logic of the commodity form.[84] Just as the commodity form levels individual use-values, so the state's legal system transforms workers into atomized "citizens." Money is the universal economic equivalent and facilitates the exchange of commodities. The law, as universal political equivalent, levels manifestly unequal individuals. The legal form supports capitalist society in an essential way by ignoring social inequalities rooted in class differences. In the state's attempt to consistently apply legal norms, citizens appear equal.

Bourgeois justice is class justice, not because of the specific content or administration of the law, as instrumentalists argue, but because of the law's form. How can there be legal justice in the absence of an underlying social and economic equality? "The systematic application of an equal scale to systemically unequal individuals necessarily tends to reinforce systemic inequalities," Balbus contends.[85]

The law would approximate justice, not by punishing capitalist and worker alike for an economic crime, for example, but by punishing capitalists more severely as they can be more rationally deterred. But this would make class background a political issue. To do so would place the social structure into question, revealing the wisdom of William Blake's aphorism in *The Marriage of Heaven and Hell*: "One law for the Lion and Ox is Oppression."

SUMMARY AND CONCLUSIONS

Radical criminology appeared during the social and political turmoil that engulfed Europe and the United States during the 1960s and early 1970s. Beginning as a critique of the "abstracted empiricism" and liberalism of conventional criminological theory and practice, the new criminology very early drew on the thought of Marx and Engels. Their thought, however, is ambiguous on many issues, and the major branches of radical criminology reflect the different interpretive currents of Marxism. "Critical," "materialist," and "structural" versions of radical criminology developed, each taking different theoretical positions concerning the nature and meaning of criminal behavior and the nature of the state. Each version has its shortcomings.

Because of the wariness of empiricism embodied in its "negative critique," the "critical" version failed to provide a convincing understanding either of the etiology of criminal behavior or the state's function in the maintenance of capitalism. Materialist accounts, which see the function of criminal law and its administration as buttressing the "free" labor market by deterrence, training, and discipline, seem cogent and have been the subject of a number of research efforts. However, by concentrating on the functional prerequisites of the capitalist system, some of these studies have ignored the complexity of politics and ideology.

Instrumentalist versions of materialism have attempted to provide social mechanisms by which the capitalist class determines state policy, but structuralists maintain that this requires the imputation of motives and largely ignores the issue of legitimacy. Moreover, they argue that capitalists are not able to act in their own long-term interest. Structuralism in turn has been criticized on the grounds that it represents a "structural super determinism," almost completely devoid of human agency.[86] While critical criminology assumed class consciousness, structuralists deny its usefulness to social change, and Mullin criticizes Pashukanis's structural model of the legal form as economistic in its reduction of law to a simple reflection of commodity exchanges.[87] The matter of voluntarism, determinism, or dialectics embedded in the science-critique opposition remains unresolved.

Today, radical criminology faces new challenges as Western nations experience deepening economic crises. Civil disorder seems imminent, especially in the United States where the recent strong movement to the right in national politics supports the somewhat older "New Realism" of criminal justice theory and practice.[88] The culprit is no longer the "correctionalism" of liberalism, but the unabashed punitiveness of neo-conservatism. And this reaction apparently has much working-class support.

NOTES

1. For a discussion of the politics involved in the termination of the school, and other aspects of academic repression at Berkeley, see "Editorial," *Crime and Social Justice* 6 (Fall-Winter 1976):1-3.

2. Tony Platt, "Prospects for a Radical Criminology in the U.S.A.," *Crime and Social Justice* 1 (Spring-Summer 1974):2-10.

3. Stanley Cohen (ed.), *Images of Deviance* (Harmondsworth: Penguin, 1971).

4. Ian Taylor and Lauri Taylor (eds.), *Politics and Deviance* (Harmondsworth: Penguin, 1973).

5. Drew Humphries, "Report on the Conference of the European Group for the Study of Deviance and Social Control," *Crime and Social Justice* 1 (Spring-Summer 1974):11-17. The proceedings of this first conference were published by H. Bianchi, et al. (eds.), *Deviance and Control in Europe* (London: Wiley, 1975).

6. For a review of two radical books on crime, the legal order, and criminology in two Latin American nations, Venezuela (J. M. Mayorca, *Criminalidad de la Burguesia*) and Colombia (F. Rojas, *Criminalidad y Constituyente*), see Argenis Riera, "Latin American Criminology," *Crime and Social Justice* 11 (Spring-Summer 1979):71-76.

7. Paul Q. Hirst, "Marx and Engels on Law, Crime and Morality," in Taylor, et al. (eds.), *Critical Criminology* (London: Routledge and Kegan Paul, 1975), pp. 203-232; and Stephen K. Mugford, "Marxism and Criminology: A Comment on the Symposium Review on 'The New Criminology'," *The Sociological Quarterly* 15 (Autumn 1974):591-596.

8. Alvin W. Gouldner, *For Sociology* (New York: Basic Books, 1973), p. 427.

9. Georg Lukács, *History and Class Consciousness* (Cambridge, Mass.: MIT Press, 1971).

10. Karl Marx, *The Eighteenth Brumaire of Louis Bonaparte* (Moscow: Progress Publishers, 1972), p. 10.

11. Karl Marx and Friedrich Engels, *The Communist Manifesto* (Moscow: Progress Publishers, 1971), p. 34.

12. Michael Burawoy, "Marxism and Sociology," *Contemporary Sociology* 6, no. 1 (January 1977):9-17.

13. Max Horkheimer, "Traditional and Critical Theory," in *Critical Theory*, 2 vols. (New York: Herder and Herder, 1973).

14. Erich Fromm, *Marx's Concept of Man* (New York: Frederick Ungar, 1961).

15. Herbert Marcuse, *One-Dimensional Man* (Boston: Beacon, 1964).

16. Herbert Marcuse, *An Essay on Liberation* (Boston: Beacon, 1969).

17. Richard Quinney, "Crime Control in Capitalist Society," *Issues in Criminology* 8 (Spring 1973):75-99.

18. Richard Quinney, *Critique of Legal Order* (Boston: Little, Brown, 1974).

19. Ibid., p. 13.

20. Tony Platt, "Prospects for a Radical Criminology in the United States," *Crime and Social Justice* 1 (Spring-Summer 1974):3.

21. Ibid.

22. Frankfurt School for Social Research, *Aspects of Sociology* (Boston: Beacon, 1972), p. 126.

23. Horkheimer, "Traditional and Critical Theory."

24. John Ainlay, "Review of the New Criminology and Critical Criminology," *Telos* 26 (1975):213-225.

25. Richard Quinney, "The Production of a Marxist Criminology," *Contemporary Crisis* 2 (1978):277-292.

26. Göran Therborn, "Critique of the Frankfurt School," *New Left Review* 63 (1970):79.

27. David F. Greenberg, "On One-Dimensional Marxist Criminology," in *Theory and Society* 3, no. 4 (Winter 1976):611.

28. Richard Quinney, *Class, State and Crime* (New York: Longman, 1980).

29. For scholarly studies documenting the suppression of radical political organization and dissent in this period, see W. Preston, *Aliens and Dissenters* (New York: Harper and Row, 1963); Max Lowenthal, *The Federal Bureau of Investigation* (New York: Sloane, 1950). For an excellent account of the private and state destruction of the Industrial Workers of the World, the reader is referred to Melvyn Dubofsky, *We Shall Be All* (New York: Quadrangle, 1969). Jeremy Brecher's *Strike!* (New York: South End Press, 1977) covers the spontaneous struggles of unorganized workers.

30. Quinney, *Class, State and Crime*, p. 65. This typology has the merit of addressing the very important problem of political consciousness. But it is limited largely to description rather than explanation. As with Robert Merton's anomie-based typology, Quinney's fails to provide criteria with which to predict particular outcomes. His theory should address the important questions of why some individuals resort to crimes of accommodation and so few others to resistance. And, just as important, why do most of the poor remain painfully law abiding? Quinney's theory is not sufficiently developed to adequately explain what gives rise to these phenomena and therefore is not very helpful in fashioning a revolutionary strategy. We need to know far more about just why the crimes he lists are supposed to be an outgrowth of capitalist society per se, especially when societies with alternative ("socialist") modes of production suffer from many of the same forms of "street" deviance and crime, including alcoholism, robbery, and rape, not to mention such "white-collar" crimes as fraud and embezzlement.

31. Douglas Hay, et al., *Albion's Fatal Tree* (New York: Pantheon, 1975).

32. E. P. Thompson, *Whigs and Hunters* (New York: Pantheon, 1975).

33. Eric Hobsbawm, *Primitive Rebels* (New York: W. W. Norton, 1959).

34. Eric Hobsbawm, *Bandits* (New York: Delacorte, 1969).

35. Anton Blok, "The Peasant and the Brigand: Social Banditry Reconsidered," *Comparative Studies in Society and History* 14, no. 4 (September 1972):496.

36. Karl Marx, "Proceedings of the Sixth Rhine Province Assembly. Third Article. Debates on the Law of the Theft of Wood," in K. Marx and F. Engels, *Collected Works*, Vol. 1 (New York: International Publishers, 1975). See also Peter Linebaugh, "Karl Marx, the Theft of Wood, and Working Class Composition: A Contribution to the Current Debate," *Crime and Social Justice* 6 (Fall-Winter 1976): 5-16.

37. Douglas Hay, "Poaching and the Game Laws on Cannock Chase," in Hay, et al., *Albion's Fatal Tree*, pp. 207-208.

38. Michael Ignatieff, *A Just Measure of Pain* (New York: Pantheon, 1978), p. 179.

39. David Rothman, *The Discovery of the Asylum* (Boston: Little, Brown, 1971), p. 248.

40. Ignatieff, *Just Measure of Pain*, p. 84.

41. For example, Taylor, et al., "Advances Toward a Critical Criminology," *Theory and Society* 1 (1974):461.

42. Jock Young, "Working Class Criminology," in Taylor et al., *Critical Criminology*, p. 71.

43. Taylor, et al., "Advances Toward a Critical Criminology," p. 449.

44. Georg Rusche, "Labor Market and Penal Sanction: Thoughts on the Sociology of Criminal Justice," translated by Gerda Dinwiddie, *Crime and Social Justice* 10 (Fall-Winter 1978):3.

45. Taylor, et al., "Advances Toward a Critical Criminology."

46. Karl Marx, *A Contribution to the Critique of Political Economy* (New York: International Publishers, 1976), p. 193.

47. Taylor, et al., "Advances Toward a Critical Criminology," p. 468.

48. Steven Spitzer, "Toward a Marxian Theory of Deviance," *Social Problems* 22, no. 5 (1975).

49. Ibid., p. 642.

50. Ibid.

51. James Stolzman and Herbert Gamberg, "Marxist Class Analysis Versus Stratification Analysis as General Approaches to Social Inequality," *Berkeley Journal of Sociology* 18 (1973-1974):105-125.

52. Friedrich Engels, *The Condition of the Working Class in England* (Stanford, Calif.: Stanford University Press, 1968), and Willem Bonger, *Criminality and Economic Conditions* (Bloomington, Ind.: Indiana University Press, 1969).

53. As paraphrased by Austin T. Turk in Bonger, *Criminality*, p. 11.

54. Taylor, et al., "Advances Toward a Critical Criminology," p. 461.

55. Ibid., p. 449.

56. Ibid., p. 467.

57. John Ainlay, "Review of the New Criminology and Critical Criminology," *Telos* 26 (1975):222.

58. G. Rusche and O. Kirchheimer, *Punishment and Social Structure* (New York: Russell and Russell, 1967).

59. Ibid., p. 5.

60. Ibid.

61. Dario Melossi, "The Penal Question in Capital," *Crime and Social Justice* 5 (Spring-Summer 1976):26-33.

62. Dario Melossi, "Georg Rusche and Otto Kirchheimer: Punishment and Social Structure," Book Review, *Crime and Social Justice* 9 (Spring-Summer 1978):73-85.

63. Karl Marx, *Capital* (New York: The Modern Library, 1906), pp. 785-786.

64. For a discussion of the disruptive social consequences attending the widespread introduction of the freely fluctuating market for labor in the United States, the reader is referred to Stephen Thernstrom, *Poverty and Progress: Social Mobility in a Nineteenth Century City* (Cambridge, Mass.: Harvard, 1964).

65. Marx, *Capital*, p. 809.

66. Karl Polanyi, *The Great Transformation* (Boston: Beacon Press, 1964).

67. Ibid., p. 73.

68. From the last quarter of the nineteenth century until the late 1930s in the United States, hundreds of private detective agencies—modeled after the Pinkerton's National Detective Agency—legally stymied labor's efforts to unionize and strike effectively by spying and providing *agents provocateur*, scabs, and strike guards. See S. Spitzer, "Privatization and Capitalist Development: The Case of the Private Police," *Social Problems* (October 1977), and Robert Weiss, "The Emergence and Transformation of Private Detective Industrial Policing in the United States, 1850-1940," *Crime and Social Justice* 9 (Spring-Summer 1978):35-48. The work of detective agencies in labor discipline was supplemented by the National Guard and the Pennsylvania State Constabulary, both of which were created expressly for the purpose. For a study of municipal police involvement in related anti-working-class activities, see Sidney L. Harring, "Class Conflict and the Suppression of Tramps in Buffalo, 1892-1894," *Law and Society Review* 11 (Summer 1977):873-911.

69. For a study of the history of vagrancy legislation in England, see W. Chambliss, "A Sociological Analysis of the Law of Vagrancy," *Social Problems* 12 (Summer 1964):67-77, and Karl Marx, "The So-Called Primitive Accumulation," *Capital*, pp. 784-837.

70. Francis S. Piven and Richard A. Cloward, *Regulating the Poor* (New York: Vintage Books, 1971).

71. Ibid., p. 33

72. Russell Hogg, "Imprisonment and Society Under Early British Capitalism," *Crime and Social Justice* 12 (Winter 1979):11.

73. Ibid., p. 12.

74. Ibid., p. 10.

75. M. Foucault, *Discipline and Punish* (London: Allen Lane, 1977), pp. 128-129.

76. Hogg, "Imprisonment and Society," p. 12.

77. "Given the economic, ideological, and social connections between prison reformers and the new industrial employers, it is not surprising that the reformers assumed that a prison should be run like a 'well-ordered manufactory,' as Buxton put it. In this way, penal and industrial discipline developed along the same trajectory of severity," Ignatieff, *Just Measure of Pain*, p. 215.

78. Althusser and Poulantzas are in the forefront of a recent movement stressing Marx as a scientist, and their effort is to reintroduce historical materialism as a "revolutionary science." They discern an "epistemological break" between his youthful (pre-1845) Hegelian years and his "mature" scientific ones. In the two periods, Marx was working with entirely different "problematics," each involving different objects of inquiry and employing different conceptual systems.

79. See Poulantzas's critique of Ralph Miliband's *The State and Capitalist Society* (New York: Basic Books, 1969) in "The Problem of the Capitalist State," and Miliband's "Reply," in Robin Blackburn (ed.), *Ideology in Social Science* (New York: Vintage, 1973):238-262. Poulantzas's criticisms also apply to such works as Quinney's revised version of *Class, State, and Crime*. Quinney continues to employ the instrumentalist approach (albeit a less voluntaristic version) rather than develop a Hegelian-Marxist approach characteristic of the Frankfurt School tradition. For an effort to develop a critical theory of the state and crime control, see Young-Hee Shim Han, "Selectivity of Crime Control and Distorted Communication: A Critique of Critical Criminology and an Alternative Critical Perspective," Ph.D. Dissertation, Department of Sociology, Southern Illinois University, Carbondale, Illinois, July 1978.

80. Piers Beirne, "Empiricism and the Critique of Marxism on Law and Crime," *Social Problems* 26 (April 1979):380.

81. "Structuralism" refers to the study of systematic functional relationships of various institutions to the process of surplus value production and appropriation. David A. Gold, et al., "Recent Developments in Marxist Theories of the Capitalist State," *Monthly Review* 27 (October 1975):29-43, and "Part 2" (November 1975):36-51.

82. According to Poulantzas, "The state is organized to present the interests of the capitalist class as the interests of all and to insert all agents of production (irrespective of their relationship to the means of production) into political and ideological activities as free and equal citizens."

83. See Isaac D. Balbus, "Commodity Form and Legal Form: An Essay on the 'Relative Autonomy' of the Law," *Law and Society Review* 11 (Winter 1977):571-588 and "Ruling Elite Theory vs. Marxist Class Analysis," *Monthly Review* (May 1971):36-46. Also, Piers Beirne, "Empiricism and the Critique of Marxism on Law and Crime," *Social Problems* 26 (April 1979):373-385; Mark Tushnet, "A Marxist Analysis of American Law," *Marxist Perspectives* 1 (Spring 1978):96-115; Falco Werkentin, et al., "Criminology as Police Science or: 'How Old Is the New Criminology?'" *Crime and Social Justice* 2 (Fall-Winter 1974):24-41, and C. B. Pashukanis, who first worked out the commodity and legal form homology in "The General Theory of Law and Marxism," in H. W. Babb (trans. and ed.), *Soviet Legal Philosophy* (Cambridge, Mass.: Harvard, 1951).

84. A commodity has a twofold character, according to Marx. On the one hand, a commodity is a "use-value" that satisfies a unique social need and represents the quantity and quality of concrete labor expended in its creation. On the other hand, a commodity has an "exchange value," its "worth" in the market place. In order for products to be exchangeable in the market, they must possess some common quality, an abstract or formal equivalence, which according to Marx's labor theory of value is abstract human labor. The concrete differences between commodities therefore are ignored, and qualitatively different objects appear equal.

85. Balbus, "Commodity Form," p. 577.

86. See Miliband's rejoinder to Poulantzas in Blackburn (ed.), *Ideology in Social Science*. Claus Offee and James O'Connor have suggested ways in which to restore the historical and dialectic elements to a structural conception of state activity. For a discussion of various political, economic, and fiscal imperatives and "crises" which beset the capitalistic state, see Claus Offee, *Strukturprobleme des Kapitalistischen Staates* (Frankfurt/Suhrkamp, 1972); "The Abolition of Market Control and the Problem of Legitimacy," *Kapitalistate*, nos. 1 and 2 (1973); and James O'Connor, *The Fiscal Crisis of the State* (New York: St. Martin's Press, 1973).

87. Neil Mullin, "Pashukanis and the Demise of the Law: An Essay Review," *Contemporary Crises* 4 (1980):433-438.

88. See Tony Platt and Paul Takagi, "Intellectuals for Law and Order: A Critique of the New 'Realists'," *Crime and Social Justice* 8 (Fall-Winter 1977):1-6; and Herman Schwendinger and Julia Schwendinger, "The New Idealism and Penal Living Standards," *Crime and Social Justice* 13 (Summer 1980):45-51.

BIBLIOGRAPHY

The literature on crime and crime control from a radical perspective is expanding rapidly. This bibliography is not intended to be exhaustive. For the most part, the works that appear below are a sample of important theoretical and empirical studies that are not discussed in the chapter.

Bernstein, Susie, et al. *The Iron Fist and the Velvet Glove: An Analysis of the U.S. Police*. Berkeley, Calif.: Center for Research on Criminal Justice, 1977.

Beginning with a short history of policing in the United States, the book argues that its origin and development are not simply responses to increasing felonious crime. The authors review the literature that documents the functions of federal, state, municipal, and private police agencies as instruments of class domination. Strikebreaking, riot control, and "order maintenance" have been the principal activities of police agencies, and in the last several decades their expertise and hardware have been exported to bolster Third World regimes.

Bunyan, Tony. *The History and Practice of Political Police in Britain*. London: Quartet Books, 1977.

Bunyan considers overt suppression of political dissent by uniformed police, their "special branches," and various intelligence and counterespionage agencies. There is a chapter-by-chapter treatment of the origin and development of these various police units, most of which have little democratic accountability.

Gordon, David M. "Class and the Economics of Crime." *Review of Radical Political Economics* 3, no.3 (1971):51-75.

This article reviews various theoretical perspectives on the nature of criminal behavior that are current in the literature of economics and finds them inadequate. The author provides a radical political-economic analysis which explains *all* types of criminal behavior as rational responses to the values and social structural pressures of capitalist society.

Greenberg, David F. (ed.). *Crime and Capitalism: Readings in Marxist Criminology*. Palo Alto, Calif.: Mayfield Publishing Co., 1981.

Divided into sections covering the issues of crime causation, criminal law, and the administration of justice, this volume is the first comprehensive criminological text from the Marxist perspective. It includes articles by Marx and Engels, as well as some of the better works by modern radical criminologists on crime historically and in contemporary times.

Hall, Stuart, et al. *Policing the Crisis: Mugging, the State, and Law and Order*. New York: Holmes and Meier, 1978.

This British Marxist contribution examines the "moral panic" in 1972-1973 of mugging as an example of the social production of crime news, and the mugger as scapegoat ("Folk Devil") for many of the ills besetting Britain during its developing capitalist crisis. Liberal social scientists failed to successfully penetrate the prevailing ideologies of crime, and the authors advance more adequate (structural and historically specific) answers.

Hay, Douglas, et al. *Albion's Fatal Tree: Crime and Society in Eighteenth Century England*. New York: Pantheon 1975.

This study of eighteenth-century English society begins with an examination of the ideological functions of English criminal law. The book gives a picture of a legal system possessing a weak enforcement apparatus that served the ruling class of property owners through the threat of Draconic penalties (judicial terror). Officials gave the appearance of fairness by their frequent acts of mercy for the poor and the occasional prosecution of nobility. This theoretical chapter is followed by a series of detailed studies of the activities of wreckers, smugglers, poachers, and highwaymen in what many historians have depicted as a stable and consensual period of English history.

Jackson, George. *Soledad Brother: The Prison Letters of George Jackson*. New York: Bantam Books, 1970.

One of America's most articulate and politically conscious black prisoners presents a collection of his letters which offers insights into his personal struggle and growth. Often presented as "the bible" of radical prison movements in the United States, this book has social significance that goes beyond the personal moments revealed in these intimate letters.

Pearce, Frank. *Crimes of the Powerful*. London: Pluto Press, 1977.

This volume examines the intimate relationship between certain kinds of crime and the capitalist system. Challenging the claim that these crimes are aberrations, Pearce argues that corporate crime, organized crime, and labor racketeering are integral parts of the normal operation of capitalist societies, tolerated and encouraged by the ruling class and the state.

Platt, Tony, and Paul Takagi (eds.). *Punishment and Penal Discipline: Studies in Crime and Social Justice*. Berkeley, Calif.: Center for Research on Criminal Justice, 1979.

This anthology of articles, drawn largely from the journal *Crime and Social Justice*, deals with historical and contemporary issues concerning punishment and rehabilitation.

Quinney, Richard. *Class, State and Crime*. 2d ed. New York: Longman, 1980.

Here Quinney explores issues in the political economy of criminal justice, advancing a theory of crime and its relation to the development of capitalism.

Quinney, Richard. *Criminology*. 2d ed. Boston: Little, Brown, 1979.

This volume represents a first attempt at a comprehensive basic text in criminology from a "critical Marxist" perspective.

Quinney, Richard. *Critique of Legal Order: Crime Control in Capitalist Society*. New York: Little, Brown, 1974.

This work examines the "law and order" policies of the Nixon administration and of the top personnel comprising the criminal justice system and its advisory committees at the federal level.

Rusche, Georg, and Otto Kirchheimer. *Punishment and Social Structure*. New York: Russell and Russell, 1967.

This 1939 study of the development of penal forms in the West over several centuries is a classic in radical theory and research.

Taylor, Ian, Paul Walton, and Jock Young. *The New Criminology: For a Social Theory of Deviance*. New York: Harper and Row, 1973.

Among the most controversial and widely known theoretical works in recent criminology, this survey and critique of the theoretical tradition in criminology helped launch the radical debate in criminology.

Taylor, Ian, Paul Walton, and Jock Young (eds.). *Critical Criminology*. London: Routledge and Kegan Paul, 1975.
A collection of some of the best articles by such radical scholars as William Chambliss, Jock Young, and Herman and Julia Schwendinger, with an essay by Taylor, Walton, and Young on the prospects of critical criminology in Great Britain.

Wright, Erik Olin (ed.). *The Politics of Punishment: A Critical Analysis of Prisons in America*. New York: Harper and Row, 1973.
In this work, written during a turbulent period of American prison history, various writers examine the conditions of prisons; their social structure; the history of prison rioting; the functions of imprisonment in capitalist society; and the prospects for prison reform.

II

THE AMERICAS

8

ARGENTINA

Pedro R. David

This chapter focuses, first, on the current status of criminological research in Argentina and, second, on the efforts of national and private universities and independent institutes to diffuse criminological knowledge in Argentina. Some recent concerns of Latin American criminology are also covered.

In Latin America, there was little activity or interest in criminology until the end of the nineteenth century. José Ingenieros, an Argentinian, was especially instrumental in awakening Latin American interest in criminology. More recently, Argentina made another special contribution to Latin American criminology by being the site of the First Pan American Congress of Criminology in November 1979, as organized by the Law School of the University of El Salvador, Buenos Aires. Almost eight hundred participants were drawn from fourteen countries of North, Central, and South America. The issues discussed and the positions taken at the congress provide many insights into Latin American criminology.

PAN AMERICAN SOCIETY OF CRIMINOLOGY

A significant event at the First Pan American Congress of Criminology was the creation of the Pan American Society of Criminology. Delegates from North, Central, and South America committed themselves to creating a professional organization that would represent their common interests in fostering criminological research and the theoretical consideration of complex issues particularly germane to the two continents. These issues are grounded in the contingencies of unbalanced or unplanned socioeconomic growth. The issues have been brought to the fore by increases in violence and economic crimes and the appearance of new kinds of crime in the region: crimes against the environment, especially air and water pollution; kidnapping for profit and terrorism by extremists of the right and left; and hoarding of foodstuffs.

Another set of purposes centered on the wish to achieve a more effective collaboration among countries in dealing with various kinds of crime. To overcome the deficiencies in criminal justice statistics, increased collaboration and interchange of information are essential. Through the new association, it will be possible to exchange experiences from various theoretical perspectives and at different levels of criminal justice systems.

The participants also agreed on the gravity of the problems of juvenile delinquency in the region. Marginalization of youth from various aspects of community life, unemployment, health problems, lack of realistic educational alternatives, unbalanced urbanization, problems of internal and international migration, and conflicting cultural patterns were also discussed. All of these phenomena point to the need for a more effective and intensive scientific cooperation among countries.

The executive committee of the new society consists of President Ricardo Levene (Argentina); Vice-Presidents Luis Rodríquez Manzanera (Mexico), M. Gonzalez Berendique (Chile), and Gerhard Mueller (United States); and General Secretary Pedro R. David (Argentina). Other prominent participants in the establishment of the society included Sinesio Buerro de Souza and Nelson Pizzotti Mendes (Brazil); Disnei Francisco Scormaiendri, Alejandro Cevallos, and Efran Torres Chavez (Ecuador); Miguel Herrera Figueroa, Horacio Maldonado, Isidro de Benedetti, Osvaldo Tieghi, Vicente Cabello, Eugenio Raul Zaffaroni, Odilon Nieva, Mario Marcopoulos, and Carlos Garcia Basalo (Argentina); Leo M. Romero (United States); Elio Gomez Grillo, Maria Christina Perez Diaz, and Dora Zerpa (Venezuela); and Luis Cousino MacIver and Maria Luisa Prieto (Chile).

FIRST PAN AMERICAN CONGRESS OF CRIMINOLOGY

The First Pan American Congress of Criminology addressed four themes: (1) "General Prevention: Delinquent Youngsters-Adults, Problems of Juvenile Justice in the Americas," reported by Elio Gomez Grillo (Venezuela) and Pedro R. David (Argentina); (2) "Drugs," which had three subthemes—"Criminal Policy and the Consumer," "The Problem of Cocaine" (*coqueo*), and "Controls and Problems at the Frontier," reported by Luis Rodríguez Manzanera (Mexico) and Carlos Norberto Cagliotti, Victor René Martínez, and Vicente Louis Alberto Ruzuela (Argentina); (3) "The Crises of Sanctions and the Deprivation of Freedom," reported by Luis Cousino MacIver (Chile) and Isidoro de Benedetti and Carlos J. Garcia Basalo (Argentina); and (4) "Psychopaths as a Criminological Factor: Prescription and Treatment," reported by Carlos Hugo Tabler (Uruguay) and Vincente P. Cabello (Argentina).

General Prevention

Latin American criminology has given impetus to the idea of linking criminological principles to strengthening social service infrastructures and to socioeconomic development in general. The congress recommended that comprehensive prevention plans be instituted at every level of government. The planning process would include detailed analysis of the problem, inventory of programs and resources available, clear definition of the values and responsibilities of the agencies or institutions responsible for prevention, mechanisms for coordinating efforts among governmental and private agencies, delineation of the strategies to be followed through continuity over time, and evaluation of all programs.

Prevention, it was agreed, should be based on community participation and alternatives. Federal, state, and local governments should cooperate closely with the private sector, representative citizens of the community to be served, and administrative and judicial bodies. The purpose, of course, would be to cultivate the collaboration essential to improved prevention. Youth should be involved throughout the process and structure of prevention.

In regard to health as a biophysical entity, the congress agreed that comprehensive and equitable public health services should be made available to youth. Health services should include preventive health care services, low-cost medical and dental programs to assist parents during prenatal and postpartum periods; a full range of community mental health services to be made available to children and their families, including parents' training programs, adequate counseling services, and protective services for children and families to facilitate raising children in permanent, cohesive, and loving family units; and adequate nutrition to children and families and information about their appropriate needs and available alternatives. The delegates urged that day-care and drop-in child-care centers for children with special needs be established with full community involvement.

The premise that criminogenesis is involved in all aspects of the social organization was carried into the sphere of education. The delegates recommended that schools assume responsibility for working with families as part of authentic responses to the realities within which pupils live. From the perspective of a balanced humanistic education, the schools would enrich the potential of the family as a learning environment and vice versa so that cultural differences would be recognized. Schools should develop programs for diagnosis and treatment of children with learning disabilities and learning problems. Close coordination with other institutions was regarded to be important to offering children basic examples of social justice, cooperation, peace, solidarity, and other basic human values.

Resolutions also recognized the importance of dealing with employment problems through comprehensive and meaningful manpower programs, tailored to the vocational needs of children and youth and to avoid discriminatory and unjust practices. Public financing should be instituted for these purposes. Finally, the media should act as a positive influence for the moral and cultural development of children and youth, avoiding indoctrination in the culture of violence.

Diversion and Decriminalization

It was recommended that state and private agencies should develop community-based programs that divert children from the juvenile justice system; decriminalization of status offenders should be the standard; and recreation programs should be an integral part of the diversionary process.

The delegates recognized that police departments should demonstrate an awareness of community needs and should help to create a community environment conducive to prevention, just practices, and fair treatment of youth. Within police departments, sections specializing in youth services should ensure citizen participation in these programs. Police departments were urged to establish training programs in juvenile matters for juvenile officers and other police personnel.

It was recommended that juvenile matters be vested in family courts at the highest general level of justice organization. Emphasis was placed on the sound professional competence of judges in the diverse areas affecting the needs of children and families. Opportunities for continuing judicial education were deemed crucial to the development by judges of an awareness of cultural differences in child-rearing practices and conduct. It was hoped that the choice among alternative dispositions would ensure cultural identity. Intervention by the family courts should be specifically defined in relation to serious child harm, actual or potential. Family courts and law enforcement and administrative agencies were urged to develop systematic working relationships while retaining the integrity of unique responsibilities and functions. The delegates called for more extensive research into diversion and decriminalization. To maximize the chances for translating findings into policy, the delegates noted the importance of making research results available to the judicial community.

Coqueo Problem and Drug Smuggling

As in other parts of the world, drug addiction and systematic traffic in narcotics are receiving increased attention in Latin America. A regional aspect of the drug problem is the chewing of the cocaine leaf known as *coqueo*, which is not deemed an antisocial act in certain regions of Latin America. A policy of simple deterrent punishment must give way to more long-term solutions. One means would be to reduce the cultivation of the coke shrub, the source of cocaine. The preventive measures discussed above—health, educational, labor, and economic policies—are also relevant.

The delegates agreed that any criminological policy must define what the drugs are and classify drug users according to their motivation. Discretion in applying sanctions to drug users should take into consideration both the kind of drug and the qualities of the user. Other matters discussed were whether or not, in lieu of suppression, drug abuse should be managed through medical prescription or treatment; the possibilities of using drugs more effectively to treat addiction; and the particular threat raised by the drug trafficker. It was recommended that the user who also trafficks in drugs to satisfy his own needs, as opposed to the professional trafficker, deserves special treatment.

Treatment was advocated as the most promising reaction to the drug addict, when compared to a policy of suppression. When security measures are necessary, therapeutic measures should not be allowed to deteriorate into a form of punishment and arbitrary social stigmatization. Legislation should provide institutional resources to solve each separate case adequately, and the judge should have the advice of specialists or should create a special magistracy for drug users. Criminal policy should defend the interests of society without exaggerating the dangerous nature of the crime. Prevention, treatment, and rehabilitation should be promoted at the same time that any legal commerce in drugs is strictly controlled and all illegal traffic vigorously prosecuted.

The international traffic in narcotics and psychotropic drugs was seen as the product of deep-rooted causes. In any society and in any period, drug traffic is a response to drug consumption which stems from cultural, economic, and political conditions. The delegates preferred that trafficking be structured basically through preventive tactics for reduction of consumption. International cooperation and coordination are especially vital to control illegal traffic because the drug subculture crosses borders, offers justifications for use of toxic substances, and broadens the market for illicit drugs.

Sentencing Policies and Alternatives to Prison

Latin American criminology has been traditionally in the legalistic mode, making sentencing a prime consideration. The trend toward criminology as a behavioral and social discipline has extended the range of attention to include the sociocultural environment within which deterrence operates. The substitution of other sanctions for orthodox imprisonment has increasingly become a topic for consideration.

The congress recommended strictly limiting sentences of preventive imprisonment to achieve the following goals: reducing the population in penal institutions, increasing the possibility of effective treatment of inmates, and keeping the fiscal costs of administering imprisonment within reasonable limits. The delegates believed that a number of actions would serve these purposes. Penal facilities should be provided in a variety of models, including a sufficient number of open and semi-open institutions. The following alternatives to imprisonment were advocated: judicial banishment, deprivation of license or permits for certain occupational activities, a fine at a level relative to income and family responsibilities, judicial pardon, and public or private warnings for minor infractions and for delinquencies of less serious character. The reintegration problems of released inmates could be eased through wider, more extensive, and more effective utilization of measures of semi-freedom, such as furloughs granted on the inmate's word of honor. By being provided opportunities for conditional freedom in the community, prisoners are expected to have better preparation for full release.

The delegates saw an increased use of alternatives to imprisonment, especially for juveniles, as a means of fitting the choice of sanction more closely to the special characteristics of the deed and the delinquent. One alternative, the conditional sentence, could provide a period of discreet observation and assistance for a convicted offender in an environment of freedom. Probation, a second alternative, constitutes a method of active treatment in freedom. Another alternative is to require the convicted offender to engage in work that benefits the community. Semi-detention permits release into the community to engage in a regular occupation but entails nightly or weekend incarceration.

The congress offered recommendations on how the substitutes for imprisonment should be administered. In selecting among alternative sanctions, the judge should make a choice consistent with the psychosocial traits of the offender, rather than considering only the type of offense or the relative leniency of the penalty. The judge should recognize the possibility of either moderating or increasing control by later substituting another measure, according to the behavior of the individual. He should also be prepared to terminate punishment when his conditions have been appreciably satisfied. The offender's reparation for damages inflicted on his victim is among the strategies possible. This choice would belong to the judge in the case and would be applicable only if no civil action were pending.

To facilitate the community reintegration of convicted offenders through effective employment, the congress recommended the issuance of certificates according to preestablished criteria. In implementing substitutes for imprisonment, the community should be informed so that all will understand their purposes and thereby lend their support and collaboration. The congress participants emphasized that the effects of the alternative measures should be evaluated and guidelines developed appropriate to each strategy and to various classes of offenders.

In some Latin American countries, terrorism has emerged in relatively new criminological forms. The delegates recognized that the principles stated above are usually applicable to all classes of offenders, but they were uncertain whether the ideological motivations of terrorists would make them appropriate candidates for resocialization measures. The delegates recommended that a future meeting consider what special penal sanctions would be most appropriate for this type of offender.

Psychopathy as an Element in Criminality

The congress recognized that it is difficult to define and identify psychopathic personalities. These personalities are not sick in the usual psychiatric sense; yet, they are neither sane nor ill and sane at the same time. Dangerous psychopaths are considered to be particularly active agents of social disturbances, but they are a great puzzle for criminology and the penal law as well. Those who become involved in social disturbances sometimes follow sublime and heroic motives, but their behaviors have been assessed as being among the lowest and most deceitful of the forms of human conduct.

The following definition for the psychopathic personality was proposed: he or she suffers great alterations of conduct, from which no intellectual damage is suffered, but which is linked to serious affective and volitional disorders. This definition stands between soma and psyche—it is anatomical-functional—by covering both a defectively balanced brain structure and the active determining factors for personality. Psychopathic personality is not regarded as a sickness but merely as a descriptive type. The psychopath eludes precise diagnostic formulas because there are no symptoms or causes specific to this category.

Some authors think that abuse of the word "psychopathy" has caused the term to lose value, except in the instance of the dangerous psychopath. The dangerous psychopathic personality, the paradigm of all psychopathies, attracts the most criminological interest, not only because with an absence of a sense of morality it exhibits the most serious and most cruel delinquent conduct but also because it opens the door to neurological investigation into the anatomical functional bases for such conduct. It is necessary to distinguish theoretically and practically between three kinds of dangerous psychopathy: the constitutional, idiopathic, or real; the pseudopsychopathies; and the symptomatic psychopathies. The first, seemingly without cause, the second, the consequence of cerebral lesions either post-encephalitic or post-traumatic, and the third, presenting a clinical picture of schizophrenics, epileptics, and manics—this range of behaviors associated with psychopathy demonstrates the importance of research to distinguish the three kinds.

The congress adopted the organic thesis of the dangerous psychopathic personality on the grounds that the anatomical-clinical approach has been fruitful, even in regard to the constitutional type. From the empirical point of view, the delegates associated themselves with Lopez Ibor, Alberca Llorente, Gustav Aschaffenburg, Hans Wetzel, Joan and William McCord, Friedrich Stumfl, Heinrich Kranz, and Langeleduk. These writers have argued that only in very serious and complex cases may psychopathy be considered a mental illness.

Principles were recommended for forensic diagnosis of the psychopathic personality, particularly the dangerous psychopath. First, available technical resources are applied to determine cerebral dysfunction or lesion which is not discounted as a cause, in contrast to pseudopsychopathy or symptomatic psychopathy. Second, evaluation would be oriented toward identifying those offenders who qualify as psychopaths in the sense that their anomalic behavior exceeds the limits of resocialization treatment because of the seriousness, dimensions, constancy, and duration of the anomalic behavior. Third, for the criminologically psychotic, the key question is the extent to which the individual can function differently than he has behaved, given his personality.

TEACHING OF CRIMINOLOGY IN ARGENTINA

It is necessary to note the incipient state of the research and teaching of criminology in Argentina. Not only is there an excessive concentration on penal studies to the detriment of criminological studies in the educational programs of state and private universities, but there is also a lack of adequate technical and economic resources to carry out exhaustive studies and impart knowledge in the field. The work that has been done reveals, with certain exceptions, individual efforts of a noncontinuous nature, rather than a systematically institutionalized effort in research and treatment.

While there is no adequate answer to the problem of criminality in Argentina, in the country's scientific and educational institutions there now exists the beginnings of a positive reaction. This tendency should be increased in the future because the study of criminology should be a prerequisite in training all professionals in law and all other roles related to the discipline.

As Jerome Hall has so brilliantly established, the various disciplines concerned with criminal conduct should engage in inquiry through multiperspective collaboration, with all inquiry centered on solving concrete problems. The basic unity of the social sciences stems from their emphasis on human conduct; it would be excessively arbitrary to separate them artificially. Progress in crime prevention demands instruction and related research in criminology which responds to today's needs.

As we shall see, the teaching of criminology is institutionalized at different levels, beginning with occasional classes in the schools of law and social science and extending to its inclusion as a specific degree program. There are also instances of postgraduate criminological studies in penal sciences and in the degree programs in sociology and social work. This diversity offers promising horizons for more serious and systematic studies in the future.

The schools of law and social science have traditionally initiated courses in criminology. At first, criminology was regularly considered only in classes on penal law where it received only passing consideration, usually without adequate recognition of its scientific possibilities. Later, postgraduate specializations in criminology were created to provide the first courses that systematically treated the topics of criminology.

As for other sciences of human behavior, criminology has suffered from the unfavorable impact of legal positivism which has prevailed almost without exception among our legal experts. There has been an almost absolute concentration on the study of the established laws, disregarding the rich possibilities which criminology offers for the training of lawyers and law students.

The conception of criminology as only an applied field is very common in legal positivism. From a neo-Kantian view of the sciences, the emphasis on applied research forestalled all possibility of criminology becoming a genuine scientific discipline and, therefore, worked against the expansion of criminological studies within the official university programs.

University of Buenos Aires

As one of the first institutes dedicated to the development of the discipline, the Institute of the School of Law and Social Sciences of Buenos Aires was the first in Argentina to offer degrees in criminology and criminal law. The courses were established by resolution in 1967, one year before the project was approved by the law school. In accord with the resolution, both the degrees in criminology and in criminal law contain the following areas of study: general criminology, biological criminology, sociological criminology, general criminal psychology, criminal psychopathology, and legal medicine.

The degree in criminology is open to persons who have earned doctorates in law or the social sciences and the equivalent as recognized by the National University; who have a law degree issued by the National University or a private accredited university; or who have doctorates in medicine, chemistry, or biochemistry. Other groups eligible for admission to the program are doctors, engineers, orthodontists, or biochemists with degrees from national or private universities and persons with degrees from foreign universities which have been approved by national or private universities. This program is also open to current or retired officials of the federal or provincial police, the National Guard, and the National Maritime Prefecture with the rank of superior officer, chief, or officer, and a minimum of three years of secondary-level education. Also eligible are officials in the careers mentioned with bachelor's, master's, or technical degrees or, if pharmacists, degrees in chemistry or biology.

The degree in criminology provides credentials for admission to four general occupational areas:

1. In judicial matters: to advise or lend expertise as designated by the courts regarding matters under discussion or specified by Articles 12, 26, and 41 of the Penal Code.
2. In extrajudicial matters: to carry out studies or research and to evaluate or advise concerning criminological problems in general, particularly those matters not presented before a public authority.
3. In administrative matters: to carry out the same technical activities mentioned above in national, provincial, or municipal administrative affairs, whether permanent or temporary, whether the work is financially compensated or of an honorary nature.
4. In educational matters: to teach and carry out research in criminology.

The degree in criminal law will qualify the graduate in dactiloscopy, the taking of hand and footprints, tracks and traces, examination of clothing, and so on; analysis and identification of soil, powders, and so on; determining proof of identity—photography, tattoos, teeth, and so on; general ballistics, including the identification of firearms and explosives; identification of all kinds of stains or markings; investigation of numberings, inscriptions, and other markings which have been erased by scraping on metals or other materials; photography and planimetry as part of visual inspection; toxicological investigations; and any skills pertaining to the discovery and solution of crime and to scientific investigation of it.

Criminology has been included in the programs of study in penal sciences at the doctoral level in the University of Salvador and the Catholic University of Santa Maria of Buenos Aires. In 1974, the John F. Kennedy University of Buenos Aires, a private institution of higher learning, established a doctorate of penal sciences that presents a multidisciplinary curriculum and is under the direction of Professor Ricardo Levene. The first year of studies draws on criminal anthropology, criminal sociology, theory of crime, forensic medicine, criminalistics, and procedural penal theory. In the second year, the student turns to criminology, penology, individual and social factors of crime, forensic psychiatry and psychology, and the judicial process.

Other centers for criminological studies operate in various areas of Argentina. Some are organized under state auspices; others are under the aegis of private institutions.

Criminological Studies Center of the Province of Mendoza

This center has an important place in the future of scientific criminology. Under the Agency of Ex-Convicts, it serves as a technical agency for planning a province's criminal policy by investigating delinquent conduct, criminality as a social phenomenon, the etiology of criminality, the penal sciences, and means of reducing and controlling criminality. In short, criminality is taught in its diverse facets.

Governed by a board of directors, the center has these departments: criminal anthropology, criminal sociology, penology and penitentiary management, corrective pedagogy, criminal policy, and social information. The program of studies provides courses for penitentiary officers, juvenile workers, and those who carry out programs for released convicts. Courses are also offered for schools of social services, social workers, and postgraduate courses in criminology. The course in criminology for social workers is of two years' duration and deals with penal law (general and specialized), general sociology, penal procedural law, research methodology, introduction to criminology, legal medicine, criminal psychology, penal methods, penology, criminal law, corrective pedagogy, social service in criminology, and legal psychiatry. Other courses are offered, a criminographic register has been created, and much important criminological research has been conducted. The *Journal of the Center of Criminological Studies* presents articles of scientific quality. Among the conferences sponsored, the center organized a very important international criminological meeting in 1969.

"Jose Ingenieros" Center of Criminological Studies

When the center was opened on June 12, 1968, at a ceremony in the Press Club of the city of Cordoba, the president of the supreme court of justice of the province of Mendoza, Dr. Juan B. Vitale Nocera, spoke on the topic "The Centers and Institutes of Criminology—The Need for Them: Criminal Policy in Mendoza."

Criminological Center of Neuquen-Zapala, Province of Neuquen

This recently opened center held a seminar in 1970 drawing outstanding professionals in the field.

OTHER INSTITUTES: APPLIED AND LEGAL PERSPECTIVES

In Argentina, most educational and research activities are carried out by organizations that are within the structure of government outside the sphere of higher education alone or are oriented toward the science of law.

Institute of Research and Teaching in Criminology

Under the Ministry of Government of the province of Buenos Aires, this institute is a technical organization at the service of criminal policy developed by the state. The institute was organized into the following sections: criminal anthropology, criminal sociology, penology and penitentiary management, criminography, criminal policy, corrective pedagogy, and social information. The institute's principal functions are to study the personality of the delinquent in its most salient characteristics; to classify the delinquent and determine a correct social prognosis for him; to study crime as a social phenomenon; to exercise an educational function through the organization of specialized courses, conferences, and classes in theory and practice, and to lend assistance to university classes and institutes; to train penitentiary personnel; to compile the results of all research; to eliminate the possible causes of crime through the formulation of a scientifically based criminal policy; to cooperate with the courts; to stimulate the study of penal science; and to maintain contact with other organizations both within and outside the field of criminal justice.

In 1958, the institute created the completion course for social workers which provides a theoretical and a practical orientation to criminology. It also created the *Journal of the Institute of Research and Teaching in Criminology* which has made very important contributions to the scientific literature.

The institute awards the degree of social worker in criminology at the secondary level. Prerequisites for admission to the two-year program are a master's, bachelor's, or technical degree. The program of studies consists of the following: criminal anthropology, corrective pedagogy, social work, general and developmental psychology, general sociology, criminal sociology, social psychology and psychology of personality, penal law and penitentiary management, law in general, legal psychiatry and applied psychology, legal medicine, and practice experience. The program qualifies the graduate for work in the Ministry of Education, the Ministry of Social Welfare, the Division of Minors, the penal institutions, the courts, the police, and the Institute of Research and Teaching in Criminology.

National University at La Plata

The Institute of Penal Law and Criminology of the School of Legal and Social Sciences of the National University of La Plata does not carry out research in criminology. In the programs of study, criminology figures neither as an independent course nor as part of the courses in legal and social sciences. The work and research are devoted to penal law and penal procedural law.

Institute of Criminology and Legal Medicine of Mendoza

This institute was created in 1953 as an official entity of the province of Mendoza and at first was under the Ministry of Government. In 1964, it became an independent entity with legal capacity to act privately, while functioning publicly under the supervision of the supreme court of justice. The governing board consists of a director, an undersecretary of justice and public instruction, the general counsel of the supreme court of justice, and the chief of police.

The institute was created in order to provide the regional courts with an advisory agency regarding matters of procedure in court judgments and police investigations. The functions of the institute are to advise and to inform the judges as the need arises concerning wounds; determination of homicide, suicide, or accident; accidents on the job and diseases inherent in certain professions; asphixiology; thanatology; legal sexology; criminal dactiloscopy; legal toxicology and autopsies; and, in general, any other consultation related to legal-medical matters. It may also offer instruction in police work.

National University of Litoral

The Institute of Penal Science and Criminology of the School of Juridical and Social Sciences of the National University of Litoral offers classes in penal law at the doctoral level. At this writing the school's program of studies is being examined with the prospect of major changes, including provision of a specialization in penal law made up of criminology, legal medicine, penology, penitentiary management, and the economics of penal law.

In October 1968, the institute sponsored the National Assemblies of Penal Law and Criminology in the city of Santa Fe under the theme "Causative Factors of Crime in Contemporary Life." Given the obvious modification of values in contemporary society, the participants called for an adjustment of legal norms to be consistent with the new norms permeating Argentinian social reality. They noted the need for revitalizing and strengthening the socialization of the family to provide mechanisms for achieving this general purpose. The conference also made recommendations in the following areas: penal reform; economic penal law; the qualifications of penal magistrates; the doctrine of penal law, authors in general, and the demands of judicial practice; the absolute necessity for the creation of institutes, centers, or departments, whether or not university affiliated, with the goal of the basic training of penal magistrates and technical personnel in institutional or post-institutional treatment of offenders; the effective adaptation of penal establishments to Argentinian penal law; the moral character of the sentenced offenders; conditional sentences and conditional freedom; and transplants of organs as related to the penal law.

Institute of Penal and Criminological Sciences

This institute was recently created and is research oriented. One of its objectives was to organize the Second Argentinian Congress of Ex-Convicts, held in November 1979.

Other Institutes

Information solicited from other institutes did not arrive for inclusion in this report, notably the Institute of Penal Law of the National University of Cordoba; the Institute of Penal Law and Criminology of the Law School of the National University of the Northeast; the Institute of Criminological Research and Comparative Penal Law of the University of the Social Museum of Argentina; and the Institute of Higher Penal Studies and Criminology of the National University of La Plata.

SOCIETIES CONCERNED WITH CRIMINOLOGY

Of many such societies in Argentina, only those that are most active in the fields of direct criminological interest are mentioned here. Nevertheless, other professional societies in the spheres of sociology and psychology are making important contributions to criminology in the course of pursuing their central disciplinary interests. An example is the Sociedad Argentina de Sociologia, prominently identified with Professor Alfredo Povina, which has devoted many of its meetings over the last two decades to the exploration of crime and deviance.

Argentinian Criminology Society

Founded on November 13, 1933, this society has the following objectives: the study of the physiopsychic personality of subjects considered to be dangerous; the external factors of crime, especially its social causes; security measures and individualized therapy for a better social readaptation of the offender; preventive criminal policy; and a scientific judicial policy.

Society of Criminal Science and Legal Medicine

Created on April 18, 1952, the society had among its founders Dr. Miguel Herrera Figueroa, as well as prominent penal lawyers, doctors of legal medicine, sociologists, psychologists, and devotees of related sciences.

The society has held numerous scientific meetings, a course in criminological topics in 1963, and conferences on legal medicine and criminology in 1954, 1960, 1964, and 1968. These conferences drew the participation of the leading Argentinian authorities in these fields. The society carried out a team study of juvenile delinquency in Tucuman in 1960.

The first conference on legal medicine and criminology was presided over by Dr. Armando Bustos, the rector of the University of Cordoba, with Dr. Pedro David as secretary. The president and secretary of the organizing committee were Drs. Marcos A. Herrera and Miguel Herrera Figueroa. The second conference was presided over by Dr. Osvaldo Loudet with Dr. Lazaro Barbieri as secretary. The third conference had Dr. José Peco as honorary president, with Dr. Isaac Freidenberg presiding and Dr. Juan Carlos Garcia Vente as secretary. The fourth conference was again presided over by the professor of legal medicine at the National University of Tucuman, Dr. Isaac Freidenberg, with Dr. Jorge V. Miguel acting as secretary. Many other important events have taken place subsequently.

Criminology Society of Rosario, Province of Santa Fe

Founded in November 1965, the society disseminates scientific knowledge through conferences and short courses. In addition, it carries out practical projects within a special area.

Society of Penal Law and Criminology of the Province of Buenos Aires

Among the principal aims of the society, created in 1968, are the promotion of the study and theory of penal law, criminal sciences, legal medicine, sociology, and other related activities. Cultural and scientific interchange at the international level is encouraged. Printing of various publications is another function. The society holds regular scientific sessions and sponsors congresses, conferences, specialized courses, and training.

Criminology Society of Mendoza

This association is private and still at an early stage of organization. Its objectives center around the scientific investigation of criminality in Argentina, especially in the province of Mendoza. Collaboration with public authorities, particularly the universities and public and private institutes, will be emphasized as a means of dealing with criminological problems through special courses, conferences, congresses, seminars, and so on. The awarding of certificates, diplomas, and other honors will be the means of acknowledging accomplishments. The society expects to issue various publications.

Society of Legal Medicine and Toxicology, Province of Mendoza

This society, also still in the organizing stage, intends to promote studies and scientific work in legal medicine and related areas. Its members will advise public and private organizations and conduct conferences and courses on matters pertaining to legal medicine.

ARGENTINA AND LATIN AMERICAN CRIMINOLOGY

The awakening of interest in criminology in Latin America may be attributed to the efforts of that extraordinary Argentinian, Jose Ingenieros. Criminology was born with his work in criminal anthropology and clinical criminology, which in turn was a byproduct of the vigorous scientific influence of positivism. The triumph of positivism in Europe had a decisive influence on Argentina's cultural development during the second half of the nineteenth century and the first quarter of the twentieth century.

One of Ingenieros's teachers was Dr. Francisco de Veyga, professor of legal medicine of the University of Buenos Aires. De Veyga introduced the teaching of criminal anthropology in 1897, and shortly thereafter he inaugurated the Service for Observation of the Socially Alienated under the supervision of the federal government. Veyga then named Ingenieros secretary of the journal *Medical Week* which Veyga edited. During those years, the internationally famous penal law specialist and anarchist leader Pietri Gori came to Buenos Aires and began to publish the *Journal of Modern Criminology* in which Ingenieros published the article, "General Criteria to Orient the Study of the Criminally Insane."

In 1900 when Ingenieros had not yet received his doctorate, de Veyga named him head of the clinic of the Service for Observation of the Socially Alienated. In 1902 the journal *Files of Criminology, Legal Medicine and Psychiatry* appeared, founded by de Veyga and edited by Ingenieros. The first issue carried an article, "The Value of Psychopathology in Criminal Anthropology," which proposed a tripartite division of criminology: criminal etiology, therapeutic criminology, and clinical criminology.

In 1905, Ingenieros participated in the Fifth International Congress of Psychology in Europe. There, in disagreement with Cesare Lombroso, he pointed out that the differentiating characteristics of the delinquent should be sought, not in their anthropometry—which is identical with that of the nondelinquents—but rather in the area of psychopathology.

Ingenieros was then named director of the Institute of Criminology; thus, Argentina became the first country to employ criminology in the area of penal law. Israel Drapkin, a prominent criminologist of Israel, has stated that what Ferri was to European criminology, Ingenieros was to Argentina and Spanish America. The work of the Institute of Criminology has since been taken over by the Institute of Classification. In discussing the program of his Institute of Criminology in 1916, Ingenieros wrote: "Until now the study of criminology has been going through a formative period. It is logical that in a science which is still not actually applied, no definite syntheses have been arrived at."

Yet, his application of criminology to penal law has not received the recognition it deserves, perhaps because his conceptual system as a whole is not adequately understood. Broadly speaking, he contended that the scientific method should be employed from three major points of view—causes, manifestations, and treatment—in studying the phenomena of human and social pathology. Therefore, to lend system to investigations, Ingenieros sketched three fields of study:

1. Criminal etiology, which studies the determining causes of crime. Instead of presupposing the free will of the delinquent, Ingenieros looks for determinism in the delinquent's antisocial act in terms of his organic makeup and the conditions of his environment.
2. Clinical criminology, which studies the multiple forms in which criminal acts are manifested and the physiopsychic character of the delinquents. This field does not try to establish the responsibility of the delinquent; rather, it would determine his or her level of potential dangerousness according to the danger that might result from his or her living in society.
3. Criminal therapy, which examines the collective and individual means for preventing and reducing crime. Punishment is not the means because of the assumption that the delinquent is free to prefer evil to good. Rather, this field of study is dedicated to assuring a "social defense" against the delinquent's unwholesome activity by administering prevention or segregation measures in correctional institutions in keeping with the qualities of the particular case.

Thereby, Ingenieros achieved a coordination among the different branches of criminology that avoided the confusion burdening the study of penal law when approached from the perspective of the classical school. The classical school did permit rather simplistic "therapy," but, even then, it operated under the basic premises of "guilt" and punishment to the exclusion of investigations related to either etiological or clinical criminology. The penal codes followed a priori logic in the mechanistic fashion of medical prescriptions appearing in almanacs; opposite the name of a disease, a standardized dosage of medicine is specified. The penal code would describe a certain type of crime and then call for a certain kind of punishment.

What would be thought of a doctor, Ingenieros asked, who tried to prescribe for his patients without finding the cause of the illness and without its clinical evolution? And an engineer who constructed a building while ignoring the features of the ground upon which it was built and without calculating the resistance of the materials used? By analogy, Ingenieros would have us similarly judge the functioning of present-day penal law.[1]

Continuing the pioneering work of José Ingenieros, Eusebio Gomez (1883-1954) made important contributions to the positivistic school of criminology in Argentina.[2] He was a judge in Buenos Aires and was one of the authors of the Argentine penal code. Among his works are *Prison Work, Argentine Criminology, Passion and Crime*, and the six-volume *Treatise of Criminal Law*.

In 1928, Miguel Figueroa Roman, a distinguished Argentine sociologist, published a sound analysis of the correctional system of Soviet Russia.[3] This analysis was produced in collaboration with Luis Jiminez de Asua, a penal law scholar from Spain, who remained in exile in Argentina until his death in 1972. Miguel Herrera Figueroa is the president of the John F. Kennedy University of Buenos Aires and is another prominent legal sociologist and criminologist. Formerly at the University of Tucuman, he is the author of *Psychology and Criminology*[4] which is remarkable for its integration of various areas of knowledge relevant to criminology. Jimenez de Asua has published extensively in penal law and criminology.[5] Enrique Aftalion, a criminologist of Buenos Aires, has opened the vast area of economic crimes for criminological research. Aftalion died in 1980 after a productive public and scientific career.[6] Ricardo Levene, at present the dean of the School of Law of the University of El Salvador of Buenos Aires, has made important contributions to criminology, procedural penal law, and penal law itself.[7]

Among criminologists of the younger generation are Osvaldo N. Thieghi, Victor Irurzun, Elias Newman, J. C. Garcia Basalo, Oscar Blarduni, and Roberto A. Teran Lomas. Many others could be named if space would allow.

Without question, the development of criminology in Argentina has mainly followed clinical orientations. In trying to combine clinical with sociological and psychological orientations, my *Sociologia Criminal Juvenil* departed from this tradition. This work attempted, for the first time, an "integrated criminology" that would harmonize various perspectives of crime and deviance, while recognizing the historical presence of facts, norms, and values in human conduct.

Nothing is gained by engaging in fierce debates about the relative merits of the "cultural" and the "natural" models of explanation and their respective methodologies, or more recently, in comparing the "clinical" and the "sociological" models for the study of crime. These polemics have traditionally plagued both the social sciences and criminology. An "integrative criminological model" can combine fruitfully a variety of methods and perspectives in the study of human conduct. The objective would be an integration—or coalescence, as Jerome Hall has suggested—of facts, values, and norms. The foundations of an integrative criminology are a balanced perspective of human conduct that constitutes one of the "regional ontologies" of a "humanistic" legal sociology. The feasibility of the integrative model is explored in my own research.[8]

FINAL COMMENT: CRIMINOLOGY AND DEVELOPMENT

Today in Argentina, increasing attention is being devoted to the complex interrelationships between crime prevention and treatment and the broader issues of socioeconomic development. The topic received considerable discussion at the Sixth United Nations Congress for the Prevention of Crime and the Treatment of Offenders in Venezuela in 1980.[9]

In this context, there is a need for an elaboration of theories and research on the interrelationships of a number of problem topics with crime and deviance. Examples of major issues are migration within rural areas, migration to cities, industrialization, modernization of rural areas, education, unemployment, housing, and tourism. Sectoral and intersectoral planning for crime prevention must be integrated with national, regional, and international plans in the context of development.

Development becomes a topic of crucial importance for the discussion of juvenile delinquency and abuses of economic and political power. The topic is also most pertinent to the choice among cultural norms for incorporation within legal norms to keep the criminal laws in keeping with the contemporary stage of socioeconomic development. Furthermore, criminal justice policy and practice can show similar consistency through establishment of administrative guidelines. Evaluation of correctional programs must follow criteria that also recognize the changing significance of crime from a macro point of view. In those various spheres, applied research must be pursued to uncover reliable information and to provide tested principles relevant to practical and pressing problems.

As in many countries, Argentina presents a number of difficulties for exploring the complex interrelationships between the problems of development and those of criminality. As one would expect, there is an insufficient supply of baseline data. More fundamental are the discrepancies between the premises of the legal system and the profile of the social realities being experienced in contemporary Argentina. As students of comparative criminology frequently point out, legal traditions imported from outside a nation are not necessarily consistent with the indigenous culture. Argentina offers an example of discrepancies between the legal code derived from European models and the Argentine culture derived from its own cultural history and social structure. The task of the future should indeed be to make a critical assessment of these disparities in order to ensure fair participation of all groups in socioeconomic and political development.

NOTES

1. Jose Ingenieros, *Criminologia* [Criminology] (Buenos Aires: Elmer Publishers, 1957), pp. 58-59.

2. Eusebio Gomez, *Enrique Ferri: Aspectos de su Personalidad* [Enrique Ferri: Aspects of His Personality] (Buenos Aires: Ediar, 1962).

3. Miguel Figueroa Roman, et al., *La Vida Penal en Rusia* [Penal Life in Russia] (Madrid: Reus, 1931).

4. Miguel Herrera Figueroa, *Psicologia y Criminologia* [Psychology and Criminology] (Tucuman: Richardet, 1956).

5. Luis Jimenez de Asua, *Tratado de Derecho Penal* [Treatise on Penal Law], Vols. 1 to 4 (Buenos Aires: Losado, 1950 to 1952); Jimenez de Asua, *El Criminalista* [The

Criminalist], Vols. 1 to 10 (Buenos Aires: La Fey and T.E.A., 1941 to 1952); Jimenez de Asua, *La Ley y el Delito* [The Law and Crime] (Buenos Aires: Hermes, 1954).

6. Enrique Aftalion, *Critica del Saber de los Juristas* [Critique of Juristic Knowledge] (La Plata: Platense, 1951).

7. R. Levene, *Codigos, procesales Penales Argentinos* [Argentine Penal Procedural Codes], 4 vols. (La Plata: Platense, 1973).

8. Pedro David, *The World of the Burglar* (Albuquerque, N. Mex.: University of New Mexico Press, 1978).

9. *New Perspectives in Crime Prevention and Criminal Justice: The Role of International Cooperation*, Sixth United Nations Congress, Caracas, Venezuela, August 25-September 5, 1980. I served as the chief consultant to the United Nations, specifically in charge of discussion of this topic at the meetings.

BIBLIOGRAPHY

These selected references from the Argentinian literature since 1945 will guide the reader with a particular interest in the topics considered in this chapter.

Treatises on Criminology

Bergalli, Roberto. *Criminología en America Latina* [Criminology in Latin America]. Buenos Aires: Pannedille, 1972.

Blarduni, Oscar C. "Estado actual de las investigaciones criminologicas en Argentina" [Present Status of Criminological Research in Argentina]. In Ricardo Levene. *Criminología* [Criminology]. Buenos Aires: Tekue, 1970, pp. 425-438.

David, Pedro. "Ideology and Criminology in Latin America." In Freda Adler and Gerhard Mueller (eds.). *Politics, Crime and the International Scene*. Puerto Rico: Centro-Sur, 1972.

David, Pedro. *Sociología Del Derecho* [Sociology of Law] Buenos Aires: Astrea, 1980.

Drapkin, Israel. "Investigación criminologica en America Latina" [Criminological Investigation in Latin America]. *International Review of Criminal Policy*, no. 23 (1965):25-30.

López-Rey Arrojo, Manuel. *Introducción al estudio de la Criminologia* [Introduction to the Study of Criminology]. Buenos Aires: El Ateneo, 1945.

Pagano, José. *Criminalidad Argentina* [Argentine Criminality]. Buenos Aires: Depalma, 1964.

Explanations for Criminality

Bajarlia, Juan Jacobo. *Sadismo y Masoquismo en la conducta criminal* [Sadism and Masochism in Criminal Conduct]. Buenos Aires: Abeledo-Perrot, 1959.

Belbey, Jose. *La Sociedad y el delito* [Society and Crime]. Buenos Aires: Claridad, 1947.

David, Pedro. *Criminología y Sociedad* [Criminology and Society]. Buenos Aires: Pensamiento Juridico, 1978.

David, Pedro. *Estructura Social y Criminología* [Social Structure and Criminology]. Maracaibo: Universidad del Zulia, 1979.

David, Pedro. *Sociología Criminal Juvenil* [Sociology of the Juvenile Criminal]. 5th ed. Buenos Aires: Depalma, 1979.

Fontan Balestra, Carlos. *Criminología y Educación* [Criminology and Education]. Buenos Aires: Libreria Hachette, 1943.

Herrera Figueroa, Miguel. *Biocriminología* [Biocriminology]. Buenos Aires: Leuka, 1978.

Herrera Figueroa, Miguel. *Psicología y Criminología* [Psychology and Criminology]. Tucuman: Richardet, 1956.

Ingenieros, José. *Obras completas—Criminología* [Complete Works—Criminology]. Buenos Aires: Elmer, 1971.

Irurzun, Victor. *La Sociología de la Conducta Desviada* [Sociology of Deviant Conduct]. Buenos Aires: Troguel, 1971.

Levene, Ricardo. *El delito de Homicidio* [The Crime of Homicide]. 3d ed. Buenos Aires: Depalma, 1977.

Treatises on Penal Law

Fontan Balestra, Carlos. *Manual de Derecho Penal, Parte General* [Manual of Penal Law, General Part]. Buenos Aires: Depalma, 1949.

Goldstein, Raul. *Diccionario de Derecho Penal* [Dictionary of Penal Law]. Buenos Aires: Bibliografia Omeba, 1962.

Jiménez de Asúa, Luis. *Tratado de Derecho Penal*, Vols. 1 to 4 [Treatise on Penal Law]. Buenos Aires: Losados, 1950 to 1952.

Levene, Ricardo. *Codigos, procesales Penales Argentinos*. 4 vols. [Argentine Penal Procedural Codes]. La Plata: Platense, 1973.

Soler, Sebastian. *Derecho Penal Argentino*. 5 vols. [Argentinian Penal Law]. Buenos Aires: Tipografia Editora, 1956.

Problem Topics Related to Criminology

David, Pedro. "Contraband at the Border." In *Problems of the Undocumented Worker*. Albuquerque, N. Mex.: Latin American Institute, University of New Mexico, 1979, pp. 51-55.

David, Pedro. "Profile of Violence in Argentina." In *Disorders and Terrorism*. Report of the U.S. Task Force on Disorders and Terrorism. Washington, D.C.: U.S. Government Printing Office, 1977, pp. 474-479.

Magulis, Mario. *Migración y marginalidad en las sociedad argentina* [Migration and Marginality in Argentinian Society]. Buenos Aires: Paidos, undated.

Mercado Villar, Olga, et al. *La marginalidad urbana: Origin, proceso y modo* [Urban Marginality: Origin, Process and Forms]. Buenos Aires: Troquel, 1970.

Miranda Gallino, Rafael. *Delitos contra el orden economico* [Crimes Against the Economic Order]. Buenos Aires: Pannedille, 1970.

Criminal Justice System

David, Pedro. "Juvenile Justice in Argentina." In Paul Friday and V. Lorne Stewart (eds.). *Youth Crime and Juvenile Justice*. New York: Praeger Publishers, 1977.

David, Pedro, and Joseph W. Scott. "A Cross-Cultural Comparison of Juvenile Offenders, Offenses, Due Processes, and Societies: The Cases of Toledo, Ohio, and Rosario, Argentina." *Criminology* 11 (August 1973):183-205.

Irurzun, Victor. *La Sociedad Carcelaria* [Prison Society]. Buenos Aires: Depalma, 1968.
Newman, Elias. *Evolución de la pena privativa de Libertad y regimenes penitenciarios* [Evolution of the Deprivation of Freedom Sanctions and Penitentiary Regimes]. Buenos Aires: Pannedille, 1971.

9

BRAZIL

Ayush Morad Amar

At the end of the nineteenth century, criminology enjoyed great prestige in Brazil, and many professionals dedicated themselves to criminological studies. Despite this promising beginning, criminology ultimately came to be excluded from Brazil's law school curricula.

ACCOMPLISHMENTS OF AN EARLIER ERA

At the turn of the century, criminal law entailed broad consideration of topics of primary interest to criminology, above all questions concerning the etiology of crime and the classification of offenders. Extreme penal dogmatism was less attractive to the intellect and more restrictive in its subject matter, and so satisfied neither the teaching staff nor the students. Instead, students were fascinated by doctrines—such as those of Cesare Lombroso, N. Pende, Gabriel Tarde, and Raffaele Garofalo—that led them beyond mere speculation in search of formulas that would explain the origin of criminal behavior and would allow them to classify criminals within well-defined and narrow guidelines.

In Italy, the repercussions of works on criminal anthropology by Lombroso, Ferri, and Garofalo were so great that physicians and penal officials all over the world began to pay more attention to the offender. This trend also appeared in Brazil where there already existed a brilliant constellation of criminal law scholars (Braz Florentino, Tomaz Alves, Joaquim Augusto de Camargo, Lima Drummond, Vieira de Araujo, Macedo Soares, Viveiros de Castro, and Esmeraldino Bandeira) and specialists in forensic medicine. Agostinho José Souza Lima (1842-1921), succeeding Ferreira de Abrue in Rio de Janiero in 1877, was an outstanding expert in forensic medicine.

The manuscript has benefited from the constructive criticisms of Professor Dr. Manoel Pedro Pimentel and Dr. Vitorino Prata Castelo Branco.

Brazilian criminologists of that time were not overly concerned with new doctrinal tendencies specifically attributable to penal science. Instead, they were attracted to anthropology, sociology, psychiatry, endocrinology, and other sciences that study the biological, psychic, and social aspects of human behavior.

An outstanding example of this tendency was the founding of the Sociedade de Anthropologia Criminal, Psiquiatria e Medicina Legal in São Paulo on October 26, 1895. Among the objectives of this society was the study of penal sciences, criminal anthropology, and forensic medicine. Members included many eminent criminologists, including Brasilio Augusto Machado de Oliveira, Cândido Motta, Reynaldo Porchat, Antonio Amâncio Pereira de Carvalho, and José Alcantara Machado. All were full professors at the São Paulo law school.

Cândido Motta's distinguished work, *Classificaçâo dos Criminosos* [Classification of Offenders], appeared in São Paulo in 1897. The name of Raimundo Nina Rodrigues (1862-1906) deserves a place as a pioneer in the history of Brazilian criminology. Lombroso himself called Raimundo Nina Rodrigues the "apostle of criminal anthropology in the New World." His works were well known in Europe, although few in Brazil knew of his international reputation. Examples of this remarkable Bahian criminologist's works are *O Problem Mēdico Judiciārio no Brasil* [The Medical-Judiciary Problem in Brazil], *O alienado no Direito Civil Brasileiro* [The Insane and the Brazilian Civil Law], *As Raças Humanas e a responsabilidade Penal* [The Human Race and Penal Responsibility], *A Loucura das Multidões* [Mass Insanity], *A Paranóia dos Negros* [The Negro's Paranoia], and *Negros Criminosos no Brasil* [The Negro Criminals in Brazil].

In 1914, the Sociedade de Medicina Legal e Criminologia (Society of Forensic Medicine and Criminology) was founded in the state of Bahia by Nina Rodrigues, Oscar Freire de Carvalho (1882-1923), Dr. Carlos Chenaud, and Jurist Felinto Bastos. This event marked the first appearance of this new science as a separate subject, independent of criminal law and forensic medicine. When Oscar Freire de Carvalho moved to São Paulo in 1918, he stimulated the foundation there of the society.

In 1892, Alcantara Machado published a work entitled *O Hipnotismo* [Hypnotism] devoted to the exegesis of Article 269 of the penal code. The well-known book *Germes do Crime* [The Source of Crime] by Aureliano Leal was published in Bahia, while Viveiros de Castro published *Ensaio sobre a Estatística Criminal* [Essay on Criminal Statistics] in Rio de Janeiro in 1894.

CRITIQUE OF MERITS OF PENAL SCIENCE

Almost all of the important Brazilian students of criminal law prided themselves on the study of criminological themes, but their conceptions of criminology did not promote the development of penal science. Their considerations of these themes were not consistent with the systematic study that qualifies as a science. Instead, juridical concepts were mixed indiscriminately with those of anthropology, psychiatry, and sociology in ways that denied careful and profound analysis of fundamental questions. "Our juridical penal bibliography was scarce, boring and thorny," Nelson Hungria has said. "It only scratched the surface of real penal science and in consequence became tedious and uninteresting."[1]

Hungria condemned the teaching approach to penal law at the university and what he regarded as simplistic jurisprudence. With only a few exceptions, jurisprudence limited its attention to questionable rules that were given such emphasis that they were treated as though they were axiomatic truths. The reaction to this penal nihilism, as Hungria called it, was charged with the superficial employment of criminological theories that led to further decay of the law expressed in an archaic code. He believed that the broad discretion granted the courts in judging crimes confused the administration of justice. The courts, Hungria said, were discredited in this era of bloodthirsty passion that was excused on the absurd grounds of the "privation of the senses."

Hungria also accused criminal lawyers of cultivating a "pathetic manner" or an "exalted style" that aggravated the penal nihilism, distorting those traces of the exact sciences borrowed from the positivism of Cesare Lombroso. Even those who were competent in penal science abandoned publication in textbooks of the rigorous interpretations of positivist law because they feared that assumption of theoretical obligations would jeopardize their professional careers. In his extensive contributions to the literature, Evaristo de Morais did not include a single study dealing specifically with technical juridical matters. Hungria summarized the consequences in this fashion:

> The law court has decayed, so profound changes must be brought about in the field of penal justice. The judgment of the majority of crimes was transferred from the jury to district judges, bringing about, in the debate and solution of criminal suits, what might be termed "juridical propriety." The vain eloquence of the jury was substituted for by ponderous dialectics, sober in the exegesis, analysis and application of legal texts.[2]

HYBRID PERSPECTIVE AND REACTION TO IT

Hungria's interpretation is correct but incomplete. It would seem that he considered only the most obvious reasons for the decline of the study of criminology in Brazil. The change of legislation, which he emphasized in his explanation, was less of a primary cause. Actually, alterations in the philosophical and juridical fields were inherent in the change of legislation, including that concerning the competence of the courts of justice. The alterations in the philosophical and juridical fields brought about the lack of prestige of criminology in the penal science area.

In the 1940s, the study of genuine penal science was set aside, but the fundamental fact was that penal science in Brazil had fallen behind developments elsewhere. Strangely, this backwardness provided the opportunity for the diversion of emergent positivism into an improper hybridization with juridical dogmatism.

As new positivist leaders gained influence, Brazilian scholars reacted culturally by disseminating new ideas and commentaries about them. In the field of penal science, the positivist theories emphasized the importance of knowing the offender's personality, and less attention was paid to the study of crime as a juridical phenomenon. The oft-repeated slogan—much in fashion at that time in the medical field and stemming from the positivist influence—states: "There are no diseases, there are only sick people." The criminologists adapted the slogan to argue: "There are no crimes, there are only criminals."

The same thing seems to have occurred in other countries, according to Roque de Brito Alves. "In the period referred to, especially after World War I," he says, "criminology turned its attention decisively to the laboratories, to penitentiaries, to psychiatric centers, shying away from closed discussions and conference controversies."[3]

Conditions were propitious for the invasion of the field of penal science by theories of anthropology, psychiatry, sociology, endocrinology, and other sciences which, mixed with juridical theories based on dogmatism, were converted into inappropriate hybrids.

The juridical and technical movement arose as a reaction against such conditions. We can date the beginning of the movement against the interference of natural sciences in the field of penal disciplines with the first quarter of the twentieth century. As a result of the movement, criminology and its correlate studies lost their place of importance in Brazilian law schools. Professor Manoel Pedro Pimentel, an eminent, respected jurist, has written the following:

> The technical juridical school, called by Ugo Spirito the "technical juridical conception," began as a reaction against the excessive intrusion of correlate or supporting sciences—philosophy, sociology, anthropology, etc.—in the field of penal science. Its main postulates were summarized by Arturo Rocco on January 15, 1910, when he lectured during the opening classes at the University of Sassari. It is beyond the intentions of this essay to make a critical analysis of Rocco's ideas, but it is necessary to emphasize his extreme aversion to philosophical questions and to *jus naturalism*. Manzi and Massari supported further the criticism Rocco had previously made on this matter and defended the position he made that the only object in the science of law is positive law.[4]

Technical and juridical postulates had enormous influence. Acceptance of the postulates was so widespread that even ardent positivists fell silent. The influence of the postulates was soon noticed in Brazil, immediately gaining many supporters. The consequence was most strongly felt in the elaboration of premises on which the 1940 Brazilian penal code was based. The premises were marked either by the points of view of juridical technicalism or of neo-juridical positivism which no longer had the slightest similarity to naturalist positivism.

At the end of a memorable lecture given at the opening session of the First National Congress of the Public Ministry in São Paulo on June 15, 1942, Hungria emphatically stated:

> In Brazil, where the study of penal law has been so careless, encouraging the dissemination of superficial ideas and grave misunderstandings, we need, now that the advent of the new code has brought the opportunity and stimulus for a broad revision of knowledge, to delineate, once and for all, the boundaries or border lines of juridical penal science. Above all, in face of new legislation which sent the so-called "criminological sciences" into limbo, it is no longer tolerable to go on referring to them as "penal sciences."[5]

This anathema was the equivalent of an official pronouncement because of the widespread knowledge of Minister Hungria's extremely strong position in regard to the Revisory Commission of the Alcantara Machado Project which produced the 1940 Brazilian penal code. On the other hand, there is no doubt that technical juridical ideas influenced this penal code, since it was based on the Italian penal code of 1933, the project elaborated by Rocco which clearly bore the technical juridical stamp.

EMPHASIS TURNS TO FORENSIC MEDICINE

Having fallen into disgrace in the juridical sphere, criminology fled to the medical schools, laboratories, mental institutions, and penitentiaries—only rarely and with extreme caution daring to call itself a science. It preferred to appear only sporadically and discreetly in forensic medicine classes or in the magistrates' courts to help elucidate some cases of homicide.

On the bookstands of criminal lawyers and district attorneys, one could still find books on criminology beside those on forensic medicine, but no law school included the subject in its curriculum.

Systematic studies of the so-called criminological sciences were thus brought to a halt over a period of forty years in Brazil's law schools. It is true that all the treatises on penal law mentioned criminology as an auxiliary science. It is also true that during this period some notable works were published in this field. Among them were *Criminologia* [Criminology] by Afranio Peixoto (1933) and *Tratado da Responsabilidade Criminal* [Treatise on Criminal Responsibility] by Valdemar Cesar da Silveira (1955) in three volumes, little known, but very valuable, erudite works. Also worthy of mention are *Estudos de Criminologia* [Studies on Criminology] by Roque de Brito Alves (1956) and especially the works of Roberto Lyra as a whole. Professor Roberto Lyra devoted himself to the criminological aspects of penal questions, bringing up in all his many books the ideas rooted in the problems of criminality and the treatment of offenders.

In Rio de Janeiro in 1931, Lyra founded the Instituto Brasileiro de Criminologia. Under his direction, the institute became the city's center of criminology, where the great Brazilian criminologists and many foreigners lectured. No work on Brazilian criminology is complete without mention of the role of Roberto Lyra, who organized the first regular course on criminology in Brazil with the help of Benjamin de Moraes, Fernando Bastos Ribeiro, Antonio Carlos Vilanova, José

Nicanor de Almeida, Joaquim de Freitas, Joacyr Bicalho Guimaraes, and Sérgio Rego Macedo. The first class graduated in 1955.

This course was offered by the Criminological Institute of the University of the Federal District, Rio de Janeiro. In organizing the course, Professor Lyra took as his model the institute founded by Enrico Ferri in Rome in 1911 "with the aim of improving graduates of law schools and giving specialization courses for doctors and lawyers." It was a two-year course, but it could be completed in a year under exceptional circumstances. The subjects were organized under three groups: the juridical group, the biological group, and the sociological group. The curriculum included criminal sociology, criminal psychology, penal law, principles of administration, and forensic medicine.

Psychiatrists made considerable progress in promoting their version of clinical criminology. Through their efforts, the penal code required that their technical expertise be employed in assessing the criminal responsibility and potentiality for further criminality of inmates of prisons and hospitals for the criminally insane. The psychiatrists regarded technical competence in determining criminal responsibility and potentiality to be vital for public safety and for avoiding penal punishment when the offender's personality necessitated treatment rather than punishment.

A whole generation of psychiatrists graduated from the Medical School of the Penal Mental Institute of Franco da Rocha near São Paulo, contributing valuable studies that are still valid and up to date. André Teixeira Lima, Eugenio Mariz de Oliveira, Tarcizo Leonce Pinheiro Cintra, and other notable doctors were part of the group of famous psychiatrists who developed the São Paulo School of Psychiatry into an educational enterprise of real quality.

STAGNATION UNDER JURIDICAL TECHNICALITY

Meanwhile, sociological criminology has stagnated; Brazilian crimologists have lagged increasingly behind the new international developments in the social sciences. In other countries, research was stepped up and great amounts of public and private monies were allocated to scientific research to find practical solutions to the growth of criminality.

Until about ten years ago, practically nothing was accomplished in sociological criminology in Brazil. No official organ was created to publish studies or to propose solutions for criminality. The country was so remote from real sociocultural conditions that Manuel Lopez Rey y Arrojo, criminological expert of the United Nations, found that the 1969 Brazilian penal code failed to recognize those realities in Brazil: "The Brazilian project, in support of the 116 articles of its general part, mentions the German project sixteen times, the Yugoslavian penal code twelve times, the Greek eight times, the Italian six times, besides occasional references to others. No mention whatsoever is made to an appreciation of national reality."[6]

At the beginning of the 1970s, a decided reaction set in favoring stronger criminological sciences and research. The trend has been towards freeing the way for introducing criminological courses and research in Brazilian law schools, rather than developing the penal science in its own terms. This new consciousness of penal law experts is marked by its universal nature as a consequence of the diminished ethical and social character of penal law. The consequence has come from the technical juridical movement's detour into excessively formal dogmatism.

"A great number of penalists, however, attempting to achieve the scientific elaboration of positive law, have consciously or unconsciously, strayed into logicist formalism," José María Stampa Braun says. "I refer to all those who, without excluding consideration of the actual content of our law, let themselves be carried away by exclusively systematic concerns, as was also the case with the majority of prewar German dogmatism—as their numerous contributions demonstrate—and many of the most faithful followers of juridical technicality."[7]

Stampa Braun describes some of the pernicious consequences of formalist dogmatism instilled by juridical technicality: the rigidity of the system, the blind faith in dogmas which translated themselves into concepts elaborated by abstract logical procedures, atomization of the concept of crime, the intention of applying to penal law the same categories as those of civil law, and preoccupation with many elegant but useless questions.

Stampa Braun speaks of a return to a position that is more suited to the aims of penal law: "Against this merely formal delimitation of the nature of law, against this laming of law and of life, against this geometric dismemberment of juridical forms, a broad ideological movement characterized by the desire to reenthrone in the jurisdictional sphere the historical and valuable sociological elements, which had been declared 'metajuridical' by *Begriffsjurisprudenz*, had to appear."[8]

Thus, conceptual jurisprudence, which was so criticized in the days of juridical positivism, repeated itself in juridical technicalism. It deserved the stigma cast on it by Américo Antolisei, S. Maggiore, Edmund Mezger, and others who attempted to revitalize dogmatism with new influences resulting from teleologism. It was refuted by Dahm and Schafftein who preached a unitary conception of crime.

Juridical technicalism improved penal science by lending it extraordinary dignity, but it was detoured from its original course. In its development, juridical technicalism did not respect Rocco's initial proposal when he spoke to the inaugural class of the law school of the University of Sassari in 1910 of "The Problems and Method of the Science of Penal Law." Many of his followers in the juridical technical movement broke the extolled pursuit of the three principles of exegesis, dogmatics, and criticism. Thus, Stampa Braun was able to say that in some sectors technicalism had degenerated into a formalism as objectionable as that of the theory of right.[9]

The new revisionist tendencies of juridical technicalism paved the way for conceptions that valorized the contribution of the criminological sciences. They opened a wide window for jurists through which they could see the reality of life and collect directly the concrete vitalizing data that are the source of the norms of positive law.

Roque Brito Alves states:

> Professor Mannheim of the University of London, one of the great contemporary authorities on juridical sociology, in a recent book, defends technical juridical reform as a solution of the precise adjustment of norms to existence—the latter undergoing in our times a "crisis in values." As he himself writes, the criminal law has, quite rightly, been called one of the most faithful mirrors of a given civilization, reflecting the fundamental values on which the latter rests. Whenever these values change, the criminal law must follow. The present crisis in values, one of the greatest in human history, cannot fail to have profound repercussions in this field.[10]

Several other factors contributed to the resurgence of interest in criminology in Brazil. First, the growth of criminality, especially in its most violent forms, has created a crisis in the penitentiary system and has upset the populations of big cities. Second, new types of offenses—such as white-collar crime and the high drug propagation rate—have emerged. Third, the crisis in the administration of justice and the overcrowded prisons have contributed to a necessity for criminological studies and research.

RESURGENCE OF BRAZILIAN CRIMINOLOGY

In 1972, under the initiative of Professor Virgilio Luis Donnici, the Brazilian Bar Association (with Dr. Theophilo de Azeredo Santos as president) brought famous professionals together in Rio de Janeiro for a symposium on "The Crisis in the Administration of Criminal Justice." Professor Donnici worked untiringly for the revival of criminological studies, taking part in various conferences, courses, seminars, and symposia and advocating the inclusion of criminology as a compulsory subject in the curricula of Brazilian law schools.

Convinced by this campaign, the Department of Penal Law of the University of São Paulo Law School, under the direction of Professor Manoel Pedro Pimentel, decided that criminology would be included in its specialization course as of 1974. Other law schools have followed this example, among them Candido Mendes Law School in Rio de Janeiro where since 1980 five criminology classes have been offered.

In São Paulo, the Faculdades Metropolitanas Unidas created an institute of criminology. The same thing has been happening in other Brazilian cities such as Londrina in the state of Paraná, where an important scientific meeting for criminological studies is held every year; important groups of professionals are brought together under the leadership of Heber Scares Vargas. As president of the Brazilian Society of Criminal Law with headquarters in São Paulo, Professor Vitorino Prata Castelo Branco must be remembered for his role in the dissemination of criminological ideas and concepts through courses held in law schools and other associations. He describes another development in the following statement:

In São Paulo, after 1972, the Oscar Freire Institute, now known as the Institute of Social Medicine and Criminology of São Paulo, under the superintendency of Professor Dr. Ayush Morad Amar, greatly advanced the study of criminology, organizing the first recognized course in São Paulo with the help of famous foreign professors and with practical training periods for students in official departments and penal mental institutions where they could see at first hand the problems of criminality, the application of sentences, and results of the penitentiaries, with written reports which were later discussed.

Professor Jean Pinatel and Georges Fully, respectively President and Secretary of the International Society for Criminology, contributed their experiences. Other participants were Franco Ferracuti and Giacomo Canepa from Italy; Severin Carlos Versele and Joris Casselman from Belgium; Alfonso Quirós Cuaron and Rafael Ruiz Harrel from Mexico; Francisco Canestri and Antonio G. Carrero from Venezuela; Israel Drapkin and Shlomo Shoham from Israel; Jacob Kahn, John Freeman and J. E. Hall Williams from England; Pablo Muñoz Gomes, Elvia Velasquez de Pabón and Maria Teresa Camargo from Colombia; Antonio Calabrese and Carlos N. Cagliotti from Argentina; José David from Uruguay; Jaime Toro Calder, Dalia Marti de Mujica and Angel Pacheco Maldonado from Puerto Rico; Gregorio Aramayo D. Medina and Roberto Palma from Bolivia; Dionísio G. Torres, Paulo Adolfo Gonzalez Petit, Emílio Gorostiaga and Encina Marin from Paraguay; Marco A.G. Berendique and J. Mardones from Chile; Julio Altmann-Smythe from Peru; Antonio Beristain and Louis Castillon Mora from Spain; Wouter Buikhuisen from Holland; Marvin Wolfgang, John Money, Saarnof Mednick, Freda Adler, Frank Ervin, Robert Rubin, Peter Manning, Peter P. Lejins, Joyce Lowinson, Raybourn Hesse and Saleem A. Shah from the United States; Denis Szabo and Reginald Smart from Canada; Marcel Ette from the Ivory Coast; M. Soueif from Egypt; Günther Kaiser from West Germany; Karl Otto Christiansen from Denmark; Eva Johansen from Sweden; Archer Tongue from the International Council on Alcohol and Addictions, Switzerland; Gerhard O.W. Mueller, Alfons Noll, James J. Moore and Manuel Lopez Rey y Arrojo from the United Nations; and many others of the same scientific stature.[11]

The Oscar Freire Institute of São Paulo, which received recognition and the denomination of "International Center for Biologic Criminology and Forensic Medicine" from the International Society for Criminology, had a vast field open for exploration and certainly did much towards the development of criminology in our country and abroad. In this sense, it replaced the Latin American Institute of Criminology, honored by the United Nations and which, through the neglect of public officials of São Paulo at that time, became extinct from their lack of understanding of the importance of such a great undertaking.

Under Professor Ayush Morad Amar's direction, the institute develops notable research in the clinical and sociological areas and has become the most advanced center for studies on drug and alcohol dependence in Brazil and, perhaps, in South America.[12]

INTERDISCIPLINARY GROUP ON CRIMINOLOGY

One important consequence of the resurgence of criminology in Brazil was the formation of the international group that has come to be known as the Interdisciplinary Group on Criminology. The initial discussion ideas were formulated during the first International Symposium on Criminology held under the sponsorship of the International Center for Biological and Medico-Forensic Criminology, São Paulo, Brazil, August 8-12, 1974. Several members of the present Interdisciplinary Group who participated in the São Paulo symposium had hoped that there would be an opportunity for small group discussions among the participants (thirty-five invited consultants from twenty countries) from several disciplines in an effort to bridge the gap among them with regard to understanding crime and delinquency. Some members of the core group thought that efforts to remedy and balance the environmentally biased approaches to criminology would not be provided by developing a biological bias. Rather, they felt the need was for a more broadly conceptualized interdisciplinary perspective that would allow consideration of relevant biological and environmental variables.

Since the basic purpose, organization, and size of the São Paulo symposium (not to mention the four languages being used) did not permit the kind of small group discussion noted above, several participants sought to cultivate an interdisciplinary perspective through informal discussions during the evenings. These initial and informal conversations led to the formulation of several ideas and recommendations to the director of the International Center for Biological and Medico-Forensic Criminology (Dr. Ayush Morad Amar). One such suggestion was that a smaller interdisciplinary group be convened to consider the development and formulation of more interdisciplinary and integrated frames of reference for studying the phenomena of crime and delinquency. It was decided that the composition of this core group should be broadened to encompass a wider range of interdisciplinary, international, and scholarly inputs.

The Fifth Workshop of the Interdisciplinary Group on Criminology was held in November 1979. This workshop was based on the four preceding workshops. It was planned, not so much to continue the theoretical discussions of an interdisciplinary focus that marked the beginning of the series of workshops, but rather to concentrate on the specific research projects being undertaken by members of the group. Specifically, these projects included the study of violent offenders in an Israeli prison, the Philadelphia collaborative perinatal project, and the cross-national comparison of delinquency in Copenhagen and Philadelphia birth cohorts. All were presented in earlier workshops as potential projects for the interest of the group. The Fifth Workshop focused primarily on methodological issues in these specific projects, which represented a considerable evolution from the philosophical and theoretical discussions concerning the interdisciplinary approach to crime and violence that characterized the first two or three workshops.

Whether or not the specific projects work out as planned remains to be determined. Nevertheless, in its eight years of continuing discussions the Interdisciplinary Group on Criminology has built a strong base for the conduct of actual interdisciplinary research in criminology. The group can make a useful contribution to knowledge in the field of criminology.

All of the studies on human subjects were carried out with meticulous attention to protecting the rights of the subjects involved, with reference both to their voluntary participation and to the confidentiality of the information obtained. The relevant human subjects experimentation committees of the participating institutions approved all projects in advance. Before these projects were conducted, it was ascertained that the risk-to-benefit ratio to the subjects was extremely small, that is, the procedures voluntarily agreed to by the subjects represented a small risk to them compared to the potential benefits to society at large from developing the integrated data that are the focus of interest and analysis.[13]

A new criminological mentality already exists in Brazil, attracting renowned professors. This development offers hope for the beginning of a new era in criminological studies in this part of the world.

NOTES

1. Nelson Hungria, *Novas questões juridico-penais* [New Juridical Penal Questions] (Rio de Janeiro: Editora Nacional da Dir. Ltda., 1945), pp. 17-18.
2. Ibid., pp. 18-19.
3. Roque de Brito Alves, *Estudos de Criminologia* [Studies in Criminology] (Recife: Imprensa Industrial Ltda., 1956), p. 20.
4. Manoel Pedro Pimentel, *Ensaio sobre a pena* [Essay on Punishment] (São Paulo: Editora Revista dos Tribunais, 1973), pp. 14-15.
5. Hungria, *Novas questões juridico-penais*, p. 15.
6. Manuel Lopez-Rey y Arrojo, "Algumas considerações analíticas sobre a Criminologia e a justica criminal" [Some Analytical Considerations on Criminology and Criminal Justice], *Revista de Direito Penal* 4 (October-December 1971): 9-29.
7. José Maréa Stampa Braun, *Introducción a la ciencia del derecho penal* [Introduction to the Penal Law Science] (Valladolid: Miñon Editora S. A., 1953), p. 72.
8. Ibid., p. 83.
9. Ibid., p. 119.
10. De Brito Alves, *Estudos de Criminologia*, p. 20.
11. Vitorino Prata Castelo Branco, *Curso Completo de Criminologia* [Complete Course on Criminology] (São Paulo: Sugestões Literárias S.A., 1975), pp. 51-56.
12. Franco Ferracuti and Ayush Morad Amar, *Temas de Criminologia I* [Themes of Criminology I] (São Paulo: Editora Resenha Universitária Ltda., 1975), pp. 2-14.
13. Ayush Morad Amar, *Temas de Criminologia II* [Themes of Criminology II] (São Paulo: Editora Resenha Universitária Ltda., undated).

BIBLIOGRAPHY

The following references are representative of works in Brazilian criminology and are grouped according to certain major topics.

Treatises on Criminology

Branco, Vitorino Prata Castelo. *Criminologia* [Criminology]. São Paulo: Sugestões Literárias, 1980.

Costa, Alvaro Mayrink. *Criminologia* [Criminology]. Rio de Janeiro: 1979.

Da Silva, Jośe Pereira. *Novos rumos da Criminologia* [The New Path of Criminology]. Rio de Janeiro: Cia. Brasil Editora, 1939.

De Castro, Olympio Augusto Viveiros. *Ensaio sobre estatística criminal* [Essay on Criminal Statistics]. Rio de Janeiro: 1913.

De Macedo, Gilberto. *As novas diretrizes da Criminologia* [The New Guidelines for Criminology]. São Paulo: Editora Leia, 1957.

De Oliveira, Elias. *Criminologia das multidões* [Mass Criminology]. Ceará: Editora Livraria Quinderé, 1934.

Donnici, Virgilio Luiz. *A Criminologia na Administração da Justiça Criminal* [Criminology and the Criminal Justice Administration]. Rio de Janeiro: Forense, 1978.

Lyra, Roberto. *Criminologia* [Criminology]. Rio de Janeiro: Editora Forense, 1964.

Peixoto, Julio Afrânio, *Criminologia* [Criminology]. Rio de Janeiro: 1933.

Rezende, Astolpho. *Nos domínos da Criminologia* [In the Domain of Criminology]. Rio de Janeiro: Cia. Brasil Editora, 1939.

Ribeiro, Leonídio. *Criminologia* [Criminology]. Rio de Janeiro: Editorial Sul América, 1957.

Santos, J.W. Sexas. *Pequeño dicionário de Criminologia* [Dictionary of Criminology]. São Paulo: Pro-Livro, 1968.

Theoretical Approaches

Amarante, Jurandyr. *Psicologia e Crime* [Psychology and Crime]. Rio de Janeiro: 1936.

Braga, Jorge. *Ensaio para a morte* [Training to the Death]. Brasília: Limitada, 1977.

D'Araujo Leal, Aureliano. *Germes do Crime* [The Source of Crime]. Bahia: Editora José Luiz F. Magalhães, 1896.

Guimarães, Ewerton Montenegro. *A Chancela do Crime* [The Mark of Crime]. Rio de Janeiro: Ambito Cultural, Edições Ltda.

Hungria, Nelson Hoffbauer. *O Código Penal e as novas teorias criminológicas* [The Penal Code and New Criminological Theories]. Rio de Janeiro: Revista Forense, 1942.

Lyra, Roberto. *Antropologia Patológica e Crime* [Pathological Anthropology and Crime]. Rio de Janeiro: Revista Forense, 1948.

Lyra, Roberto. *O methodo estatístico e as causas econômicas da criminalidade* [The Statistical Method and Economic Causes of Criminality]. Rio de Janeiro: 1934.

Mendes, Antonio Evaristo. *Ensaios de Pathologia Social* [Essay on Social Pathology]. Rio de Janeiro: Livraria Editora Leite Ribeiro and Maurillo, 1921.

Peixoto, Isadora Durval. *Superstição e crime no Brasil* [Superstition and Crime in Brazil]. São Paulo: Revista dos Tribunais, 1980.

Peixoto, Julio Afranio. *Epilepsia e Crime* [Epilepsy and Crime]. Bahia: Editora V. Oliveira, 1898.

Ribeiro, Leonídio. *Antropologia Criminal* [Criminal Anthropology]. Rio de Janeiro: Editora Imp. Nacional, 1937.

Rodrigues, Raimundo Nina. *As raças humanas e a responsabilidade penal no Brasil* [The Human Race and Penal Responsibility]. São Paulo: Editora Nacional, 1938.

Rodrigues, Raimundo Nina. *A paranóia dos negros* [Negro Paranoia]. São Paulo: Associação Cultural do Negro, 1931.

Rodrigues, Raimundo Nina. *As coletividades anormais* [Mass Insanity]. Rio de Janeiro: Editora Civilização Brasileira, 1939.

Soares, F. *Causas da Criminalidade e fatores criminogenos* [Causes of Criminality and Criminogenic Factors]. Rio de Janeiro: Científica Ltda., 1978.

Tubenchiek, G. *Teoria do Crime* [Theory of Crime]. Rio de Janeiro: Forense, 1978.

Studies of Criminality

De Azevedo Marques, Joaó Benedito. *Marginalizacao do menor e Criminalidade* [Minors and Criminality]. McGraw-Hill do Brasil Ltda., 1976.

Hungria, Nelson Hoffbauer. *A Criminalidade dos homens de cor no Brasil* [Criminality Among Blacks in Brazil]. Rio de Janeiro: Revista Forense, 1951.

Lyra, Roberto. *Criminalidade Econômica* [Economic Criminality]. Rio de Janeiro: Forense, 1978.

Mendes, Antonio Evaristo. *Criminalidade Passional* [Passionate Criminality]. São Paulo: Editora Saraiva, 1933.

Mendes, Antonio Evaristo. *Criminalidade da infância e da adolêscencia* [Child and Adolescent Criminality]. Rio de Janeiro: Editora Francisco Alves, 1927.

Mendonca, Yolanda. *O Crime de Furto* [Theft]. Rio de Janeiro: São José, 1971.

Neves, Akair Metzker Coutinho Serrano. *Violência e Criminalidade* [Violence and Criminality]. Rio de Janeiro: 1980.

Noronha, E. Magalhães. *Do Crime culposo* [Negligent Crime]. São Paulo: Editora Savaira, 1955.

Rodrigues, Raimundo Nina. *Negros criminosos no Brasil* [Negro Criminals in Brazil]. São Paulo: Editora Nacional, 1945.

Salles, Romeu de Aleida, Jr. *Do crime* [Crime]. São Paulo: Brasilivros Ed. e Distribuidora Ltd., 1980.

Santos, Ary dos. *Como nascem, como vivem e como morrem os criminosos* [How Criminals Are Born, Live and Die]. São Paulo: Livraria Acadêmica, 1939.

Silva, Juary C. *A Macro Criminalidade* [The Macro Criminality]. São Paulo: Revista dos Tribunals, 1980.

Penal Code and the Courts

André, Antenor. *Prova Pericial* [The Expertise Evidence]. Rio de Janeiro: Editora Rio, 1978.

De Jesus, Damãsio E. *Da Co. Delinquencia em face do Novo Código Penal* [Co-delinquency and the New Penal Code]. São Paulo: Revista dos Tribunals, 1976.

Fayet, Ney. *A Sentença criminal* [Criminal Sentence]. Porto Alagre: Síntese, 1980.

Ferreira, Ovídio Inácio. *A Instrução Criminal* [Court Proceedings]. Sen Editor.

Hungria, Nelson Hoffbauer. *Comentarios ao Codigo Penal* (Remarks on the Penal Code]. Rio de Janeiro: Editora Revista Forense, 1951.

Loureiro, Osman. *Introdução aos Crimes Contra o Património e Estudos de Direito Penal* [Introduction to the Crimes Against Property and Penal Law Studies]. José Konfino, 1972.

Lyra, Roberto. *Noções de Direito Criminal* [Notions of Criminal Law]. Rio de Janeiro: Editora Nacional Dir. Ltda., 1944.

Nogueira, Paulo Lúcio. *Questões Processuals Penais e Controvérsias* [Criminal Procedure and Controversies]. São Paulo: Sugestões Literárias, 1979.

Rodrigues, Raimundo Nina. *O alienado no Direito Civil Brasileiro* [The Insane and Brazilian Civil Law]. São Paulo: Editora Nacional, 1939.

Contributions to Criminal Justice Administration

Da Motta, Candido Nazianzeno Nogueira. *Classificação os Criminosos* [Classification of Offenders]. São Paulo: J. Rosetti, 1897.

Da Silveira, Baldemar Cesar. *Trado de Responsabilidade Criminal* [Treatise on Criminal Responsibility]. São Paulo: Editora Saraiva, 1955.

De Barros, Orlando Mara. *Dicionãrio de Classificação de Crimes* [Dictionary of Crime Classification]. Rio de Janeiro: Rio.

Hungria, Nelson Hoffbauer. *Classificação Criminosos* [Classification of Offenders]. Rio de Janeiro: Revista Forense, 1958.

Lyra, Roberto. *Classificação de Crimes* [Classification of Crimes]. Rio de Janeiro: Revista Forense, 1943.

Lyra, Roberto. *O memor e a responsabilidade criminal* [The Minor and Criminal Responsibility]. São Paulo: Editora Saraiva, 1932.

Peixoto, Julio Afranio. *Psicopatologia Forense* [Forensic Psychopathology]. Rio de Janeiro: Editora Francisco Alves, 1923.

Rodrigues, Raimundo Nina. "O problema médico-jurídico no Brasil" [The Medical-Judiciary Problem in Brazil]. *Editora Revista Brasil* 14, no. 4 (1898):327.

Soares, Orlando. *Justiça e Criminalidade* [Justice and Criminality]. Rio de Janeiro: Forense, 1974.

Thompson, Augusto. *A Questão Penitenciária* [The Penitentiary Question]. Rio de Janeiro: Forense, 1980.

10

CANADA

Jim Hackler

The long-range goal of this book might be best served by a frank (and somewhat opinionated) appraisal of how criminology has developed in Canada. To that end, several patterns are noteworthy.

PATTERNS IN CANADIAN CRIMINOLOGY

First, any review of the substantive work must distinguish between anglophone criminology and francophone criminology. To a large degree, work in anglophone Canada is integrated with the thinking that goes on in the United States and England. Francophone criminologists in Quebec share the thinking of criminologists in France, Belgium, and other francophone centers of criminology. Criminologists in Quebec tend to be bilingual and are also familiar with the literature in English. Regrettably, anglophone scholars in Canada have relatively little knowledge of the francophone literature.

Second, the centers for teaching and research in criminology differ in their origins and orientations. Montreal has a broad base of teaching, academic research, and applied criminology. Initially without a teaching mission, Toronto established a sophisticated research unit from its beginning. Alberta has a heavy commitment to teaching at undergraduate and graduate levels and to academic research; applied criminology has drawn interest only recently. Alberta and Toronto also draw on the established disciplines through courses outside their centers, whereas Montreal and Simon Fraser universities favor strengthening criminology as a discipline in itself. Both Regina and Ottawa emphasize applied programs.

The author would like to thank Louise Biron, Hans Mohr, David Perrier, Richard Ericson, Otto Driedger, P. J. Giffen, and others for suggestions on this chapter. Any interpretations or errors, however, are the responsibility of the author.

Third, most of the criminological research done in Canada is not uniquely Canadian but deals, rather, with larger issues. Studies done by John Hagan[1] on the criminal justice system in Alberta and by John Hogarth on the provincial courts in Ontario[2] are part of a larger body of literature on the criminal justice system that is shared with the United States. Similarly, the recent findings in Ontario by Byles and Maurice,[3] and also by Annis,[4] that various forms of treatment do not have much impact on clients are consistent with similar experiences in the United States. In Alberta, the growing interest in brain damage and learning disabilities is reflected in work by Lorne Yeudall.[5] Studies of the police by Shearing and Leon,[6] Koenig,[7] Klein et al.,[8] and others are part of the larger body of literature shared with the United States and England.

Even the debates over the evaluation of prevention programs appeal to the larger North American audience. Gendreau and Ross emphasize areas where psychologists have brought about change in institutional settings.[9] By contrast, Hackler emphasizes some of the potentially negative aspects of evaluating research.[10] Roesch favors more rigor in the evaluation of programs, reflecting a common theme in some U.S. writings.[11] Some of the Quebec scholars will make an impact both in anglophone and francophone circles with projects like the careful evaluation of the Boscoville project which bases therapy on principles well known in Europe and in North America.[12] The assessment of the social costs of prisons by Landreville, Menghile, and Pepin[13] and the extensive work done by Marc LeBlanc and Louise Biron on juvenile delinquency[14] are illustrations of Quebeçois contributions to these particular topics.

Fourth, as with Canadian physics and Canadian medicine, criminology, although differing across Canada, reflects worldwide developments. The emergence of centers of teaching and research in Canada has been characterized by interaction with colleagues in other parts of the world. This consideration of Canadian criminological research will also reveal weaknesses shared elsewhere and thereby suggests cross-cultural comparisons. Objective self-criticism, no matter how dedicated it is to the long-term enrichment of the field, wins few friends, but such controversial issues are not limited by national boundaries. The discussion of deficiencies in the way Canadians do research might be instructive for readers seeking parallels to research problems in their own cultural settings.

Fifth, criminological research in Canada should be seen within the context of the larger research picture. The *Financial Times of Canada* tells us that only Canada among Western industrialized nations spends less than 1 percent of its gross national product on research and development.[15] Obviously, research and intellectual leadership are not spread evenly in all disciplines. Canada has shown leadership in nuclear power, various aspects of medicine, and petroleum engineering, but in criminological research has lagged behind the Scandinavian and other countries of comparable size and wealth.

Sixth, Canada has nevertheless demonstrated an innovative spirit in some aspects of criminology. For example, in 1967 the province of Alberta borrowed the ombudsman system from the Scandinavian countries and applied it to the criminal justice system and other areas of governmental activities. By 1979, provincial ombudsmen were established in all provinces except Prince Edward Island and the Northwest Territories. In 1973, a correctional investigator was established for the Canadian penitentiary service.

CENTERS OF TEACHING AND RESEARCH IN CANADA

It is appropriate that this survey of criminological centers, dedicated to teaching and research, should begin with the first to be established in Canada.

Ecole de Criminologie, Université de Montréal

The School of Criminology was established at the University of Montreal in 1960 by Denis Szabo who was its director for many years. Szabo attended the universities of Budapest, Louvain, and Paris. He obtained his doctorate in social and political science at the University of Louvain and a diploma at the Sorbonne. He is now the director of the International Center for Comparative Criminology at the University of Montreal.

The School of Criminology has approximately twenty professors and 350 students, and offers sixty courses in criminology. The director until 1979, André Normandeau, obtained his doctorate at the University of Pennsylvania under Marvin Wolfgang. The current director, Jean Trepanier, took his doctorate at the London School of Economics. The criminologists at Montreal participate fully in francophone criminology as well as anglophone developments and represent a broad spectrum of perspectives from radical to conservative. This range of perspectives has not led to polarization or antagonisms at Montreal. The School of Criminology has an interdisciplinary approach and an orientation toward applied criminology. The range of activities is probably greater than in any other center in Canada; a full academic program offers bachelor's, master's, and doctoral degrees and programs of an applied nature. A wide range of research has been part of the picture for years.

Members of the department have also been actively involved in public life. Guy Tardif, after doing his doctorate at the University of Montreal, became a professor in the School of Criminology and wrote a best selling book from his dissertation on police and politics in Quebec.[16] He then ran for the legislative assembly in Quebec under the Parti Quebeçois and, after winning his seat, became the minister of urban affairs under the premiership of René Levesque. André Normandeau has stood as a Parti Quebeçois candidate in two elections. Marie André Bertrand was active in the LeDain Commission (the Commission of Inquiry into the Nonmedical Use of Drugs) sponsored by the Ministry of National Health and Welfare, and Maurice Cusson was a member of the Batshaw Committee investigating juvenile institutions. Jean-Paul Brodeur and Jean-Pierre Lussier were active with the Keable Commission which had a mandate to look into questionable police activities. Related to the School of Criminology are other organizations offering additional breadth. The International Centre for Comparative Criminology brings criminologists from other parts of the world to work in Montreal, including some who are not part of the francophone sphere. The Groupe de Recherche sur l'Inadaption Juvenile (GRIJ) was founded in 1973 to study juvenile delinquency.

The University of Montreal has had a tendency to become somewhat "ingrown," partly because of limited sources of francophone scholars in North America. Thirteen of the twenty staff members have taken their doctorates at the University of Montreal. Anglophones have always been welcome, but only a few, such as Malcolm Spector of McGill University, have the necessary language skills.

Center of Criminology, University of Toronto

This center was first established at the Dalhousie University Law School and moved to Toronto in 1963 under the leadership of J. Ll. J. Edwards who came from a law background in England. Unlike the School of Criminology in Montreal, the Toronto center was initially a research organization with no teaching responsibilities, but there were cross-appointments with teaching departments. Although a legalistic orientation influenced part of the research, informal links with the Clark Institute of Psychiatry provided other perspectives, such as work on sexual offenders by J. J. Mohr, Alex Gigeroff, and R. E. Turner.[17] Perspectives other than the legal have been followed in the work of P. J. Giffen on criminal statistics,[18] Peter McNaughton-Smith on parole,[19] and Irvin Waller on parole.[20] John Hogarth's work on courts illustrates a blend of law and sociology.[21] The Toronto Center has made a particular effort to remain politically independent of funding sources.

The center moved into the teaching area, with students taking courses at Woodsworth College, and now offers an M.A. program in criminology. In addition, Ph.D. students in basic disciplines can be doctoral student fellows at the center. The organization of the teaching of criminology at the University of Toronto contrasts sharply with the teaching at the University of Montreal and Simon Fraser University. At the latter two, students concentrate on criminology, while at Toronto they have greater opportunities to maintain their ties with other basic disciplines. The criminology library facilities at Toronto are the best in Canada, at least for materials in English.

Center for Criminological Research, University of Alberta

The development of criminology at the University of Alberta has differed from that in Montreal and Toronto in that this center grew within the Department of Sociology. When Gwynn Nettler, author of the most widely used criminology text in Canada,[22] arrived at the University of Alberta in 1963, the criminology enrollment was already growing. His lectures were popular, and by the mid-

1970s approximately one thousand students were enrolled in five sections of introductory criminology and approximately one thousand other students were enrolled in deviance courses, advanced criminology, and graduate seminars. The program has remained highly academic, rather than applied, and largely restricted to the Sociology Department. Teaching and graduate training played a major role during the 1970s. By 1980, Nettler had probably supervised the largest number of doctoral dissertations of those teaching criminology in anglophone universities in Canada. While M.A.s and Ph.D.s in the sociology of deviance were frequent, the emphasis was on research rather than practice.

Interest in interdisciplinary study and in applied programs as alternatives led to the establishment of an M.A. program in corrections in 1975 in the Sociology Department, with courses drawn from other departments. An undergraduate degree in criminology continues to be discussed as a means of qualifying students for such jobs as probation officers.

The Center for Criminological Research at the University of Alberta was not established until 1977. The need for a research center was less pressing than elsewhere because research grants are administered rather easily through individual professors, and the availability of the Population Research Laboratory within the Department of Sociology provided the necessary facilities for most research needs.

Department of Criminology, University of Ottawa

The Department of Criminology at the University of Ottawa established a master's program in 1967 under the leadership of Tadeusz Grygier. This graduate program is unique in that it is not preceded by undergraduate teaching. Approximately twelve professors, plus part-time staff, offer an interdisciplinary program in both French and English. It is the closest to a truly bilingual program in criminology in Canada.

A master of arts in criminology stresses research, while a master's of correctional administration (M.C.A.) concentrates on practice. Both degrees include field work. The candidate for the M.A. degree prepares and presents a thesis, while the candidate for the M.C.A. degree obtains more practical training.

The Department of Criminology at Ottawa offers a truly multicultural faculty. With degrees from Cracow, Warsaw, and London, Grygier has competence in both psychology and law. Cleobis Jayewardene took his first degree in Sri Lanka, was a medical doctor, and then went to the University of Pennsylvania where he did an M.A. and Ph.D. in criminology. Some of the staff, such as Justin Ciale, Yvon Dandurand, Jacques LaPlante, and Ludwik Koś-Rabcewicz-Zubkowski, provide links with francophone Canada.

Department of Criminology, Simon Fraser University

With no criminology courses or professors in 1973, the Department of Criminology in the Faculty of Interdisciplinary Studies at Simon Fraser University grew to approximately twenty members by 1979 and now has one of the largest enrollments of any department at the university. This dramatic growth was instigated by financial support from the British Columbia government. The expansion at Simon Fraser includes library facilities, a new building, and a variety of research activities. An M.A. program is in place, and a Ph.D. program is being planned.

Ezzat Fattah came from the University of Montreal in 1974 to launch the new program. Simon Fraser recruited faculty on a worldwide basis. The Australian influence is reflected in Duncan Chappell who arrived in 1980. The current chair, Simon Verdun-Jones, has degrees from Cambridge and Yale. Four other criminologists at Simon Fraser did their graduate work under Gwynn Nettler at Alberta. Marvin Wolfgang, Cleo Jayewardene, and Leslie Wilkins have been visiting professors.

School of Human Justice and Prairie Justice Research Consortium, University of Regina

In 1977, the solicitor general of Canada provided a grant to initiate a human justice program at the University of Regina under the leadership of Otto Driedger. Matching funds came from the province of Saskatchewan. The activities at Regina might be viewed in three parts: (1) an undergraduate degree program leading to work in the criminal justice field, (2) contract research within Saskatchewan, and (3) shared communication within the prairie region. The first and second areas of activity are probably parallel to those of other centers and universities in Canada, but the Prairie Justice Research Consortium is attempting to develop a better communication network across the provinces of Alberta, Saskatchewan, and Manitoba. To achieve this goal, the consortium commissioned three state-of-the art reviews for a workshop in March 1979. The reviews were on the mentally disordered offender (Steve Wormith), policing (Stuart Johnson), and natives and justice (Melanie Lautt); the reviews were published and circulated to interested scholars.[23] The consortium has inventoried research completed or in process in the three prairie provinces, and an information service is available on request.

Other Centers in Canada

The programs mentioned above represent systematic efforts to stimulate criminological research or a traditional concern with this area. Other programs have developed at Carleton University in Ottawa, the University of Windsor, and the University of Manitoba. A police administration program was introduced at Saint Mary's University in Halifax, Nova Scotia.

CANADIAN CRIME STATISTICS

As in most countries of the world, crime statistics must be viewed as problematic. Criminal statistics are generated by several different organizations in Canada. The Royal Canadian Mounted Police (RCMP) gather most of the data because they police small towns and rural areas for eight of the ten provinces. Ontario and Quebec have their own provincial police forces, and most major cities and numerous small ones have separate municipal police forces.

Because each organization has its own data collection strategy, statistics for comparisons should be treated with caution. A small community of four thousand in central Alberta with an RCMP detachment generates crime statistics that differ considerably from those of a nearby community which has its own police department. Official statistics would give the impression that Manitoba has a very high rate of juvenile delinquency while the neighboring province of Saskatchewan has an extremely low rate, but the comparison is not valid. The age limit for juveniles is eighteen in Manitoba and sixteen in Saskatchewan. In addition, many juveniles are handled by the welfare system in Saskatchewan but by the court system in Manitoba. Thus, the data provide more insights into the differential operation of the juvenile justice system than information on the relative extent of delinquency.

Canada holds the potential for better criminal statistics. The census division of Statistics Canada is a very sophisticated data-gathering organization, and the experience and expertise are available for exploiting criminal statistics more efficiently. In addition, many Canadian city police forces are sophisticated users of the computer and process data in a manner that would lend itself to effective research use.

Some of the problems of Canadian crime statistics have been reviewed by Nicholas Zay[24] and by P. J. Giffen.[25] Here we limit our discussion to two reasons for the limitations of Canadian crime statistics. First, because Canadian social scientists do not use the official data extensively, errors and questions of interpretation remain concealed. Their hesitancy is derived from doubts that official data are a reliable tool for meaningful interpretations about human behavior. At the International Symposium on Selected Criminological Topics in Stockholm in 1978, Delbert Elliott expressed such reservations, but Carl Gunnar Jansson of the University of Stockholm pointed out that criminologists have used official data effectively in the Scandinavian countries in a number of ways. Although Canadian crime statistics probably do not match the Scandinavian in quality, usage would provide the feedback and discussion that lead to better statistics. In Canada, Lynn McDonald, [26] Lorne Tepperman,[27] and Ezzat Fattah[28] have attempted to use crime statistics to study trends.

Second, research directed toward the data-gathering process itself is just beginning. Victimization studies might provide a check on official studies, but these studies in Canada are limited.[29] Canada has not properly recognized that the many elements of criminal statistics—as Stanton Wheeler and others have noted[30]—tell us as much about the criminal justice system as about criminal behavior. For example, when major cities are compared according to official crime rates, the conclusions do not compare with general observations of their normative ambience.

According to the official 1977 crime statistics, both Montreal and Toronto had property crime rates of approximately 4,500 per 100,000 population. Regina, Saskatchewan, had a rate of 8,950; Gatineau, Quebec, a rate of 15,800; and Victoria, British Columbia, a rate of 10,900. For crimes of violence per 100,000, the rates in 1977 were Montreal 667, Toronto 605, Regina 705, Gatineau 1,214, and Victoria 1,029.[31] It is hard to imagine Victoria as a more violent city than Montreal and Toronto. Calgary and Edmonton are almost identical in size, population growth, age structure, and a variety of other characteristics that might be related to crime rates. Yet, Edmonton has historically higher crime rates than Calgary. A comparison of the two cities by Robert Silverman[32] did not resolve this mystery, but he learned that assault rates in Edmonton were inflated over those of Calgary because of certain reporting practices.

Other gaps in the system were illustrated by a study by Jilek and Roy on homicide in British Columbia.[33] They noted that native Indians in British Columbia die from homicidal violence ten times as frequently as the non-Indian population. When they turned to criminal statistics, they searched in vain for figures on homicidal and other offenses committed by Canadian Indians. Ethnic or racial categories are apparently not applied in the official recording of criminal data in Canada. Similarly, juvenile court data in many areas do not include any information on social class or ethnicity.

CRIMINOLOGICAL RESEARCH AND JUSTICE POLICY

Researchers disagree on whether their findings have an impact on public policy.[34] Experienced as both a Canadian civil servant and a scholar, Gordon Cassidy has examined the planning process in France, Britain, Canada, and the United States. He notes that the English Home Office has a planning unit that works directly with a crime policy planning committee of second-level bureaucrats.[35] In Canada, the Ministry of the Solicitor General has a research division, but its research and that sponsored by the unit have had little impact on policy so far.

Compared to France and England, Cassidy finds that the operations of the criminal justice system are more locally controlled in Canada. The percentage of contributions by the various levels of government for justice services in Canada in 1975-1976 were 26.2 percent at the federal level, 38.4 percent at the provincial, and 35.4 percent at the municipal. Municipal expenditures are chiefly for the police, with the exceptions of court expenditures in Nova Scotia, Quebec, and Saskatchewan, and corrections expenditures in Nova Scotia. In the United States control is even more decentralized. Compared to the other three countries,

Cassidy notes the United States has practically no relations between research activities and policymaking. The staff secretariat in Canada attempts to coordinate policy within the Ministry of the Solicitor General of Canada (the Canadian Correctional Service, which includes the former penitentiary service and the national parole board, and the Royal Canadian Mounted Police). It would be interesting to compare this situation with the attempts of the U.S. Department of Justice to coordinate the twenty-three agencies under its jurisdiction. The inability to have effective coordination on federal policy initiatives might lead to versatility or to chaos. A cross-cultural study might determine if closer links between policymaking and research endeavors lead to poorer quality research and to the entrenchment of certain patterns.

At the present time, the research division of the Ministry of the Solicitor General establishes "guidelines" in the centralized French model, but the more wide open, poorly integrated, but vigorous strategy in the United States might be more rewarding and might avoid value conflicts raised by government-directed criminological research. Should research have a direct impact on public policy, or should policy issues provide the major thrust to certain social research? The first half of this question leads to another question: can social policy be determined on scientific grounds? Most policy issues involving the criminal justice system appear to deal with moral issues rather than scientific ones. This point might be illustrated by the work done by Paul Whitehead on the relationship between automobile accidents and lowering the drinking age in Ontario.[36] Our society pays an extremely high price for alcohol consumption, but other values concerning individual freedom are also involved. Essentially, Whitehead tried to test two incompatible theories about alcoholism. The *sociocultural model* argues that the rate of alcoholism will be lower when a culture is characterized by prescriptions for moderate drinking and proscriptions against excessive drinking.[37] That is, learning how to use alcohol creates fewer problems than trying to keep people from drinking at all.

The second perspective, the *distribution of consumption model*, argues that there is a positive relationship between the overall level of consumption of alcoholic beverages and the incidence of alcohol-related problems. It is not how you drink but how much is consumed. Lowering the drinking age for young people would be compatible with the sociocultural model but not with the distribution of consumption model. Since alcohol would no longer be considered "forbidden fruit" to young people between the ages of eighteen and twenty, the sociocultural perspective would suggest that they would learn to use it more intelligently. Whitehead's study, sponsored by the Department of National Health and Welfare, did not support the sociocultural model but found instead that the lowered drinking age seemed to result in more consumption, which persisted even after the initial period, and in more accidents.

Few research projects are more directly linked to public policy decisions than Whitehead's work, but it is unrealistic to think that scientific research will, or should be, the guiding factor in public policy decisions. Canadian governmental officials, at both federal and provincial levels, are exerting increased efforts to "direct" criminological research and may be walking into this trap.

Law Reform Commission

Space does not permit the description of the activities of individual researchers at many other Canadian universities, but a review of criminology in Canada should definitely include the role played by Hans Mohr with the Law Reform Commission in Canada. Mohr is the only criminologist in Canada who holds joint appointments in sociology and law and is involved in this type of public role. In 1972, he took a leave of absence from York University to join the Law Reform Commission established by the Department of Justice. Canada and the United States tend to use judges and lawyers more than any other profession to staff commissions concerned with criminology. Mohr's contribution to the Law Reform Commission was that he argued for debate on crucial topics and resisted the pressure to draft legislation. This strategy was in contrast to the tendency of most Canadian commissions to collect public opinion and then spell out a long list of specific recommendations.

Ministry of the Solicitor General

Although a number of federal agencies have been involved in criminological research, usually it has been a contract with researchers outside of government. An illustration of in-house research done directly by the solicitor general's department is the study by Brian Murphy assessing the effect of a treatment program for opium addicts in British Columbia.[38] The work done by Parlett and Ayers on criminal personality in the penitentiary service in British Columbia illustrates the collaboration between federal employees and academics.[39] Until the recent development of the Research Division of the Ministry of the Solicitor General, research done directly by the federal government in criminology was relatively modest. While in-house research is becoming more common, the bulk of research activity sponsored by the solicitor general of Canada is still through contracts with other individuals and organizations.

The Research Division has made a significant contribution to criminology in Canada by producing comprehensive reviews on certain topics. For example, in 1977 the Research Division prepared the only annotated bibliography of Canadian criminology.[40] It also produced review essays on deterrence and the death penalty,[41] crime prevention through environmental design,[42] community-based preventive policing,[43] and bibliographies on policing[44] and the economics of crime.[45] In spite of their major information links with the United States, France, or England, Canadian criminologists have difficulty otherwise in learning what is happening in their own country. The Research Division has expedited this flow of information.

Research at the Provincial Level

Except for some activities in Ontario, British Columbia, and Quebec, there is little systematic research at the provincial level. The Ministry of Correctional Services in Ontario has contributed meaningful research on the use of volunteers,[46] assessing the classification system for the placement of wards in training schools[47] and examining the social milieu in a woman's institution,[48] but these activities have been very modest. In Quebec, some research is done by the Ministry of Social Affairs and the Ministry of Justice.

Ground work being done at various provincial and municipal levels should establish a useful base for future criminological research. For example, the Research and Planning Division of the solicitor general's department in Alberta has been cleaning up data that could be very useful for future research.[49] Ontario has also recognized the difficulties with national data and now produces annually Justice Statistics Ontario. Similarly, researchers have not taken sufficient advantage of data accumulated by the RCMP and various municipal police forces.

FUNDING CRIMINOLOGICAL RESEARCH

"Encouragement and support of research will in itself," Hans Mohr says, "be a measure of the extent to which a society is willing to look at itself critically and to understand its failings."[50] At this stage, Canada cannot claim leadership.

The 1969 Report of the Canadian Committee on Corrections (Ouimet Report) recommended that 2 percent of the total law enforcement, judicial, and correctional budgets be allocated to research. Hans Mohr notes that the Ouimet Report estimated that in 1966 Canada spent $18 million in operating its prisons.[51] In 1977-1978, the cost of the penitentiary service was approximately $227 million. Obviously, nothing like $4 million is invested in prison research in Canada, and as Mohr tells us, the cost of policing is many times higher than the cost of prisons, and relatively little money has been spent systematically on police research.[52]

Three Modes of Funding

Although policymaking should be a factor in financing research, short-run policy considerations risk stifling the creativity that stimulates inquiry into matters beyond the immediate concerns of policymakers. Three major types of research funding may be considered.

First, unrestricted and sustained criminological research funding is provided by the Social Sciences and Humanities Research Council and certain programs of the solicitor general's department. The object here would be to pursue promising lines of thought while having few misgivings about abandoning less promising directions when this becomes advantageous. Naturally, academic researchers prefer unfettered funding, but alteration of the direction of research does not jeopardize the accountability with which those in political office are understandably concerned.

Second, policy-oriented research funding would focus on specific areas of concern. Although more restricted than the first mode of financing, policy-oriented funding is more effective when the researcher has time and room for maneuvers to pursue unanticipated insights gained in the course of investigations.

Third, various governmental agencies would offer short-term contracts from time to time. This mode of financing lends itself to the exploration of immediate issues amenable to straightforward answers, but less to the examination of broad questions. Canada appears to be shifting in the direction of short-term contracts rather than toward sustained funding. (Notable exceptions are the program grants from the Social Sciences and Humanities Research Council to the University of Montreal and the University of Toronto and the foundation grants provided to five centers of criminological research by the solicitor general of Canada.) One might ask if the costs of administering research grew faster during the 1970s than the actual cost of doing research.

Social Sciences and Humanities Research Council

As a more specialized outgrowth of the early Canada Council, the Social Sciences and Humanities Research Council (SSHRC) is a federal agency that supports a wide variety of "pure" and "applied" research. As in most granting agencies, a number of factors will influence funding, but in Canada the SSHRC is the closest approximation of fellow experts in criminology deciding who shall get research support through peer review. Not being bound to a rigid contract, researchers are free to abandon unprofitable directions and shift to more promising aspects of their research program. This flexible policy tends to generate more and better quality research for the dollar spent than the research sponsored by most other governmental agencies. However, SSHRC funding may not always permit salaries or graduate student stipends that are competitive. Furthermore, unlike other governmental agencies, the SSHRC does not pay an honorarium to the principal investigator. These problems do not seem to exist with the five-year program grants, such as the $1 million sustaining grant provided to the Center of Criminology at the University of Toronto.

Commercialization of Criminological Research

During the latter part of the 1970s, there was an increased use of consulting firms and contract research, including work by academics. This trend has stimulated concern that less support will go to long-term research at universities and research centers. The expression of this concern should be interpreted within the context of the particular inclination in Canada to assume that a governmental commission or committee will provide incisive, reliable research. While commissions may serve an important political role, they may be a questionable method of generating genuine research. For example, in 1965 some policymakers were waiting for the Department of Justice to complete its report on juvenile delinquency before taking action.[53] Seventeen years later, it is clear that the impact of this report was negligible.

Some Canadian provinces turned to consulting firms for reports on social issues during the 1970s. Research reports prepared by consulting firms, especially at the provincial level, are sometimes read by only a few people. By contrast, research that leads to published articles exposes weaknesses, has the potential of generating different perspectives, and stimulates better work in the future.

Contract research may encourage researchers to adjust their strategies to financial considerations and simple conclusions to the detriment of contributions to knowledge and objective analyses which expose weaknesses in current policies. Meaningful breakthroughs cannot be predicted in advance, and contract research does not provide a sustained quest for answers to basic questions.

For obvious reasons, consulting firms doing research for profit favor projects that draw large funds and thereby overlook opportunities for inexpensive but useful studies. John Hagan's important study of the criminal justice system in Alberta cost approximately $8,000. A consulting firm could not afford to do so much work for so little money.

Funding by the Research Division, Ministry of the Solicitor General

Differences in opinion between academic criminologists and members of the Ministry of the Solicitor General are not based on differences in backgrounds. Both the director and second in command of the Research Division are respected scholars whose contributions are well received by the academic community. They illustrate the pattern of movement of personnel in both directions between academia and government; those in government are frequently fellow scholars from time to time. In fact, the director returned to academia in 1980. Those working for the Research Division frequently attend and participate in scholarly conferences and collaborate with scholars who do not work for government. In addition, critics of government policy are frequently working with the division at the same time.

In other words, to view the following criticisms in terms of some sort of animosity between individuals would be a gross misreading of this section. Rather, the basic argument is that the rigid imposition of "guidelines" from above and the use of rigid contracts has weakened the effectiveness of the research teams within the Research Division, lowered the productivity and quality of work of researchers in the field, and consumed excessive amounts of time for all concerned. Researchers within the division spend a major part of their time negotiating a working relationship between specialists in the field and those who are setting policy or controlling funds from above.

A study of juvenile diversion initiated in Kingston, Ontario, illustrates the unreasonableness of rigid guidelines established in advance. Gordon West and Mary Morton were supposed to "evaluate" the project, but their interviews soon indicated that the main impact of the project involved the nature of relationships among different agencies. Attempts to channel juveniles from one stream of processing to another led to potential conflict among and within these organizations. These "implications" could not have been clearly defined in advance.

In a sense, policies imposed on the Research Division from above ignore many of the realities of doing research. The Research Division itself is caught between demands for accountability from above and the conditions necessary to do quality research in the field. However, a movement toward systematic and sustained research was signaled in 1978 when the solicitor general committed $900,000 to support long-term research at centers for criminological research at Canadian universities. The Social Science and Humanities Research Council, like its predecessor, the Canada Council, traditionally channels a higher percentage of its funds directly into research.

Other Funding Agencies

Except for Ontario and Quebec and, to a lesser degree, British Columbia, most provinces provide very little direct support for criminological research as distinct from legal research. When provinces and municipal governments engage in criminological research, they are more inclined to use the short-term contract approach. However, there is a considerable degree of indirect support, as illustrated by the funding from the province of Saskatchewan for the Human Justice program at the University of Regina and the funding from the province of British Columbia for the Criminology Department at Simon Fraser University. In addition, the close working relationships between programs such as the criminology certificate program at Saint Mary's University in Halifax, Nova Scotia, and provincial agencies have facilitated research even when funds are minimal. Considerable research has been undertaken at most Canadian universities with internal funds and occasional small outside grants.

In Ontario, the Ministry of Correctional Services and the Ministry of Justice have funded research projects, frequently at the Center of Criminology at the University of Toronto, and have launched a number of in-house projects related to probation and institutional settings.[54]

Private foundations make some contributions to criminological research in Canada, but most of these funds are directed toward action programs. The Donner Foundation contributed to Hogarth's study of provincial judges in Ontario and Wilkins' work on legal aid,[55] and occasionally makes contributions to criminological research, primarily in Ontario. With the growing wealth in Alberta, private foundations are becoming more visible, but criminological research has not received funding priority. However, the provincial government has supported a number of programs for legally oriented research, such as that of the Institute of Law Research and Reform at the University of Alberta. Those who share the biases of social scientists would argue that in Alberta legal research has received support to a greater degree than research reflecting a behavioral science orientation.

Typically, opposition parties at the provincial level do not initiate criminological studies, but the official opposition in Alberta commissioned a study of violent crime in 1980.[56]

DISSEMINATION OF RESEARCH FINDINGS

Communication patterns in Canada are probably as strong outside the country as they are within. This is certainly true of communication from east to west. In the 1970s, the Canadian Association for Criminological Research attempted to expedite this sharing of information, but Canadian researchers still learn more about Canadian criminology at the American Society of Criminology meetings and other gatherings outside of Canada. In general, Canadians must maintain contacts with both U.S. and Canadian networks to keep up with the changes in the field. The University of Ottawa has been sponsoring workshops in applied criminology for several years which has improved the Canadian network.

This communication pattern also affects the reporting of Canadian research in Canadian journals. Much of the sophisticated work in Canada appears in prestigious American journals. Unfortunately, this tendency works against thorough coverage of Canadian criminological research in Canadian journals. There is also the possibility that Canada is trying to support too many journals for the amount of criminological research being done.

In anglophone Canada the *Canadian Journal of Criminology* has been the main journal for over twenty years. Until 1977, it went by the title *The Canadian Journal of Criminology and Corrections*. In 1973 a new journal, attempting a balance between French and English materials, was introduced at the University of Ottawa under the editorship of Yvon Dandurand. The initial title was *Criminologie-Criminology Made in Canada*. This title was later changed to *Crime et/and Justice*. (As the reader can see, developing titles of journals that are compatible with French and English provides a challenge in Canada.) In 1979, students at the Center for Criminology, University of Toronto, launched the *Canadian Criminology Forum* under the editorship of Ruth-Ellen Grimes. Articles on criminology also appear in the *Canadian Journal of Sociology* and the *Canadian Review of Sociology and Anthropology*. Naturally, criminology articles appear in numerous law journals across Canada, but *The Criminal Law Quarterly* is the journal most specialized in this area. There are also three criminological journals in Quebec.

In general, publishing presents a different set of problems in Canada than it does in the United States. Although the University of Toronto Press has published relatively expensive criminology books in small quantities, most of the commercial presses find that specialized books dealing primarily with the Canadian scene are marginal economic endeavors. However, McGraw-Hill Ryerson has published *The Disreputable Pleasure* by John Hagan and *Crime Control* by Lorne Tepperman. Methuen has also launched a number of semi-specialized books in the criminology area, including *Violence in Canada* by Mary Alice Byer Gammon, *The Prevention of Youthful Crime: The Great Stumble Forward* by James Hackler, and *An Introduction to Criminal Law* by Graham Parker. A number of collections of readings have been published in Canada, aimed at criminology courses, but with a relatively modest collection of articles and materials to draw from, it has been difficult to maintain quality. Butterworths has been a publisher of Canadian legal materials and is now moving into criminology with *New Directions in Sentencing* by Brian Grosman, *Effective Correctional Treatment* by Robert Ross and Paul Gendreau, *Criminal Justice in Canada* by Curt Griffiths, John Klein, and Simon Verdun-Jones, and *Crime in Canadian Society* by Robert Silverman and James Teevan.

It is highly likely that the dissemination of information on criminology will continue to be a somewhat *ad hoc* process in the near future. The very useful annotated bibliography prepared at the International Center for Comparative Criminology at the University of Montreal (one of the appropriate uses of a contract from the solicitor general of Canada) was completed in 1976. We hope that later editions of the bibliography will appear.

PROMISING DIRECTIONS FOR CRIMINOLOGY IN CANADA

Canada has clearly provided leadership in criminological research in the area of drug and alcohol addiction. The Addiction Research Foundation in Ontario has produced internationally significant studies under the authorship of Smart, LaForest, Whitehead, Giffen, Small, and several others.[57] The Health Protection Branch, Health and Welfare Canada, has also made meaningful research contributions in this area as illustrated in the work of Alex Richman and Irving Rootman.[58]

The ecological studies of Paul and Pat Brantingham show particular promise because of other skills and resources available in Canada.[59] The census division of Statistics Canada has expertise in records linking, where individual cases from one data set, such as police files, could be linked with another set, such as census data, and then reproduced as grouped data. Naturally, the concern for privacy will play an important role in such studies, but several scholars in Statistics Canada have been working on strategies to provide such protection. One illustration is the random-rounding of figures in tables to 0s or 5s.[60] In other words, this is an area where Canada could draw on skills that are already available.

Canada could profitably replicate studies done in the United States while at the same time introducing some cross-cultural elements. Victimization studies could offer interesting parallels and differences with the United States. Both the similarities and subtle differences between agencies of social control in Canada, the

United States, and England could make replications particularly valuable. Studies of the police, such as those cited by Shearing, Klein, Koenig, and their colleagues, have already moved in this direction. The receptivity for criminological research on the part of the RCMP and other police units in Canada may be greater than in some other countries. Other aspects of the criminal justice system, such as the courts, are just beginning to get the attention of social scientists. While legal research has focused on the formal aspects of the system, there has been relatively little empirical work attempting to analyze the informal systems. We know little about the subcultural patterns in Canadian prisons, although the work by Peter Letkeman[61] on the careers of criminals shows that Canadian prisons also function as "schools for crime." Is there a native Indian subculture that plays a similar role in Canadian prisons as do minority groups in American prisons? Some work has been done on economic development and deviance among native populations,[62] but Canada could make a useful contribution to cross-cultural comparisons.

General agreement on the state of Canadian criminology today is unlikely. The centers of teaching and research have grown in different ways across Canada depending on local conditions and the philosophy of various academic entrepreneurs. Usually, there are favored pipelines of communication from other countries like France, England, and the United States which influence the orientation of criminological research and government agencies. With the exception of a few areas, Canada's overall contribution in this area has thus far been modest. Funding has certainly been rather small; criticisms of the funding procedure may be justified, but one aspect of Canadian criminology must be viewed as a definite plus. Unlike some countries, the relationship among criminologists, as well as between academic and government officials, is frequently very cooperative in spite of differing methodological approaches and perspectives. Canadian criminologists are both heterogeneous and congenial.

NOTES

1. John Hagan, "The Social and Legal Construction of Criminal Justice," *Social Problems* 22, no. 5 (1975):620-637.

2. John Hogarth, *Sentencing as a Human Process* (Toronto: University of Toronto Press, 1971).

3. J. A. Byles and A. Maurice, "The Juvenile Services Project: An Experiment in Delinquency Control," *Canadian Journal of Criminology* 21 (April 1979):155-165.

4. Helen M. Annis, "Group Treatment of Incarcerated Offenders with Alcohol and Drug Problems: A Controlled Evaluation," *Canadian Journal of Criminology* 21 (January 1979):3-15.

5. Lorne Yeudall, "Neuropsychological Assessment of Forensic Disorders," *Canada's Mental Health* 25, no. 2 (1977):7-15.

6. Clifford D. Shearing and Jeffrey S. Leon, "Reconsidering the Police Role," *Canadian Journal of Criminology* 19 (October 1977):331-345.

7. Daniel Koenig, "Police Perceptions of Public Respect and Extra-Legal Use of Force," *Canadian Journal of Sociology* 1 (Fall 1975):313-324.

8. John F. Klein, Jim R. Webb, and J. E. DiSanto, "Experience with the Police and Attitude Towards the Police," *Canadian Journal of Sociology* 3, no. 4 (1978):441-456.

9. Paul Gendreau and Bob Ross, "Effective Correctional Treatment: Bibliography for Cynics," *Crime and Delinquency* 25 (October 1979):463-489.

10. James C. Hackler, *The Great Stumble Forward: The Prevention of Youthful Crime* (Toronto: Methuen, 1978); James C. Hackler, "The Dangers of Political Naivete and Excessive Complexity in Evaluating Delinquency Prevention Programs," *Evaluation and Program Planning* 1 (December 1978):273-283; James C. Hackler, "Invention to Error: The Dangers of Evaluation and Some Alternatives," *Canadian Journal of Criminology* 24 (January 1979):39-51.

11. Ronald Roesch, "Does Adult Diversion Work?" *Crime and Delinquency* 24 (January 1978):72-80.

12. Marc LeBlanc, "The Evaluation of Boscoville," presented at the meetings of the Canadian Association for Advancement of Research in Crime and Criminal Justice, Calgary, 1977.

13. P. Landreville, C. Menghile, and P. Pepin, "Description de la population de l'establissement de detention de Montréal" [Description of the Population of the Detention Facility of Montreal], funded by the Donner Foundation of the League of the Rights of Man of Quebec, 1974; P. Landreville, *La Prison de Montréal (Bordeaux) 1913-1940* (Montreal: Counseil des Arts, 1974); P. Landreville, V. Blankevoort, and A. Pires, "Les Cout Sociaux du Système Penal" [The Social Cost of the Penal System], *Crime et/and Justice*, 7-8, nos. 3 and 4 (1979-1980):180-189.

14. Louise Biron and Marc LeBlanc, "La Delinquance Cachée à Montréal" [Hidden Delinquency in Montreal], *Criminologie: Made in Canada* 3, no. 1 (1976):5-16: Marc LeBlanc, "Le Système de Justice pour mineurs au Quebec: Quelques données statistiques" [The System of Justice for Minors of Quebec: Some Statistical Data], *Criminologie: Made in Canada* 3, no. 1 (1976):47-66; Marc LeBlanc, Louise Biron, G. Cote, and L. Pronovost, "Le Delinquance Juvenile: son Developpement en Regard du Developpement Psychosocial durant l'Adolescence" [Juvenile Delinquency: Its Development in Regard to Psychosocial Development During Adolescence], *Annales de Vaucresson* 15 (1978).

15. *The Financial Times of Canada*, September 3, 1979.

16. G. Tardiff, *Police et Politique au Quebec* [Police and Politics in Quebec] (Montreal: L'Aurore, 1974).

17. J. J. Mohr, A. K. Gigeroff, and R. E. Turner, "Sex Offenders on Probation: An Overview," *Federal Probation* 33 (June 1969):22-26. Other articles on sex offenders appeared in the September and December 1978 and March 1969 issues.

18. P. J. Giffen, "Official Rates of Crime and Delinquency," in W. T. McGrath (ed.), *Crime and Its Treatment in Canada* (Toronto: Macmillan of Canada, 1976).

19. Peter McNaughton-Smith, *Permission to Be Slightly Free* (Ottawa: Law Reform Commission of Canada, 1976).

20. Irvin Waller, *Men Released from Prison* (Toronto: University of Toronto Press, 1974).

21. Hogarth, *Sentencing as a Human Process*.

22. Gwynn Nettler, *Explaining Crime*, 2nd ed. (New York: McGraw-Hill, 1978).

23. Dorothy Hepworth (ed.), *Explorations in Prairie Justice Research* (Regina: Canadian Plains Research Center, 1979).

24. Nicholas Zay, "Gaps in Available Statistics in Crime and Delinquency in Canada," *Canadian Journal of Economics and Political Science* 29 (February 1963):75-89.

25. Giffen, "Official Rates of Crime and Delinquency."

26. Lynn McDonald, "Crime and Punishment in Canada: A Statistical Test of the Conventional Wisdom," *Canadian Review of Sociology and Anthropology* 6, no. 4 (1969):212-236.

27. Lorne Tepperman, *Crime Control: The Urge Toward Authority* (Toronto: McGraw-Hill Ryerson, 1977).

28. Ezzat Fattah, *A Study of the Deterrent Effect of Capital Punishment with Special Reference to the Canadian Situation* (Ottawa: Information Canada, 1972).

29. M. C. Courtis, "Victimization in Toronto," in Robert Silverman and James Teevan (eds.), *Crime in Canadian Society* (Toronto: Butterworths, 1975).

30. Stanton Wheeler, "Criminal Statistics: A Reformulation of the Problem," *Journal of Criminal Law, Criminology and Police Science* 58, no. 3 (1967):317-324.

31. Statistics Canada, Justice Statistics Division, *Crime and Traffic Enforcement Statistics 1977* (Ottawa: Ministry of Industry, Trade, and Commerce, 1979).

32. Robert Silverman, *Criminal Statistics: A Comparison of Two Cities* (Edmonton: Solicitor General of Alberta, 1977).

33. Wolfgang Jilek and Chunilal Roy, "Homicide Committed by Canadian Indians and Non-Indians," *International Journal of Offender Therapy and Comparative Criminology* 20, no. 3 (1976): no pagination in reprint.

34. See Chapter 6, "Who Shall Lead Us?" in Hackler, *The Great Stumble Forward.*

35. R. Gordon Cassidy, "A Cross National Comparison of Criminal Justice Policy Processes," unpublished paper, School of Business, Queen's University [1978].

36. Paul Whitehead, *Alcohol and Young Drivers: Impact and Implications of Lowering the Drinking Age* (Ottawa: Department of National Health and Welfare, 1977).

37. Donald Larsen and Baha Abu-Laban, "Norm Qualities and Deviant Drinking Behavior," *Social Problems* 15 (Spring 1968):441-450.

38. Brian C. Murphy, "A Quantitative Test of the Effectiveness of an Experimental Treatment Program for Delinquent Opiate Addicts," *Research Centre Report #4*, Solicitor General of Canada, 1972.

39. T.A.A. Parlett and J. D. Ayers, "The Modification of Criminal Personality Through Massed Learning by Programmed Instruction," *Canadian Journal of Criminology and Corrections* 13 (April 1971):155-165.

40. Gertrude Rosenberg, Katia Mayer, and Lise Brunet-Aubry, *Canadian Criminology: Annotated Bibliography* (Montreal: Centre International de Criminologie Comparée, 1976).

41. Fattah, *Deterrent Effect of Capital Punishment.*

42. Paul R.A. Stanley, *Crime Prevention Through Environmental Design* (Ottawa: Solicitor General of Canada, 1976).

43. David K. Wasson, *Community-Based Preventive Policing* (Ottawa: Solicitor General of Canada, 1977).

44. Clifford Shearing, Jennifer Lynch, and Catherine Matthews, *Policing in Canada: A Bibliography* (Ottawa: Solicitor General of Canada, 1979).

45. Samir Rizkalla, Robert Bernier, and Rosette Gagnon, *Bibliographic Guide: The Economics of Crime and Planning of Resources in the Criminal Justice System* (Montreal: Centre International de Criminologie Comparée, 1978).

46. Susan Pirs, "Assessment of the Probation Volunteer Program in Metropolitan Toronto" (Ontario: Ministry of Correctional Services, 1975).

47. Leah R. Lambert and Andrew C. Birkenmayer, "An Assessment of the Classification System for Placement of Wards on Training Schools: II. Factors Related to Classification and Community Adjustment" (Ontario: Ministry of Correctional Services, 1972).

48. Leah R. Lambert and Patrick G. Madden, "The Vanier Centre for Women, Research Report no. 1: An Examination of the Social Milieu" (Ontario: Ministry of Correctional Services, 1974).

49. Donald Cook and Carolyn Daniel, *A Compendium of Criminal Justice Statistics: Alberta* (Edmonton: Solicitor General of Alberta, 1978).

50. Hans Mohr, "Research into Crime and Its Treatment in Canada," in McGrath, *Crime and Its Treatment in Canada*, p. 568.

51. Ibid.

52. Ibid.

53. Department of Justice, *Juvenile Delinquency in Canada* (Ottawa: Report of the Committee on Juvenile Delinquency, 1965).

54. John Gandy, Ruth Pitman, Margaret Strecker, and Candace Yip, "Parents' Perceptions of the Effect of Volunteer Probation Officers on Juvenile Probationers," *Canadian Journal of Criminology and Corrections* 17 (January 1975):5-19; Lambert and Madden, "The Vanier Centre."

55. James L. Wilkins, *Legal Aid in the Criminal Courts* (Toronto: University of Toronto Press, 1975).

56. Jim Hackler and Laurel Gauld, "Violent Crime in Alberta: Some Background Statistics" (Edmonton: Office of the Official Opposition, 1980); "Sentencing Strategies and Violent Crime" (Edmonton: Office of the Official Opposition, 1980); "Strategies for the Prevention of Violent Crime" (Edmonton: Office of the Official Opposition, 1980).

57. R. G. Smart, D. Fejer, and W. J. White, "Medical Use of Drugs: Trends in Drug Use Among Metropolitan Toronto High School Students," *Addictions* 20, no. 1 (1973):62-72; P. J. Giffen, *The Chronic Drunkenness Offender* (Toronto: Alcoholism and Drug Addiction Research Foundation, 1978); Shirley Small, "Canadian Narcotics Legislation, 1968-1973: A Conflict Model Interpretation," in W. K. Greenway and S. L. Brickey (eds.), *Law and Social Control in Canada* (Scarborough: Prentice-Hall of Ottawa, 1978); R. G. Smart, L. LaForest, and P. Whitehead, "The Epidemiology of Drug Use in Three Canadian Cities," *British Journal of Addictions* 66, no. 4 (1971):107-115; and much additional work coming from the Addiction Research Foundation of Ontario.

58. Alex Richman, "Follow-up of Criminal Narcotic Addicts," *Canadian Psychiatric Association Journal* 11, no. 2 (1966):107-115; Irving Rootman and Alex Richman, "Trends in Reported Illegal Narcotic Use in Canada: 1956-1973," *Bulletin on Narcotics* 27 (October-December 1975):27-40.

59. Patricia Brantingham and Paul Brantingham, "Notes on the Geometry of Crime." Paper presented at the International Symposium on Selected Criminological Topics, Stockholm, 1978.

60. M. S. Magundkar and Walter Saveland, "Random-rounding to Prevent Statistical Disclosures," *Canadian Statistical Review* (February 1973).

61. Peter Letkeman, *Crime as Work* (Englewood Cliffs, N.J.: Prentice-Hall, 1973).

62. Charles W. Hobart, "Economic Development, Liquor Consumption and Offender Rates in the Northwest Territories," *Canadian Journal of Criminology* 20 (July 1978):259-278.

BIBLIOGRAPHY

This annotated bibliography obviously leaves many gaps. Different types of work have been chosen to represent the range of Canadian work. Those works that are not particularly Canadian, but more international in focus, such as the writings of Gwynn Nettler, are also neglected. Works in English are favored over those in French, so the reader should note the rather complete bibliography by Rosenberg, et al. listed below.

Frechette, Marcel, and Marc LeBlanc. *La Delinquance Cachée a l'adolescence* [Hidden Delinquency During Adolescence]. Montreal: Groupe de Recherche sur l'Indaptation Juvenile, 1979.

The Research Group for Juvenile Deviance at the University of Montreal has been a major producer of research in juvenile delinquency, juvenile courts, and juvenile treatment programs in Quebec. This publication is one of many completed by that research team.

Gammon, Mary Alice Beyer. *Violence in Canada.* Toronto: Methuen, 1978.

This collection of readings emphasizes violent crime and other aspects of Canadian society that provide an underlying basis for violence.

Hackler, James C. *The Great Stumble Forward: The Prevention of Youthful Crime.* Toronto: Methuen, 1978.

This book is concerned with societal responses to delinquency. It argues that many governmental policies are not based on logical or scientific arguments and that the work of social scientists can also be misleading. After reviewing a range of programs that have been relatively unsuccessful in delinquency prevention, the author suggests a few strategies that would not lead to a great leap forward, but perhaps an occasional stumble forward.

Hagan, John. *Disreputable Pleasures.* Toronto: McGraw-Hill Ryerson, 1977.

Although this is a general text on deviant behavior and criminology in Canada, Hagan makes explicit attempts to compare crime in Canada with the United States.

Hogarth, John. *Sentencing as a Human Process.* Toronto: University of Toronto Press, 1971.

Although trained as a lawyer, Hogarth has actually done a sociological study of the dynamics of judicial processes in the lower courts in Ontario.

Klein, John, and Arthur Montague. *Check Forgers.* Lexington, Ky.: Lexington Books, 1977.

Based on interviews with convicted check passers, this study focuses on various stages in criminal careers. The perspective emphasizes parallels between these activities and those of "normal" people.

Letkeman, Peter. *Crime as Work.* Englewood Cliffs, N.J.: Prentice-Hall, 1973.

In this study of safecrackers and armed robbers, Letkeman views criminal activities as a career. He argues that serving time is part of the learning and socialization process. The pattern for penitentiary inmates in Vancouver seems to parallel findings in the United States.

Mann, Edward, and John Lee. *The R.C.M.P. vs. the People*. Don Mills, Ontario: General Publishing Co., 1979.

This is a rather direct attack on one of the most respected police forces in the world, the Royal Canadian Mounted Police. The authors argue that reforms are needed while acknowledging that the RCMP enjoys the support of most Canadians because of efficient, honest, and evenhanded law enforcement. The focus is on the Security Service which is Canada's major intelligence service with responsibility for national security. Using the proceedings from three investigative commissions (MacDonald, MacKenzie, and Keable), they describe how "dirty tricks" become part of "doing the job."

Parker, Graham. *An Introduction to Criminal Law*. Toronto: Methuen, 1977.

This general overview of Canadian criminal law is primarily for the nonlawyer. It describes philosophical, historical, and technical influences on Canadian criminal law and uses cases to illustrate some of the points under discussion.

Prus, Robert, and Styllianoss Irini. *Hookers, Rounders, and Desk Clerks*. Toronto: Gage, 1980.

This participant observer study is of hookers, strippers, bartenders, cocktail waitresses, bouncers, desk clerks, bar patrons, and rounders—those who form the "hotel community" and a subculture that is rarely recognized as developing unique interactional patterns.

Rosenberg, Gertrude, Katia Luce Mayer, and Lise Brunet-Aubrey. *Canadian Criminology: Annotated Bibliography*. Montreal: International Center for Comparative Criminology, [1976].

This is the most complete bibliography available on Canadian criminology. Some of the materials are annotated. Since this chapter does not concentrate on specific research and neglects francophone work, this bibliography would be the logical starting point for anyone attempting to become familiar with a specific area of research in Canada.

Vincent, Claude L. *Policeman*. Toronto: Gage, 1979.

Vincent describes the world of the policeman in Windsor, Ontario, in the early 1970s. Done originally as an M.A. thesis, this participant observation study focuses on the way the police are socialized into their occupation.

Waller, Irvin. *Men Released from Prison*. Toronto: University of Toronto Press, 1974.

This study of 423 men released from Canadian prisons concentrates on their reintegration into society. The focus is on the interrelationships among their previous histories, prison experience, the dynamics of compulsory or voluntary supervision, and a variety of post-release problems. Interviews were made at the time of release and periodically up to twenty-four months. The study questions some assumptions about after-care programs.

11

CHILE

Marco A. González-Berendique

In Chile, criminology is understood to be a science that studies crime in its factual dimensions and establishes a basis for a reasonable degree of control of criminality through measures of prevention and treatment. The development of this conception of criminology has been grounded in historical circumstances. The first criminological studies were aimed toward social, penal, and correctional reforms. The first field investigations were based on the clinical orientation. Therefore, Chile's criminology includes both etiological and penological investigations, "fundamental" research and evaluations of measures or programs, "pure" teaching in the universities, and "problem-oriented" teaching in the spheres of the police, penal justice, and corrections.

CRIMINOLOGY: THE CONCEPT AND ITS PROFILE

At the turn of the century, Chile—intimately related to Latin Europe and scarcely linked to the Anglo-Saxon world—received the sonorous messages of Lombroso, Ferri, and Garofalo with great interest. In examining the development of Chile's criminology, attention might be drawn to the internal ideological contradictions of the Italian school, to the slightly pragmatic Chilean way of thinking, and to the country's insufficient instruments for empirical exploration (departments of sociology appeared only in the late 1950s). The consequence was a rationalistic and discursive positivism that substituted outdated references and statistics for the experimental method.[1] In those years some studies stemmed from the field of law; they asked for the study of causes of crimes, emphasized crime prevention, and criticized the social structure and penal system. As these claims were insufficiently grounded in national factual data, the reform proposal was barely fertile.[2]

Translated by Susan Hunt, Department of Foreign Languages and Literatures, Southern Illinois University at Carbondale.

The crime problem also aroused the interest of some physicians, mainly psychiatrists, who, after 1900, began to study the individual delinquent. The excessive emphasis they could have applied to genetic and biological aspects was neutralized to some extent by the unavoidable consideration of the socioeconomic handicaps of some criminals, by the study of the relationship between crime and certain national problems such as alcoholism, and by the greater influence of Ferri's biosocial determinism than Lombroso's "anthropologism." Thus, the first attempt of clinical criminology in 1919 combined several elements of law, anthropology, experimental psychology, and sociology. In the same line, the Institute of Criminology—Prison Service, founded in 1936—has had social workers since its inception; in 1946, Teeters praised this feature as exceptional.[3] The institute progressively withdrew from biological criminology and moved toward a more psychosocial perspective, favored by the creation of the first departments of psychology in the 1940s.

The first Latin American school of social work was founded in Chile in 1925, supplying the sociological perspective which was not to be emphasized by departments of sociology until the 1950s. The delayed arrival of the latter schools, their diffusive attention to many social problems, and their only relative interest in criminology made difficult both the access to social theory and the development of sound research. In regard to law, only the chairs of legal medicine (which appeared in 1906) approximated to a certain degree the normative and factual sciences. Criminology would not be taught until 1957. Only in 1966 did a broad university reform and adoption of the principle of "law in action" inspire the jurists to the scientific study of reality, with partial subordination of the logical-abstract method.

Thus, criminology has emerged separately in the diverse disciplines involved, in very different periods, and with very wide-ranging characteristics, limitations, and importance. In recent years, qualitative and quantitative changes of the crime problem have stimulated a technical strengthening of law enforcement, the courts, and corrections, and have expanded the range and significance of research. New chairs of criminology have been established in the universities and the professional academies (devoted to police and corrections), with lawyers, psychologists, and sociologists as professors and a broadened demand for academic or professional activities.

In spite of these developments, no decision has been made as to whether to establish a specialized degree in criminology as an autonomous field of theoretical knowledge. That degree could undoubtedly contribute to a "diverse" professional career. Chilean criminologists—lawyers, psychologists, sociologists, plus some physicians and social workers—thus continue to be qualified in the field and continue to be "kings without a kingdom" as Sellin has described them. Those circumstances suggest that certain professionals contribute their particular perspectives and intellectual tools, but the absence of a typically criminological viewpoint implies segmentation rather than intellectual integration in academia, research, and practice. Yet, the greater availability of criminological literature and a fuller dialogue imply genuine progress when compared with the status of Chile's criminology at the beginning of the twentieth century.

PARAMETERS OF CHILEAN SOCIETY

In a number of respects, Chile is unique among Latin American nations. The country is remarkably homogeneous ethnically because of facile interbreeding of natives and Hispanic conquistadors and the easy absorption of immigrants, mainly Europeans, in the last half of the nineteenth century and the early part of the twentieth. Today there are no more than 250,000 "pure" Indians in a population of approximately 11 million. A long period of political independence (the Republic was founded in 1810) and far-sighted leadership in the nineteenth century have produced a strong institutional maturity represented in general terms by democratic traditions, free exchange of ideas, distinct separation of the branches of government, sound administration, and an effective educational system.

By Latin American standards, the socioeconomic indicators in Chile are favorable. Among the employed population, 13.5 percent have ten to twelve years of formal education, the highest percentage in Latin America.[4] According to the 1970 census, only 11.6 percent of the inhabitants are illiterate. There are high enrollments in primary and secondary schools and in institutions of higher learning.

Chile's population grew from 8,884,768 inhabitants in 1970 to 10,917,465 on June 30, 1979, according to population estimates.[5] The annual growth rate has declined from 2.20 percent in the 1952-1960 period to 1.71 percent for the 1970-1979 period.[6] In regard to risk of criminalization or victimization, it has to be noted that Chile has a large number of youngsters, but the population is aging demographically. As Tacla points out for 1970, "Chile with 39 percent of the population under fifteen years and 5 percent over sixty-five years, can be considered a country with a structure in transition. Therefore, the age structure will alter significantly in the next approximately fifteen years."[7] Her prediction was confirmed by the population estimate: by June 1979 that share of the population had been reduced to 33 percent.

Until 1940, the population was predominantly rural; since 1952, however, urbanites have been most numerous, representing 75.1 percent of the total population in 1970.[8] The metropolitan region, including the capital of Santiago, held 38.2 percent of the total population in 1979.[9] In comparison with the country's three large cities in 1952, Chile had seven cities with more than 100,000 inhabitants in 1970.

Using fourteen socioeconomic indicators, a 1969 UNICEF report ranked Chile among the first group of Latin American countries, following only Argentina and Uruguay.[10] Recent progress has been recorded in Chile in this regard. The illiteracy rate fell from 16.4 percent in 1966 to 11.9 percent in 1970.[11] Life expectancy was fifty-nine years in 1960-1965, 60.5 years in 1965-1970, 62.6 years in 1970-1975,[12] and 65.6 years in 1975-1980.[13] Infant mortality was 101.9 per 1,000 live births in 1960-1965 and 52.1 in 1977.[14]

Chile is frequently credited with ample but undeveloped natural resources and is considered to be undergoing socioeconomic development. It was the first of the Latin American countries (1939) to create a planning organization, the Corporation for the Promotion of Production (CORFO), which recognized social variables and the reform of the social structure as elements in its strategy for economic growth in the 1960s. In spite of ideological differences, the last two governmental regimes since 1972 have emphasized socially oriented politics and a unified focus of development.

The liberal technocracy of President Jorge Alessandri (1958-1964) produced a ten-year development plan and began agricultural reform. The Christian-Democrat regime of President Eduardo Frei (1964-1970) created the Office of National Planning of the Presidency of the Republic (ODEPLAN), emphasizing state intervention in the development process, social variables, and intensified agricultural reform. President Salvador Allende (1970-1973) took a socialist perspective toward extreme state intervention in noting economic stagnation, external dependence, and inequitable income distribution. The present administration is taking an absolutely opposing stance, underlining only subsidiary state intervention and the advantages of free market economy.

Prolonged application of the last-named policy has reduced public spending, denationalized corporations, ended price controls, and removed most restrictions of custom duties. As a result, by 1979, exports were diversified to reduce the heavy dependence on copper, inflation was controlled and reduced, and the gross internal product increased very significantly. Inflation was 508.1 percent in 1973,[15] 375.9 percent in 1974, 340.7 percent in 1975, 174.3 percent in 1976, 63.5 percent in 1977, and 30.3 percent in 1978.[16] The GPI (Gross Personal Income) had an annual growth rate of minus 0.6 in 1975, 4.5 in 1976, 8.6 in 1977, and 5.0 in 1978. The per capita GPI had the following percentage changes: minus 2.2 in 1975, 2.8 in 1976, 6.8 in 1977, and 3.0 in 1978.[17]

In spite of socioeconomic progress, the endemic problem of Latin America, extreme poverty, persists in Chile, although it is the target of the Planning Office, which has adopted the goals of the ILPES (Latin American Institute for Economic and Social Planning).[18] The 1974 "map of extreme poverty," based on the 1970 census, places 22 percent of the population in this category.[19] In a 1978 study, Oscar Altimir found 20 percent of the households below the poverty line ($180 USA) and 6 percent below the "destitution line" ($90 USA). Chile, however, is inferior only to Argentina among Latin American nations in reducing the dimensions of economic deprivation. Unemployment in Greater Santiago for August-October 1978 was 17 percent, in 1978 14.4 percent, and in 1979 13.2 percent for the same months.[20] In the last figure, it should be noted, 2.6 percent represented persons looking for their first jobs.

INSTITUTIONS OF THE CRIMINAL JUSTICE SYSTEM

The republican, democratic, and representative system of government has persisted in Chile except for brief periods. Before 1973 in this century, except for the period 1920-1932, ardent social movements favored de facto regimes.

In spite of political freedom and the controlling authority of the House of Representatives, the Parliament has demonstrated little scientific and pragmatic concern about the crime problem. In this respect, only a few parliamentary debates and the enactment of only some penal legislation should be mentioned. The classical Penal Code of 1874 still stands with only superficial modifications. The 1906 Penal Procedural Code did not accept the jury system, prescribed that judges had to be lawyers, established written procedure, and combined two functions—investigation and sentencing—under one judge to save expenses. A 1954 law, defining certain minor antisocial acts (vagrancy, beggary, and so on) in a positivistic style, has not been enforced. Various liquor laws have been enacted, the last one in 1969. Suspended sentences ("sursis") were authorized by a 1944 law. Two laws in 1969 and 1973 dealt with drugs. Generally, the philosophy of retribution predominates in all this legislation.

The executive branch of the government, especially the Department of Justice, has been somewhat uneasy about the crime problem but not intensively or persistently. Economic criteria, conservatism, and debatable priorities have closed the way to wide innovation. In regard to the protection of minors since 1928, when a special law was enacted, only one genuine change was accomplished in 1961: an interdepartmental commission was created in that year to coordinate the sectoral programs. The commission later assumed executive functions. In regard to crime prevention and treatment of offenders, the government has not framed a sound criminal policy and has not designed an overall organizational scheme. The programs have been merely sectoral, have lacked sufficient resources, and have not been based on scientific principles. The criminogenic side-effects of the development process have been overlooked. Although proposed several times, an interdepartmental council of social defense has not been implemented with a capacity to elaborate policies and to coordinate plans and programs.

Although frequently announced, correctional reform has not been undertaken seriously. Since the end of the nineteenth century, when the Balmaceda administration constructed numerous penal facilities, the reforms have consisted mainly of slow but persistent renovation of the most antiquated jails. Nevertheless, some partial institutional advances deserve mention. In 1963, Sunday furloughs were authorized for long-term sentenced inmates under their word of honor. Since 1964, daily work-furloughs have facilitated the reintegration of prisoners within the free world. An open urban prison was established in 1969, and various open prison camps started in 1973. Widespread use of the special pardon—which in several cities in addition to Santiago is based on clinical-criminological investigations—has mitigated the harshness of the 1874 Penal Code. To the same effect, parole was introduced by a 1925 decree-law.

The judges, all of whom are lawyers, enjoy tenured careers. Through the principle of *ratio legis*, the higher courts have harmonized legal precepts with new social conditions. Psychiatric reports have been used intensively for many years, expediting the employment of neo-classical hermeneuticism and substituting the concept of free will for psychic normality. Sometimes the concept of psychopathic personality has been used in the positivistic sense to aggravate public fears of "the criminal." Since approximately 1940, clinical-criminological "dossiers" have allowed courts to consider the social and personality traits of offenders in serious cases and in a certain amount ("dosage"). For years, lawyers aspiring to become juvenile judges have received special training, and an advanced course has been given for criminal court judges. In 1979, the University of Chile created the School for Judges awarding a master's degree in judicial law. The Medical-Legal Service created in 1930 and other special organizations advise judges in certain technical aspects.

There are two branches of police: a preventive uniformed branch and an investigatory civil branch. They are well organized, in accord with the continental system. The officers of the uniformed branch are required to have twelve years of previous instruction and two years of training. The subofficers are required to have six years of previous instruction and one year of training. The investigatory branch is manned by officers only. Both branches provide a sound technical base for personnel through special training schools for applicants and academies for higher officers. The first chairs of criminology were created in these institutions in 1942 and 1948, respectively. In recent years, the increase of crime has exceeded police resources, and thousands of arrest warrants probably go without official action.

The Prison Service, today known as the Gendarmeria de Chile, was established in 1931 when it was separated from the police force. Since then, improved organization and greater resources have been provided. An institute of criminology was created in 1936 at the penitentiary in Santiago, with subsidiaries added at some of the other major penal facilities. Since 1953, all custodial, treatment, and administrative personnel, except for professionals and technicians, have been trained in a technical school.

Within the Prison Service, the recently created Division of Treatment in the Community supervises "sursis" (suspended sentences) and parole, and will be in charge of certain alternatives to imprisonment (community service orders, weekend and nightly imprisonment, and probation) expected to be introduced in 1981.

The personnel and material resources of the Prison Service are insufficient. More than one hundred penal facilities widely distributed around the country contain more than fifteen thousand inmates under conditions of serious overcrowding and promiscuity. Personnel shortages, especially of technically trained persons, make "treatment" more a hope than a reality. The same can be said for the after-care under "sursis" and parole.

The preceding review presents a paradox. On one hand, Chile has achieved institutional and administrative maturity and favorable cultural and educational levels. On the other hand, the country has an archaic penal code emphasizing retribution and imprisonment, a faulty criminal justice system with delayed decisions, an impossible work burden for well-trained personnel in penal justice and law enforcement, a sharply restricted treatment program, high levels of recidivism, and scant official interest in the scientific analysis of the crime problem. Seeing these patterns, Teeters said in 1946: "When one views the signal progress made

crime for Chile—were means of gaining resources "to promote the revolution." From 1969 until September 1973, political groups drawn from either the extreme left or the extreme right tried either to increase the pace of change or to reduce it through bombings, and some homicides and attempted kidnappings. In August 1973 alone, more than two hundred terrorist attacks were recorded.

The estimated population in 1975 was 10,196,423, and the courts received 180,591 new cases, a rate of 1,177 per 100,000 population. The percentage distribution of cases included larceny 16 percent, robbery and burglary together 10 percent, worthless checks 7 percent, rape and other sex crimes 1 percent, and homicide 0.32 percent. Larceny, robbery, and burglary were the leading reasons for arrest, but drug offenses gained in importance. The Allende administration strengthened legal weapons to deal with drug trafficking. The present government has used those weapons intensively, while improving legislation against economic crimes. The decline in the number of robberies may be attributed especially to the higher level of public order attained in the first two years of the present administration, clearly in contrast to the permissiveness previously existing. Another important development in 1975 was the significant number of traffic offenses. The number of prison inmates at the end of the year declined to 13,575, or a rate of 133 per 100,000 inhabitants.

In 1978, the population reached 10,917,465 persons, double the number in 1940, and the courts received 221,019 cases, or a rate of 2,024 per 100,000 population. The charges included larceny 14 percent, robbery and burglary together 10 percent, checks without sufficient funds 9 percent, bodily injuries 6 percent, fraud 4 percent, rape 0.85 percent, and homicide 0.30 percent. The leading reasons for arrests were robbery and burglary together 20 percent, bodily injuries 17 percent, larceny 14 percent, and drug-law violations 7 percent. There were 12,331 persons in jail at the end of the year, or a rate of 112 per 100,000 population.[24]

In 1979, political and economic factors provoked a greater number of audacious and violent raids by gangs on banks and large merchantile establishments. This type of robbery offered easy access to money. In the case of burglaries or larcenies, access to loot was favored by a plentiful market of goods because of governmental policies encouraging imports and credit lines.

The preceding analysis is only a general review because official criminal statistics, regardless of their relative quality, cannot show the qualitative aspects of crime and capture the "dark figure." Moreover, white-collar offenses are underrepresented. In addition, in the necessarily brief space available here, a complete and searching analysis of demographic and socioeconomic indicators is not possible.

Changes in the number of new criminal cases since 1939 have been related to increases in Chile's total population. In the 1939-1979 period, some types of offenses became more important. Larceny consistently dominated the crime picture. Crimes against persons were of minor statistical significance, especially homicide and bodily injuries. Embezzlement became progressively more noteworthy, especially when worthless checks are counted in these law violations. Sex crimes were of little importance. More recent years have witnessed the appearance of economic crimes, drug-law violations, some terrorist attacks, and increased traffic offenses. Common criminality showed no perceptible organization or sophistication.

Alcohol is related to Chilean criminality and delinquency. Some forms of misdemeanant violation of liquor laws hold a major share of arrests. In 1940, 42 percent of all arrests were for drunkenness, a figure that decreased to 32 percent in 1978. Illegal sale of liquor and drunken driving were also proportionally important. Two research projects conducted in 1963 pointed to the presence of alcohol in common crimes and misdemeanors.[25] An investigation of homicides in Greater Santiago for a three-year period found that 43 percent of all murderers and 64 percent of all victims were under the influence of alcohol at the time of the crime, 26 percent of murders were committed in a bar or nearby, and trivial motives were involved in 32 percent of cases.[26]

An analysis of police investigations conducted in 1974-1978 in metropolitan Santiago[27] shows that men accounted for 84 percent of all offenders, fifteen to twenty-eight year olds predominated, and only 20 percent of those apprehended had previous criminal records. The large proportion of first offenders is remarkable when one considers that 59 percent of contemporary convicted inmates are recidivists.[28] Most persons arrested were unemployed, a pattern reported by other researchers as well. For example, in 1971, a sample of 512 inmates in the Santiago Penitentiary demonstrated marks of socioeconomic handicaps, such as illiteracy (18 percent), no skills (43 percent), and economic disadvantage (54 percent). Nevertheless, proneness to crime is not exclusive to the underprivileged. Other social strata are certainly underrepresented in criminal statistics.

CRIMINOLOGY AND PROFESSIONAL ACTIVITIES

In spite of Chile's obvious economic and sociocultural progress in the last forty years, criminology is more an academic than a professional activity, has not gained an increased number of followers, has not developed as a clearcut occupational sphere, and has not obtained independent research resources. As already stated, criminology in Chile has not emerged as an autonomous branch of learning. Criminologists are primarily jurists, psychologists, and sociologists who became qualified through occupational experience without being exposed to criminology as a special discipline. Some professionals have studied criminology abroad and perform as judges or have become specialists in fields not associated with the problem of crime. These circumstances certainly are hampering any attempt to deal with the great increases in criminality and delinquency through scientific principles.

The development of criminology has been impeded first because the multiplicity of socioeconomic problems in Chile has caused human and material resources to be diverted to problems other than crime, and second because the typical perspective taken in studies of criminal phenomena has been more intellectual than social and more academic than pragmatic.

Criminologists have little access to contemporary foreign bibliography, restricted professional opportunities, and persistent research difficulties. In contrast, specialists in penal law have enjoyed easy access to up-to-date references and intellectual and professional rewards. Criminological publications are meager in comparison with the many penal law texts widely disseminated in Latin America. Academic meetings are diverted from criminological issues toward logical-juridical analysis. In contrast with timid attempts to develop theoretical criminology, penal law professors propose and conduct the design of a model criminal code for all Latin America.[29]

This tendency appears to be common in Latin America and for the international congresses on criminology,[30] where little empirical research is reported. Debates tend to follow old biological models or merely criticize social structures. Their conclusions are based on faulty data, impressionistic opinions, or foreign experiences or research that are not necessarily relevant to Latin American situations. These shortcomings are of primary practical importance because dogmatic points of view dominate programs, and ongoing action projects seldom allow for evaluation.

Under these circumstances, the criminologist is not easily identifiable as a specialist, and parallel disciplines are frequently favored in the search for a more productive dialogue. In this vein, conferences on criminological subjects have been held by the Institute of Penal Sciences since 1949. In the same all-embracing approach, the Society of Criminalistics, Legal Medicine and Criminology was created in 1956. The First National Conference on Criminology and Social Psychiatry in 1974 focused on the theme "Social Defense Planning and Deviant Behavior." The conference participants recommended the foundation of an academic entity that would be devoted not only to criminology but also to social psychiatry and criminalistics.

INTERACTION RELEVANT TO CRIMINOLOGY

Chilean criminologists regularly interact with one another in congresses, conferences, seminars, and symposia. They also engage in the activities of various scientific societies and in permanent or transitory work teams.

Particularly active has been the Institute of Penal Sciences which was created in 1937.[31] It assembles professionals from various disciplines—jurists, psychologists, sociologists, and physicians—interested in crime. The essential orientation is that of law, but the institute has actively promoted penal sciences from a broad point of view. The national conferences organized by the institute have sometimes centered on criminological subjects: the penal process, antisocial personalities, and abandoned, abnormal, and delinquent minors (1949); public health crimes, institutional treatment, and mass media and crime (1954); juvenile delinquency (1960); economic crimes (1962); and medical responsibility (1979). Together with the University of Chile, the institute organized the Second Latin American Congress on Criminology in 1941 and an international colloquium in 1973 on penalties and deviant behavior.

The University of Chile has sponsored several seminars, including the International Seminar on Juvenile Probation (1976) and the Seminar on Criminal Behavior (1979). A number of agencies—the Ministry of Justice, the Medical-Legal Service, the Mental Hospital, and the police—participated in the First National Conference on Criminology and Social Psychiatry (1976) which focused on "Social Defense Planning and Deviant Behavior." A number of significant and up-to-date recommendations formulated then are consistent with the conclusions of the 1975 United Nations Congress on Prevention of Crime.[32] A noteworthy product of this conference was the establishment in 1979 of the Chilean Society of Criminology, Social Psychiatry, and Criminalistics.

Among the working sessions organized by scientific societies, special mention should be given to the lectures, workshops, and other academic activities sponsored by the Institute of Penal Sciences on topics such as "New Trends in Corrections," "The Work Furlough Program: A Penological Experience," and "Criminal Statistics." Also worthy of note are the contributions of the old Society of Criminalistics, Legal Medicine and Criminology that was replaced in 1979 by the Chilean Society of Criminology, Social Psychiatry and Criminalistics.[33] In spite of its recent creation, the Chilean Society of Criminology has performed numerous services through panels, lectures, and working sessions on topics such as the following: "Victimology: An Interdisciplinary Approach," "Victims as Faced by the Police, the Courts and the Experts," "The Prison Crisis," "Criminology in Latin America," "Behaviorism and Punishment: The Santiago Penitentiary Project," "The Subculture of Violence," "Child Abuse and Neglect," "Rape: A Comprehensive Analysis," "Female Criminality," and "Spouse Abuse."

The term "work team" used above refers, first, to those organizations created specifically and permanently to deal with criminological matters and, second, to the *ad hoc* groups organized to manage a particular action program or a scholarly investigation. Several permanent "work teams" should be mentioned:

1. The Institute of Criminology of the Prison Service was created in the Santiago Penitentiary in 1936, after several experiences in criminological case study undertaken since 1919. Today the institute has subsidiary centers in major penal facilities, such as those at Temuco and Valparaiso. Although originally conceived to manage classification and criminological case studies, the institute has promoted diverse penological reforms, such as Sunday furloughs, daily work-furloughs, an open urban prison, and open prison camps.

2. The Section of Criminology and Criminal Psychology, afterwards named the Institute of Social Pathology, had been attached to the School of Philosophy and Education, University of Chile, and was active from 1943

to 1969. Through a predominantly functionalist perspective, the institute applied several "medium-range theories," such as anomie, to deviant behavior and also tried to measure the magnitude of crime. Its contributions included two criminological annals and one research report on crime and alcohol relationships.

3. The Center for Research in Criminology at the School of Law, University of Chile, was created in 1959. In a first stage, under the influence of Kurt Lewin, Ralph Linton, and interactionism, the center explored the psychosocial characteristics of habitual offenders and urged the development of criminal typologies appropriate to Chile. After 1970, it became engulfed in deep epistemological troubles and was attracted to radical criminology. This orientation could be perceived in an unorthodox rehabilitation program for inmates recommended to the Allende administration. Reduced resources and a more pragmatic approach since 1974 have turned the center to a problem orientation that includes exploration of serious offenses and evalution of the efficacy of penalties.
4. Between 1968 and 1973, the Section of Criminology within the civil police administration explored the psychological traits of offenders and mounted a program that contributed significantly to the positive reintegration of medium-risk releasees.
5. The Social Defense Division, within the Ministry of Justice since 1975, does research and proposes projects in crime prevention and the treatment of offenders. Its work was basic in framing a drug law bill, a project for computerizing crime statistics, and a bill introducing community service orders, probation, and discontinuous imprisonment as alternatives to prison.

Among transitory work groups are those that guide university theses or research projects and those organized to examine a particular criminological issue. In the University of Concepción, a group evaluated the efficacy of suspended sentences.[34] In the Prison Service, a special committee examined the future implementation of the bill for alternatives to prison, which is expected to be enacted.

FORMAL EDUCATION AND CRIMINOLOGY

As mentioned earlier, criminology has not attained the status of an autonomous branch of learning, and those who have criminological occupations or conduct university research are basically jurists, psychologists, sociologists, physicians, or social workers. Only some have had the chance to obtain a limited formal education in criminology because the subject is being handled only in some university departments.

In the Law School, University of Chile, legal medicine was introduced into the curriculum in 1906 and criminology only in 1957. In departments of sociology in the universities, courses in social disorganization appeared first and courses in social deviance came later. In the Department of Psychology, University of Chile, two chairs are designated for criminology and social pathology. The term "social pathology" reminds us of archaic bio-organicism. Criminology has been taught in the social work departments of some universities. Although psychiatrists were interested in the study of crime at the beginning of this century, medical departments show only occasional interest in the subject, in spite of some symposia being devoted to abortion and child abuse. The lack of interest in courses in criminology is remarkable because the first directors of the Institute of Criminology were physicians.

Chilean criminologists acquire their basic knowledge through on-the-job performance of their tasks in education, research, or correctional work. This self-education favors the preservation of unidisciplinary perspectives, with little recognition of other approaches. A limited number of professionals have carried out advanced study in other countries at the University of Pennsylvania, the Free University of Brussels, the University of Montreal, the University of Rome, and the University of Madrid. Almost all of them end up as judges or in other activities far removed from criminology.

Some fields within the sphere of criminological work have attained modest and gradual progress. The juvenile justice system has been upgrading the educational credentials of personnel. For many years, the entrance requirements have called for "specialized accredited knowledge in psychology." Since 1974, special preparatory courses in juvenile law, including criminology, have been offered by the University of Chile, the Catholic University of Chile, and the University of Concepción. The Catholic University of Valparaiso and the University of Chile plan similar courses. In the field of criminal justice, the University of Chile has offered special courses for judges and in 1979 instituted a master's degree in judicial law favoring a deeper knowledge of the behavioral sciences. The School of Law, University of Chile, is now considering a master's degree in criminology or in penal sciences which would offer courses to graduates in law, psychology, sociology, education, medicine, and social work.

If the academic situation in teaching and occupational qualifications is unsatisfactory, it is even more so in research activities. Resources are markedly limited when compared with those of other fields of study. The implementation of research depends heavily on nonprofessionals, such as university students preparing theses in law, psychology, sociology, and other disciplines.

Sociology and its research tools appeared rather recently in Chilean criminology. The traditional sociologists' and psychologists' preference for Latin-European theoretical sources may be attributed to their limited competence in the English language; this is even more true among jurists. Latin-European works are more accessible and more likely to be translated, but they tend to be less grounded in data-based theory, less pragmatic, and less concerned with the social aspects of criminality. These circumstances complicate the development of a criminology soundly related to national requirements. The obsolescence of criminological works in the Spanish language[35] and the students' difficulties in obtaining materials originally published in English have been alleviated to some extent by books of readings that include translations made for teaching purposes.[36]

Courses in criminology have existed for many years in the training schools and academies of both branches of the Chilean police. Cultivation of a scientific perspective has been achieved to a degree in the correctional field; prison officers attend a two-year qualification curriculum at the technical school that includes a course in criminology.

LEVEL AND DIRECTION OF RESEARCH

In 1962, Radzinowicz said that the concept of modern criminological investigation was still virtually unknown in South America.[37] In 1965, Israel Drapkin, a Chilean professor, wrote that in the Latin American bibliography on crime the predominant themes are juridical, biological, and bio-typological.[38] He relates works based on modern criminological theories of sociology to the European ancestry of the juridical and biological philosophies of Latin America, to the late appearance of modern psychology and sociology, to a degree of rejection of North American criminology, and to the preference to divert available research funds into "more productive" areas.

Today we cannot subscribe to Radzinowicz's harsh judgment. Chile does offer the credentials of modern criminological research, including more than one program dedicated to objective and free inquiry, a number of field investigations, and serious consideration of research issues such as the question of "hard versus soft methodology." Drapkin's critique is more on the mark: the necessity of Chilean criminologists to educate themselves, the conservatism of the dominant juridical and criminological ideologies, the postponement of reactions to the crime problem, the limited diffusion of the empirical methodology, and the antipragmatic rhetoric characteristic of Latin America. In light of the events of the last fifteen years, these criticisms probably have decreasing merit, however.

Implementation of criminological research entails various types of major choices. First, one must select the *area* for research: delinquents or victims, primary or secondary prevention, or treatment of offenders. Second, one must select the *type* of investigation: fundamental versus applied research, perceived as a continuum including exploratory, descriptive, etiological, evaluative, "field-induced," and other modalities. Third, one must select the *method* from far-ranging alternatives from either "soft" or "hard" methodologies, according to ideographical or nomothetical orientations and the peculiarities of the basic discipline involved. Fourth, one must select the *theoretical framework*: whether micro- or macro-approaches, segmentalism versus integration, one-factor versus multiple-factor theories or medium-range hypotheses, determinism versus probabilism, delinquent-oriented versus situation-oriented studies, and so on.

Faced with these options, Chilean criminologists, until the middle of the century, opted for targeting the individual delinquent, the etiological and descriptive approaches, and the biological orientation. The method was essentially clinical, although there was a certain desire for "hard" data in some data collections or samples. The social reaction to deviance came up only in doctrinal discussions and in bibliographic works.

By 1950, the Institute of Criminology had completed over three thousand case studies. Some post-facto studies used them in looking for some degree of generalizations, predominantly in terms of the psychological-psychiatric aspects of personality.[39] Other studies resorted to projective techniques in trying to reveal "the offender's personality"; control groups were sometimes used.[40] Even as late as the 1950s, the image of the "criminal man" persisted among many researchers. This image was expressed in the development of "profiles" which, in some Latin American research, included consideration of blood traits.[41]

This period also reflected the influences of psychoanalysis, endocrinology, and bio-typology as effects of the writings of Alexander and Staub, Pende, Di Tullio, Kretschmer, Mezger, and Exner. In this period—since the beginning of the century—some writers have sharply criticized the penal system: court processes are faulty and time-consuming, correctional treatment does not exist, and prisons fail as a "panacea," being unable to "redeem" or to "rehabilitate."[42] Those claims, however, were not derived from rigorous empirical analysis.

Of more recent creation are the new university departments of psychology, sociology, and economics, the Latin American School of Social Sciences (FLACSO), and entities such as the Center for Research in Criminology in the School of Law, University of Chile. Their appearance has signaled new scientific perspectives which have contributed to an expanded supply of bibliographic and empirical materials on socioeconomic phenomena related to criminality, and have also provided more openness in criminological research. Departments of economics have examined urbanization, migration, and income distribution. Departments of sociology have investigated social disorganization, social aspects of economic development, stratification, marginality, culture and subcultures. Departments of psychology have followed new theoretical perspectives and have analyzed new trends in diagnosis and treatment among other things.

Research of a specifically criminological nature can be perceived in this most recent stage as lacking craftsmanship and having a broader range of interests. Thus, in studies of delinquents—whether case studies or more or less sophisticated samples—social factors are being stressed and the research does not try to get "profiles" but rather bases for criminal policies.

Various studies have stressed the serious frustrations and socioeconomic handicaps of the criminals that generally come to official attention.[43] Using a diachronic perspective, with psychological, or socio-anthropological orientations, other researchers look for "chains of internal events" that can determine criminal behavior systems.[44] Scholars with a psychological bent are either skeptical of or thoroughly reject the possibility of capturing, by way of certain techniques, the "type profiles" of categories of offenders.[45] Finally, although describing diverse personality traits, other researchers limit their inquiries to a certain type of lawbreaker found within a special type of offense.[46]

The more or less implicit "multiple causation" viewpoint of some of those studies has given way in other research projects to a more focused etiological pespective stemming from medium-range theories. An example is an investigation by FLACSO on juvenile delinquency in lower class urban families in transition. Some research has been grounded in the containment theory of Reckless and the anomie approach of Merton and Srole.[47]

In other topical areas, some studies have been oriented toward improved measurement and interpretation of criminality and its sources,[48] toward perceptions of the prevalence and characteristics of new deviant phenomena or of crimes especially prone to "dark figure" invisibility,[49] and toward the evaluation of the economic costs of criminality.[50]

The sphere of control and treatment is represented by FLACSO research on the social reaction to deviance and some studies of the penal process and the juvenile courts. An interdisciplinary investigation has dealt with the criteria employed in handling minors from sixteen to eighteen years of age.[51] The penal process has been evaluated in terms of equity—granting of bail, for example—efficiency, efficacy of sanctions, levels of restitution, and average length of time required for disposition.[52] Those studies may be regarded as problem-oriented and somewhat linked to reform. The demonstrated high impunity of drug traffickers, for example, has brought efforts to achieve more effective control and to improve legislation. Evaluative research has contributed to the expansion of innovative strategies. A study of suspended sentences[53] stimulated the extension of the boundaries of their utilization. Studies of Sunday furloughs provided the basis for daily work-furloughs and for open prisons.[54] A rigorous followup study of the open prison has been part of the documentation for proposals of alternatives to imprisonment, especially probation.[55]

Other important investigations range from an old research project on psychosurgery and criminal behavior[56] to more recent evaluative studies on prisonization, institutionalization of juveniles, subcultures, and the possibilities and efficacy of the token economy.[57] Finally, the School of Law, University of Chile, has examined the effectiveness and efficacy of certain penalties, thus offering scientific guidance for changes in criminal policy.[58]

In conclusion, Chile's criminological research has been influenced in recent years by a wide range of interests, in spite of the scarcity of human and economic resources and the inferior coordination of efforts. Methodological bias has sometimes weakened conclusions. Effort has not always been applied to topics of the highest priority. Inquiries have not been synchronized with vital reform goals. Nevertheless, efforts of the most recent years generally follow the 1969 Guidelines of the United Nations[59] and the standards enunciated by Chilean experts at a number of international meetings. Only a beginning has been made in the search for ways to adapt Chilean criminology to historical realities, to the peculiarity of their problems, and to the richness of their potentialities.[60] When resorting to "soft" methodology in matters of drugs and juvenile delinquency, for example, the Chilean criminologist has been only partly motivated by limitations of resources. In a continent with so many problems and uncertainties that dramatically demand action, frequently the criminologist believes it is better "to stop counting" and to try to know more.[61] A few but relevant and reliable figures should be sufficient to demonstrate some painful realities, to stimulate a profound change, and to open a new path for criminology.

NOTES

1. Concerning the ideological contradictions of positivism and its "scholastic" nuance in Latin America, see Marco A. González, "La Ideología en la Criminología Latinoamericana: Chile y Panamá" [The Ideology of Latin American Criminology: Chile and Panama], in F. Adler and G.O.W. Mueller (eds.), *Politics, Crime, and the International Science: An Inter-American Focus* (San Juan, Puerto Rico: North-South Center Press, 1972), pp. 214-233.

2. For example: Francisco J. Herboso, *Estudios Penitenciarios* [Penitentiary Studies] (Santiago: Imprenta Ercilla, 1892); Manuel D. Valenzuela, *El delito y su represión* [Crime and Its Repression] (Santiago: Encuardernación San Pablo, 1907); Valentín Brandau, *De la represión y prevención del delito en Chile* [Repression and Prevention of Crime in Chile] (Santiago: Imprenta La Ilustración, 1910); Alfredo Guillermo Bravo, *Sobre el delito y su represión en Chile* [Concerning Crime and Its Repression in Chile] (Santiago: Imprenta Chile, 1913). The last three works contain numerous references to Ferri, Lombroso, and Garofala and very scanty national data.

3. "While the personnel of the clinic is heavily weighted by those following the biological approach and in this respect parallels the conventional clinic in South American prisons, it is nevertheless balanced by the presence of two social workers and the good judgment of the director." From Negley K. Teeters, *Penology from Panama to Cape Horn* (Philadelphia: University of Pennsylvania Press, 1946), p. 174.

4. United Nations, *Statistical Yearbook for Latin America*, 1978, p. 59.

5. Instituto Nacional de Estadísticas, *Compendio Estadístico 1979* (Santiago: Imprenta INE, May 1979), p. 13.

6. Ibid.

7. Odette Tacla, Instituto Nacional de Estadísticas, *Panorama Demográfico de Chile y su evolución en el presente siglo* [Demographic Panorama of Chile and Its Evolution in the Present Century] (Santiago: Imprenta INE, 1975), p. 23.

8. *Compendio Estadístico 1979*, Vol. VIII.

9. Ibid., pp. 12, 31.

10. UNICEF, *La Infancia y la Juventud en América Latina* [Children and Juveniles in Latin America] (Santiago: CEPAL, 1969), p. 73.

11. *Statistical Yearbook for Latin America*, 1978, p. 43.

12. Ibid., p. 11.

13. *Compendio Estadístico 1979*, p. 49.

14. Ibid., p. 48.

15. *Banco Central de Chile, Boletin Mensual* [Central Bank of Chile, Monthly Bulletin], November 1974, p. 1496.

16. Ibid., October 1979, p. 1828.

17. *Statistical Yearbook for Latin America, 1979*, pp. 65-66; concerning socioeconomic evolution and perspectives, see *Progreso económico y social en América Latina, Informo*

1977 del Banco Interamericano de Desarrolo [Economic and Social Progress in Latin America, 1977 Report of the Development Interamerican Bank], pp. 229-237.

18. The goals are per capita increase in income, better distribution of income, full employment, real equal opportunities, well-balanced social development, respect for the dignity of man, true achievement of personal development, and cultural integration. See Instituto Latinamericano de Plantificación Económica y Social, *Progreso Cientifico y Técnico en América Latina* [Scientific and Technical Progress in Latin America], 1974.

19. Cited by Ivan Lavados in "Plantificación y Políticas Públicas referentes a la infancia en América Latina" [Planning and Public Policies in Relation to Childhood in Latin America], *Revista de Derecho Económico*, Universidad de Chile, Santiago, No. 42-43 (July-December 1978):114.

20. Instituto Nacional de Estadísticas, Report 4-Xii, 1979.

21. Teeters, *Penology from Panama to Cape Horn*, p. 187.

22. In my essay, "The Ideologies of Latin American Criminology: Chile and Panama" (Note 1), an explanation is advanced for the persistence of the biological model, the neo-Lombrosian perspective, and the neglect of sociological research in Latin America that amazed Teeters in 1944. See his lecture in "Nuevos horizontes en Criminología" [New Horizons in Criminology], *Revista de Ciencias Penales* 7 (October-December 1944):338-344.

23. Don Martindale, *La Teoría Sociológica* [Sociological Theory] (Madrid: Aguilar, 1968), p. 175.

24. For the above-mentioned data, the sources are *Anuarios Estadísticos* [Statistical Yearbooks]; for 1940: *Política, Administración, Justicia y Educación* [Policy, Administration, Justice and Education], Dirección General de Estadística; for 1952, *Educación, Justicia, Política y Administración* [Education, Justice, Policy and Administration], Servicio Nacional de Estadística y Censos; for 1971, 1975, and 1978, *Justicia y Policía* [Justice and Police], Instituto Nacional de Estadísticas.

25. Instituto de Patología Social, Universidad de Chile, *Anuario Criminológico de Chile, 1963* [Criminological Yearbook of Chile, 1963] (Santiago: Editorial Universitaria, 1966).

26. Marco A. González, Eduardo Muñoz, et al., *El Delito de homicidio en el Gran Santiago, 1970-1971-1972* [Homicide in Greater Santiago, 1970-1971-1972], in press. Also see Marco A. González, "Alcohol, drogas y criminalidad en Chile: epidemiologia, actitud comunitaria, políticas de control" [Alcohol, Drugs, and Criminality in Chile: Epidemiology, Community Attitude, Control Policies], *Anales del III Symposium Internacional de Criminología* (San Pablo, Brazil: Centro Internacionale de Criminología Biológica y Médico-Legal, 1976), pp. 121-156.

27. Elías Escaff, "Descripción de la criminalidad en Chile y su relación con algunas variables" [Description of the Criminality in Chile and Its Relation with Some Variables], *Revista Institucional de Investigaciones de Chile* (December 1978):16.

28. Report of Gendarmería de Chile to the Ministry of Justice (Santiago: November 1978), mimeo, Vol. 1, p. 9.

29. Initiative of the Instituto de Ciencias Penales, 1963. After many meetings in several capitals, the general part was completed at the San Pablo meeting in 1971. See *Código Penal Tipo para Latinamérica* [Model Penal Code for Latin America], 2 vols., edited by Juridica de Chile, Santiago, 1973.

30. For example, the First and Second Latin American Congresses on Criminology, Buenos Aires, 1938, and Santiago, 1941. The Pan American Congress on Criminology, 1979, was held in Buenos Aires.

31. Instituto de Ciencias Penales; the address is Huérfanos 1147 of 546 Santiago. Miguel Schweitzer Speisky is president.

32. Published in *Revista de Neuro Psiquiatría*, January, February, and March 1977.

33. Chilean Society of Criminology, Social Psychiatry and Criminalistics; Marco A. González-Berendique is president; the address is Avenue Providencia 835, dep. 64, Santiago.

34. See Bernardo Gesche, et al., *La Remisión condicional de la pena* [The Suspended Sentence] (Santiago: Editorial Juridica de Chile, 1975).

35. The only really modern treatises in the Spanish language are those of López-Rey and Göppinger. A deplorable translation of Sellin's *Culture, Conflict and Crime* (1938) appeared in 1969, under the title *Cultura, Conflicto y Crimen*. The well-known work by Merton, *Social Theory and Social Structure*, was translated only in 1964. *Crime and Personality* by Eysenck (1964) was translated in Spain only in 1976. We know no Spanish version of the *Principles of Criminology* by Sutherland, nor of the works by Cloward and Ohlin, Clinard, Reckless, Vold, Shoham, Cohen, Glaser, the Gluecks, Mednick, Christiansen, Szabo, Mannheim, Christie, Wilkins, Sykes, Matza, and so on. Students tend to cite the works of Exner, Hurwitz, di Tullio, or the most recent work by Seelig. All of them are available in Spanish. The French texts, such as those of Heuyer, Ellenberger, Szabo, and Pinatel, appear to be more accessible.

36. See my *Criminología: Materiales de Enseñanza* [Criminology: Teaching Materials] (Santiago: 1970), 2 vols., which brings nearer to the students the thoughts of some of the authors cited in the previous note.

37. Leon Radzinowicz, *In Search of Criminology* (Cambridge, Mass.: Harvard University Press, 1962), p. 170.

38. Israel Drapkin, "Investigación criminológica en América Latina" [Criminological Research in Latin America], *Revista Internacional de Política Criminal*, United Nations, No. 23, 1965, p. 25.

39. For example: Eduardo Brücher and Manuel Zamorano, "Estudio psiciólogico, psicopathológico y psiquiátrico sobre 100 delincuentes chilenos" [Psychological, Psychopathological and Psychiatric Study of 100 Chilean Criminals], *Revista de Ciencias Penales* 6 (January-March 1943):5-14; Guillermo Agüero, "Aspecto de nuestra delincuencia femenina" [Aspect of Our Female Criminality], *Revista de Ciencias Penales* 4 (January-June 1938):61-78, with more emphasis on the socioeconomic aspects to which are partially attributed the intellectual and moral deficits.

40. For example: Hernán Brücher, *Estudio de la personalidad de delincuentes chilenos* [Study of the Personalities of Chilean Criminals] (Santiago: LaSalle, 1944), tests by Rorschach, Benreuter, and PMK by Mira and López; Loreley Friedman, *Estudio de la personalidad de mujeres delincuentes y de diversos grupos de mujeres que no han estado en conflicto con la Justicia* [Study of the Personalities of Female Criminals and of Law-abiding Women] (Santiago: Jurídica de Chile, 1950), tests by Rorschach and Mira and López.

41. Israel Drapkin and Luis Sandoval studied more than one thousand criminals to demonstrate they had a distribution of blood traits similar to that of the general population. See "Grupos sanguíneos de la población penitenciara de Santiago" [Blood Traits in the Inmates of the Penitentiary of Santiago], *Revista de Ciencias Penales* 8 (January-March 1945):5-18.

42. Benjamin Vicuna Mackenna, a distinguished public figure of the nineteenth century, devoted his thesis for the law degree to "El sistema penitenciaro en general y su mejor

aplicación en Chile" [The Penitentiary System in General and Its Better Application in Chile] (Santiago: Anales de la Universidad de Chile, January-June 1857); also see note 2 above.

43. For example: Salvador Cifuentes, et al., "Estudio sobre caracteristicas psico-sociales y jurídicas de los menores recluídos en la Penitenciaría de Santiago" [Study on Psychosocial and Juridical Characteristics of Juvenile Inmates of the Santiago Penitentiary], *Revista Chilena de Ciencia Penitenciara y de Derecho Penal* 10, no. 4 (1960):35-54.

44. For example: Claudio Naranjo, "La historia psicológica del delincuente" [The Psychological History of the Offender], *Revista de Ciencias Penales* 23 (January-April 1964):57-90; Loreley Friedman, et al., "Trayectoria de vida de delincuentes habituales y de grupo control" [Life Course of Habitual Offenders and a Control Group], *Revista de Ciencias Penales* 23 (May-August 1964):208-240.

45. For example, Manuel Problete, "Resultados de una serie de aplicaciónes del P.M.K. de Mira y López en delincuentes adultos" [Results of a Series of Applications of the P.M.K. of Mira and López to Adult Offenders], *Revista de Ciencias Penales* 17 (September-December 1958):130-136; Salvador Cifuentes, "Aplicación del test de Szondi en homicidas chilenos" [Application of the Szondi Test to Chilean Murderers], *Revista de Ciencias Penales* 18 (January-April 1959):59-73.

46. For example: Doris Banchik and Jacobo Pasmaik, "Aspectos psiquiátricos y psichológicos del infanticidio" [Psychiatric and Psychological Aspects of Infanticide], *Revista Psiquis*, no. 3 (March 1965):31-37; Luis Weinstein, "Estudio sobre la vagancia juvenil" [Study on Juvenile Vagrants], *Revista de Ciencias Penales* 19 (May-December 1960):250-252.

47. For example: Oscar Karadima, "Factores sociales de la delincuentia en Chile: Un estudio sociológico" [Social Factors in the Delinquency of Chile: A Sociological Study] (Santiago: mimeo, 1967). It is interesting that this study was sponsored by the National Planning Office.

48. For instance, *Anuario Criminologico de Chile 1963* (Note 25); Hernán Montenegro, Guillermo Adriasola, Gloria Jaramillo, and Patricio de la Puente, "El menor en situación irregular en un distrito del Gran Santiago. Medición de su frecuencia y de la asociación con algunas variables" [Minors in Need of Supervision in a District of Greater Santiago. A Measurement of Its Frequency and Its Relation with Some Variables] (Santiago: Consejo Nacional de Menores, mimeo, 1970); Marco A. González and Eduardo Muñoz, "Diseño de una Estadística Correccional Mecanizaca para Internos Condenados" [Design of Computerized Correctional Statistics for Sentenced Inmates] (Santiago: mimeo, 1978); Elías Escaff, *Descripción de la criminalidad en Chile en relación con algunas variables* (Note 27).

49. For example: Patricia Richard, Ana Viveros, and Liana Ortiz, *¿Fuma marihuana el estudiante chileno?* [Does the Chilean Student Smoke Marihuana?] (Santiago: Editorial Nueva Universidad, 1972); Mario Gomberoff, R. Florenzano, and J. Thomas, "Algunas caracteristicas de adolescentes que inician recientemente el consumo de marihuana" [Some Characteristics of Adolescents Beginning Marihuana Use], *Revista Argentina de Psiquiatría y Psicología de la infancia y de la adolescencia* 4, no. 1 (1943); and Jaime Náquira, et al., "El síndrome del niño maltratado" [The Battered Child Syndrome] (Thesis, Santiago, 1978).

50. Beatriz Pinto, "Incidencia económica de los actos antisociales" [The Economic Cost of Crimes] (Santiago: Editorial Universitaria, mimeo, 1962).

51. Antonio Bascuñán, et al., "La Responsabilidad Penal del Menor" [Penal Responsibility

of Delinquents] (Santiago: Instituto de Docencia e Investigación Jurídica, mimeo, 1974).

52. For instance: Manuel Urrutia, et al., "Investigación de expedientes penales sobre los objetivos del sumario" [Research on Penal Trials Concerning the "Summary"—First Stage—Goals] (Santiago: various university theses, 1974, 1975); Felipe Sáez, "La libertad provisional" [Release on Bail] (Santiago: Thesis, 1977); Manuel Guzmán, et al., "El tráfico de estupefacientes en la realidad nacional" [Drug Traffic in the National Reality], *Revista de Ciencias Penales* 31 (May-December 1972):139-156; Antonio Bascuñán, et al., "El delito de incendio" [The Crime of Arson] (Santiago: Editorial Jurídica, 1974).

53. Gesche, et al., *La remisión condicional de la pena*. Law 7821 of 1944 allows penalties up to one year; the 1972 law raised the limit to a maximum of three years.

54. Partially included in my essay, "Una experiencia penológica: el permiso bajo palabia de honor" [A Penological Experience: The Sunday-Furlough and Work-Furlough Programs], *Revista de Ciencias Penales* 26, no. 2 (May-August 1967):206-228.

55. Latin American countries, with a shameful overpopulation in their penal facilities, are not aware of noninstitutional treatment. Since the 1940s, as an alternative to prison, they have used only the "suspended sentence" or French-Belgian "sursis," limited surveillance and assistance, which in fact is an equivalent of the judicial pardon. Not many years ago, juvenile probation was introduced in only some countries. See Joan Reimer, Graciela Weinstein, and Gloria Jaramillo, "Evaluación de las experiencias sobre libertad vigilada en Chile" [Evaluation of Experiences Concerning Juvenile Probation in Chile] in Seminario Internacional sobre Libertad Vigilada (Santiago: 1976); and Alvaro Troncoso and Germán San Martín, "Sistema de Libertad Vigilada en Chile" [System of Juvenile Probation in Chile] in Seminario sobre Conducta Delictual (Santiago: Universidad de Chile, 1979). In my paper presented at the Pan American Congress of Criminology (Buenos Aires: 1979), "Tras una mayor eficacia de la pena: prisión y alternatives, algunos indicadores" [Towards a Greater Efficacy of Penalties: Prison and Alternatives, Some Indicators], in press, I included several evaluations of Chilean experiences in the correctional field. They give a strong empirical basis to my project on adult probation, community service orders, and weekend and nightly imprisonment as alternatives to prison. The conclusions of the Buenos Aires Congress point at adult probation and other alternatives that should be introduced in the Latin American countries.

56. Constantino Chuaqui, "Leucotomía en psicóticos criminales" [Leukotomy in Criminal Psychotics] (Thesis, Santiago: Imprenta Stanley, 1952).

57. Ana Ottenberger, et al., "Una alternativa de Servicio Social frente al menor en conflicto con la Justicia" [A Social Work Alternative in Relation to Juvenile Delinquents] (Thesis, mimeo, 1975); Regina Buckuk and Irene Gómez, "Modificación de conductas desadaptadas en menores en situación irregular" [Maladaptive Behavior Modification in Minors in Need of Supervision] (Santiago: Thesis, mimeo, 1974); Kuperman and Messina, "Instauración de conductas adaptativas en menores en situación irregular en función de la contingencia del refuerzo" [Building of Adaptive Responses Through Contingent Reinforcement in Juveniles in Need of Supervision] (Santiago: Thesis, 1972).

58. For example: Joan Reimer, Graciela Carvajal, and Carolos Vila, "Investigación empírica acerca de la eficacia de las penas de presidio y reclusión perpetuas" [Empirical Research on Life Penalties Efficacy] (Santiago: Thesis, 1978).

59. Franco Ferracuti and R. Bergalli, *Tendencies y necesidades de la investigación criminológica en América Latina* [Trends and Necessities of Criminological Research in Latin America] (Rome: UNSDRI, 1969), pp. 27-42.

60. For example, lines of action are clearly formulated in my essay, "Consecuencias económicas y sociales del delito. Nuevos desafíos para la investigación y el planeamiento" [Economic and Social Consequences of Crime: New Challenges for Research and Planning], *Revista de Informaçao Legislativa*, Brasilia, no. 47 (July-September 1975): 162-192. This essay was used as a working paper in the Seminario sobre Planificación de la Defensa Social organized by ILANUD (Latin American Institute of the United Nations for the Prevention of Crime and Treatment of Criminals) in San Jose, Costa Rica, July 1975. Of great value and current relevance are the suggestions formulated by the Chilean expert Julio Peña-Núñez in "Evaluación de los métodos usados para la prevención de la delincuencia juvenil en América Latina" [Evaluation of the Methods Used for Delinquency Prevention in Latin America], *Revista Internacional de Política Criminal*, United Nations, no. 21, 1963; and "La Planificación Intersectorial de la Defensa Social en América Latina" [Intersectoral Planning of Social Defense in Latin America], *Revista de Informaçao Legislativa*, Brasilia, no. 47 (July-September 1975):111-144, also a working document of the aforementioned San José seminar.

61. See Nils Christie, "Is It Time to Stop Counting" in *Evaluation Research in Criminal Justice* (Rome: UNSDRI, 1976), p. 63; and David L. Bazelon, "The Hidden Politics of American Criminology," *Federal Probation* 42 (June 1978):3.

BIBLIOGRAPHY

Banchik, Doris, and Jacobo Pasmaik. "Aspectos psiquiátricos y psicológicos del infanticidio" [Psychiatric and Psychological Aspects of Infanticide]. *Revista Psiquis*, no. 3 (March 1965):31-37.

Cifuentes, Salvador, et al. "Estudio sobre caracteristicas psico-sociales y jurídicas de los menores recluídos en la Penitenciaría de Santiago" [Study on Psychosocial and Juridical Characteristics of Juvenile Inmates of the Santiago Penitentiary]. *Revista Chilena de Ciencia Penitenciaria y de Derecho Penal* 10, no. 4 (1960):35-54.

Drapkin, Israel. "Investigación criminológica en América Latina" [Criminological Research in Latin America]. *Revista Internacional de Política Criminal*, United Nations, no. 23 (1965).

Drapkin, Israel, and Luis Sandoval. "Grupos sanguíneos de la población penitenciaria de Santiago" [Blood Traits in the Inmates of the Penitentiary of Santiago]. *Revista de Ciencias Penales* 8 (January-February 1945):5-18.

Ferracuti, Franco, and R. Bergalli. *Tendencies y necesidades de la investigación criminológica en América Latina* [Trends and Necessities of Criminological Research in Latin America]. Rome: UNSDRI, 1969.

Friedman, Loreley, et al. "Trayectoria de vida de delincuentes habituales y de grupo control" [Life Course of Habitual Offenders and a Control Group]. *Revista de Ciencias Penales* 23 (May-August 1964):208-240.

Gesche, Bernardo, et al. *La Remisión Condicional de la pena* [The Suspended Sentence]. Santiago: Editorial Juridica de Chile, 1975.

Gonzalez, Marco A. "La Ideología en la Criminología Latinoamericana: Chile y Panamá" [The Ideology of Latin American Criminology: Chile and Panama]. In F. Adler and G.O.W. Mueller (eds.). *Politics, Crime, and the International Science: An Inter-American Focus*. San Juan, Puerto Rico: North-South Center Press, 1972. Pp. 214-233.

Naranjo, Claudio. "La historia psicológica del delincuente" [The Psychological History of the Offender]. *Revista de Ciencias Penales* 23 (May-August 1964):208-240.

Teeters, Negley K. *Penology from Panama to Cape Horn*. Philadelphia: University of Pennsylvania Press, 1946.

12

COSTA RICA

Jorge A. Montero

As in other areas of the world, the crime problem of Costa Rica is omnipresent but appears to be more acute at one time than another. To determine specific sources of the problem and the nature of societal responses to it, it is necessary to examine the historic background and patterns of the country's recent development along social, economic, and political dimensions. In this way, Costa Rica can be used as a case example for other nations with similar sociohistorical characteristics.

To delineate the development of criminology in Costa Rica, a number of professors and practitioners were consulted. Their contributions were integrated into the analysis that follows. To orient the readers, the chapter begins with a review of the history of Costa Rica from the discovery of the continent to the present.

CONQUEST, COLONIZATION, AND DEVELOPMENT

The Spanish conquest has not had the profound effects on the development of Costa Rica that it has had on the history of other Latin American countries. As a small country with limited resources, the area now known as Costa Rica offered little temptation to the Spanish conquerors in search of riches for themselves and the Spanish Crown. The Indians first seen by Christopher Columbus wore precious jewels, lending the impression of much gold and thereby explaining the name "Costa Rica." The impression was soon discarded because the Indians gave no information on the sources of gold and the Spaniards became bored with their searches. Furthermore, the conqueror, Governor Juan Vásquez de Coronado, effected a code forbidding the ill treatment and enslavement of Indians. Although the Indians were forced to work for the Spaniards by doing the so-called *encomiendas*, the colonial society soon developed the characteristics of frugality, industriousness, and democratic relationships.[1]

The Costa Ricans gained their independence without violence under a proclamation for all the territories under the general capitaincy of Guatemala. Nevertheless, some of the population preferred to remain under the Spanish Crown, and so they kept the proclamation secret. Other persons wanted the country to be annexed to the empire of Agustin de Iturbide of Mexico.[2] These conflicts provoked a brief war between the Costa Rican provinces, culminating in the battle of Ochomago pitting the provinces of Cartago and Heredia against San Jose and Alajuela which sought independence.[3] Independence was proclaimed in 1821, and the foundations for nationhood and government were laid. Civil wars and coups d'état were avoided through prudent administration and legislation oriented toward the public interest.

The peace of the country was disturbed in 1856 when both Nicaragua and Costa Rica were invaded by North American filibusters commanded by William Walker. The filibusters intended to take possession of all Central America and annex the territory to a Confederation of the Southern United States, based on the practice of slavery. They also sought to establish a political entity linking the Pacific and Atlantic oceans. This territory presents the shortest distance between the oceans. The San Juan River connects the Atlantic Ocean to the Nicaraguan Lake; only a small stretch of land would have to be spanned with a canal to open a water route between the lake and the Pacific Ocean. The Costa Ricans defeated the filibusters, forcing them to abandon their plans.[4]

During the nineteenth century and the first three decades of the twentieth, Costa Rica enjoyed a provincial, family life with a very low crime rate. There were very few homicides; the most common forms of crime were larceny and various misdemeanors.

Costa Rica has experienced important changes from 1948 to date, when the second and last revolution in this century took place. The revolution in 1948 broke out largely because of political and electoral problems and doubts about administrative honesty. Because of the sociopolitical changes of the 1940s, the government enacted advanced social legislation in response to serious confrontations between the middle and working classes.[5] The revolution partially changed the political and administrative system—changes that culminated in a new constitution in 1949. The social legislation favoring the poorest classes remained, and social insurance and housing programs were introduced.

FORCES OF CHANGE IN RECENT DECADES

Other facets of Costa Rica's institutional structure have undergone changes. The last forty years have witnessed the release of socioeconomic forces that have undermined the country's provincial tranquility and social stability. These developments were partly the consequence of military cooperation with the United States as an ally in World War II, the opening in 1942 of the international airport at the capital, San Jose, and the inclusion of Costa Ricans in the "consumer society." The United States was permitted to establish a small military base in Costa Rica during World War II.

During the 1970s, Costa Rica was admitted to the Central American Common Market, creating a necessity for an industrialization policy, which was almost nonexistent before. The gross national product has increased, reaching $1,240 per inhabitant in 1977.[6] Although the industrialization process never reached Europe's level, many rural people were stimulated to migrate to towns in search of factory jobs. In the absence of coordinated industrial development planning, the factors have been concentrated in the metropolitan area rather than distributed throughout the territory of the Republic.

In the search for new markets following World War II, some countries followed commercial policies that have contributed to the appearance of the consumer society in Costa Rica, with the economic fluctuations that it entails. Partly through advertising and the mass media, the people's desires for consumer goods and all the material comforts of "modern life" reached unprecedented proportions. Business and industry were encouraged to seek fast and certain profits. Beginning in 1950, the slogan "buy now and pay later" provoked a sharp increase in consumer expenditures among the upper and middle classes.

These new trends must be assessed against the backdrop of the Costa Ricans' traditional inclination to spend the money they have and to go into debt when they lack money. These trends fomented class discontent and sharpened the social differences which had always existed but had not been visible under previous social conditions. Previously, the landlord or wealthy coffee grower led a relatively modest and simple life. The new desires for conspicuous consumption now undermined the social tranquility.

Beginning in the 1950s, a population explosion ensued, culminating in an annual gross birth rate of 47.5 per thousand inhabitants (1960).[7] The population growth added to the concentration of people in the principal cities, such as San Jose. The population of the capital city burgeoned from 200,000 to 400,000 inhabitants.[8] San Jose had exhibited few of the features of a developed metropolis; it had only one building over five stories. Now its physical development parallels the population increase.

Rapid modernization has also released important institutional and socioeconomic changes at all levels of the social structure. The traditional customs and thought patterns of Costa Ricans have been seriously challenged. The establishment of the University of Costa Rica in the 1940s was an important reflection of this cultural impact and a major attempt to prepare Costa Rican society to deal with its consequences.

The profound effects on social institutions can also be attributed to improvements in communications and in national and international transport, and to the introduction of television. At the same time, these improvements destroyed the rustic way of life found in Costa Rica before the 1950s and introduced life-styles found in all developing countries.

INCIDENCE OF CRIME IN COSTA RICA

Costa Rica's general crime rate remains low compared with that of many other countries because most towns are small with a low population density. Nevertheless, Costa Rica is experiencing a modest increase in the overall crime rate as a reflection of the anonymity of the larger cities and of the greater difficulty of identifying criminals. From a broader perspective, Costa Rica is being subjected to the influences of decreased insulation from external cultural forces that have weakened traditions of respect for others and for family obligations. The concentration of new industries in the metropolitan area—a consequence of inadequate economic planning, as mentioned above—has produced slum pockets of extreme poverty in the environs of San Jose as a result of rural-to-urban migration.

TABLE 12-1
REPORTED CRIMES IN COSTA RICA, 1974-1979

Year	Number of Reported Crimes	Index: 1974 Equals 100	Crimes Per 100,000 Persons
1974	23,083	1.00	1,186.4
1975	24,144	1.04	1,210.9
1976	25,842	1.12	1,264.2
1977	31,931	1.38	1,521.6
1978	30,484	1.32	1,453.6
1979	30,331	1.31	1,406.8

Source: Supreme Court of Justice, Statistical Department.

As Table 12-1 indicates, the overall annual crime rate for Costa Rica increased with some consistency between the years 1974 and 1979 (years for which reasonably accurate data are available), but most of the increase came before 1978 when a modest decline in annual rates began. For the years 1974 through 1977, there was a consistent increase, with the greatest upsurge recorded for 1977 over 1976. If we take the number of reported crimes in 1974 as the base, the index figures show that the number in 1977 exceeded that of 1974 by 38 percent, whereas that for 1976 was only 12 percent higher. After 1977 the annual number tapered off. One explanation is that, effective in 1976, an unprecedented number of violations of consumer protection laws were reported.[9]

The emergence of a seemingly opulent society—standing in sharp contrast to the existence of groups with very low incomes—has had its effects on crime, although Costa Rica has a smaller proportion of low-income persons than some countries. One particular type of criminality entails petty larceny and housebreaking to obtain electrical appliances, money, jewels, and other items easy to sell. Seldom reported are thefts of clothing hanging to dry after laundering, toys children leave abandoned, and milk and bread of peddlers.

One adverse consequence of economic progress during the 1970s was a dramatic upsurge in traffic offenses. Traffic deaths numbered 251 in 1979 and injuries resulting from automobiles totaled 4,827—alarming statistics for a population of some 2.2 million persons.[10]

Juvenile gangs were almost unknown before the 1970s. The highest crime rate among all age groups is recorded for those persons seventeen to twenty-five years of age, a pattern common among contemporary societies.[11]

Drug consumption is limited mostly to marijuana; abuse of narcotics is quite unusual. However, development of international communications has resulted in drug traffic in recent years.

A particularly noteworthy offense in Costa Rica has been the looting and smuggling of pre-Columbian treasures. New laws have been enacted in an attempt to cope with this new offense. Along with outright criminal activities, foreigners have purchased legitimately and taken treasures from Costa Rica to be added to private and museum collections in developed countries.

THE CRIMINAL JUSTICE SYSTEM

In Costa Rica, the criminal justice system may be best understood by examining each of its integrated subsystems—the police, courts of justice, and penitentiary subsystems.

Police Subsystem

The administration of law enforcement is directly under the executive authority of the Ministry of Interior, Police, and Public Security. The police functions are performed by two components: the Rural Assistance Guard which fulfills its duties in the countryside and in small towns; and the Civil Guard which is responsible for the capital city and the most important cities. However, all of the national territory is under the direction of both guards. The main duties of the two forces are to preserve national sovereignty; to ensure the maintenance of order and public calmness; and to safeguard the security of persons and property. Under the constitution, the president of the Republic holds supreme control over all the police forces of the country.[12]

Courts of Justice

The organization of the state is based on three kinds of power—legislative, executive, and judicial—with judicial power exerted by the supreme court of justice as the higher body to which all courts and judicial officers are responsible in their administration of justice in the country. Jurisdiction is allocated on the basis of the territory within which the offenses occur, the quantity of cases, and the matters involved. The constitution provides for the functional and fiscal independence of the courts. It calls for the annual assignment of funds in an amount no less than 6 percent of the entire national budget.[13]

The Department of the Public Prosecutor is in charge of criminal action[14] and initiates prosecution. The department is responsible for ensuring criminal and procedural orders affecting parties interested in public suits. Among other functions, the department promotes and carries out public actions and the practice of summary information, provides evidence, and establishes the appeals. The public prosecutor and his agents, however, do not make decisions, which are the exclusive responsibility of judges or the courts. The total convictions won by the courts for the years 1977-1979 are shown in Table 12-2.

TABLE 12-2
NUMBER OF CONVICTED PERSONS IN COSTA RICA BY YEAR AND TYPE OF COURT, 1977-1979

Year	Total	Tribunal	Court
1977	4,484	1,896	2,588
1978	4,546	1,947	2,599
1979	4,290	1,752	2,538

Source: Statistical Yearbooks of the Judicial Power, Costa Rica.

The Judicial Investigation Body (judicial police) conducts inquiries and investigations aimed at clarifying the reported criminal deeds and at determining the alleged offenders. The judicial policemen are charged with apprehending the offenders and seizing various types of evidence (arms, drugs, and so on) for disposition by appropriate judicial authorities. The body is auxiliary to the criminal courts, with jurisdictions covering the entire territory of the Republic.[15]

Penitentiary Subsystem

Within the executive branch of government, the penitentiary regime is directly under the Ministry of Justice. Its functions are carried out through a body called the General Department of Social Adjustment and Crime Prevention.[16] Among its functions is the implementation of measures—adopted by competent authorities—that deprive or restrict the freedom of accused and sentenced persons, that entail their custody and treatment, and that require administration of prisons. The number of persons imprisoned in Costa Rica during 1978-1980, by juridical status, is shown in Table 12-3.

In recent years, Costa Rica has initiated extensive reform of the criminal justice system and the execution of sanctions. The reforms have been expressed in the new Penal Code (1970), the Criminal Procedures (1975), and the Law

TABLE 12-3
NUMBER OF PRISONERS IN COSTA RICA BY JURIDICAL STATUS, 1978-1980

Juridical Status	1978		1979		1980	
	No.	*Pct.*	*No.*	*Pct.*	*No.*	*Pct.*
Juvenile	184	8.8	152	6.6	182	7.2
Sentenced	972	46.7	942	40.8	1,079	42.4
Pretrial detention	801	38.5	981	42.5	1,025	40.3
Security measures	54	2.6	79	3.4	55	2.2
Sentenced and pretrial	9	0.4	29	1.3	42	1.6
Infringer	53	2.5	124	5.4	157	6.2
Unreported	10	0.5	1	0.04	3	0.1
Total	2,083	100.0	2,308	100.0	2,543	100.0

Source: *Penal Demographic Yearbook* (San Jose: Ministry of Justice, General Department of Social Adjustment, 1980).

Concerning the Execution of Sentences (1971). New penal establishments for both accused and convicted offenders and new correctional centers for juveniles, females and males, have been constructed. A new system for rehabilitation of the convicted offender includes diagnosis, prognosis, and individual and collective treatment. An after-care service, including treatment within the community, is being established in open institutions. Inmates are selected according to interdisciplinary technical measures for work or study outside the institution.

Sentence to conditional execution is similar to probation. When the sentence does not exceed either three-years' imprisonment or banishment for a first offender, the judge may suspend the sentence under certain circumstances and at a fixed date, after analysis of the prisoner's personality and the reasons for and nature of the crime. If the convicted person does not fulfill the state requirements or if he/she commits another crime during the "probation" period, the suspension is revoked and he/she must serve the sentence.[17]

Under conditional release (parole), any person condemned to imprisonment has the right to ask the judge for parole after serving half of the imposed sentence. To be eligible, the prisoner must not have been previously sentenced for an offense, must display good behavior, must have a profession or a job, and must have received a favorable report from the penitentiary institution. When granting parole, the judge can impose certain conditions. If the conditions are not satisfied or a new punishable offense is committed during the parole period, the parole can be modified or revoked.[18]

WHAT DOES CRIMINOLOGY MEAN?

From a scientific perspective, Costa Rican criminology appeared and developed under the influence of foreign experts. Criminology is considered the sum of all the studies that deal with crime, the criminal as a human being, the explanations for criminality, crime prevention, and the treatment of offenders. Crime is defined as antisocial behavior penalized by criminal law.

Costa Rican criminology is based essentially on knowledge acquired from European and North American scholars. However, each country deals with the science of criminology by adjusting research methods, the occupational system of criminology, and the interpretation of scientific principles according to its own idiosyncrasy.

The general opinion in Costa Rica is that advantage should be taken of foreign experiences in dealing with crime through exchange of knowledge. In this respect, Costa Rican criminology covers the academic and research fields and the managerial and professional practices within the criminal justice system: police, judicial inquiry, forensic medicine, courts, public prosecution, and correctional institutions.

In this vein, applied criminology has been an important facet of the Costa Rican interest in crime and criminals. Criminology as a profession generally means public service with two exceptions: university teaching and research, and the activities of the Latin American Institute of the United Nations for the Prevention of Crime and the Treatment of Offenders (ILANUD). In the last two instances, criminology is considered a science. Nevertheless, those who see themselves as criminologists agree that applied criminology must have a scientific basis and that the continuous renewal of theories comes from their empirical application.

The applied emphasis was expressed early through an interest in penitentiaries. In 1890, Octavio Beeche published a report on penitentiary studies derived from his visit to penal establishments in Europe.[19] However, serious interest in penitentiary reform has been more characteristic of the years since 1968. Effective in 1972, Costa Rica has become involved in the modification of physical facilities, the development of progressive treatment programs for prisoners, and the training of personnel in law enforcement, courts, and the penitentiary. Reform of criminal laws and procedures has also been undertaken.[20]

WHAT IS THE CRIMINOLOGIST? SOME ISSUES

Those in Costa Rica who identify themselves as criminologists devote themselves primarily to teaching or to individual research, sometimes as part of their duties in governmental or other public institutions and sometimes to gratify their personal interests. Criminologists include those who are officials and advisers within the penitentiary system. Regardless of the particular field of primary activity, they share dedication to preparing articles and other materials recording their impressions, insights, knowledge, and experiences.

There is considerable dispute in Costa Rica over whether or not any scientist could be considered to be primarily a criminologist and whether or not criminology is more of a pastime than a profession. Those persons who see it as a science and profession agree that criminology should be followed as a full-time occupation for a number of reasons. The scientific quest for profound understanding is an arduous endeavor. The subject matter of criminology blankets the variegated aspects of human behavior and the complex effects of social change as well. To gain insights particularly relevant to crime and criminal justice in Costa Rica, the criminologists would have to place any theory within the Costa Rican context. Then, the theories of the behavioral and social sciences, if developed in Europe or North America, could be accommodated to the special features of the sociocultural and political context of Costa Rica. Ideally, the criminologist would have the theoretical knowledge and the methodological competence to employ fundamental concepts, probably developed elsewhere, in an incisive manner. On the basis of such arguments, the criminologist may be viewed as primarily a trained professional capable of employing a multifaceted social and behavioral discipline, although his or her work operates within elements provided by law.

Nevertheless, the institutional prerequisites for a regular, well-defined role for the criminologist are lacking in Costa Rica. Development of criminology has been rather limited from an academic point of view. There are few criminologists in the universities where criminal law has been the dominant consideration when crime and criminals are brought into scholarly discussion. Specialized publications are in short supply. The occupational market does not present a demand specifically directed toward the criminologist's functions. When such specialization is required, the criminological tasks are often performed by persons trained in other subject matters.

Costa Rica has no association specifically formed and conducted to bring criminologists together as criminologists. Their interaction with one another is incidental to their membership in other organizations of lawyers, social workers, physicians, and so on.

TOWARDS A RICHER CRIMINOLOGY

Traditionally, criminology in Costa Rica was considered to be a branch of the law rather than constituting an autonomous sphere with its own subject matter and research interests. This emphasis may be seen in the book *American Criminal Archeology*, originally published in 1898, in which Anastasio Alfaro drew on legal and criminal records in the National Files.[21] Also important to the early Costa Rican literature was the 1940 study by Ricardo Jinesta, *Penitentiary Evolution in Costa Rica*, in which he traced the history of penal institutions from colonial times to 1918.[22]

The last ten years have produced evidence of more tangible recognition of criminology's potentialities as an autonomous science rather as merely an appendage of criminal law. The signs of this movement were first dimly discernible in the 1940s, but, for reasons to be given below, the movement can be assessed with more confidence today.

There are tentative signs of a change of attitude in universities and among those persons with a special interest in criminology. Already, students of law are given the benefit of lectures on the subject. When participating in national and international meetings, the experts always stress the importance of the interdisciplinary perspective in evaluating offenders, assessing criminality, and framing measures to deal with criminality.

In the period after World War II, the social defense approach was supported by professionals, such as Hector Beeche, Manuel Guerre, Joaquin Vargas Gene, Enrique Benavides, Shanti Quiros, Alfonso Acosta Guzman, and Victor Manuel Obando. Also influential was the criminal policy of the United Nations which was aimed at crime prevention and treatment of offenders. A number of specialists appeared to devote themselves to criminological surveys and research in a more professional way. Among them should be mentioned Fray Alberto Izabuirre, Enrique Castillo, Francisco Castillo, Iza El Kouri, Minor Calvo, Luis Lachner, and Jorge A. Montero.

Latin American criminologists had been peculiarly isolated from work carried out in other Latin American countries, in spite of geographic proximity and idiomatic identity. This tendency has existed even in those countries—such as Argentina, Chile, Venezuela, and Mexico—that have been outstanding in this hemisphere. The last few years have brought the establishment of more effective channels of communication.

The Criminal Code published in 1972, when put into full effect, would require the specialized services of persons educated in criminology. For example, the progressive orientation of this set of laws requires that sentencing judges take into consideration the principles of behavioral theory in determining whether the convicted offender should receive probation, a suspended sentence, or imprisonment. Crime prevention is appropriate for those urban districts experiencing greater criminality under circumstances outlined earlier in this chapter. Community surveys and the implementation of crime prevention programs call for well-trained professionals.

FORMAL EDUCATION AND CRIMINOLOGY

If a Costa Rican seeks specialized education in criminology, he or she must attend a foreign university because, as already stated, criminology is considered a minor branch of the criminal law and an activity that requires only incidental attention in a curriculum. An institute for criminological sciences was proposed for the University of Costa Rica, with interdisciplinary research to be followed, but the idea has not been implemented. One argument in support of the proposal was that a larger number of persons would benefit from an indigenous program.

It would be feasible to bring professors and other specialists to Costa Rica—as the first step toward developing a full-fledged faculty of Costa Rican professors—as a means of expanding the student clientele beyond that provided by the practice of sending potential criminologists abroad.

The proposed center for criminological research was conceived in 1976 as an organizational platform, within the Faculty of Law, whereby instruction in criminology by specialists would be available to students in law, education, and the social sciences. Another idea has been that an institute for multidisciplinary research be established, but again this plan has not been implemented. The instruction of criminology-related subjects, available now in Costa Rica, may be outlined as follows:

University of Costa Rica

The Faculty of Law offers courses in criminology, criminalistics, criminal sociology, legal psychiatry, tutelary law for juveniles, and penitentiary law, when students want to specialize in criminal law. The School of Sociology instructs criminal sociology. The School of Psychology has courses in criminal psychology as part of its curriculum. The School of Social Work also has a course in criminal sociology. Since 1961, the Faculty of Medicine has made forensic medicine a required subject.

University College in Cartago

This college is one of the provincial institutions of higher learning. Students pursuing a professional career have the opportunity to take courses in criminology, criminal psychology, criminal sociology, forensic medicine, criminalistics, and penitentiary law.

National Autonomous University

For the last three years, the School of Sociology has given courses in criminology in the summer semester for university students and employees of the Social Adaptation Department. This university, located in Heredis province, does not give regular courses in criminology, but there are plans for a master's in clinical social sciences which would include criminology.

Autonomous University of Central America

The Free School of Law includes some elements of criminology in its law curriculum. The law career of the Collegium Academicum includes courses in criminology and forensic medicine.

Other Institutions

The School of Penitentiary Training (Social Adaptation) provides in-service training through two-month courses known as Principles of Criminology for personnel involved in the treatment of offenders. The Training School of the Judicial Investigation Agency is a specialized arm of the supreme court; it has short courses.

ILANUD

The institute organizes national and international courses and seminars on several subjects related to the prevention of crime, the planning of criminal policies, and the treatment of offenders.

STATUS AND TRENDS OF RESEARCH

Research in the criminological field certainly exists in Costa Rica, but it is poorly organized and coordinated. Research is carried out in universities and state agencies responsible for criminal policy. Some individuals and private groups engage in research. The establishment of ILANUD was a significant event for Costa Rican criminological research.

In 1973, a meeting was held at Brasilia to prepare for the Fifth United Nations Congress on the Prevention of Crime and the Treatment of Offenders. The United Nations was strongly urged to create a criminological institute in Latin America to deal with these topics. The result was the establishment in 1975 of the Latin American Institute of the United Nations for the Prevention of Crime and the Treatment of Offenders, located in San Jose. The institute is designed to be a means of collaboration among countries in Latin America by encouraging research activities, inquiries, meetings of experts, and otherwise expanding the resources of comparative criminology.[23]

ILANUD has also been of service to Costa Rica, the country within which it is located. It has lent support to the Ministry of Justice in sponsoring several surveys. Of course, such efforts are minor compared with the participation of the University of Costa Rica, a central national institution of higher learning.

Among those who have accomplished research in Costa Rica, Enrique Castillo and Luis Lachner may be cited as examples.[24] They have responded theoretically to the sociological and anthropological implications of the clash of cultures. In Costa Rica, researchers are well aware that the forces of urbanization and modernization, as discussed above, are vital topics for analysis of the roots of delinquency and crime and of the potentialities for societal reactions to the problems illustrated by delinquency and crime.

The researchers, however, face serious handicaps because of conditions also found in other nations undergoing economic development. Of course, acquiring the necessary funding is always a basic difficulty. There are many high priority needs that compete for available resources. A well-established system for recruiting, educating, and utilizing qualified criminologists is fundamental to any long-term program of theoretical and applied research. Costa Rica, as we have seen, lacks this institutionalized foundation. It will be necessary to expand the coverage and to improve the reliability of official data on crime, criminals, and the administration of criminal justice. At present, the collection of available data sources is the responsibility of several agencies: the Social Adaptation Department, the annual prisoner census of the Ministry of Justice, and the Statistics Department of the supreme court. ILANUD also plays a role.

In conclusion, all of these difficulties stem from the complexities of cultivating the rational thought endemic to the research process within the dynamic environment of a society undergoing a rapid rate of socioeconomic and cultural change. Caught in the bewildering environment, the average Costa Rican is unprepared to recognize the long-term importance of basic and operational research. Striving to meet burgeoning needs in the face of limited fiscal and manpower resources, policymakers have difficulty allocating available resources so that research and the establishment of criminology as an occupational system can receive due attention. Perhaps the ultimate conclusion is that Costa Rica illustrates the same dilemmas as similar nations that are facing the 1980s under conditions that did not exist forty years ago. Criminology has much to offer for understanding the socioeconomic difficulties, but, to take advantage of this potentiality, the effects of the difficulties on the development of criminology must be overcome.

NOTES

1. Juan Vásquez de Coronado, *Letters Reporting the Conquest of Costa Rica*, Costa Rican Academy of Geography and History (San Jose: University of Costa Rica Press, 1964).

2. Ricardo Fernández Guardia, *Independence* (San Jose: National Commission of the 150th Anniversary of the Independence of Central America, Publications Dept., University of Costa Rica, 1971).

3. Ibid., pp. 78-80.

4. Rafael Obregón Loría, *The Transition Campaign* (San Jose: University Editorial, Lehmann Press, 1956).

5. John Patrick Bell, *Crisis in Costa Rica* (Austin, Texas: University of Texas Press, 1971).

6. The total population of San Jose province is 695,163. See *Population Census* Vol. 1 (San Jose: General Department of Statistics and Census, 1973).

7. In 1960, the birth rate was 53.6 per 1,000 inhabitants. In 1959, it was 49.6 (General Department for Statistics and Census).

8. The gross national product was 25,675.6 million colones in 1977, while the gross national product per capita was 12,400 (General Department for Statistics and Census).

9. Supreme Court of Justice, Statistics Department.

10. Ibid.

11. Ibid.

12. *Political Constitution of Costa Rica* (San Jose: National Publishing House, 1980), Art. 139, para. 3.

13. Ibid., Art. 9, para. 7.

14. *Code of Criminal Procedure* (San Jose: Metropolitan Publishing House, 1974), Art. 5.

15. Legislative Assembly, *Organic Law of the Judicial Power* (San Jose: Lehmann, 1979), Art. 125, para. 138.

16. *Law of the General Department for Social Adjustment*, No. 4762, May 8, 1971 (San Jose: Atilio Vincenzi, 1972).

17. Legislative Assembly, *Penal Code* (San Jose: National Publishing House, 1979), Art. 59 and following, p. 57.

18. Ibid., Art. 64 and following, p. 58.

19. Octavio Beeche, *Penitentiary Surveys: Report to the Costa Rican Government* (San Jose: National Publishing House, 1890).

20. In 1968, according to Law No. 4120, the commission in charge of reviewing the penal laws was set up. It is still at work (1981). Among the many reforms the commission initiated are the Penal Code (1970) and the Penal Procedure Code (1973).

21. Anastasio Alfaro, *American Criminal Archeology*, Foreword by Carlos Melendez (San Jose: Costa Rica Publishing House, 1961).

22. Ricardo Jinesta, *Penitentiary Evolution in Costa Rica* (San Jose: Costa Rica Publishing House, 1940).

23. The Latin American Institute of the United Nations for the Prevention of Crime and the Treatment of Offenders (ILANUD) was created by agreement between the Costa Rican government and the United Nations, as signed in New York on July 11, 1975.

24. Among Enrique Castillo's papers are: "Status of the Defendants in Costa Rica," *Review Fore*, no. 3 (1980):4-9; "Values, Perception and Society" (mimeo), Publications Department, University of Costa Rica, 1968, p. 20; "Institute for Criminological Expertise and Social Pathology," Publications Department, University of Costa Rica, 1972; "Schools of Criminology," *Review of Juridical Sciences*, no. 37 (January-April 1979):243-256; "Becker and Chapman, Interactionist Criminologists. Symbolic Interactionism in Criminology and Two of Its Representatives," ILANUD, Essay Series, no. 6, 1979 (also published in the *Review of Juridical Sciences*, no. 38 [May-August 1979]:63-138).

Luis Lachner has conducted, among others, the following investigations: *Compendium of Criminal Statistics in Latin America and the Caribbean, 1950-1977* (San Jose: National Publishing House, ILANUD, 1979) and, with Vaino Kannisto, *Comparative Analysis of Latin American and Caribbean Criminal Statistics, 1950-1977* (San Jose: National Publishing House, 1981).

Eduardo Vargas Alvarado, professor at the University of Costa Rica and head of the Department of Forensic Medicine within the Judicial Power, should be mentioned as representative of schools in forensic medicine. Dr. Vargas Alvarado has published several research works. He is the author of a textbook, *Forensic Medicine: Compendium of Forensic Sciences for Doctors and Lawyers*, 2d ed. (San Jose: Lehmann, 1980).

BIBLIOGRAPHY

Acosta Guzman, Alfonso, and Rudolph Muelling. *Forensic Medicine and Toxicology*. 4th ed. 2 vols. San Jose: University of Costa Rica, 1969-1970.

The two volumes cover forensic medicine, toxicology, forensic psychiatry, criminalistics, and criminology (including penitentiary science). They were written for students in the Faculty of Law and for lawyers. Starting with the third edition (1961), the work was extended, thanks to the collaboration of Professor Muelling from the University of Louisiana, to make it appropriate for students of the Faculty of Medicine, University of Costa Rica. The fourth edition has additional collaborating specialists, such as Professors Eduard Vargas, Roberto Chaves, and Manuel Antonio Molina from the Forensic Medicine Department of the Judicial Power and Professor Gonzalo Gonzalez Murillo, the chair of psychiatry at the University of Costa Rica.

Alfaro, Anastasio. *American Criminal Archeology*. 2d ed. San Jose: Costa Rica Publishing House, 1961.

This historical and anecdotal work is based on data of the National Files and is addressed primarily to the public at large. At time of publication, it met the concerns aroused in Costa Rica by the reorganization of the criminal law programs as a result of Héctor Beeche's travel to Europe to study penitentiary systems (see below). Many chapters were originally published in several national newspapers. Comparative analysis is promoted by statistics from 1686 to 1859 and more explicatory statistics from 1850 to the end of the century.

Beeche, Héctor. "Penitentiary Treatment." (Offprint.) *Review of the College of Barristers*, Vol. 6 (April 1951).

The author delineates the principles of the penitentiary treatment of the 1950s as set by criminology and penitentiary science: Treatment should be based on an integral study of the individual and on the characteristics of the environment. Juvenile delinquency should be excluded from the common penal proceedings, and a specialized juvenile court should be established. Treatment of women should prepare them for handicrafts as well as the field of domestic service, so that rehabilitation would be more likely. Treatment of men should be individual and progressive, inspired by the principles of order, discipline, and rewards. It is necessary to set up a board for released prisoners to ensure their development within the community; a national institute for criminology should be established to conduct criminological surveys on prisoners and changes in criminality; a penitentiary school should be established.

Beeche, Héctor. *Social Defense and the Penal Procedure*. San Jose: Falcó Printing House, 1956.

In the spirit of social defense and an orientation towards prevention, the author recommends reorganization of penal procedure and of criminal policy. The application of scientific treatment for rehabilitation is preferred; long-term segregation would be imposed only on unadaptable offenders. Among his recommendations are the following: Juvenile offenders should be subjected to a tutelary procedure, and a new jurisdiction consisting of special juvenile courts should be created. A collegiate technico-administrative council would supervise the execution of sanctions and the development of penitentiary treatment.

Beeche, Octavio. *Penitentiary Surveys*. San Jose: National Publishing House, 1890.

The author reported to the Costa Rican government after his visits in 1889 to the most important penitentiary establishments of Europe in search of the ideal system for Costa Rica. His survey covered Belgium (Louvain), Italy (Torino, Rome, Venice), France

(Paris, Melun), Switzerland (Neutchatel), England (Millbank, Wormwood Scrubs), and Germany (Hamburg, Berlin). His investigation compared the systems, their premises, and regimes. The Philadelphia, Auburn, Irish, and continuous separation models were applied in the several countries. The author included statistical tables and reports about advances in the penitentiary field in Frankfurt (1846), Brussels (1847), Stockholm (1876), and Rome (1885).

Castillo Barrantes, Enrique. *Institute for Criminological Expertise and Social Pathology.* 1st ed. San Jose: University of Costa Rica Press, 1972.
To meet the needs of criminal justice, the author urges the setting up of an institute for criminological expertise and social pathology which would furnish support and counseling for courts in regard to sentencing. The proposal specifies the theoretical and philosophical framework, the functions of sciences and disciplines, and the way in which the institute would operate.

Jinesta, Ricardo. *Penitentiary Evolution in Costa Rica.* San Jose: Falcó Printing House, 1940.
The history of imposed punishments is traced from the first stages of human societies when revenge was an important motive. During the last century, several scholars made possible humanitarian modification of punishment. Offenders have come to be viewed in light of their lack of education, possible insanity, and the baneful effects of environment. The book also reviews the evolution of social institutions, under different systems, which has had both direct and indirect influence on the persons living within their environments. One chapter deals with penal developments in Costa Rica through the indigenous, conquest, and colonial periods. Discussion is complemented by statistics covering the twentieth century and proposed legislation for reform and regulation of prisons.

Latin American Institute for the Prevention and Treatment of Delinquency (ILANUD). *Crime and Delinquency in San Ramon: A Diagnosis.* San Jose: National Publishing House, 1977.
This survey of crime in the area of San Ramon, a Costa Rican city, was carried out by a team of professionals in social science and fifty secondary-school students. The interview schedules were designed to determine the general and specific criminogenic factors in a rural society obtaining increased access to higher education.

Montero, Jorge A. *Problems and Needs of Criminal Policy in Latin America.* San Jose: National Publishing House, 1976.
Montero states that increases in delinquency and the reactions of society to delinquency call for better governmental control under a criminal policy based primarily on crime prevention in connection with national development. No plan, no matter how well conceived and supported by research, can be definitive unless allowance is made for the constant evaluation of the effects of social change. This survey of criminality and its sources makes the important reassertion that criminal policy planning should be integrative. The police, the judicial power, and the penitentiary subsystem should operate in close coordination with national development. Latin American countries, Montero argues, have failed to develop criminal policy in this fashion.

Montero, Jorge A., and Elías Carranz. *Training of Personnel Specialized in Crime Prevention.* San Jose: ILANUD, 1980.

The authors contend that combining the modern concepts of prevention and training is essential. To achieve real crime prevention, certain groups must receive specialized training suitable to their particular place and function in either general or special prevention: the population at large, the police, the judicial power, penitentiary institutions, and after-care staff. The authors examine the required type of training in terms of specialization and interdisciplinary subject matter. Specific action-oriented tasks are envisaged. The possibilities for ILANUD to act in this field are analyzed.

13

MEXICO

Antonio Sanchez Galindo

Alcoholism was of extreme concern to the Aztecs, Cuarón[1] tells us in his review of diseases that were mentioned by the early residents of the area now known as Mexico. To combat alcoholism, the Aztec emperor recommended that *octli* not be consumed and that alcoholics be repudiated and exposed to punishments amounting to public shame. Corporal punishment was inflicted—beatings that could culminate in death—when the alcoholic was a notable person or priest. Nevertheless, elderly people were permitted to imbibe. With the conquest of Mexico by the Spaniards, punishments for inebriation were eliminated and prohibition relaxed.

CRIME AND PUNISHMENT IN "NEW SPAIN"

The response to alcoholics is only one illustration of the multiple preoccupations of the aborigines of Mexico with the control of criminal conduct within their different communities. In addition to inebriation, the Aztecs were confronted with other forms of deviance that were considered criminal acts: abortion, abuse of trust, accusation, concealment, assault, slander, judicial slander, damage to another's property, rape, sheltering a criminal, false testimony, falsification of measures, witchcraft, homicide, incest, misappropriation of funds, embezzlement, pederasty, fighting, robbery, insurrection, and treason. In addition, there were particular crimes with configurations determined by situational factors. For example, prostitution was considered a crime, but, when practiced by a noble Aztec woman, the charge was reduced to an unlawful act.

A diversity of punishment was applied; the chief sanctions were slavery, opprobrious and corporal punishments, exile, confiscation of property, fine, imprisonment, dismissal from employment or office, and capital punishment. Punishment by death was applied very frequently and with rigor. The diverse forms of execution were imposed in accordance with the gravity and type of crime committed. As generally understood, the prison was a place of custody while awaiting the imposition of another sanction, but it was also a sanction in itself for minor offenses.

Criminal justice became a "criminology of the powerful conqueror and invader" with the onset of the colonial period that began with the conquest of Mexico by the Spaniards in 1521 and ended with the gaining of independence from Spain in 1821. "From a purely ideal point of view," Eohánove Trujillo says, "the laws which Spain gave to its American colonies were excellent."[2] Many of the cases for Indians were so favorable to them that, as a collection of laws, they were known as a "code of exemptions and privileges."

The fundamental vice of the Spanish colonial administration, however, was the interpretation of the Spanish Criminal Code. The discrepancies between the legal norms and their applications in reality became flagrant because the code developed for the colonies demoralized the officials who already believed that the legal ideals could not be accomplished. Hypocrisy was encouraged, even when the intentions were commendable, because the decision-makers were convinced that the legal precepts as presented in the laws could not be carried out. If we also consider the voracity of the conquerors who sought only to enrich themselves, corruption was the product of the combination of breach of legal norms and ardor for private profit. The sense of justice and associated values were undermined increasingly by the buying and selling of judicial decisions, with the cost of buying "justice" subject to changes in the current level of economic payments.

In addition, the Inquisition, a religious tribunal imported from Spain by the viceroys and established in Mexico City on November 4, 1571, instilled fear among all inhabitants. The tribunal of the Inquisition relied on several prisons: Cárcel de Perpétua or la Misercordia (The Perpetual or the Compassionate), la Cárcel Secreta (the Secret Prison), and la Cárcel de la Roperiá (the Prison of the Wardrobe). Sentences were imposed for heresy, libel, slander, blasphemy, idolatry, Judaizing, rebelliousness, and Frenchification. The tribunal employed very brief trials which usually concluded with the penalty of death. With the passage of time, respect for the tribunal diminished, and ridicule eventually replaced awe.

The struggle for political independence lasted from September 27, 1821, through September 15, 1910. During this period, both the insurgents and the colonial authorities practiced great cruelty, each faction following its own form of summary justice. Executions at the wall and decapitations were public and widely publicized in efforts to dissuade resistance and to intimidate opponents. Instant jails were filled with dissidents. Assaults without warning, unpunished homicides, ravenous plunder, and acts of personal revenge were rampant.

EARLY CRIMINOLOGY AND CRIMINAL POLICY

By 1871, Mexico was moving toward participation in the worldwide development of criminology and penology. The second phase of national independence, instigated by Benito Juárez, began to produce results. The positive school of criminology made a strong impression on Mexican thought which was favorable to liberalism. From this point in history, although in an incipient form, the scientific perspective gained a foothold in Mexico through the dynamic influence on the study of criminals from the perspectives of Lombroso, Garofalo, Ferri, and Lacassagne.

In addition to the beginning of appreciation for the principle of legality, the state of the prisons received serious consideration. Dr. Enoch C. Wines represented Mexico at the Conference on Penitentiaries in London through appointment by Benito Juárez. As the representative of "a commission of distinguished and intelligent citizens" (1871) named by the Supreme Government of the Mexican Republic, Dr. Wines reported:

> This Commission announces that the capital of the Republic has a prison for the detained, another for sentenced adult prisoners, and a facility for the poor now serving as a detention center for condemned children. In addition there is a special establishment for young people from nine to eighteen years of age, in which they receive a moral education, and a vocation is taught to them.[3]

Until 1872, the year in which Juárez died, the principal prisons in Mexico were the jails in the capital cities. Especially prominent were those in Puebla and Guadalajara. The crimes most frequently resulting in imprisonment were predominantly those of violence (homicide, infliction of serious injuries, and rape) and secondarily, crimes against property, robbery, assault, cattle theft, fraud, and embezzlement. This period was one of nation-building and grave economic deprivation.

After the death of Juárez and with the increasing influence of positivism, the scientific approach experienced significant expansion. The urgent need for prison construction was met more by providing physical facilities than by serving humanitarian purposes. Under the direction of Carlos Roumagnac, the development of a modern police force was begun, with the establishment of fingerprinting and identification systems. Anthropological methods of biotypology and studies of tattooing—including group testing as used by Martínez Bacca—were practiced. Scientific seminars were conducted with international scholars among the participants. The administration of Porfirio Díaz (1875-1910) supported this early flowering of scientific activity. One tangible product of this support was the permanent incorporation of medical services in the prisons.[4]

Then came the Revolution which, as Rodríquez Manzanera says, was "the most important movement, psychologically speaking, in the history of Mexico, since a true independence succeeded. . . . The Mexican people could not support a dictatorship for long; their individualism was impeded."[5] By 1917, a new constitution was promulgated; its Article 18 set forth for the first time a penitentiary policy consistent with criminological principles. Two penal codes appeared:

the Almaraz of 1929 and that of 1931. Article 18 was amended in 1975 in support of penal reform.

The administration of General Lázaro Cárdenas (1934-1940) did not ignore crime prevention and treatment of offenders, but the interest was perfunctory. There were fewer innovations than in the previous decade; those that were attempted had a precarious existence.

THE "MIRACLE OF TOLUCA"

Not until 1967 did the State of Mexico[6] create an authentic system of penitentiary treatment. The Minimum Standards of the United Nations were influential, but other features of modern penology were also heeded: establishing legal legitimacy for the prisons, creating standards for the recruitment and hiring of personnel, design of suitable physical facilities, introduction of progressive techniques, individualized treatment, indeterminate sentencing, introduction of parole, after-care services, and assistance to victims of crime.

Within the short period of four years, the governor of the State of Mexico, Juan Fernández Albarrán, had attained results that in 1971 stimulated a penal reform movement at the national level. It is fitting that what has been known as the "miracle of Toluca"[7] was implemented by Dr. Alfonso Quiroz Cuarón and Dr. Sergio García Ramírez. García Ramírez has said that it was his lot to continue the work of Dr. Quiroz Cuarón. Unusual innovations were accomplished in the penitentiaries that previously had been implemented in only incomplete and fortuitous ways. García Ramírez summarizes the accomplishments of the "miracle of Toluca."[8]

> During the period of the organization and consolidation of the Central Penitentiary, the State of Mexico has enriched its index of elements for the treatment of delinquents with physical and juridical instruments which mutually complement each other as follows: 1) Law for execution of penalties for full confinement and for limited restriction of liberty; 2) the Central Penitentiary of the State of Mexico; 3) law for rehabilitative treatment of juveniles; 4) a school for rehabilitation of juveniles; 5) a system of prerelease treatment, including furloughs; 6) partial remission of penalties in exchange for work and affording educational and psychological intervention programs for prisoners; 7) a statute authorizing open institutions; and 8) aftercare for released inmates. . . .[9] The real consequence of these elements was the completeness of the changes in the criminal policy of the State.

In more detail, García Ramírez lists the specific contributions that the Central Penitentiary has made to its inmates and in some instances to Mexico's penology:

> For the first time, carefully formulated treatment plans have been carried out after integrated diagnoses of prisoners in accord with the practical purposes of the individualization of penal treatment. In conformity with Article 18 of the Federal Constitution and the Law for the Execution of Penalties of the State of Mexico, treatment of untried defendants, and especially of sentenced prisoners, has met standards in regard to medical, psychiatric, psychological, labor, pedagogic, and social programs.

A genuinely progressive penitentiary system, as opposed to one of classical character, has been based on study of the inmate's personality and the introduction of successive stages of treatment. The techniques of observation in classification stand out among those typical of Mexico.

Introduction of weekend leaves and day-time furloughs for inmates in the final stage of confinement previous to their release from prison.

Construction of the first full-fledged open prison in the Republic of Mexico.

Creation of pilot treatment groups, a unique experiment for Mexico, which emphasize individualization of the inmates' experiences while in prison.

A technical counsel panel is composed of the chiefs of various divisions, other technical personnel, and advisors from outside the penitentiary. In clinical sessions, individual cases are discussed to suggest treatment plans for inmates, to offer opinions on partial remission of sentences, and to recommend improvements in prison operations.

Selection and training of custodial personnel is conducted at a technical level not matched elsewhere in Mexico.

The system of prisoner classification takes maximum advantage of the available physical facilities to separate inmates according to the following categories: sex status, juridical circumstances, recidivism, felonious potential, dangerousness, conduct record, and age.

Classification proceedings are conducted to meet an integrated set of standards that serve juridical, correctional, medical, psychological, pedagogical, social work, and prerelease purposes.

Formal communication to all new inmates admitted to prison, in keeping with recommendations of the United Nations and the requirements of law, their rights and obligations and the nature of life in prison.

Strict and just administration of prison regulations in regard to infractions and rewards for meritorious conduct, including informing inmates of charges against them, providing a proper hearing, and permitting the inmate the opportunity to present a defense.

Work assignment of inmates that is unprecedented in Mexico for achieving the matching of inmate with tasks useful to him and are remunerated in accordance with the quality of work accomplished.

Increase in the level of inmate wage payments, in keeping with quality of work productivity, that is constantly adjusted to exceed the legal minimum of pay for equipment free labor in the area.

Management of all aspects of prison labor—assignment to tasks; acquisition of tools, machinery, and raw materials; distribution and sale of products—to avoid competition with free labor and industry by following the state-use system.

Inmate wages are used to support dependents, placed in a savings account with interest credited to the inmate, use for reparation of damages to victims, or to meet the immediate needs of the inmate. These policies are not typical of all penal systems in Mexico.

Vocational training of inmates is emphasized, not only high productivity, as the purpose of workshop instructors who are free persons employed by the government for this purpose.

An academic program, unique in Mexico, assumes that adult prisoners requiring formal education require a program differing from that designed for children if the purpose of social rehabilitation is to be achieved. Primary academic instruction is important but is supplemented by instruction in work attitudes, hygiene, physical education, civics, artistic activities, ethics, and social behavior.

Within the scope of education, plans have been developed for a library of books and periodicals, and a recreational program of music, artistic performances, and sports in the prison.

The medical services of the penitentiary include general medicine, dentistry, and psychiatry; when specialized care is necessary, hospitals outside the prison are used. Among the latter are institutions for detention of the criminally insane.

The psychiatrist and the psychologists apply group psychotherapy in pilot groups of long-term prisoners and for women requiring such treatment.

The Office of Social Work endeavors to sustain and promote healthy relationships between inmates and family members through visitation and social assistance. Conjugal visits are authorized but under careful control. Although this practice is not necessarily followed by all prisons in Mexico, permission is contingent upon proof of marriage or of a stable marital relationship as a safeguard against the exercise of prostitution. Absence of venereal disease must be officially verified by the penitentiary medical service for inmates and by a health center for visitors.

The dominance of inmate subcultures and subterranean "business" transactions—including the involvement of staff members—have been suppressed. Prison-operated canteens provide for inmate purchases of personal items under state management. Incidentally, the awarding of honor-grade status to inmates is based on rehabilitative criteria, rather than the customary distribution of this distinction according to the economic capacity of the inmate.

An administrative segregation unit shelters those inmates with acute personality problems. The Central Penitentiary has abolished the sanctioning system that employs special dungeons for physical and psychological management because it has been demonstrated that many of the rule violators require psychiatric help more than disciplinary correction.

To avoid criminogenic influences, the detainees are isolated from the convicted prisoners. Here "detainees" are individuals for whom an order of either imprisonment or release has not been issued within the 72 hours required by law.

A steady increase of the productivity of industrial programs has permitted reinvestment in new workshops and acquisition of machinery and equipment. This surplus accumulated in addition to the payment of inmate wages. The surplus has been used also for construction of an open facility, renovation of sections of the penitentiary, financing of services for released prisoners, and assistance to various district jails.

Close coordination and technical counsel for the development of the prison programs has been gained from various agencies and institutions, public and private, state and federal.

Inservice training of the staff of the Central Penitentiary has also served officials of other prisons. Research projects of scientific quality unprecedented in Mexican penology have been concerned chiefly with penitentiary problems and genetic anthropology.[10]

PENOLOGY AND CRIMINOLOGY AT THE NATIONAL LEVEL

As already stated, the "miracle of Toluca" stimulated reform at the national level beginning in 1971, one hundred years after the first penal code. The Penitentiary of the Federal District was constructed in 1957. The Prison for Women and the Institution of Michoacán were built in 1952.[11] The Law of

Minimum Standards for the Social Rehabilitation of the Sentenced was promulgated. The detailed and profound reform of penal codes followed the principles of deinstitutionalization, decriminalization, and avoidance of criminal stigmatization. New penitentiary buildings were constructed; construction continued to replace old and obsolete facilities. The Preventive Centers of the Federal District began to function.

Provisions for training personnel have been expanded; examples are the Training Center for the Preventive Detention Centers of the Federal District, the Training Center for Coordinated Services of Prevention and Social Rehabilitation, the National Institute of Penal Sciences, and several schools in some states such as Mexico and Jalisco.[12] The National Institute of Penal Sciences now offers postgraduate education at a very high level and sponsors conferences on criminology such as the 1979 conference in Mexico City, D.F., attended by prominent criminologists of Latin America.

Recent years have revived the penitentiary conventions that had been practically suspended. They were held from 1923 to 1932 and then were suspended until 1952. The next convention was held in 1969, sponsored in Toluca by the State of Mexico. They were held in Morelia[13] in 1972, Sonora[14] in 1974, and Monterrey[15] in 1976.

The professional institutionalization of criminology has been advanced by the development of associations of criminology. The Mexican Society of Criminology in some measure continues the activities initiated in 1932 by the Mexican Academy of Penal Sciences. Javier Piña y Palacios is the president of the Mexican Society of Criminology and the director of the Mexican Academy of Penal Sciences. There is also the Institute of Criminology for the Procurement of Justice of the Federal District, directed by Dr. Juan Pablo de Tavira y Noriega. The Mexican Library of Prevention and Social Rehabilitation has given prestige to Mexico in its field.

Systematic research of scientific quality has been undertaken into diverse topics, including frequency of felonious crimes, violence, genetic sources of violent crimes, and the rhythm of criminality. A national study of penitentiaries was launched as the important basis for policymaking.

Criminology as an applied science came to Mexico rather late. It was the 1920s when applied studies were undertaken by José Gómez Robleda, Alfonso Quiroz Cuarón, Edmundo Buentello, Francisco Núñez Chávez, and Matilde Rodríguez Cabo of the Supreme Council of Social Prevention that later was made a department. Their work was in criminal psychology, anthropology, forensic psychiatry, and social work in prisons. Their significant research was to have applications and implications a decade later. They created criminological experience for the first time in Mexico, before Laudet succeeded in giving it legitimacy in 1939.

Gómez Robleda predicted that the judges of the future would be physicians, not lawyers. In novel form, he published two criminological studies based on his research: *El Güero* [The Blonde] and *El Ladrón* [The Thief]. Carrancá y Rivas said these novels inspired experimental studies.

From this base, Mexican criminology in practical terms presented Dr. Alfonso Quiroz Cuarón as the only criminologist who was developed and was graduated in Mexico.[16] By the 1960s, a new generation of criminologists, educated in various European countries, was to emerge as a well-prepared and prestigious nucleus for scientific criminology. In the history of Mexican criminology, Dr. Quiroz Cuarón stands out as the master criminologist. One of his students was Dr. Luis Rodríguez Manzanera[17]—a jurist, psychologist, and criminologist—who said: "Utilizing a term coined in the origins of criminology, we should risk describing Master Quiroz Cuarón as a born criminologist!"

From childhood, Quiroz Cuarón appeared to be attracted to the mysteries of criminal conduct. This attraction launched him upon an interdisciplinary education in medicine, psychology, and law. He considered criminology to be a scientific synthesis, causal explicative, natural, and cultural in its examination of criminal behavior. Criminology was to be scientifically rigorous with precise definitions; as a man of science, he opposed "literary criminology." In the hundred articles and dozen books he authored, Quiroz Cuarón demonstrated the potentialities of criminology as a union of the natural and cultural sciences. In this chapter, his work is used as a framework for presenting a panoramic view of Mexico's criminology.

The base of knowledge established by Professor Quiroz Cuarón is being expanded by a new generation of Mexican criminologists, including Sergio García Ramírez, Luis Rodríguez Manzanera, Gustavo Barreto Rangel, Rafael Ruiz Harrell, Victoria Adato de Ibarra, Gustavo Malo Camacho, Javier Piña y Palacios, Raúl Carrancá y Rivas, Salvador López Calderon, Ricardo Franco Guzman, and Hilda Marchiori. A rising generation of young criminologists is being oriented under the direction of Dr. Sergio García Ramírez at the Institute of Penal Sciences.

From a broader point of view, Dr. Quiroz Cuarón played an important role in the development of Mexico's criminal justice: formation of the Banking Police; creation and development of the national police under the direction of persons such as Iturbide Alvirez and Piña y Palacios; founding of Los Patronatos para Reos Liberados, an organization that assists released prisoners directed by Buentello y Villa; appointment of qualified judges; reducing the disparity of sentences; creation of a national judicial cabinet; introduction of skills and laboratories for criminalistics with the collaboration of Rafael Moreno and Homero Villarreal; establishment of the Forensic Medical Service providing a corps of experts, with the participation of Fernández Pérez; creation of a central office to manage information for criminal identification; abolition of capital punishment; standardization of penal codes; reform of the juvenile courts; enactment of laws to coordinate the National Penitentiary System, with the collaboration of Sergio García Ramírez and Antonio Sánchez Galindo; removal of military personnel from the staff of the penitentiary; enlisting Mexico among the countries in INTERPOL; and establishing Centers for Juvenile Integration that specialize in preparing youth for work as pharmacy clerks.

FORENSIC MEDICINE AND VICTIMOLOGY

Quiroz Cuarón's final work was *Medicina Forense* (1977) [Forensic Medicine], which was also his most complete book. The voluminous and exhaustive treatise deals with the classic problems of forensic medicine, such as injuries, abortion, and violent deaths, but it goes beyond these topics to constitute a genuine analysis of criminological medicine. It is the most complete work on medical criminology known in the Spanish language. Forensic medicine is conceived, not as a science of medical skill in the service of justice, but as a theory of prevention integrating study of the criminal's personality with study of his victims.

Quiroz Cuarón's approach to victimology is illustrated by his book *Asaltos a Bancos en Venezuela y América* (1964) [Assaults on Banks in Venezuela and America], in which he draws on his long experience in the service of the Central Bank of America in an analysis of violence in Mexico as well as other Latin American countries. As was his custom, the work is oriented toward prevention. He emphasizes selection and training of bank personnel, as well as employing techniques within the bank's internal environment and its broader environment. He also emphasizes the role of the victim:

> Psychologically, many robberies result, not because of the ability, shrewdness or daring of the criminals, but because of the action or oversight of the victims themselves, whose subconscious motives allow themselves to indulge in excessive inattention. Negligence in the management of money or its equivalent is a chronic habit of their daily life. To let oneself be robbed is conduct that is the equivalent of a frustrated act, which like all frustrated conduct is active, sought and desired. The hidden forces in the unconscious of the owners of property, set free by a sentiment of guilt, leads them to work against their interests and their fortunes.
>
> It is taken into account, of course, by criminals in their diverse behavioral patterns but principally when they act as a group. The criminal action of the criminal gang is the revealing sign of the serious criminality of a collectivity, in whose bosom are hidden other acts of social, political and economic dispositions most grave, which serve as a support for the aggressive criminality of the young people. The distinctive shadings of differences between the criminal gang, riots, skirmishes and wars, rebellions or revolutions, are perceptible only to the most penetrating scrutiny.[18]

Forensic medicine and victimology also were combined in a study, in collaboration with Samuel Maynes Puentes, of notorious crimes: *Psicoanálisis del Magnicidio* (1965) [Psychology of Violent Murders of Very Important Persons].[19] They conducted investigations of murders that especially captured public attention, the characteristics of the slayers, and the characteristics of the victims. The notorious murderers were classified as either mentally ill or those who "are symptomatic of strong psychological tensions, especially when the 'magnicide' is preceded by other criminal acts that reflect problems—whether religious, racial, or political-economic—that undermine the society." Quiroz Cuarón and

Puentes emphasize psychiatric variables in explaining these crimes and in their recommendations for preventing assassinations:

Envy is only sick admiration.... Only when resentment accumulates and completely poisons the soul can it express itself through a criminal act.... Envy and hate are sins of strictly individual projection. It (the crime) always assumes a duel between the one who hates or envies and the hated or envied. Resentment is a passion that has much of the impersonal, of the social.

Protecting the life of a chief of state never should be the function of impulsive or violent types, as generally are those persons who accompany him (the chief of state) but should be a problem of selection and careful disciplining of those to whom these delicate missions are entrusted.... Exaggerated protection, of course, expresses the conscience and the sentiments of guilt.[20]

As a remarkable clinician, Quiroz Cuarón conducted some of the most publicized criminological clinical examinations in Mexico, including those of Ramón Mercader ("Jacques Mornard"), the assassin of Leon Trotsky, Gregorio Cardenas, and Sobera de la Flor. From these studies, a number of books and articles were published: *El Asesino de Leon Trotzky y su Peligrosidad* (1957) [The Assassin of Leon Trotsky and His Dangerousness], *Un Estrangulador de Mujeres* [A Strangler of Women], and *Dictamen sobre la Personalidad del Delincuente* [Judgment on the Personality of the Delinquent]. Quiroz Cuarón's qualifications were first developed during his education in the School of Medicine where he presented his master's thesis in 1939, "Examen Somático-Funcional: Su Técnica" [Somatic-Functional Examination: Its Technique]. Subsequently, he practiced his clinical skills in juvenile and adult courts and in private practice.

ECONOMIC FACTORS AND CRIMINALITY

The social-psychological elements implied above were supplemented by Quiroz Cuarón's examination of the relationships between economics and criminality, as especially revealed in his *Teoría Exonomica de los Disturbios* (1970) [Economic Theory of Disturbances]. His analysis may be summarized by stating his four principles:

1. Criminality is directly proportional to size of the population and inversely proportional to level of income.
2. In whatever human concentration, sociopolitical stability will be broken if the rate of increase of net income is less than double the rate of increase of population numbers plus the square of this rate.
3. Criminality is determined fundamentally by the rate of change in size of the population and of net per capita income.
4. It is less difficult, more congenial to understanding—perhaps more complex to manage but certainly more promising for reaching conclusions

quickly—to consider the effects of the rate of income rather than of the rate of population change.

Supporting these principles with a profusion of statistical data, Quiroz Cuarón predicted that the society that is experiencing social unrest will experience the disturbances of crime. In this sense, crime represents a cost borne by the host society. In collaboration with his brother Raúl, he conducted a sophisticated and complete investigation of this facet of economic analysis. The book, *Costo Social del Delito* (1970) [The Social Cost of Crime], calculates the total social cost of crime in Mexico by taking many variables into consideration: The intrinsic cost of crime; the economic goods the criminal fails to produce; the economic goods the victim fails to produce; loss of productivity to the victim's family; loss of productivity to the criminal's family; payments of the criminal and his victims to intermediaries and the authorities in the official processing of the criminal case, plus what was paid by the victims; wages, salaries, compensations, and social security contributions for personnel involved in the investigation and prosecution of crime; amortization, maintenance, and upkeep of buildings and equipment of the police and public administrators; illicit payments by criminals and victims to corrupt officials; salaries of court personnel; amortization, maintenance, and upkeep of buildings and equipment of the courts and pretrial detention facilities; costs of public defenders, experts employed in evaluating evidence and giving trial testimony, servers of legal documents, and legal counsel for victims; wages of penitentiary personnel; amortization, maintenance, and upkeep of penitentiary buildings and equipment; payments of criminals and their relatives to various intermediaries and penitentiary employees; and a variety of more minor and miscellaneous factors.[21]

It was argued that prevention would be less costly to society than sole reliance on repression. For homicide alone, it was estimated that a single homicide in 1965 on the average would cost $499,040 (Mexican dollars), or an annual total of $2,759,080 for the known homicides of that year. For 72.8 percent of all crimes registered in the Republic in 1965, the total cost of $3,650,500 exceeded by $122,880 the federal budget of 1970 for the decentralized departments of the Republic and represented 7.3 percent of the total public debt of all Latin American countries.

BIOMEDICAL INVESTIGATION

As for many criminologists in Latin America and elsewhere in the world, Mexican criminologists have a keen interest in the biotypical study of criminals. Here too, Quiroz Cuarón—in collaboration with his teacher José Gómez Robleda—contributed a notable biomedical study: *El Tipo Sumario* (1949) [The Summary Type]. They succeeded in simplifying the complex biotypological systems developed by others in different parts of the world. Among these others were G. Viola, N. Pende, W. H. Sheldon, Mario Bárbara, and Ernest Kretschmer.

The study began with the premise that, with height governed by laws of heredity and weight modified by environmental changes, height is the best index of the constitution and weight is the best index of temperament. Taking only those two factors into consideration—weight and height—Gómez Robleda and Quiroz Cuarón launched into the experimental field, measuring and weighing thousands of subjects of Mexican nationality. They wanted to identify the summary type of Mexican. By studying the population of Mexico, they sought to avoid the common error of reaching false conclusions for Mexico by using foreign studies.

They concluded that the two variables were enough to establish valid results. Their conclusion set them into opposition to other authors who had made complex measurements of many variables: weight, height, length of the arms, legs, and thorax, partial height, perimeters, diameters, and so on.

From their data, Gómez Robleda and Quiroz Cuarón constructed a table with sigma units in which the formula $P - E = D$ ($W - H = D$)[22] was contrived; that is, weight minus height equals deviation. If the deviation is positive (=), it will be treated as a brachytype. If it is negative (-), we find a longtype. When there is no deviation (0), the person is a normal type.

In addition to developing a table for calculating the summary type, Gómez Robleda and Quiroz Cuarón elaborated on differentiated morphological characteristics and their psychosomatic correlates. They related a large number of morphological and psychosomatic characteristics to prognosticate those relationships that were strongly typical.

From a broader perspective, physical anthropology and archaeology excited Quiroz Cuarón's research interest because of his passion for the history of his fatherland. Two of his books continue to arouse debate: *El Estudio de los Huesos de Hernán Cortés* (1956) [Study of the Bones of Hernan Cortes] and *El Descumbrimiento y Estudio de los Restos de Cuauhtémoc* (1950) [The Discovery and Study of the Remains of Cuauhtemoc].

PATTERNS OF CRIME IN MEXICO

It is appropriate to conclude this chapter with a review of some of the patterns of crime in Mexico as reported by Professor Quiroz Cuarón in a study covering thirty-eight years of criminality: *La Criminalidad en la Republica Mexicana* (1969) [Criminality in the Mexican Republic].

The annual average number of crimes reported was 43,161, of which 25,138 (or 58 percent) resulted in the imposition of a sanction. On an average day, thirty homicides were committed, or 48.1 per 100,000 inhabitants for the given year, of which seventeen homicides go unpunished. Over the years the situation has improved, but it is still unsatisfactory. Violent crimes constitute about 53 percent of the total number. Of one hundred reported offenses, ninety-two are perpetrated by males, or 12.5 men for each female offender. Of those persons convicted of a crime and sentenced, 93 percent are males, or 14.8 males per female offender.

On an average, a crime occurs in Mexico every twelve minutes. A homicide takes place every eighty minutes, a crime resulting in physical injuries every thirty-eight minutes, a sexual offense every ten hours and ten minutes, an abduction and/or rape every three hours and twelve minutes, a robbery every forty-eight minutes, damage to another person's property every seven hours and forty-eight minutes, and a fraud every nine hours and twenty-one minutes.

Obviously, criminology in Mexico does not lack for subject matter. As recent developments testify, Mexican criminology will likely continue to grow. In the applied sectors, there have been encouraging developments, but there is need for further progress because, as Dr. Quiroz Cuarón said, "penalty without treatment is not justice, it is vengeance."

NOTES

1. Alfonso Quiroz Cuarón, "Fray Bernardio de Shagun" [History of Things in New Spain] in *Medicina Forense* [Forensic Medicine] (Mexico City: Editorial Porrúa, 1977).
2. Carlos A. Echánove Trujillo, *Sociología Mexicana* [Mexican Sociology] (Mexico City: Editorial Porrúa, 1963).
3. Enoch C. Wines, "Informe que acerca de los Sistemas Penitenciarios rinde ante el Supremo Gobierno de la Republica Mexicana" (Information on the Penitentiary Systems Submitted to the Supreme Governor of the Republic of Mexico), translated into Spanish by Enrique de Olavarria y Ferrari (Mexico City: Government Printing, 1873), pp. 48, 78, 99, 119, 132, 150, 181, 206, 222, and 238. Enoch Cobb Wines was the first president of the National Prison Association, organized in Cincinnati in 1870, and was an official delegate at the International Penitentiary Congress in London.
4. Dr. Roberto Peimbert, Jr., *Evolución Histórica de los Servicos Médicos Penales y su Progrección Actual* [Historical Evolution of Penal Medical Services and Their Projection Today] (Mexico City: Printed by the Department of the Federal District, 1972). The report was prepared under the direction of the Neuropsychiatric Unit, Central Hospital of the Penal Medical Services.
5. Dr. Luis Rodríguez Manzanera, *Ejecución Penal y Adaptación Social en los Países en Desarrollo. Eu la Reforma Penal en los Países en Desarrollo* [Penal Execution and Social Adaptation in the Developing Countries. On Penal Reform in the Developing Countries] (Mexico City: Universidad Nacional Autónoma de Mexico, 1978).
6. The State of Mexico is one of the twenty-eight states of the Republic of Mexico. It is located west and north of the Federal District; the capital city of the Republic, Mexico, D.F., is located within the Federal District.
7. Toluca is the capital of the State of Mexico.
8. Dr. Sergio García Ramírez, *Balance y Resumen sobre el Centro Penitenciario del Estado de Mexico* [Balance Sheet and Summary of the Central Penitentiary of the State of Mexico] (Toluca: Government of the State of Mexico, 1969), pp. 17-22.
9. I add that later legislation was enacted for the assistance of the victims of crime.
10. Garcia Ramírez, *Balance y Resumen*, pp. 17-22.

11. Michoacán, a state in the Republic, borders the State of Mexico to the north and west. Morelia is the capital of Michoacán.

12. One of the states of the Republic, Jalisco, borders on the State of Michoacán to the north and west. Guadalajara is the capital of Jalisco.

13. Morelia is the capital of the State of Michoacán.

14. Sonora, a state of the Republic in the northwest, is bordered on the north by Arizona in the United States.

15. Monterrey is the capital of the State of Nuevo León which is in the northeastern part of the Republic.

16. The bibliography at the end of this chapter lists some of his many publications.

17. The bibliography lists some of Dr. Rodríguez Manzanera's publications.

18. Alfonso Quiroz Cuarón, *Asaltos a Bancos en Venezuela y América* [Assaults on Banks in Venezuela and America] (Mexico City: Editorial Morales Hermanos, 1964). For the sake of brevity, the flavor of the analysis has been summarized without direct quotation.

19. "Magnicidio" is a coined expression describing "great" violent murders of very important persons in the sense of the prefix *magni* in English.

20. Alfonso Quiroz Cuarón and Samuel Maynes Puente, *Psicoanálisis del Magnicidio* [Psychology of Violent Murders of Very Important Persons] (Mexico City: Editorial Juridica Mexicana, 1965), pp. 27-31.

21. For purposes of comparative criminology, these variables and the estimates for Mexico could be related to similar studies conducted elsewhere, including the following: E. R. Hawkins and Willard Waller, "Critical Notes on the Cost of Crime," *Journal of Criminal Law and Criminology* 46 (January-February 1956):657-672; J. P. Martin and J. Bradley, "Design of a Study of the Cost of Crime," *British Journal of Criminology* 4 (October 1964):591-603; President's Commission on Law Enforcement and Administration of Justice, *The Challenge of Crime in a Free Society* (Washington, D.C.: U.S. Government Printing Office, 1967), pp. 33-34.

22. In Spanish $P - E = D$ refers to Peso - Estatura = Desviación; in English the formula would read $W - H = D$, or Weight minus Height equals Deviation.

BIBLIOGRAPHY

From the extensive criminological literature of Mexico, the following works have been selected to represent the range of scholarly interests and of practical concerns. These items supplement the literature drawn upon in preparing the chapter proper.

TREATISES ON CRIMINOLOGY

Beccaria, César Bonesana. *Tratados de los Delitos y de las Penas* [An Essay on Crime and Punishment]. Trans. Constancio Bernaldo de Quirós. Pubebla: Editorial José M. Cajica, 1957.

Bergalli, Roberto. *Criminología en América Latina* [Criminology in Latin America]. Buenos Aires: Editorial Pannedille, 1972.

Bernaldo de Quirós, Constancio. *Lecciones de Criminología* [Readings on Criminology]. Puebla: Editorial Cajica, 1948.

Bernaldo de Quirós, Constancio. *Criminología* [Criminology]. Puebla: Editorial Cajica, 1956.

Cuello Calón, Eugenio. *La Moderna Penología* [Modern Penology]. Reprinted. Barcelona: Casa Editorial Bosch, Inc., 1958.

Laignel-Lavastine, M., and V. V. Stanciu. *Compendio de Criminología* [Abstract on Criminology]. Trans. Alfonso Quiroz Cuarón. Mexico City: Jurídica Mexicana, 1959.

Marchiori, Hilda. *Psicología de la Conducta Delictiva* [Psychology of Criminal Conduct]. Buenos Aires: Edicionnes Pannedille Saecic, 1973.

Marcó del Pont, Luis. *Penología y Sistemas Carcelarios.* [Penology and Prison Systems]. Vols. 1 and 2. Buenos Aires: Ediciones Depalma, 1975.

Martínez de Castro, Antonio. "Exposición de Motivos de Código Penal" [Interpretation of Penal Code Motives]. *Revista de Derecho Penal Contemporaneo*, Volumen Especial, 1971.

Ortiz, Orlando. *La Violencia en México—Antologias Temáticas* [Violence in Mexico—Thematic Anthologies]. Mexico City: Editorial Diógenes, S.A., 1971.

Quiroz Cuarón, Alfonso. *La Pena de Muerte en México* [The Death Penalty in Mexico]. Mexico City: Ediciones Botas, 1962.

Quiroz Cuarón, Alfonso. "Crimen en México" [Crime in Mexico]. *Criminalia* 26, No. 1.

Quiroz Cuarón, Alfonso, and Raúl Quiroz Cuarón. *El Costo Social del Delito en México.* [The Social Cost of Crime in Mexico]. Mexico City: Ediciones Botas, 1970.

Quiroz Cuarón, Alfonso, and Samuel Maynes Puente. *El Psicoanálisis del Magnicidio* [Psychoanalysis of Magnicide]. Mexico City: Editorial Jurídica Mexicana, 1965.

Veiga da Carvallo, Hilario. *Compendio de Criminología* [Abstract on Criminology] José Bushatsky (ed.) (São Paulo, Brazil: 1973).

Principles of Criminal Law

Bernaldo de Quirós, Constancio. *Lecciones de Derecho Penitenciaro* [Readings on Penitentiary Law]. Mexico City: Imprenta Universitaria, 1952.

Carrancá y Rivas, Raúl. *Derecho Penitenciaro, Cárcel y Penas en México* [Penitentiary Law, Prison and Punishment in Mexico]. Mexico City: Editorial Porrúa, 1974.

Carrancá y Trujillo, Raúl. *Derecho Penal Mexicano, Parte General* [Mexican Penal Law, General Statement]. Mexico City: Editorial Porrúa, 1974.

Florian, Eugenio. *Tratado de Derecho Penal* [Treatise on Penal Law]. Buenos Aires, Argentina: EDIASA, 1970.

García Maynes, Eduardo. *Introducción al Estudio del Derecho* [Introduction to the Study of Law]. 5th ed. Mexico City: Editorial Porrúa, 1953.

García Ramírez, Sergio. *La Imputabilidad en el Derecho Penal Federal Mexicano* [Imputability of Mexican Federal Penal Law]. Mexico City: Universidad Nacional Autónoma de México, Instituto de Investigaciones Jurídicas, 1968.

González Bustamante, Juan José. *Principios de Derecho Procesal Penal Mexicano* [Principles of the Mexican Legal Process]. 2d ed. Mexico City: Editorial Porrúa, 1947.

Jiménez de Azúa, Luis. *La Ley y el Delito* [Law and Crime]. 2d ed. Mexico City: Editorial Hermes, 1945.

Tena Ramírez, Felipe. *Derecho Constitucional Mexicano* [Mexican Constitutional Law]. Mexico City: Editorial Porrúa, 1955.

Facets of Penitentiary Administration

Adato de Ibarra, Victoria. *La Cárcel Preventiva de la Ciudad México* [The Preventive Prison of the City of Mexico]. Mexico City, Ediciones Botas, 1972.

Bergamini Miotto, Armida. *Curso de Derecho Penitenciaro* [Course on Penitentiary Law]. São Paulo, Brazil: Saraiva, S.A., Libreios Ediciones, 1975.

El Centra Penitencia del Estadio de México [The Central Penitentiary of the State of Mexico]. Toluca: Estado de México, 1969.

García Ramírez, Sergio. *Represión y Tratamiento Penitenciaro de Criminales* [Repression and Penitentiary Treatment of Criminals]. Mexico City: Editorial Logos, S. de R.L., 1962.

García Ramírez, Sergio. *Asistencia a Reos Liberados* [Assistance to Released Prisoners]. Mexico City: Ediciones Botas, 1966.

García Ramírez, Sergio. *El Articulo 18 Constitucional: Prisión Preventiva, Sistema Penitenciaro, Menores Infractones* [Constitutional Article 18: Preventive Confinement, The Penitentiary System, Minor Law Breakers]. Mexico City: Universidad Nacional Autónoma de México, Coordinación de Humanidades, 1967.

García Ramírez, Sergio. *La Reforma Penal de 1971* [The Penal Reform of 1971]. Mexico City: Ediciones Botas, 1971.

Kent, Jorge. *El Patronato de Liberados y el Instituto de la Libertad Condicional* [Patronage for Former Prisoners and the Concept of Conditional Freedom]. Buenos Aires: Astrea, 1974.

Kent, Victoria. "Sobre Tratamiento Penitenciario Femenino" [On the Penitentiary Treatment of Women]. *Criminalia* 20, no. 11 (1952):325-337.

Piña y Palacios, Javier. *La Cárcel Perpétua de la Inquisición y la Real Cárcel de Corte de la Nueva España* [The "Perpetua" Prison of the Inquisition and the Royal Prison of the Court of New Spain]. Mexico City: Ediciones Botas, 1971.

Ruiz Funes, Mariano. *La Crisis de la Prisión* [The Prison Crisis]. Havana: Jesús Montero, 1949.

Sánchez Galindo, Antonia. *Manual de Conociminentos Basicos de Personal Penitenciaro* [Manual of Basic Knowledge for Penitentiary Staff]. Toluca: Ediciones Goberno del Estado de México, 1974.

Sánchez Galindo, Antonia. "El Trabajo en el Centro Penitenciario del Estado de México" [Work in the Penitentiary Complex of the State of Mexico]. *Cuardernos de Criminología del Centro Penitenciaro del Estado México*. Toluca: 1970.

Sánchez Galindo, Antonia. "Estudio Sobre la Reincidencia en el Centro Penitenciaro del Estado de México." [Study of Repeated Offenses in the Penitentiary Complex of Mexico]. *Cuardernos de Criminología del Centro del Estado de México*. Toluca; 1970.

Sánchez Galindo, Antonia. "El Trabajo Social en los Sistemas Penitenciarios Modernos" [Social Work in Modern Penitentiary Systems]. *Cuardernos de Criminología del Centro Penitenciaro del Estado de México*. Toluca; 1971.

14

UNITED STATES OF AMERICA

Robert F. Meier

Perhaps the most unmistakable feature of criminology in the United States is its diversity. This diversity extends to such matters as the disciplinary backgrounds of criminologists, the boundaries of that body of knowledge called "criminology," and many of the presumed facts upon which criminology as an area of study rests. In spite (or because) of the disputes this diversity breeds, criminology in the United States is among the world's most vibrant. This chapter attempts to trace lightly the changing character of American[1] criminology by sketching, first, the structure within which criminology in the United States is practiced, and, second, selected trends in criminological work since 1945.

THE DEVELOPMENT AND STRUCTURE OF AMERICAN CRIMINOLOGY

There is disagreement on whether any activity that is somehow connected with crime constitutes "criminology" and whether any person with an occupational relationship with crime or criminals is a "criminologist." While this confusion may not have retarded progress toward a deeper understanding of either crime or criminality, this is surely a nagging problem for persons who identify with criminology professionally.

Early Development with Sociology

This discomfiture has resulted, at least in part, from criminology's historical association with the discipline of sociology. Much criminology in the nineteenth century in the United States was essentially ameliorative; criminology was social work and charity with "paupers"[2] and other unfortunates who were said sometimes to commit crimes out of the need generated by economic misery. There were some "empirical" (or, more accurately, quantitative) studies of crime during this period, but such work reflected a style of "research" popular during the preceding century in England. A philanthropist or reformer who was deeply disturbed about a problem would gather and publicize data to make others aware of it.[3]

The lack of reliable empirical work seems not to have hindered greatly the early development of criminology. Curiously, criminology textbooks were written without sophisticated research by following a social activist orientation. As late as 1893, one of the first discussions of crime in an American textbook placed criminology within the larger sphere of social activism with "dependents, defectives, and delinquents."[4] But criminology was expected to go beyond advocacy of reformist values by producing the gist of reform activities. Charles Richmond Henderson stated this position: "We seek the ethical basis of charity, the ideals of philanthropy, and the social mechanisms for attaining in larger measure what ought to be."[5] Criminologists, of course, would decide what "ought to be."

Henderson, one of the four original faculty members of the first Department of Sociology in the United States,[6] seemed initially to have brought criminology into sociology by calling for better scientific understanding of crime so that it could be more reasonably attacked. Criminology was originally to be the study *and* the correction of crime. In this sense, Henderson was extending to criminology nineteenth-century ideas about the role of social research in general as a utilitarian device for improving society. "Social research was predominantly a tool for social reformers."[7]

Henderson's interest in crime had two important implications for the later development of criminology. First, criminology began to be associated with departments of sociology; however, as we shall see, the influence of sociology may have been exaggerated. Sociologists began to do all the teaching, textbook writing, and the majority of the research on crime. Originally, this association seemed quite natural since sociology itself was conceived in the United States as the scientific study of the social problems of urban, industrial society.

Second, because of this association, the developments in criminology paralleled those in sociology. Well into the twentieth century, sociologists gradually withdrew from their social problems orientation, eschewing social activism and dissociating themselves from such practical concerns as social work.[8] The history of the administrative titles of sociology departments from 1920 through the 1960s traces this trend (from Department of Sociology and Social Work to Department of Sociology). However, unlike the case of sociology and social work, which developed separate affiliations, both academic criminologists and crime control practitioners retained an identification with criminology. As a result, one group of self-identified criminologists did the teaching and much of the research, while another group engaged in direct therapy and other intervention efforts.

Both of these groups were affected by an "applied" label in their professional associations, and the field of criminology, as Wheeler has noted, may have suffered:

> One of the pervasive qualities of American criminology has been the tendency for participants in the process to be drawn from the lower echelons of their respective fields. The criminal lawyer lacks the status and prestige of other lawyers. The psychiatrist who works primarily with criminals is not at the apex of the psychiatric profession. Social workers or clinical psychologists are likely to prefer medical to correctional settings. After all, the clients of all these groups are typically drawn from the lower reaches of society. Even the expensive private mental hospital for upper class patients, where students or practitioners of mental health may be located, is lacking in the field of criminology. In addition, the social scientists who concern themselves primarily with applied fields such as criminology are less likely to have the prestige of their counterparts in the areas of pure or basic research. Thus despite the presence of some outstanding contributors in each area, the *rate* of talent flow into crime control practice and research has been somewhat lower than for other fields. This condition has affected both the quality of crime control programs and the quality of research on crime.[9]

Wheeler's observations should not be taken to mean that both the world of crime control practice and that of scholarship were drawing personnel from the same pool of candidates. Some persons with research training have taken up careers in criminal justice practice, and some scholars have had "practical experience" in various crime control agencies. Nevertheless, communication between the worlds of practice and scholarship is incomplete and faulty. Probation and parole agents, police administrators, correctional officials, and others pay little attention to the writings and research of academic criminologists, perhaps because criminology has yet to develop more than a few practical insights.[10]

For these reasons, the development of criminology diverges from the history provided by other disciplines (for example, psychology) that claim both scholars and practitioners.[11] This divergence is reflected in competing definitions of criminology and the criminologist.

DEFINITIONS OF THE FIELD

Definitions of the term "criminology" differ mainly in one major respect: the extent to which they incorporate a social activist role for the field. There seems to be no convenient way to resolve definitions that do and do not view social action as inherent in criminology. Some writers have shunned the issue of varying definitions of criminology and refer merely to the content of research and theory that has accumulated on crime.[12] Others, if they recognize the disagreements, have apparently surrendered to the task of attempting to resolve the disputes, as though no meaningful solution were possible.[13]

An Organizational Definition

The central professional organization for criminologists in the United States should be able to specify the nature of criminology and who appropriately may be considered a criminologist. The American Society of Criminology (ASC) describes itself as a body consisting of "persons interested in the advancement of criminology, including scholarly, scientific and professional knowledge of the etiology, prevention, control, and treatment of crime and delinquency, the measurement and detection of crime, legislation, and the practice of criminal law, the law enforcement, judicial, and corrections systems." In short, virtually anyone who has a "professional" interest in or knowledge about crime and its control can be considered a criminologist, including presumably criminals themselves to the extent that they take a "professional" interest in such matters.

The central professional organization of criminologists may not be able to provide satisfactory definitions. First, organizational statements of purpose and membership are necessarily compromise products among early founders of such societies and may or may not reflect contemporary opinion. Second, the nature of professional organizations changes over time; later developments may make obsolete the statements that were valid at an earlier time. Moreover, growth makes subsequent reform of statements of purpose organizationally cumbersome. Third, the ASC was formed primarily by persons who were interested in aspects of crime control (professors of criminal law, police administrators, and so on), and their concern with including practitioners and even interested laymen in the organization is understandable.[14] In this regard, it could be argued that the scope of the organization was simply a function of who (scholars or practitioners) got there first and laid claim to the term "criminology" by founding the organization.

If one examines the composition of the ASC and the kinds of activities with which these persons have been concerned over the years, one sees that it has been primarily an academic organization since the 1960s. Academics have dominated such aspects of the organization as speakers at annual meetings, editorial control of the society's journal (*Criminology: An Interdisciplinary Journal*), and leadership positions in the association. This is not to deny that practitioners have been influential in terms of participation and maintenance of the organization between annual meetings. However, the society's journal has a distinctly scholarly emphasis with little trace of "bread and butter" discussions that interest practitioners.

Individual Definitions

Among textbooks writers and others the central issue, again, is the extent to which criminology is, or should be, ameliorative. The activist orientation is reflected in a recent definition by Glaser who says:

> Since criminology, as viewed here, seeks scientific explanation not only for violations of criminal law but also for past and prospective changes in this law. . . its interests include: (1) studying the relationships among what is currently defined as crime, reactions to it, and other social concerns; and (2) studying the possibility of alleviating various social problems by revising criminal law (including international law), or by enforcing it differently. Criminology, as thus conceived, can be a distinct complement to the other social

sciences in helping to achieve a better world, precisely because of its focus on crime as behavior lawfully punished by the courts.[15]

A slightly more ambiguous definition claims that "criminology as a discipline should embrace not only the etiology of crime, which has been the traditional emphasis of sociologists, but the system of criminal justice and the field of penology, or corrections, as well."[16] Perhaps the definition that is most encompassing is that which defines the criminologist as anyone who displays an objective attitude toward crime and criminality. "By our definition, the criminologist is an intellectually disciplined observer. The practitioner and the criminal are included when they are able to harness the emotions engendered by the frustrations of either dealing with 'troublesome' persons or being subject to penalties imposed in the administration of justice."[17] Thus, being a criminologist amounts to little more than exerting some measure of self-control over one's feelings about crime.

The definitions cited above share a concern with the control of crime and, as such, are value-laden. Most persons view criminality as undesirable. But to incorporate a formal statement of disapproval into the definition of a discipline is curious indeed. Most demographers are personally concerned about population problems; yet, the counselor in the birth control clinic does not identify with demography professionally, nor does this discipline claim the counselor as a demographer.[18] Why, then, should there be confusion regarding criminology and practitioners who attempt to control crime?

Part of the answer, as pointed out earlier, is historical and has to do with the close association of criminology with a specific problem orientation and the self-identification of practitioners as criminologists. Another explanation relates to the confusion as to the mission of criminology and its scientific status. Knowledge that criminality is closely associated with learning in intimate or primary groups does not translate *automatically* into any particular ameliorative program; it may be the basis for group counseling, for community reorganization, or for in-depth individual psychotherapy, all depending on the views of the practitioner. Criminology is concerned with the generation of knowledge about crime; in contrast, practice is concerned with the application of that, or some other, knowledge to immediate social situations with the objective of reducing crime. Criminological knowledge sometimes has practical implications, but it could as easily be used by someone who wished to generate, rather than retard, criminality;[19] there is nothing that precludes such a use.

Criminology Viewed as a Science

To view criminology as anything other than the creation of scientific knowledge about crime and criminality is to introduce personal preferences. Values are disagreeable features of criminology, not because most criminologists wish to increase crime, but because any discipline has enough difficulty with the interference of values without making them *formally* part of the scope and objective of study.

The most defensible definition of criminology is one that views it as a scientific enterprise. No recognized science defines itself in terms of the kinds of practical implications that are likely to flow from its work. Indeed, what makes science distinctive (*inter alia*) is the fact that it is concerned exclusively with the generation of new knowledge through commonly accepted techniques, usually termed scientific method. Birth control counselors may have some knowledge that demographers do not; Don Juans may have some knowledge that social psychologists interested in interpersonal attraction may not; marriage counselors may have some knowledge about problems of husbands and wives that students of family systems do not; and probation officers, prison wardens, and police administrators may have some knowledge about criminals that criminologists may not.[20] The question in each case is whether the knowledge possessed by the practitioner is the kind necessary to pose and solve scientific questions. (If it is, of course, the scientist had better get busy and acquire that knowledge.)

Criminology can be defined as the scientific study of laws, lawbreaking, and responses to lawbreaking.[21] This definition does not preclude personal preferences for crime control on the part of criminologists (that is, the persons engaged in generating that knowledge), but neither does it preclude someone who is interested in increasing crime. The important dimension is the manner in which criminologists go about their work. That work may include evaluative research on the effectiveness of crime control programs, studies designed to tease out etiological clues of criminality, the process by which some norms but not others become laws, or the relationships among crime and various aspects of social or economic structures. What matters is not the content of the work, but the manner used to go about that work.

CRIMINOLOGY AND CRIMINAL JUSTICE EDUCATION

Most training for criminologists takes place within university settings in departments of behavioral science that share some interest in crime (for example, sociology, psychology, political science, and anthropology). After graduation, criminologists take positions either in a university (as teachers and/or researchers), in a private organization devoted exclusively to conducting research on crime (commonly funded by grants), or in some governmental bureau that deals with crime. Not all criminologists, however, are engaged in research or the training of researchers. Some have become associated with criminal justice education programs that train students for quite different careers. The rapid increase in the number and quality of criminal justice education programs is one of the most notable features affecting criminology in the past decade.

Upsurge of Criminal Justice Programs

The 1970s witnessed a tremendous upsurge in the number of criminal justice education programs in American colleges and universities. There had been some graduate level programs before this time, but they were comparatively rare. There were also a number of undergraduate departments of criminal justice before 1970, although many of these units organized their curricula more around police methods of crime detection and evidence-gathering than around criminology as defined here. Most of these departments were not research units, nor did they engage in the training of criminologists.

The rapid growth in the number of criminal justice programs was spurred by two developments: (1) The availability of federal funds, primarily those generated by the Omnibus Crime Control Act of 1968, as amended, and administered by the Law Enforcement Assistance Administration; and (2) the keener vocational interest among students who perceived crime control as a potential occupational career. Throughout the 1970s, departments of sociology, as well as other liberal arts departments, experienced declines in undergraduate enrollments, while more vocational programs such as journalism, engineering, and preprofessional courses experienced increases.

Common Themes in Programs

The content of the curriculum of criminal justice programs displays substantial variation, although there are common themes. First, the typical subjects of courses are related to crime control. Many programs do offer courses dealing with criminology, but this body of knowledge is generally not taken as the central core of learning. Rather, one is more apt to find concentration on public administration, criminal procedure, social work, or "criminal justice" (which refers to the examination of the criminal and/or juvenile justice apparatus as "systems," or the interrelationships among decisions made by the police, prosecutor, judge, and correctional personnel).

Second, and related to the first theme, there is a clear vocational emphasis within criminal justice programs on preparing students for positions that do not require research competence. Most criminal justice programs do not offer a Ph.D. degree, although many do offer master's degrees for study beyond the baccalaureate. It is often unclear, however, precisely what positions students are being trained for. Many college catalogue descriptions suggest that criminal justice programs prepare students for positions within the criminal justice system, but, with some notable exceptions, most of these positions actually require either professional training (for example, law) or are initially obtainable without any specified line of advanced study (for example, police officer, correctional guard).

Third, criminal justice programs generally emphasize experiential learning. This comes through participation in internship programs during the regular school year, or longer, more intensive, placements over the summer months. Students may be assigned to an agency (for example, probation department, correctional facility) to experience at first-hand the kind of work persons in the field accomplish and the problems they encounter. Another form of this kind of study is the "study tour" usually to foreign countries in conjunction with universities there.

Criminal justice programs may also confer college credit for previous work experience in the community.

Such features do not exhaust the differences between criminal justice programs and the nature of criminological training in the United States, but they do illustrate the contrast. Criminology and criminal justice are not irrelevant to one another, but they have yet to develop a common basis for systematic understanding beyond the fact that they are ostensibly concerned with the same general problem.[22]

SUBSTANTIVE INTERESTS SINCE WORLD WAR II

As noted earlier, a split between academicians and practitioners, both of whom identified themselves as criminologists, fostered a reformist tendency within criminology by providing it with a social activist component. Early criminologists exercised a belief in the existence and desirability of social consensus concerning the predictability of social relationships, a predictability that arose from agreement on fundamental values and norms. In this view, criminality was abnormal (the result of some pathology or social disorganization within communities).

The combination of its reformist and consensual elements, according to Johnson, helped to produce a set of ideas that formed the core of criminological work for the first part of this century:

> First, crime was regarded as an alien phenomenon that exists *outside* of and preys *on* society. Crime was attributed to some "strange" group; for example, immigrants not of white Anglo-Saxon Protestant origin were the favorite explanation in the early decades of this century. Second, protection of the society was selected as the primary purpose of the criminal law and its administration. "Society" usually was identified with the interests of elite groups who were presumed to represent consensual values and norms. Thus, the purposes of criminal justice administration were grouped around the general objective of controlling "evil" criminals. Third, science-based treatment would be directed against these pathological *individuals*. Research would discover the causes of crime lurking in the physiology, psychology, or immediate social environment of "the criminal." Science-based treatment would employ psychological knowledge and educational techniques to counter the effects of the selected cause deemed relevant to the given offender.[23]

These ideas are basic to the so-called "medical model" of crime, a perspective followed in much research. A recent survey of the criminological literature concludes that most empirical research done on offenders since 1945 has been psychologically oriented, presumably for this reason.[24] The medical model has been under vigorous attack for some time,[25] although there are still contemporary examples of this approach.[26]

The medical model has been used for some time by practitioners as well as academics. Practitioners wish to know how to deal with the offenders they encounter daily. Partly to serve this end, a particular style of theorizing was popularized in American criminology that asked about the conditions under which individuals came to commit criminal acts. This concern with etiology has a long and respected history in criminology, although one is hard pressed to find precise counterparts in other social science fields. Demographers have gotten along for some time without asking why males and females have sexual intercourse that produces babies; the reasons for such events are taken as self-evident and trivial.

Criminologists before 1945 placed substantial confidence in their ability to generate etiological theories that would explain the origin of all crime. But, perhaps persuaded by Merton's call for theories of "middle-range,"[27] criminologists found less sanguine the prospect that one theory would be able to explain such a heterogeneous mass of conduct as "crime." As a result, criminology in the past several decades has involved less the study of the origins of *all* lawbreaking, and more the study of *forms* of lawbreaking, the origins of laws that define those crimes, and the social and legal responses to crime.

At the risk of oversimplification, some of the main currents of criminological work can be summarized as follows. Through the 1940s, the most pressing theoretical questions in criminology seemed to be how some persons, but not others, came to commit crimes and how these crimes were distributed in social space (Shaw and McKay, Merton, Sutherland). During the 1950s, the theoretical questions seemed to revolve around the origins of criminal and delinquent norms and how some persons came to subscribe to these norms (Cohen, Miller, Cloward and Ohlin). During the 1960s, the issues included the origin of "conventional" norms (both social rules and laws), the process by which some rules became laws while others did not, and the consequences on criminal careers of enforcing these rules (Becker, Kitsuse, Schur). The work in the 1970s has been in part a reaction against the labeling tradition, with attention turning to the role of sanctions (Gibbs, Waldo and Chiricos, Tittle) and the effectiveness of crime control agencies (Wilson, van den Haag) in producing compliance with legal norms. While not all criminologists during each of these decades pursued these general questions, the theory and research of those who did eventually became very influential.

The direct reformist stance of earlier criminologists was substantially diminished, although some criminologists were influenced by a revival of a version of reformism during the 1960s brought about by sociologists who implored their colleagues to "use" their research to advance nonelite interests.[28] Gone too was the consensual perspective on social order. Even the commitment to positivism would undergo change, as some sociologists would question whether such methods could reasonably address the "pressing" issues of the day; ethnomethodologists, for example, would advocate a quite different strategy of "knowing" that required making explicit one's values and incorporating them formally into their research. In short, criminology began searching for new intellectual roots and problems, leaving to the practitioners the task of reducing crime as best they could.

THEORETICAL DEVELOPMENTS SINCE 1945

The period immediately following World War II was one of theoretical ferment in criminology. While there are notable exceptions, scholarly work beginning in the 1950s turned attention away from "criminals" to the behavior defined as "crime." Beginning with the work of Cohen,[29] and continuing through that of Bloch and Neiderhoffer,[30] Miller,[31] Cloward and Ohlin,[32] and Short and Strodtbeck,[33] there was less interest in identifying factors that would differentiate criminals from noncriminals, and more in exploring the meaning of criminal acts. Cohen's theory is not so much a theory of delinquent conduct, but of the conditions under which delinquent *norms* arise. Delinquency, in Cohen's view, was simply behavior that conformed not to conventional but to delinquent norms. Subsequent writers built upon Cohen's ideas by addressing such issues as the location of delinquent norms in social space. (Miller's analysis locates them in lower class settings; Cloward and Ohlin find them arising from specific neighborhood conditions; Bloch and Neiderhoffer in cleavages in the age-generation structure; and Short and Strodtbeck in patterns of interaction among delinquent gang members and in status struggles within gangs.)

If criminologists in the 1950s focused on the origins of criminal and delinquent norms, those in the 1960s shifted their attention to a broader problem: the consequences of social control efforts for behavior that departs from conventional norms. The "labeling" perspective concentrated attention not on the actions of criminals in isolation, but on criminality as part of an interaction with other parts of society. Criminal careers were not simply the results of a criminal's behavior, but the responses to that behavior by others, particularly formal agents of social control.

It soon became obvious in this work that analyses of the origins of criminal norms were only a subset of the study of the origins of all norms. The study of rule-making and rule-enforcement thereby became a major focus of interactionist and labeling theorists. Overall, the predominant issue became how one version of conventional rules came to take precedence over others. Examples of work in this tradition include Becker's[34] studies of the role of the Federal Bureau of Narcotics in creating a "new class of outsiders—marijuana users" and the role of moral entrepreneurs generally in creating rules defining deviance; Duster's[35] examination of "The Legislation of Morality" with respect to opiates; Chambliss's[36] interpretation of historical records concerning the law of vagrancy in England; studies of interest groups promoting specific changes in laws relating, for example, to prostitution[37] and marijuana;[38] historical inquiries into "the invention of delinquency";[39] studies of the role of professional groups in defining and implementing deviance, for example, delinquency,[40] and of governments with respect to political crime.[41]

The nature and meaning of research on crime changed as well. Since crime was not a quality of persons but of rules (laws) and their enforcement, research was needed to explicate how these rules came about and the consequences of rule enforcement. Criminality was still largely class specific, but this was now interpreted in a different manner: there are not more criminals in the lower classes, merely more criminal law enforcement. Official statistics did not measure "criminals," but the actions of social control agents in enforcing conventional rules.

Police statistics measured the actions and interests of the police, not criminals,[42] just as mental hospital admissions measured the behavior not of patients but of psychiatrists.[43]

Since the labeling perspective focused attention on the consequences of social control efforts for deviant careers, it is not surprising that this tradition spurred considerable research on social control agencies. Studies of the police by sociologists,[44] persons trained in public administration,[45] history,[46] and law[47] explored such topics as the history and development of modern policing, the occupational and subcultural characteristics of the police, the use and abuse of police discretion, the interaction of the police and the community, and the philosophical and legal dilemmas posed by the police in a democratic society. While criminological interest in the police seems to have ebbed slightly in recent years, it remains an important research topic. Criminological interest in prisons is of an older vintage,[48] but the labeling perspective provided fresh impetus to this literature.[49] Criminological work on prisons has included studies of inmate social systems and subcultures,[50] the consequences of the prison experience and the effects of specific treatment programs,[51] the historical origins of prisons as oficially prescribed places of punishment,[52] and the administratative structure of prisons and its relation to prison programs.[53] Studies of the court system in the United States by criminologists have not been quite as numerous as those of other agencies of social control,[54] although some court processes (for example, plea bargaining[55]) have received scholarly attention.

In addition to giving rise to new theoretical insights, the labeling conception of deviance also prompted a positivistic resurgence in the field. Critiques of labeling,[56] and ethnomethodology and phenomenology,[57] and radical perspectives (to be discussed presently) made strong demands for empirical evidence long the cornerstone of positivistic criminology. When such tests were forthcoming, however, they were seldom unambiguous. "Tests" of propositions of the radical perspective, for example, generated renewed debates and often raised more questions than they resolved.[58] Critics and defenders of these perspectives disagreed as to the nature of "critical" tests, and even as to what might be considered relevant evidence. Some scholars even expressed the uneasy feeling that relativistic conceptions of crime and deviance might prove to be unfalsifiable.[59] Thus, major empirical and methodological advances of the post-World War II period were applied more to questions posed prior to the war than to newer perspectives.

EXPANSION OF THE EMPIRICAL BASE

Criminologists have long been dissatisfied with the validity and the reliability of available data on crime and delinquency. They were active in support of efforts to secure more reliable and valid data on common crime (as in an advisory capacity in establishing the Uniform Crime Report system of the Federal Bureau of Investigation) and in efforts to identify types of behavior inadequately conceptualized in law and reported by official agencies (for example, white-collar crime). Early studies of "hidden crime" had documented the fact that behavior for which youth might be apprehended, brought before the courts, and incarcerated was engaged in by many who never became involved with official agencies charged with juvenile and criminal justice responsibilities.[60]

It was not until the 1950s, however, that self-reported delinquency studies became common. These studies revealed both points of agreement and difference with reports from official agencies. Studies conducted during the 1950s found delinquent behavior (adult crime has never been studied systematically by means of self-reports) to be virtually universal among populations studied. However, greater frequency and more serious involvement were found to characterize officially defined delinquents, and males reported greater involvement than females, though the differences were smaller than reflected in official data. Social class and racial differences were smaller still.

Recent research has studied more representative samples of youngsters and a broader range of delinquencies than did earlier inquiries. Findings generally confirm the earlier work, with some exceptions. A study conducted by the Illinois Institute for Juvenile Research in 1972, for example, found that black boys report more involvement in serious offenses of violence than do white boys, in some measure supporting official statistics in this regard.[61] A smaller national sample in 1972 found no such differences, but some of the more serious violent offenses studied in Illinois were not included in the national sample.[62] Social class differences in the incidence and prevalence of delinquent behaviors were small and in some studies nonexistent. Such findings cast considerable doubt on theories that fail to account for wide sex-linked disparities (and for their narrowing[63]) as well as theories that emphasize class and race differences.

The President's Commission on Law Enforcement and Administration of Justice[64] added still another component to the measurement of crime when it sponsored studies of criminal victimization.[65] These studies were continued, in cooperation with the U.S. Bureau of Census, after the President's Commission was disbanded.[66] Concern over victims of crime has led to still other state and local studies. As a result, the data base for studying the extent and social distribution of crime has been greatly expanded. The fact that most common crime is committed by young males has permitted comparisons of official data, self-reports, and victim reports.[67]Together with critical assessments of each methodology,[68] these have contributed to a greater appreciation of the complexity of even the simplest questions regarding the extent and nature of criminal and delinquent behavior.

The empirical base of sociological studies of crime and delinquency has also been enhanced in recent years by a few longitudinal studies. Based chiefly on police contacts, these studies have focused primarily on descriptions of the involvement of cohorts of young people rather than on theory testing.[69] Findings to date have been reasonably consistent and, in general, confirmatory of findings concerning the social distribution of crime based on cross-sectional data. Large-scale studies employing self-reports and observational techniques have been employed to test a variety of hypotheses drawn from theoretical problems posed prior to 1945, as well as those that have emerged since.[70]

With criminologists increasingly using more sophisticated methodologies and statistical analyses, a number of issues that had been of concern prior to World War II have again been reopened. There is, for example, a conscious return to the "basics" of the field with extended studies of the correlates of criminality, including the relationship between crime and socioeconomic status,[71] I.Q.,[72] age,[73] sex,[74] and race.[75] The recent interest in female criminality, long a neglected topic among criminologists, can also be interpreted within the context of using recent data-gathering and analytical techniques to examine older, still unresolved, problems.[76] Such work may have enormous implications for the future of criminological theory in the United States since it could introduce a serious reconceptualization of the "facts a theory must fit."[77]

RECENT TRENDS IN CRIMINOLOGICAL WORK

The most recent work in criminology in the United States, while still displaying overall the diversity of interests characteristic of earlier work, seems to have concentrated on several areas of substantive interest: white-collar and corporate illegalities, aspects of violent crime (particularly the nature of violent criminal careers), and theoretical and empirical work on philosophical justifications for the imposition of legal punishment. Moreover, recent work has reflected the continuing decline of interest in criminal etiology compared to that found in earlier decades, and the continued expansion of the empirical base through the use of such techniques as historical analyses. There is also some evidence of a broader theoretical split between Marxist perspectives and revivals of classical penal philosophy.

A Short Summary of Empirical Interests

The past five years or so have witnessed a growing commitment on the part of criminologists to understand and study more carefully than in the past the criminality of both upper status persons[78] and organizations.[79] This renascence of work begun by Sutherland in the 1940s has included discussions of the seriousness of these forms of criminality,[80] case studies of individual white-collar offenders,[81] and theoretical perspectives that may prove helpful in understanding the nature of this problem.[82] Large-scale research projects presently underway may expand knowledge of corporate violations and the legal and social responses to them.

More than any form of criminality, violent crime (including white-collar crimes of violence) evokes public apprehension and condemnation.[83] Recent work has been concerned largely with analyses of violent crime[84] and violent criminal careers.[85] There is also some concern that racial factors may be more important than previously thought.[86] Recent publications have also examined violent adolescent criminality[87] as well as in gang delinquency, particularly its more violent components.[88]

The large amount of empirical work on the deterrent effects of legal threats has fostered considerable doubts about so-called liberal strategies of seeking the social causes of criminality and addressing reform efforts to control crime around those causes.[89] The work on deterrence suggests, but nothing more, that the manipulation of legal threats, without regard for the social causes of crime, may constitute a partial means to combat some forms of crime. Unfortunately, the most reasonable conclusion from this research (that some persons are deterred from some crimes by some punishments some of the time) has not yet lent itself to further systematic study and policy recommendations.[90]

The possibility of deterring crime has led to other, equally "pragmatic," criminological interests. The prevention of crime through the manipulation of selected facets of the physical environment[91] reflects the continuing decline in the perceived importance of etiological theorizing in criminology. This approach largely ignores criminal motivation—often a core element of most theories of crime causation—and concentrates instead on the physical prevention of crime.

Another line of research, and one that has more discernible theoretical implications, is the investigation of biosocial bases of criminality. A number of empirical studies in the past decade have addressed the relationship among genetic, physiological, and endocrinological factors and criminality.[92] The return to biologically based explanations of criminality seems to have been prompted by (1) an intuitive appeal of biological factors in accounting for crime, especially those crimes that are otherwise apparently unexplainable (such as a mass murder), and (2) the development of new research tools for more precise measurement of biological factors.These conditions have led some criminologists to suggest that biological and social forces interact in ways still unspecified to produce certain types of crime. Some studies, for example, have suggested that genetic and physiological factors are linked with the origins of crime, but that their influence is more pronounced for middle-class offenders and quite weak for lower-class offenders.[93] While such studies are not beyond criticism, the future acceptance of this research may depend ultimately on the extent to which it is dissociated from the biological studies that marked the early development of criminology.

Short Summary of Theoretical Interests

A case can be made that American criminology faces an impoverishment of theory. Dissatisfaction with previous theoretical perspectives is reflected in the seeming exhaustion of new insights and concepts. Elliott, Ageton, and Canter observe that there have been few major theoretical advances in the etiology of criminality since the work of Cloward and Ohlin, and Hirschi.[94] Moreover, what little theory can be said to dominate the work of criminologists is either (1) previous perspectives, such as control theory, social learning theory, anomie perspective, or combinations of these;[95] (2) criminological perspectives based on several interpretations of Marxist social and economic thought;[96] or (3) perspectives derived from classical legal or philosophical conceptions of crime, largely recast into economic terms.[97] A recent review of criminological theory by Gibbons suggests that future theoretical work will concentrate largely on relatively minor puzzles left over from earlier theories or on questions that may eventually bring criminology closer to conventionally conceived sociological theory.[98]

The rise of radical or critical criminology in the United States seems to reflect a combination of historically specific events, such as the urban riots of the 1960s,[99] and the need to supplant existing theory.[100] Radical criminology seeks explanations for crime in features of economic structure and the power of a few to control for the many the criminal definition (lawmaking) process and procedures (the criminal justice system). At present, radical criminology is not a generalized perspective for American criminologists for a number of reasons. (1) Some versions of Marxist thought applied to crime tend to make only obvious statements about the structure of American society (for example, some have more power than others, this power is used to protect the elite—capitalist—interests, laws come about because of the dominance of state interest over others). To quote one writer: "The overall impression the reader takes away is one of enormous simplification, reification, and an almost appalling absence of sensitivity to the complexity of human interaction."[101] (2) Radical criminologists, with few exceptions, have yet to develop a vocabulary or procedure by which they can examine their own ideas and, as such, have no basis by which they can maintain sustained dialogue with others. Nonradical criminologists have felt comfortable dismissing radical criminology as merely doctrinaire and dogmatic. (3) More recent statements by radical criminologists have gone little beyond those offered during the early 1970s, leading some criminologists to suggest that radical criminology is as theoretically bankrupt as those perspectives radical criminologists criticize.[102] Still, radical criminology has provided a large-scale conceptual critique of macrosocial and -economic structures and processes in the causation of crime.

Criminologists have also begun to examine more closely than in the past the theoretical rationale by which the state intervenes in crime. Rehabilitation as a motive for state intervention has rapidly been losing adherents as evidence accumulates to suggest the seeming failure of such efforts.[103] More and more, such goals as retribution are being heralded as legitimate—and perhaps the only morally justifiable—goals of penal punishment.[104] At present, however, it is arguable whether retribution is being touted on its own merits or because it seems to represent the only alternative available with rehabilitation in disrepute and the efficacy of criminal law to deter crimes still poorly understood.[105] Disputes will likely continue until a retributivist penal philosophy can be conceptualized and operationalized to permit empirical testing and evaluation. Retribution, unlike other goals of criminal law, is not utilitarian in the direct sense that it fails to espouse a crime control function. It is achieved, if at all, based on abstract conceptions of "justice" (usually termed "desert" and "proportionality") rather than an empirical consequence of reducing crime.[106]

Debates concerning the role of etiological theorizing in criminology continue without foreseeable resolution.[107] Criminologists who prefer a policy-oriented approach advocate an abandonment of etiological theorizing,[108] while others press for continued work in this area.[109] What seems to be needed at this point is some idea of how these positions can be reconciled, if they can be at all.

QUALITY OF AMERICAN CRIMINOLOGY SINCE 1945

It is much easier to highlight a small portion of the criminological literature since World War II than to make defensible statements about the quality of that work. No agreed-upon set of criteria exists to judge the "quality" of scientific work, although it does appear that scientists are able to make judgments about the relative merits of scientific work in a number of fields that are surprisingly consistent in the absence of such standards.[110]

A very useful study on the quality of criminological work in the United States by Marvin Wolfgang, Robert Figlio, and Terence Thornberry examines this literature between 1945 and 1972.[111] Their review covers all scientific criminological literature, excluding for reasons of space that on the police, courts, and corrections, that is, that literature that might be considered in some sense "criminal justice." Wolfgang and his associates found that the literature in criminology parallels the exponential growth of other scientific disciplines; at present, the literature in criminology is growing at about 7 percent annually, and the literature as a whole doubles every ten years.[112] In spite of this rapid increase, the authors were able to detect little evidence that this literature was cumulative. Of the 3,690 items they examined, 2.2 percent received one-half and 0.5 percent one-quarter of all citations in criminology. Some of the literature in the field is enormously influential, most is not.

Turning to the judged quality of this literature, the study indicated that "the methodological sophistication and competency of most publications in criminology is dismally low."[113] One possible reason for this poor quality has been noted by Greenberg: "Having been taught in college that crime statistics contain errors, criminologists assume that nothing can be learned from quantitative methods and do not study them. This, in turn, discourages other criminologists from undertaking quantitative research. Criminology journals, for example, are reluctant to publish papers that their readers will not be able to understand."[114] On a slightly more optimistic note, Wolfgang, Figlio, and Thornberry conclude that, while the quality of criminology publications has been low, it has been improving over time.

Empirical work in criminology has been dominated by a psychological orientation; this is an unexpected situation for sociologists who have claimed criminology as their own. As Wolfgang and his associates state: "It is probably safe to assume that sociologists have made wider claims of influence, impact or utilization of sociology to empirical studies of criminology than is deserved."[115] The theoretical work has been characterized by a tendency to divorce theory from empiricism.[116] In fact, "of the theoretical work in criminology, nearly half (49.2 percent) are polemical without much structure and with little capacity for generating hypotheses."[117]

Whether one is buoyed by the prospects that criminologists are becoming more sophisticated, or depressed that criminologists still have much progress to make, one must surely take seriously another finding from this study—that criminology has benefited substantially from a multidisciplinary base.[118] The recent additions to the literature by economists, political scientists, historians, psychologists, sociologists, and anthropologists (and others) have contributed a wide range of theoretical insights and methods by which to study crime and criminals.

CONCLUSIONS AND FINAL COMMENT

Criminology in the United States is a multidisciplinary scientific field concerned with the generation of knowledge about lawmaking, lawbreaking, and responses (both legal and social) to lawbreaking. As conceived originally, criminology would provide, through its research emphasis, a practical technology to persons engaged in crime control practice. Since World War II, however, it has become increasingly clear that criminology, with few notable exceptions, has not supplied practitioners with the insights and skills necessary to control crime. To date, crime control practitioners have not benefited from the results of criminological research in the way that, for example, physicians have from the results of medical research. For this reason, it could be argued that the "applied" label that is often attached to criminology is misleading.

Perhaps the most noteworthy theoretical feature of criminology since 1945 is that interest in the etiology of criminal behavior has declined significantly. Fewer criminologists now ask "Why do they do it?," and more have turned to such issues as the conditions under which laws come about, the nature of different forms of criminality, and the consequences—both to society and the individual offender—of responses to lawbreaking, particularly in the form of legal social control. At present, it appears that criminologists are unsure of precisely what kind of theory should replace etiological theory (for example, theories of law, theories of different forms of criminality, theories of social control, or simply different etiological theories).

The vitality of American criminology lies in its uncertain future. The requirement to develop new theory and to continue research on virtually every dimension of the lawbreaking process guarantees such a future. The broad range of work to be done, coupled with the recent use of new data-gathering and data-analytic techniques, explains why most criminologists in the United States find their work challenging and exciting.

NOTES

1. Gibbons has noted that using the term "American" as a substitute for "United States" is highly questionable in that American includes Canada, Mexico, and a number of South and Central American countries. While this is true, "it is the case that writers do often equate American with the United States." Don C. Gibbons, *The Criminological Enterprise: Theories and Perspectives* (Englewood Cliffs, N.J.: Prentice-Hall, 1979), pp. 1-2.

2. See Harold Finestone, *Victims of Change: Juvenile Delinquents in American Society* (Westport, Conn.: Greenwood Press, 1976).

3. Stephen Cole, "Continuity and Institutionalization in Science: A Case Study of Failure," in Anthony Oberschall (ed.), *The Establishment of Empirical Sociology* (New York: Harper and Row, 1972), p. 74.

4. Charles Richmond Henderson, *An Introduction to the Study of the Dependent, Defective and Delinquent Classes and Their Treatment* (Boston: D. C. Heath, 1893). The first full textbook in criminology from a sociological viewpoint is Maurice Parmelee, *Criminology* (New York: Macmillan, 1918).

5. Henderson, *An Introduction to the Study of the Dependent, Defective and Delinquent Classes and Their Treatment*, 2d ed. (1908) p. iii.

6. The University of Chicago is usually given credit (and sometimes blame) for instituting the first Sociology Department in the United States. See Robert E.L. Faris, *Chicago Sociology, 1920-1932* (Chicago: University of Chicago Press, 1971).

7. Cole, "Continuity and Institutionalization," p. 104.

8. See Roscoe C. and Gisela Hinkle, *The Development of Modern Sociology* (New York: Random House, 1954), pp. 18-43. There is some evidence that sociology in the United States may be attempting to rekindle its practical component. See Barney Glassner and Jonathan A. Freedman, *Clinical Sociology* (New York: Longman, 1979).

9. Stanton Wheeler, *The Social Sources of Criminology," Sociological Inquiry* 32 (Spring 1962): 158.

10. See Robert F. Meier and Gilbert Geis, "Is Criminology a Policy Science?" *Journal of Sociology and Social Welfare* 4 (1977): 1273-1283

11. Few persons doubt that a clinical psychologist is as much a "psychologist" as an experimentalist. Yet, the argument that crime control practitioners are criminologists is questionable because psychology has a licensing procedure to signal the acquisition of a new member, a practice also common in law, medicine, and social work. There is, however, no officially sanctioned procedure to signify when someone is a "criminologist." Practitioners of crime control occupy their positions by virtue of having been hired by some agency, not through the completion of some prescribed course of study. See Edward Sagarin, "The Egghead, the Flatfoot, and the Screw," *Criminology* 18 (November 1980): 291-302.

12. See, for example, John F. Galliher and James L. McCartney, *Criminology: Power, Crime, and Criminal Law* (Homewood, Ill.: Dorsey Press, 1977).

13. See, for example, Hugh D. Barlow, *Introduction to Criminology* (Boston: Little, Brown, 1978), p. 25.

14. Albert Morris, "The American Society of Criminology: A History, 1941-1974," *Criminology* 13 (August 1975):123-167.

15. Daniel Glaser, *Crime in Our Changing Society* (New York: Holt, Rinehart and Winston, 1978), pp. 5-6.

16. Sue Titus Reid, *Crime and Criminology* (New York: Holt, Rinehart and Winston, 1976), p. 22.

17. Elmer H. Johnson, *Crime, Correction and Criminology*, 4th ed. (Homewood, Ill.: Dorsey Press, 1978), p. 56.

18. Graham and Taylor have pointed out that criminologists and demographers have much in common, including corresponding scientific problems. See Hilary Graham and Laurie Taylor, "Conceptions and Commissions: Parallels in the Development of Demography and Criminology," *The Sociological Review* 23 (1975):629-644.

19. As Hirschi notes, quoting a fictitious sociologist: "I study deviant behavior because I am interested in quadrupling the rate at which people engage in it. The oldtimers may have wanted to reduce the rate of deviance, but not me. I want to increase it. I want to make one big cat house of the world. In pursuit of this goal, I will ask the question students of deviance have always asked: Why do they do it? Once I find the answer to this question, I will flood the market." Travis Hirschi, "Procedural Rules and the Study of Deviant Behavior," *Social Problems* 21 (Fall 1973):171.

20. Similarly, an alcoholic is a good source of information about that person's experiences (maybe), but if the issue is the nature and extent of alcoholism in the United States, the social processes that generate and retard alcoholism, or the most effective means of treatment for the widest variety of alcoholics, one of the most unreliable sources of information would be local skid row alcoholics. See also Robert K. Merton, "Insiders and Outsiders: A Chapter in the Sociology of Knowledge," *American Journal of Sociology* 78 (July 1972):9-47.

21. Similar definitions are offered by Edwin H. Sutherland and Donald R. Cressey, *Criminology*, 10th ed. (Philadelphia: Lippincott, 1978); Marvin E. Wolfgang, "Crime, Criminology and the Criminologist," *Journal of Criminal Law, Criminology and Police Science* 54 (June 1963):155-162; and Marvin E. Wolfgang and Franco Ferracuti, *The Subculture of Violence: Towards an Integrated Theory in Criminology* (London: Tavistock, 1967), Chapter 2.

22. The disciplinary status of criminal justice is discussed in Vincent J. Webb and Dennis E. Hoffman, "Criminal Justice as an Academic Discipline," *Journal of Criminal Justice* 6 (Winter 1978): 347-355; and Don C. Gibbons and Gerald E. Blake, Jr., "Perspectives in Criminology and Criminal Justice: Implications for Higher Education Programs," *Criminal Justice Review* 2 (Spring 1977):23-40. For an analysis of the emphasis in criminology and criminal justice on comparative crime problems, see Leonard J. Hippchen, "The Teaching of Comparative and World Criminology in Graduate Schools of Sociology and Criminal Justice," *International Journal of Comparative and Applied Criminal Justice* 1 (Spring 1977):57-71.

23. Elmer H. Johnson, "American Criminology: A Brief Review of Its History and Contemporary Trends," unpublished paper, Southern Illinois University at Carbondale, 1978, pp. 8-9.

24. Marvin E. Wolfgang, Robert M. Figlio, and Terence Thornberry, *Evaluating Criminology* (New York: Elsevier, 1978).

25. See, for example, Marshall B. Clinard and Robert F. Meier, *Sociology of Deviant Behavior*, 5th ed. (New York: Holt, Rinehart and Winston, 1979), pp. 119-122.

26. See Samuel Yochelson and Stanton E. Samenow, *The Criminal Personality*, Vols. 1 and 2 (New York: Jason Aronson, 1976 and 1977).

27. Robert K. Merton, *Social Theory and Social Structure*, enl. ed. (New York: Free Press, 1968), Chapter 2.

28. See Howard S. Becker, "Whose Side Are We On?" *Social Problems* 14 (1967):239-247.

29. Albert K. Cohen, *Delinquent Boys: The Culture of the Gang* (New York: Free Press, 1955).

30. Herbert Bloch and Arthur Neiderhoffer, *The Gang: A Study in Adolescent Behavior* (New York: Philosophical LIbrary, 1958).

31. Walter B. Miller, "Lower Class Culture as a Generating Milieu of Gang Delinquency," *Journal of Social Issues* 14 (November 1958):5-19.

32. Richard A. Cloward and Lloyd E. Ohlin, *Delinquency and Opportunity: A Theory of Delinquent Gangs* (New York: Free Press, 1960).

33. James F. Short, Jr., and Fred L. Strodtbeck, *Group Process and Gang Delinquency* (Chicago: University of Chicago Press, 1965).

34. Howard S. Becker, *Outsiders: Studies in the Sociology of Deviance*, enl. ed. (New York: Free Press, 1973), especially Chapters 7 and 8.

35. Troy Duster, *The Legislation of Morality* (New York: Free Press, 1970).

36. William J. Chambliss, "A Sociological Analysis of the Law of Vagrancy," *Social Problems*, 12 (Summer 1964):67-77.

37. Pamela A. Roby, "Politics and Criminal Law: Revision of the New York State Penal Law on Prostitution," *Social Problems* 17 (Summer 1969):83-109.

38. John F. Galliher, James L. McCartney, and Barbara Baum, "Nebraska's Marijuana Law: A Case of Unexpected Legislative Innovation," *Law and Society Review* 8 (Spring 1974):441-455.

39. Anthony Platt, *The Child Savers* (Chicago: University of Chicago Press, 1969).

40. John Hagan and Jeffrey Leon, "Rediscovering Delinquency: Social History, Political Ideology, and the Sociology of Law," *American Sociological Review* 42 (1977):587-598.

41. Walter D. Connor, "The Manufacture of Deviance: The Case of the Soviet Purge, 1936-1938," *American Sociological Review* 37 (1972):403-413.

42. John I. Kitsuse and Aaron V. Cicourel, "A Note on the Uses of Official Statistics," *Social Problems* 9 (1963):131-139.

43. Thomas J. Scheff, *Being Mentally Ill* (Chicago: Aldine, 1966).

44. See, for example, Jerome Skolnick, *Justice Without Trial*, 2d ed. (New York: Wiley, 1975; originally published 1966); Egon Bittner, *The Function of the Police in Modern Society* (Washington, D.C.: U.S. Government Printing Office, 1970); and Albert J. Reiss, Jr., *The Police and the Public* (New Haven, Conn.: Yale University Press, 1971). For a recent analysis, see Peter K. Manning, *Police Work: The Social Organization of Policing* (Cambridge, Mass.: MIT Press, 1977).

45. See Herman Goldstein, *Policing a Free Society* (Cambridge, Mass.: Ballinger, 1977).

46. James F. Richardson, *Urban Police in the United States* (Port Washington, N.Y.: Kennikat Press, 1974); and Jonathan Rubenstein, *City Police* (New York: Farrar, Straus and Giroux, 1973.

47. Wayne R. LaFave, *Arrest: The Decision to Take a Suspect into Custody* (Boston: Little, Brown, 1965); and Kenneth Culp Davis, *Police Discretion* (Minneapolis, Minn.: West Publishing Company, 1975).

48. See, for example, Donald Clemmer, *The Prison Community* (New York: Holt, Rinehart and Winston, 1958; originally published 1940).

49. See the review contained in Neal Shover, *A Sociology of American Corrections* (Homewood, Ill.: Dorsey Press, 1979).

50. This literature is reviewed in Charles W. Thomas and David M. Petersen, *Prison Organization and Inmate Subcultures* (Indianapolis, Ind.: Bobbs Merrill, 1977).

51. See Daniel Glaser, *The Effectiveness of a Prison and Parole System* (Indianapolis, Ind.: Bobbs Merrill, 1964); and Gene Kassebaum, David A. Ward, and Daniel Wilner, *Prison Treatment and Parole Survival* (New York: Wiley, 1972).

52. See the recent analysis by Michel Foucault, *Discipline and Punish: The Birth of the Prison* (New York: Pantheon, 1977).

53. James B. Jacobs, *Stateville: The Penitentiary in Mass Society* (Chicago: University of Chicago Press, 1976).

54. Notable exceptions are Abraham Blumberg, *Criminal Justice* 2d ed. (New York: New Viewpoints, 1979); Maureen Mileski, "Courtroom Encounters: An Observational Study of a Lower Criminal Court," *Law and Society Review* 5 (1971):473-538; and David Sudnow, "Normal Crimes: Sociological Features of the Penal Code in a Public Defender Office," *Social Problems* 12 (1965):255-276.

55. See Donald Newman, *Conviction: The Determination of Guilt or Innocence Without Trial* (Boston: Little, Brown, 1967); and Arthur Rosett and Donald R. Cressey, *Justice by Consent: Plea Bargains in the American Courthouse* (Philadelphia: Lippincott, 1976).

56. Jack P. Gibbs, "Conceptions of Deviant Behavior: The Old and the New," *Pacific Sociological Review* 9 (1966):9-14.

57. Lewis Coser, "Two Methods in Search of a Substance," *American Sociological Review* 40 (1975):691-700.

58. See, for example, Theodore G. Chiricos, and Gordon P. Waldo, "Socioeconomic Status and Criminal Sentencing: An Empirical Assessment of a Conflict Proposition," *American Sociological Review* 40 (1975):753-772; Graeme Newman, *Comparative Deviance* (New York: Elsevier, 1976); and Lynn McDonald, *The Sociology of Law and Order* (Boulder, Colo.: Westview Press, 1976).

59. Jack P. Gibbs and Maynard L. Erickson, "Major Developments in the Sociological Study of Deviance," *Annual Review of Sociology* 1 (1975):21-42.

60. See F. J. Murphy, et al., "The Incidence of Hidden Delinquency," *American Journal of Orthopsychiatry* 16 (1946):686-695; and Austin L. Porterfield, *Youth in Trouble* (Austin, Tex.: Leo Potishman Foundation, 1946).

61. Illinois Institute for Juvenile Research, *Juvenile Delinquency in Illinois* (Chicago: State of Illinois Department of Mental Health, 1972).

62. Martin Gold and David J. Reimer, "Changing Patterns of Delinquent Behavior Among Americans 13 Through 16 Years Old," *Crime and Delinquency Literature* 7 (1975):438-517.

63. Anthony R. Harris and G. Hill, "Changes in the Gender Patterning of Crime, 1953-1974," Paper presented at the annual meetings of the American Sociological Association, Chicago, Illinois, 1977.

64. President's Commission on Law Enforcement and Administration of Justice, *The Challenge of Crime in a Free Society* (Washington, D.C.: U.S. Government Printing Office, 1967); and the Commission's *Task Force Report: Crime and Its Impact—An Assessment* (Washington, D.C.: U.S. Government Printing Office, 1967).

65. Philip H. Ennis, "Criminal Victimization in the United States: A Report of a National Survey," University of Chicago, National Opinion Research Center, 1967.

66. Michael J. Hindelang, *Criminal Victimization in Eight American Cities: A Descriptive Analysis of Common Theft and Assault* (Cambridge, Mass.: Ballinger, 1976).

67. In recent years, such work has taken on a decidedly international flavor. See Marshall B. Clinard, "Comparative Crime Victimization Surveys: Some Problems and Results," *International Journal of Criminology and Penology* 6 (1978):221-231; and Richard F. Sparks, Hazel G. Genn, and David J. Rodd, *Surveying Victims: A Study of the Measurement of Criminal Victimization* (New York: Wiley, 1977).

68. See, for example, Albert J. Reiss, Jr., "Inappropriate Theories and Inadequate Methods as Policy Plagues: Self-Reported Delinquency and the Law," in N. J. Demerath III, Otto Larson, and Karl Schuessler (eds.), *Social Policy and Sociology* (New York: Academic Press, 1975), pp. 211-222.

69. See Marvin E. Wolfgang, Robert M. Figlio, and Thorsten Sellin, *Delinquency in a Birth Cohort* (Chicago: University of Chicago Press, 1972); Center for Studies of Crime and Delinquency, *Teenage Delinquency in Small Town America* (Washington, D.C.: National Institute of Mental Health Research Report 5, U.S. Government Printing Office, 1974); Lyle W. Shannon, "A Longitudinal Study of Delinquency and Crime," in Charles Wellford (ed.), *Quantitative Studies in Criminology* (Beverly Hills, Calif.: Sage Publications, 1978), pp. 121-146; and Delbert S. Elliott and Harwin L. Voss, *Delinquency and Dropout* (Lexington, Mass.: Lexington Books, 1974).

70. Note, however, that self-report and victimization data are not relevant to a labeling conception of deviance since here crime is defined in terms of official reactions which in some sense are measured accurately for this purpose by official statistics. However, some of these data are pertinent to several issues posed earlier. Some of these earlier issues are identified by a sociologist and a psychiatrist. See Marshall B. Clinard, "Sociologists and American Criminology," *Journal of Criminal Law, Criminology and Police Science* 41 (1951):549-576; and Walter Bromberg, "American Achievements in Criminology," *Journal of Criminal Law, Criminology and Police Science* 44 (1953):166-176.

71. See Charles R. Tittle, Wayne L. Villemez, and Douglas A. Smith, "The Myth of Social Class and Criminality: An Empirical Assessment of the Empirical Evidence," *American Sociological Review* 43 (1978):643-656.

72. Travis Hirschi and Michael J. Hindelang, "Intelligence and Delinquency: A Revisionist View," *American Sociological Review* 42 (1977):571-587.

73. David Greenberg, "Delinquency and the Age Structure of Society," *Contemporary Crises* 1 (1977):189-223.

74. Harris and Hill, "Changes in the Gender Patterning of Crime"; and Anthony R. Harris, "Sex and Theories of Deviance: Toward a Functional Theory of Deviant Typescripts," *American Sociological Review* 42 (1977):3-16.

75. Michael J. Hindelang, "Race and Involvement in Common Law Personal Crimes," *American Sociological Review* 43 (1978):93-109.

76. See Freda Adler, *Sisters in Crime* (New York: McGraw-Hill, 1975); Rita J. Simon, *Women and Crime* (Lexington, Mass.: D. C. Heath, 1975); Freda Adler and Rita J. Simon (eds.), *The Criminology of Deviant Women* (Boston: Houghton Mifflin, 1979); and Lee Bowker (ed.), *Women and Crime in America* (New York: Macmillan, 1981).

77. Cohen, *Delinquent Boys*, Chapter 2.

78. See Gilbert Geis and Robert F. Meier (eds.), *White-Collar Crime: Offenses in Business, Politics and the Professions* (New York: Free Press, 1977); John M. Johnson and Jack D. Douglas (eds.), *Crime at the Top* (Philadelphia: Lippincott, 1978); and M. David Erdman and Richard L. Lundman, *Corporate Deviance* (New York: Holt, Rinehart and Winston, 1981).

79. Donald R. Cressey, "Restraint of Trade, Recidivism and Delinquent Neighbor-

hoods," in James F. Short, Jr. (ed.), *Delinquency, Crime and Society* (Chicago: University of Chicago Press, 1976), pp. 209-238.

80. See, for example, John E. Conklin, *"Illegal But Not Criminal": Business Crime in America* (Englewood Cliffs, N.J.: Prentice-Hall, 1977).

81. Diane Vaughan and Carlo Giovanna, "The Appliance Repairman: A Study of Victim-Responsiveness and Fraud," *Journal of Research in Crime and Delinquency* 12 (1975):153-161.

82. Pat Lauderdale, Harold Grasmick, and John P. Clark, "Corporate Environments, Corporate Crime and Deterrence," in Marvin D. Krohn and Ronald L. Akers (eds.), *Crime, Law and Sanctions* (Beverly Hills, Calif.: Sage Publications, 1978), pp. 137-158.

83. Peter K. Rossi, Emily Waite, Christine E. Bose, and Richard E. Berk, "The Seriousness of Crimes: Normative Structures and Individual Differences," *American Sociological Review* 39 (1974):224-237.

84. Graeme Newman, *Understanding Violence* (New York: Harper and Row/Lippincott, 1979).

85. Wolfgang, et al., *Delinquency in a Birth Cohort.*

86. Lynn A. Curtis, *Violence, Race and Culture* (Lexington, Mass.: D. C. Heath, 1975); and Charles E. Silberman, *Criminal Violence, Criminal Justice* (New York: Random House, 1979).

87. Paul A. Strasburg, *Violent Delinquents* (New York: Simon and Schuster, 1979).

88. Walter B. Miller, *Violence by Youth Gangs and Youth Groups as a Crime Problem in Major American Cities* (Washington, D.C.: National Institute for Juvenile Justice and Delinquency Prevention, U.S. Government Printing Office, 1975).

89. See also John F. Galliher, "The Life and Death of Liberal Criminology," *Contemporary Crises* 2 (1978):245-263.

90. See the summary contained in Jack P. Gibbs, *Crime, Punishment and Deterrence* (New York: Elsevier, 1975).

91. See C. Ray Jeffery, *Crime Prevention Through Environmental Design*, 2d ed. (Beverly Hills, Calif.: Sage Publications, 1977).

92. Much of this work is ably reviewed in Saleem A. Shah and Loren H. Roth, "Biological and Psychophysiological Factors in Criminality," in Daniel Glaser, ed., *Handbook of Criminology* (Chicago: Rand McNally, 1974), pp. 101-173.

93. Sarnoff A. Mednick and Karl O. Christiansen (eds.), *Biosocial Bases of Criminal Behavior* (New York: Gardner Press, 1977).

94. Delbert S. Elliott, Suzanne S. Ageton, and Rachelle J. Canter, "An Integrated Theoretical Perspective on Delinquent Behavior," *Journal of Research in Crime and Delinquency* 16 (1979):3.

95. A valuable study of the influence of theories formulated prior to 1945 on subsequent research (anomie was found to be particularly influential in this regard) can be found in Stephen Cole, "The Growth of Scientific Knowledge: Theories of Deviance as a Case Study," in Lewis Coser (ed.), *The Idea of Social Structure* (New York: Harcourt Brace Jovanovich, 1975), pp. 175-220. Examples of reformulations of these earlier theories can be found in Elliott, et al., "An Integrated Theoretical Perspective on Delinquent Behavior"; Robert L. Burgess and Ronald L. Akers, "A Differential Association-Reinforcement Theory of Criminal Behavior," *Social Problems* 14 (1966):128-147; William Simon and John H. Gagnon, "The Anomie of Affluence: A Post Merton Conception," *American Journal of Sociology* 82 (1976):356-378; and Rand Conger, "From

Social Learning to Criminal Behavior," in Krohn and Akers (eds.), *Crime, Law and Sanctions*, pp. 91-104.

96. See Richard Quinney, "The Production of a Marxist Criminology," *Contemporary Crises* 2 (1978):277-292; and Richard Quinney, *Class, Crime and State* (New York: David McKay, 1977).

97. One of the first and most important papers is Gary Becker's "Crime and Punishment: An Economic Approach," *Journal of Political Economy* 76 (1968):169-217. Also see the recent, and controversial, work of Isaac Ehrlich, "The Deterrent Effect of Capital Punishment: A Question of Life and Death," *American Economic Review* 65 (1975):397-417; and Ehrlich, "Capital Punishment and Deterrence: Some Further Thoughts and Additional Evidence," *Journal of Political Economy* 85 (1977):741-788.

98. Gibbons, *The Criminological Enterprise*.

99. Gresham Sykes, "The Rise of Critical Criminology," *Journal of Criminal Law and Criminology* 65 (1974):204-213.

100. Robert F. Meier, "The New Criminology: Continuity in Criminological Theory," *Journal of Criminal Law and Criminology* 67 (1976):461-469.

101. Peter K. Manning, "Deviance and Dogma," *British Journal of Criminology* 15 (1975):12.

102. Carl Klockars, "The Contemporary Crisis of Marxist Criminology," *Criminology* 16 (1979):477-515.

103. Douglas Lipton, Robert Martinson, and Judith Wilks, *The Effectiveness of Correctional Treatment* (New York: Praeger, 1975); and Francis A. Allen, *The Decline of the Rehabilitative Ideal* (New Haven, Conn.: Yale University Press, 1981).

104. Andrew von Hirsch, *Doing Justice: The Choice of Punishments* (New York: Hill and Wang, 1976); and Graeme Newman, *The Punishment Response* (Philadelphia: Lippincott, 1978).

105. See Jack P. Gibbs, "The Death Penalty, Retribution, and Penal Policy," *Journal of Criminal Law and Criminology* 69 (1978):291-299.

106. One version of utilitarian argument with respect to retribution states that the imposition of legal punishment is necessary to uphold the moral and social order as embodied in the law. As such, the reaffirmation of community standards and values constitutes the "desired" outcome of a punishment system based on retributivist principles. See Walter Berns, *For Capital Punishment: Crime and the Morality of the Death Penalty* (New York: Basic Books, 1979).

107. See Robert F. Meier, "The Arrested Development of Criminological Theory," *Contemporary Sociology* 9 (May 1980):374-383.

108. See James Q. Wilson, *Thinking About Crime* (New York: Basic Books, 1975); and Earnest van den Haag, *Punishing Criminals: Concerning and Old and Painful Question* (New York: Basic Books, 1975).

109. Glaser, *Crime in Our Changing Society*; and Donald R. Cressey, "Criminological Theory, Social Science and the Repression of Crime," *Criminology* 16 (1978):171-191.

110. The literature on peer evaluation and its reliability is reviewed and assessed in Wolfgang, et al., *Evaluating Criminology*.

111. Ibid.

112. Ibid., pp. 244-248.

113. Ibid., p. 173.

114. David F. Greenberg, *Mathematical Criminology* (New Brunswick, N.J.: Rutgers University Press, 1979), p. xv.

115. Wolfgang, et al., *Evaluating Criminology*, p. 136.
116. Ibid., p. 140.
117. Ibid., p. 143.
118. Ibid., p. 11.

BIBLIOGRAPHY

The literature on criminology in the United States is very large and is growing annually. The statement is all the more true for recent years with the incursion of economists, psychologists, historians, anthropologists, and political scientists into the field. What is resulting is a diverse literature, filled with many insights from different disciplines and from different viewpoints within those disciplines. For this reason alone, an adequate, representative bibliography of the American criminological literature is impossible, and, were it possible, the list would be unmanageably long.

What follows is a short list of works, both books and articles, that have been chosen to reflect only a part of this diverse literature. Although faults can be found with it, the list provides a reasonable starting point for exploring this literature. For this purpose, both works that offer original insights into theory and method and works that attempt to summarize and review specific areas within criminology are included.

Allen, Francis A. *The Decline of the Rehabilitative Ideal*. New Haven, Conn.: Yale University Press, 1981.
This prominent critic of the rehabilitation philosophy that dominated American penal policy in earlier decades, explores its premises, ideological foundations, and failures.

Becker, Howard S. *Outsiders: Studies in the Sociology of Deviance*. Enlarged edition. New York: Free Press, 1973). (Originally published in 1963).
This highly influential book "founded" the labeling perspective on crime and deviance. Becker employs a reactive definition of deviance, and subsequent writers in this tradition have produced a large, if slightly confusing, literature.

Blumberg, Abraham. *Criminal Justice*. 2d ed. New York: New Viewpoints, 1979.
Blumberg, a social scientist with legal training, has written one of the better, most comprehensive discussions of criminal justice as a topic of theory and research among criminologists.

Chambliss, William J. and Robert B. Seidman. *Law, Order, and Power*. 2d ed. Reading, Mass.: Addison-Wesley, 1982.
This "conflict" oriented discussion of law, its development and administration, is now more than a decade old, but remains one of the better treatments of law from the theoretical perspective.

Bowker, Lee (ed.). *Women and Crime in America*. New York: Macmillan, 1981.
A collection of papers on women as offenders, victims, and defendants in the criminal justice system.

Clinard, Marshall B., and Peter C. Yeager. *Corporate Crime* New York: Free Press, 1980.

This report on a large-scale study of legal violations by economic organizations (corporations) updates Sutherland's classic study (1949) with substantially better data and interpretation.

Cloward, Richard, and Lloyd E. Ohlin. *Delinquency and Opportunity*. New York: Free Press, 1960.

This major extension and integration of the theoretical traditions of Merton and Sutherland, brought to bear on gang delinquency, provide a rationale for a number of social action programs in the 1960s in the United States.

Cohen, Albert K. *Delinquent Boys*. New York: Free Press, 1965.

Cohen's book initiated criminological interest in delinquent subcultures and, subsequently, delinquent gangs in the 1950s and 1960s. It can still be read with interest since it addresses one of the most important problems of criminology: the origin of delinquent norms.

Cressey, Donald R. "Fifty Years of Criminology: From Sociological Theory to Political Control." *Pacific Sociological Review* 22, no. 4 (1979):457-480.

This necessarily brief review of selected developments in criminology and criminal justice is by a noted criminologist.

Elliott, Delbert S., Suzanne E. Ageton, and Rachelle J. Canter. "An Integrated Theoretical Perspective on Delinquent Behavior." *Journal of Research in Crime and Delinquency* 16 (January 1979):3-27.

The authors attempt to integrate diverse theoretical traditions and to align the result with data. Also see the comments by Short and Hirschi following this article for evaluative comments.

Finestone, Harold. *Victims of Change*. Westport, Conn.: Greenwood Press, 1976.

This excellent well-written historical account of the "creation" of delinquency ties delinquency and the juvenile court into nineteenth-century social conditions in the United States.

Geis, Gilbert, and Robert F. Meier (eds.). *White-Collar Crime: Offenses in Business, Politics and the Professions*. New York: Free Press 1977.

Geis and Meier present a collection of major papers—with editorial introduction—that shaped the conception and present study of white-collar and corporate criminality.

Gibbons, Don C. *The Criminological Enterprise*. Englewood Cliffs, N.J.: Prentice-Hall, 1979.

This recent review of major theories and perspectives on crime also contains commentary and evaluation.

Gibbs, Jack P. *Crime, Punishment and Deterrence*. New York: Elsevier, 1975.

This book contains a careful analysis of the conceptual status and the empirical literature on deterrence. It is issue oriented and quite comprehensive.

Gibbs, Jack P., and Maynard L. Erickson. "Major Developments in the Sociological Study of Deviance." *Annual Review of Sociology* 1 (1975):21-42.

Gibbs and Erickson review theoretical and empirical developments in the study of crime and deviance, with particular attention given to the influence of labeling theory.

Glaser, Daniel. *Crime in Our Changing Society*. New York: Holt, Rinehart and Winston, 1978.
This book is useful not only for its review of the criminological literature (but not criminal justice literature) but also for its original insights into such issues as explaining the crime peak during adolescence, long a perennial problem in the field.

Goldstein, Herman. *Policing a Free Society*. Cambridge, Mass.: Ballinger, 1977.
This insightful analysis of policing by a former police administrator examines central philosophical, sociological, and legal issues of policing.

Gordon, David M. "Capitalism, Class, and Crime in America." *Crime and Delinquency* 19 (April 1973):163-186.
Gordon sketches the relation between crime and social and economic structure within a Marxist tradition.

Gove, Walter R. (ed.). *The Labelling of Deviant Behavior*. 2d ed. Beverly Hills, Calif.: Sage Publications, 1980.
This collection of original papers attempts to evaluate propositions derived from a labeling perspective.

Greenberg, David F. "Deliquency and the Age Structure of Society." *Contemporary Crises* 1 (April 1977):189-223.
In this interesting attempt to deal theoretically with the pronounced relationship between crime and age in U.S. society, Greenberg shows the relevance of historical factors and research.

Hindelang, Michael J. *Criminal Victimization in Eight American Cities*. Cambridge, Mass.: Ballinger, 1976.
This study of crime patterns in eight large U.S. cities employs one of the newer techniques for discerning crime trends: victimization data.

Hirschi, Travis. *Causes of Delinquency*. Berkeley, Calif.: University of California Press, 1969.
Hirschi presents perhaps the most cited version of "control theory" which tests that theory with self-reported delinquency data from a large sample of California adolescents.

Irwin, John. *Prisons in Turmoil*. Boston: Little, Brown 1980.
After analyzing the social organization and patterned activities of the "Big House," Irwin reviews the upheavals of the 1950s and 1960s that disrupted this system. He analyzes administrative reactions, community corrections as a proposed solution, features of the American prisons of the 1980s, and possible future trends.

Klockars, Carl. "The Contemporary Crisis of Marxist Criminology." *Criminology* 16 (February 1979):477-515.
This is a recent critique of Marxist criminology.

Klockars, Carl. *The Professional Fence*. New York: Free Press, 1974.
This fine account of one "marginal" criminal uses participant observation methods and contains some excellent descriptive material.

Kornhauser, Ruth Rosner. *Social Sources of Delinquency*. Chicago: University of Chicago Press, 1978.
Kornhauser presents an excellent, though controversial, examination of strain, social disorganization, cultural transmission, and control theories of delinquency.

Lauderdale, Pat, Harold Grasmick, and John P. Clark. "Corporate Environments, Corporate Crime and Deterrence." In Marvin D. Krohn and Ronald L. Akers (eds.) *Crime, Law and Sanctions* Beverly Hills, Calif.: Sage Publications, 1978. Pp. 137-158.
The authors seek to account for violations of law by corporate bodies using a perspective developed from the study of formal organizations in sociology.

Lipton, Douglas, Robert Martinson, and Judith Wilks. *The Effectiveness of Correctional Treatment*. New York: Praeger, 1975.
In this extensive summary and review of studies that have evaluated correctional treatment programs, the authors conclude that correctional treatment as implemented has been seemingly ineffective.

Manning, Peter K. *Police Work*. Cambridge, Mass.: MIT Press, 1977.
This dramaturgical analysis of policing uses data from the United States and England. It is one example of what sociologists might look at with respect to the police, rather than what an attorney or administrator might be interested in.

Matza, David. *Becoming Deviant*. Englewood Cliffs, N.J.: Prentice-Hall, 1969.
A phenomenological analysis of deviance occupies the second half of this book, while the first half is concerned with providing trenchant observations on the ideological influences that shaped the study of deviance.

Meier, Robert F. "The New Criminology: Continuity in Criminological Theory." *Journal of Criminal Law and Criminology* 67 (December 1976):461-469.
This study traces elements of modern radical or conflict criminology to earlier issues and perspectives.

Miller, Walter R. "Lower Class Culture as a Generating Milieu of Gang Delinquency." *Journal of Social Issues* 14 (November 1958):5-19.
This analysis of lower class delinquency locates its origins in larger features of lower class life and culture.

Morris, Albert. "The American Society of Criminology: A History, 1941-1974." *Criminology* 13 (August 1975):123-167.
Morris presents a reminiscent account of the American Society of Criminology, the major professional organization of criminologists in the United States.

Nettler, Gwynn. *Explaining Crime*. 2d ed. New York: McGraw-Hill 1978.
This excellent summary contains penetrating critiques and commentary on most of the major ideas about crime.

Newman, Graeme. *The Punishment Response*. Philadelphia: Lippincott, 1978.
This historical examination of punishment provides a rationale, though not an exact, formulation of practical implementation, of retribution as the basis of a penal philosophy.

Quinney, Richard. *Class, State and Crime*. 2d ed. New York: Longman, 1980.
The latest volume by the most widely quoted American Marxist criminologist, this edition has a decided religious influence.

Schur, Edwin M. *Interpreting Deviance*. New York: Harper and Row, 1979.
Schur presents an interpretation of deviance, including crime, from an interactionist and labeling perspective.

Short, James F., Jr., and Robert F. Meier. "Criminology and the Study of Deviance." *American Behavioral Scientist* 24 (January/February 1981):462-478.
The shifts in theoretical focus since 1950 are interpreted for related fields of criminology and deviance. Before 1950, Short and Meier say, scholars asked: Why do criminals and deviants act the way they do? Since 1950 sociologists have asked more frequently: What is the social meaning of rule breaking, and why do these particular persons evoke negative sanctions?

Short, James F., Jr., and Fred L. Strodtbeck. *Group Process and Gang Delinquency*. Chicago: University of Chicago Press, 1965.
This work is a major empirical study of gang behavior in the 1960s. It tests ideas derived from Cohen, Miller, and Cloward and Ohlin, among others.

Shover, Neal. *A Sociology of American Corrections*. Homewood, Ill. Dorsey Press, 1979.
Shover gives a fine summary of the sociological and legal issues dealing with corrections.

Sutherland, Edwin H. and Donald R. Cressey. *Criminology*. 10th ed. Philadelphia: Lippincott, 1978.
This book, perhaps the oldest social science text (first published in 1950 and certainly the oldest criminology text) still in print, was revised by Sutherland's last graduate student.

Sykes, Gresham M., and David Matza. "Techniques of Neutralization." *American Sociological Review* 22 (December 1957):664-670.
Originally intended as an alternative to Cohen's theory (see above), the notion of neutralization may be compatible with most perspectives on crime but has received little conceptual or theoretical attention.

Toch, Hans (ed.). *Psychology of Crime and Criminal Justice*. New York: Holt, Rinehart and Winston, 1979.
This collection of original papers covers important aspects of crime and criminal justice, many from a psychological viewpoint.

Turk, Austin T. *Criminality and the Legal Order*. Chicago: Rand McNally, 1969.
Turk presents a "conflict" (but not Marxist) account and interpretation of the etiology and epidemiology of crime in the United States.

Wilson, James Q. *Thinking About Crime*. New York: Basis Books, 1975.
This conservative analysis of crime and criminal justice advocates more stringent penalties and more active enforcement efforts to combat street crime.

Wolfgang, Marvin E., Robert Figlio, and Thorsten Sellin. *Delinquency in a Birth Cohort*. Chicago: University of Chicago Press, 1972.
This longitudinal analysis, based on police records and other official sources, deals with a large group of boys from Philadelphia.

Wolfgang, Marvin E., Robert M. Figlio, and Terence Thornberry. *Evaluating Criminology*. New York: Elsevier, 1978.
This study of the criminology literature from 1945 to 1972 charts trends and offers content observations about that literature.

Zimring, Franklin E., and Gordon Hawkins. *Deterrence*. Chicago: University of Chicago Press, 1973.
Many of the issues that still concern deterrence researchers are identified in this volume, although, not unexpectedly, the authors tend to emphasize jurisprudential problems and concerns.

INDEX

Abbott, Daniel J., 81, 96
Abortion, 251, 259
Abstentionalism, 126, 127
Abu-Laban, Baha, 205
Acosta Guzman, Alfonso, 242, 246
Adato de Ibarra, Victoria, 258, 266
Addiction Research Foundation, Canada, 202
Adler, Freda, 102, 103, 105-6, 107, 115, 116, 117, 169, 181, 226, 231, 288
Adorno, Theodor, 123
Adriasola, Guillermo, 229
Advanced International Institute of Criminal Science, 51
Affluence, 72, 73, 85, 93, 235, 236
Aftalion, Enrique, 167, 169
Aftercare, 239, 254, 258
Age: and crime, 101, 102; status, 218, 278, 279
Ageton, Suzanne S., 280, 289, 292
Agüero, Guillermo, 228
Ainlay, John, 133, 142, 143
Akerknecht, Erwin H., 25
Akers, Ronald L., 289, 290, 294
Albarrán, Juan Fernández, 254
Alcohol offenses, 51, 72, 73, 113, 195, 202, 218, 251
Alessandri, Jorge, 212
Alexander, Franz, 224
Alfaro, Anastasio, 241, 246, 247
Alienation, 122, 124
Allen, Francis A., 290, 291
Allende, Salvador, 212
Alliance of NGOS on Crime Prevention and Criminal Justice, 49
Almeida, José Nicanor, 177-78
Alper, Benedict S., 36, 81
Althusser, Louis, 138, 144
Altimir, Oscar, 212
Altmann-Smythe, Julio, 181
Alvarado, Eduardo Vargas, 246
Alves, Tomaz, 173
Alvirez, Iturbide, 258
Amar, Ayush Morad, 44, 181, 182, 183
Amarante, Jurandyr, 184
American Society of Criminology, 18, 201, 269-70
Amin, Idi, 84, 91
Amnesty International, 80
Ancel, Marc, 52
Andenaes, Johs., 36
André, Antenor, 185
Andry, R. G., 47, 59
Anglo-American criminology, 10-11, 13, 187, 188
Aniyarde Castro, L., 44, 58
Annis, Helen M., 188, 203
Anomie, 88, 93, 281
Anthropology, 7, 9, 13, 22, 41-42, 86, 160, 161, 165, 174, 175, 176, 210, 244, 253, 257, 261-62, 272
Antolisei, Américo, 179

Applied criminology, 17, 18-21, 23, 42, 187, 189-90, 192, 195-202, 240, 267-69, 270-71
Applied research, 125-26, 158, 189, 220, 221, 282
Araujo, Vieira, 173
Argentina, 151-68
Argentinian Criminology Society, 163
Aschoffenburg, Gustav, 157
Asia and Far East Institute, United Nations, 83, 93
Assaults, 70, 72, 101, 129, 251, 253
Asuni, Tolani, 44, 64
Aubert, Vilhelm, 27
Australian Institute of Criminology, 93
Automobile theft, 216
Ayers, J. D., 196-205
Aztecs, 251

Babb, H. W., 145
Bacca, Martínez, 253
Badu, S. N., 64
Bailey, David H., 95
Bajarlia, Juan Jacobo, 169
Balbus, Isaac, 139, 145
Banchik, Doris, 229, 231
Bandeira, Esmeraldino, 173
Bandini, T., 47, 59
Banditry, 85, 127-28
Banishment, 155, 239, 251
Baquerizo, G. Zavala, 44
Bárbara, Mario, 262
Barbieri, Lazardo, 164
Barkum, Michael, 27
Barlow, Hugh D., 284
Barreto Rangel, Gustavo, 258
Basalo, Carlos Garcia, 152, 167
Bascuñán, Antonio, 229, 230
Bassiouni, M. Cherif, 81
Bastos, Felinto, 174
Baum, Barbara, 286
Bazelon, David L., 231
Beccaria, Cesar Bonesana, 264
Becker, Gary, 290
Becker, Howard S., 275, 285, 286, 291
Beeche, Octavio, 240, 242, 246, 247
Beirne, Piers, 139, 145
Belbey, Jose, 169
Bell, John Patrick, 245
Benavides, Enrique, 242
Ben-David, Joseph, 25, 26
Bendix, Reinhard, 8, 9, 24
Bennett, Richard R., 26
Berendique, M. Gonzalez, 152
Bergalli, Roberto, 169, 230, 231, 264
Bergamini Miotto, Armida, 266
Beristain, Antonio, 44, 58, 181
Berk, Richard E., 289
Bernaldo de Quirós, Constancio, 264, 265
Bernier, Robert, 205
Berns, Walter, 290
Bernstein, Susie, 146
Bertrand, Marie André, 189
Bianchi, Herman, 36, 141
Biles, David, 98
Biological approaches, 22, 40, 42, 157, 188, 210, 223, 224, 231, 261-62, 280
Birkenmayer, Andrew C., 206
Birmingham Center for Cultural Studies, 121
Biron, Louise, 187, 188, 204
Bittner, Egon, 286
Black, Donald, 7, 24
Blackburn, Robin, 144, 145
Blake, Gerald E., 285
Blake, William, 140
Blankevoort, V., 204
Blarduni, Oscar, 167, 169
Bloch, Herbert, 276, 286
Blok, Anton, 128, 142
Blumberg, Abraham, 287, 291
Boehringer, G. H., 96, 98
Bohannan, Paul, 95
Bonger, William A., 25, 132, 133, 143
Boni, A., 44
Borden, Jerry F., 81
Boren, Jerry F., 36
Borodin, Stanislav V., 64
Bose, Christine E., 289
Bouzat, Pierre, 51
Bovet, L., 60
Bowker, Lee H., 102, 105, 116, 117, 288, 291
Bradley, J., 264

Braga, Jorge, 184
Branco, Vitorino Prata Castelo, 173, 180-81, 183
Brandau, Valentín, 226
Brantingham, Patricia, 202, 206
Brantingham, Paul, 202, 206
Bravo, Alfredo Guillermo, 226
Brazil, 173-83
Brazilian Bar Association, 180
Brazilian Society of Criminal Law, 180
Brecher, Jeremy, 142
Brennan, Anthony, J. E., 64
Brickey, S. L., 206
Brierly, John E. C., 25
Brodeur, Jean-Paul, 189
Bromberg, Walter, 288
Brücher, Eduardo, 228
Brücher, Hernán, 228
Brunet-Aubry, Lise, 205, 208
Buchuk, Regina, 230
Buentello y Villa, Edmundo, 257, 258
Buikhuisen, Wouter, 181
Bunyan, Tony, 146
Buraway, Michael, 141
Burgess, Robert L., 289
Burglary, 100, 102, 113, 115, 216-17, 236
Bustos, Armando, 164
Byles, J. A., 188, 203

Cabello, Vincente, 152
Cagliotti, Carlos Norberto, 152, 181
Calabrese, Antonio, 181
Calder, Jaime Toro, 181
Calvo, Minor, 242
Camargo, Joaquim Augusto, 173
Camargo, Maria Teresa, 181
Cambounet, Ch., 41
Canada, 102, 187-203
Canadian Association for Criminological Research, 201
Canepa, Giacomo, 43, 57, 181
Canestri, Francisco, 48, 181
Canter, Rachelle J., 280, 289, 292
Capitalism, 73, 120, 123, 126, 127, 128, 131, 132, 134-38
Capital punishment, 31, 74, 76, 90, 91, 134, 196, 251, 252, 258
Cardenas, Gregorio, 260
Cárdenas, Lázaro, 254
Carrancá y Rivas, Raúl, 257, 258, 265
Carrancá y Trujillo, Raúl, 265
Carranz, Elías, 248
Carrero, Antonio G., 181
Carroll, Denis, 38, 39, 41, 42, 44, 54
Carvajal, Graciela, 230
Carvalho, Oscar Freire, 174
Casselman, Joris, 181
Cassidy, R. Gordon, 194-95, 205
Castillo, Francisco, 242
Castillo Barrantes, Enrique, 242, 244, 246, 248
Central American Common Market, 235
Centro Nazionale di Prevenzione a Difesa Sociale of Milan, 52
Cevallos, Alejandro, 152
Chambliss, William J., 144, 148, 286, 291
Chang, Dae H., 13, 25
Chappell, Duncan, 192
Chaves, Roberto, 247
Chavez, Efran Torres, 152
Cheddadi, Mohammed, 95
Chenaud, Carlos, 174
Children's court judges, 32
Chile, 209-26; society of, 211-12
Chiricos, Theodore C., 275, 287
Choosup, Dlavee, 64
Christiansen, Karl Otto, 36, 121, 228, 289
Christie, Nils, 47, 59, 228, 231
Chuaqui, Constantino, 230
Chubin, David E., 25
Ciale, Justin, 191
Cicourel, Aaron V., 286
Cifuentes, Salvador, 229, 231
Cintra, Tarcizo Leonce Pinheiro, 178
Clark, John P., 289, 294
Class conflict, 128, 129
Classical school, 166, 215
Classification: of nations, 12-13; of prisoners, 255
Clemmer, Donald, 286
Clifford, William, 81, 95, 96, 98
Clinard, Marshall B., 81, 96, 228, 285, 288, 291

Clinical Criminology, 40, 42, 43, 44, 165, 166, 167, 178, 209-10, 213, 223-24, 260
Cloward, Richard, 47, 59, 137, 144, 228, 275, 276, 280, 286, 291, 295
Cohen, Albert H., 228, 275, 276, 288, 291, 295
Cohen, Jerome Alan, 96
Cohen, Stanley, 120, 141
Cole, Stephen, 284, 289
Colin, M., 44, 58
Collins, Randall, 25
Colonialism, 70, 91, 223-34, 251-52
Columbus, Christopher, 233
Commission on Human Rights, United States, 66, 68
Commission on Narcotic Drugs, United Nations, 66, 68
Commission on Transnational Corporations, United Nations, 66, 68
Committee on Crime Prevention and Control, 63-65, 66, 67-68, 76-78, 78-79
Community service orders, 221
Comparative criminology, 6, 7, 8-9, 11, 13-14, 22-23, 40, 43, 44, 86-87, 92, 168; method, 6-7, 8-11, 13-14, 22-23; research 23-24, 69-70, 86-87, 182; studies, 32, 70-76, 85-86, 102-6, 194-95, 202-3
Compensation, 90
Conference for Critical Legal Studies, 121
Confucius, 92
Conger, Rand D., 97, 289-90
Conjugal visits, 256
Conklin, John E., 289
Connor, Walter D., 286
Consensus perspective, 33, 120, 129, 274-75
Control theory, 281
Cook, Donald, 206
Cornil, P., 44
Corporal punishment, 31, 90, 91, 134, 251
Correctionalism, 125
Corrections, 74-76, 268, 269, 272
Corruption, 84, 88, 89, 91-92, 234, 252, 261
Coser, Lewis, 287, 289
Costa, Alvaro Mayrinit, 184
Costa, J. L., 60
Costa Rica, 233-45; history of, 233-34
Cote, G., 204
Cotic, Dušan, 64
Council for the Coordination of International Congresses of Medical Sciences, 53
Council of Europe, 33, 34, 49, 51, 79
Courtis, M. C., 205
Courts, 46, 90, 188, 203, 237-38, 240, 277
Crane, Diana, 26
Cressey, Donald R., 285, 287, 288, 290, 292, 295
Crime: against persons, 70-72, 101, 215-18, 251; against property, 70-72, 84, 100, 101, 102, 106, 108, 111, 194, 215, 216-18, 234, 236-37, 251, 253, 262-63; rates, 70-74, 215-18, 236-37, 262-63; rates by sex status, 100, 101, 102, 107, 112-13; revolutionary potential of, 131, 132; statistics, 10, 52-53, 70-74, 85-86, 91, 102, 151-52, 190, 193-94, 197, 202, 215-18, 236-37, 238, 244-45, 277-79, 282
Crime control, 34, 46, 269-70, 271, 273, 275, 276-77, 283
Crime Prevention and Criminal Justice Branch, 66, 67, 68, 78-79, 68-80
Criminal stereotypes, 113-14
Criminal tribes, 93
Criminalistics, 159, 162, 243, 253, 258
Criminalization, 34-35, 211
Criminological Research Council, 33
Criminologies-in-societies, 17-18
Criminology: autonomous or specialty? 15, 18, 21-22; critical, 124-30; definition of, 9, 15, 17-24, 157, 173-74, 175-78, 209, 218-19, 221-22, 240, 241-42, 252-53, 257, 258, 267, 269-72; as a discipline, 15-24, 86-87; elements of, 5-6, 15-17, 23; and female crime, 99-100, 113, 115; future of, 18, 22-24, 35-36, 283; as idiographic discipline, 9, 11;

institutionalization of, 15-21, 22-24, 257; interdisciplinary span, 7, 9, 15, 18; mainstream (liberal), 120; as nomothetic discipline, 9, 11, 16-17, 19-22; obstacles to, 6, 10, 23-24; and policy, 18, 19, 32, 33, 34, 51, 73, 76-77; as science, 125-126, 131, 158, 242, 271-72; and social control, 7-8, 16-17, 31-32; theoretical and applied, 17, 18-21, 23, 42; transnational, 6, 9-11, 15, 17-18, 20-21, 22, 23-24; vicarious experience of, 5-6
Critical criminology, 124-30
Critique, Marxist, 121-22
Cross-cultural perspective, 99, 102, 203
Cuaron, Alfonso Quiros, 181
Cuello Calón, Eugenio, 265
Culture, 40, 46, 86, 87, 88, 89-90, 92, 99, 102, 108-9, 152
Curriculums, criminological, 158-61, 177-78, 180, 189-94, 221-23, 272-74
Curtis, Lynn A., 289
Cusson, Maurice, 189

Dacoits, 93
Dahm, J., 179
d'Alleaume, Piprot, 38, 39
d'Amelio, M., 42
Da Motta, Candido Nazianzeno Nogueira, 186
Dandurand, Yvon, 191, 201
Dangerous criminals, 156-57, 163
Daniel, Carolyn, 206
D'Araujo Leal, Aureliano, 184
Dark figure of crime, 85, 217, 225, 278
Darwin, Charles, 13
Da Silva, José Pereira, 184
David, José, 181
David, Pedro R., 152, 164, 169, 170
David, Rene, 25
Davis, Kenneth Culp, 286
De Abrue, Ferreira, 173
De Azevedo Marques, João Benedito, 185
De Barros, Orlando Mara, 186
De Benedetti, Isodore, 152
De Brito, Roque Alves, 176, 177, 180, 183
Debuyst, Ch., 47, 59
De Carvalho, Antonio Amâncio Pereira, 174
De Castro, Olympio Augusto Viveiros, 173, 174, 184
De Coronado, Juan Vasquez Juan, 233, 245
Decriminalization, 52, 153-54, 257
De Freitas, Joaquim, 178
De Greeff, Etienne, 38, 39
Deinstitutionalization, 47, 257
De Iturbide, Agustin, 234
De Jesus, Damásio E., 185
De La Puente, Patricio, 229
del Campillo, Ortega, 44
del Rosal, J., 42, 44
De Macedo, Gilberto, 184
Demerath, N. J., III, 288
Democracy, 139, 211, 215, 277
Demography, 92-93, 194, 211-12, 235, 260, 271, 272
De Moraes, Benjamin, 177
De Morais, Evaristo, 175
Demystification, 122
Denis Carroll Prize, 41, 45, 47, 59
De Olavarria y Ferrari, Enrique, 263
De Oliveira, Brasílio Augusto Machado, 174
De Oliveira, Elias, 184
De Oliviera, Eugenio Mariz, 178
De Silveira, Valdemar Cesar, 177, 186
De Souza, Sinesio Buerro, 152
Deterrence, 134-35, 138, 140, 154, 196, 280
De Tocqueville, Alexis, 30
de Vabres, H. Donnedieu, 42
Developed nations, 70-74
Developing nations, 6, 19, 34, 46, 70-72, 83-95, 235; and crime, 84-85, 87-88
Development, socioeconomic, 16, 73, 78-79, 83-86, 92-42, 103, 105, 151, 152, 168, 203, 212, 213, 235, 244
De Veyga, Francisco, 165
De Villalaz, Aura Guerra, 64
De Vos, George, 27

De Waele, J. P., 47, 59
Dharmashastra, Manava, 92
Di Argentine, Beria, 52
Dias, Maria Christina Perez, 152
Díaz, Porfirio, 253
di Gennaro, Giuseppe, 64
Dinwiddie, Gerda, 143
Di Santo, J. E., 204
Disciplines, development, 14-17, 19, 21
Di Tullio, Benigno, 224, 228
Diversion, 94, 153-54, 200
Donnici, Virgilio Luis, 180, 184
Dore, R. P., 27
Douglas, Jack D., 288
Drapkin, Israel, 44, 165, 169, 181, 223, 228, 231
Driedger, Otto, 187, 192
Drugs: abuse, 51, 68, 70, 71, 73, 85, 89, 93-94, 101, 111, 152, 154-55, 180, 189, 196, 202, 216, 217, 218, 237, 276; trafficking, 89, 93-94, 101, 154-55, 216, 217, 218, 225
Drummond, Lima, 173
Dubofsky, Melvyn, 142
Dubow, Fredrick L., 14, 25
Ducloux, L., 54
Dupreel, J., 52
Durkheim, Emile, 6, 24, 89
Duster, Troy, 276, 286

Echanove Trujillo, Carlos A., 252, 263
Ecology, 202
Economic and Social Council, 63, 64-65, 66, 69, 77, 78, 80
Economics, 120, 196, 224, 260-61, 281; determinism, 122, 123; exploitation, 84, 89, 92, 93
Education, 153, 211
Educational opportunity, 152
Edwards, J. Ll. J., 190
Ehrlich, Isaac, 290
El Kouri, Iza, 242
Ellenberger, Henri, 228
Elliott, Delbert S., 193, 280, 288, 289, 292
Elliott, Mabel, 114, 116
Embezzlement, 100, 101, 251, 253
Employment, 153, 156
Endocrinology, 174
Engels, Frederick, 121, 122, 132, 140, 141, 142, 143, 146
Ennis, Philip H., 287
Epistemology, 42, 125, 221
Erickson, Maynard L., 287, 292
Ericson, Richard, 187
Erlanger, H. S., 114, 117
Ermann, M. David, 288
Erra, C., 44
Ervin, Frank, 181
Escaff, Elias, 227, 229
Ethnic groups, 192, 194, 203
Ette, Marcel, 181
Etzioni, Amitai, 14, 25
European Committee on Crime Problems, 33
European Group for the Study of Deviance and Social Control, 34, 120
Evaluation, 13, 188, 209, 221, 225
Exner, Franz, 224, 228
Eysenck, H. J., 228

Family, 47, 73, 87, 90, 105, 108-9, 110-12, 153, 162
Faris, Robert E.L., 284
Farrell, R., 113, 116
Fattah, Ezzat, 192, 193, 205
Fayet, Ney, 185
Fejer, D., 206
Females and crime, 6, 23-27, 73, 99-115, 220, 279; in Britain, 102; in Canada, 102; interaction patterns, 108-13; international patterns, 100-106; role changes, 100, 102, 108-13; in United States, 100-101
Females and criminology, 23, 27, 99-100, 113, 115
Feminist movement, 99, 100, 102, 106-7, 108, 111-12
Fernandez Guardia, Ricardo, 245
Ferracuti, Franco, 181, 183, 230, 231, 285
Ferreira, Ovídio Inácio, 185
Ferri, Enrico, 40, 165, 173, 174, 178, 209, 226, 253
Figlio, Robert M., 282, 285, 288, 289, 290, 291, 296

Figueroa, Miguel Herrera, 152
Filibusters, 234
Fines, 134, 155, 251
Finestone, Harold, 284, 292
Fliegal, Frederick C., 29
Florentino, Braz, 173
Florenzano, R., 229
Florian, Eugenio, 265
Fontan Balestra, Carlos, 170
Forgery, 100, 108
Foucault, Michel, 138, 144, 287
Franco Guzman, Ricardo, 258
Francophone criminology, 187-88, 189-90, 191
Frankfurt Institute for Social Research, 123-24, 125, 126, 130, 134
Fraud, 70, 72, 100, 101, 102, 108, 253
Frechette, Marcel, 207
Freedman, Jonathan A., 284
Freeman, John, 181
Frei, Eduardo, 212
Freidenberg, Isaac, 164
Friday, Paul C., 21, 26
Friedman, Loreley, 228, 229, 231
Fromm, Erich, 123, 124, 141
Fully, Georges, 39, 55, 181
Furloughs, 155, 213, 220, 225, 254
Future of criminology, 18, 22-24, 35-36, 283

Gagnon, John H., 289
Gagnon, Rosette, 205
Gainer, Ronald L., 64
Galliher, John F., 284, 286, 289
Gamberg, Herbert, 143
Gammon, Mary Alice Byer, 202, 207
Gandy, John, 206
Gangs, 47, 237, 259, 280
García Maynes, Eduardo, 265
García Ramírez, Sergio, 254, 258, 263, 265, 266
Garofalo, Raffaele, 40, 173, 209, 226, 253
Gassin, Raymond, 59
Gatti, V., 47, 59
Gauld, Laurel, 206
Geis, Gilbert, 26, 284, 288, 290
Gemeinschaft, 234, 235, 236
Gendreau, Paul, 188, 202, 204
Genn, Hazel G., 288
Gesche, Bernardo, 228, 230, 231
Gibbens, Trevor, 39, 46, 59
Gibbons, Don C., 267, 284, 285, 290, 292
Gibbs, Jack P., 275, 287, 289, 290, 292
Giffen, P. J., 187, 190, 193, 202, 204, 205, 206
Gigeroff, Alex K., 190, 204
Giovanna, Carlo, 280
Glaser, Daniel, 228, 270, 284, 287, 289, 290, 293
Glassner, Barney, 284
Glick, R. M., 116
Glueck, Eleanor, 24, 228
Glueck, Sheldon, 13, 22, 24, 29, 42, 228
Godony, Josef, 64
Gokhale, S. D., 98
Gold, David A., 145
Gold, Martin, 287
Goldstein, Herman, 286, 293
Goldstein, Raul, 170
Gomberoff, Mario, 229
Gomes, Pablo Munhoz, 181
Gómez, Eusebio, 167, 168
Gómez, Irene, 230
Gómez Robleda, José, 257, 261, 262
Gonin, D., 47, 59
González-Berendique, Mario A., 152, 181, 226, 227, 227, 229, 230, 231
González Bustamante, Juan José, 265
González Murillo, Gonzalo, 247
Gonzalez Petit, Paulo Afonso, 181
Göppinger, H., 228
Gordon, David M., 146, 293
Gori, Pietri, 165
Gorostiaga, Emílio, 181
Gouldner, Alvin, 121-22, 141
Gove, Walter R., 293
Graham, Hilary, 285
Gramatica, Felippo, 52
Grasmick, Harold, 289, 294
Grassberger, R., 44
Graven, Jean, 40
Greenberg, David F., 126-27, 146, 282, 288, 290, 293
Greenway, W. K., 206

Griffiths, Curt, 202
Grillo, Elio Gomez, 152
Grimes, Ruth-Ellen, 201
Grispigni, F., 44
Grosman, Brian, 202
Grünhut, Max, 60
Grygier, Tadeusz, 191
Guerre, Manuel, 242
Guimarães, Ewerton Montenegro, 184
Guimaraes, Joacyr Bicalho, 178
Guzmán, Manuel, 230

Hackler, James C., 188, 202, 204, 205, 206, 207
Hagan, John, 188, 199, 202, 203, 207, 286
Hall, Jerome, 27, 158, 167
Hall, Stuart, 146
Hall Williams, John Eryl, 39, 46, 49, 56, 59, 181
Harrell, Rafael Ruiz, 181
Harring, Sidney L., 144
Harris, Anthony R., 113, 116, 287, 288
Haussling, J., 44, 58
Hawkins, E. R., 264
Hawkins, Gordon, 296
Hay, Douglas, 142, 146
Heidensohn, F., 166
Henderson, Charles R., 267, 284
Hepworth, Dorothy, 204
Herboso, Francisco J., 226
Hermassi, Elbaki, 96
Herrera, Marcos A., 164
Herrera Figueroa, Miguel, 152, 163, 164, 167, 168, 170
Hesse, Raybourn, 181
Heuyer, Georges, 44, 57, 228
Hill, G., 287, 288
Hindelang, Michael J., 287, 288, 293
Hinkle, Gisela, 284
Hinkle, Roscoe C., 284
Hippchen, Leonard J., 285
Hirschi, Travis, 280, 284, 288, 292, 293
Hirst, Paul, 132, 141
History, 7, 42, 267-69, 276, 277
Hobart, Charles W., 206
Hobsbawm, Eric, 127-28, 142
Hoffman, Dennis E., 285
Hogarth, John, 47, 59, 188, 190, 200, 203, 204, 207
Hogg, Russell, 137, 138, 144
Homicide, 47, 70, 72, 73, 89, 101, 105, 111, 194, 216-17, 234, 251, 253, 261, 262-63
Horkheimer, Max, 123, 124, 126, 141
Howard League for Penal Reform, 35, 53, 80
Hughes, H. Stuart, 27
Human rights, 66, 68, 77-78
Humphries, Drew, 120, 141
Hungria, Nelson Hoffbauer, 175, 176-77, 183, 184, 185, 186
Hurwitz, Stephan, 228

Ibor, Lopez, 157
Idiographic discipline, criminology as, 9, 11
Ignatieff, Michael, 129, 138, 143, 144
Imprisonment, 74-76, 90, 155, 242, 251-52
Imprisonment, alternatives to, 155-56, 214
Imprisonment rates, 216-17
Income, per capita, 73
Individual orientation, 31, 33, 133, 223-24
Individualization, 254
Industrialization, 11, 72, 73, 84, 88, 93, 106, 168, 235
Infant mortality, 73, 211
Ingenieros, Jose, 151, 165-67, 168, 170
Inquisition, 252
Institute of Criminal Anthropology, Genoa, 43
Institute of Statistics, 53
Institutionalization of criminology, 15-21, 22-24, 257
Institutes, criminological, 19, 38, 42-43, 52, 53, 55, 69, 83, 93, 160-63, 165-66, 177, 178, 180-81, 189-94, 198, 200-201, 202, 210, 214, 219, 220-21, 224, 240, 244, 257, 258, 278
Interactional approach, 33, 42
Interdisciplinary Group on Criminology, Brazil, 181-83

Interdisciplinary perspective, 7, 9, 15, 18
International Academy of Legal and Social Medicine, 53
International Association of Educators of Maladapted Youth, 52
International Association of Judges for Juveniles, 52
International Association of Magistrates for Juveniles, 52
International Association of Penal Law, 35, 51, 80
International Association of Workers with Maladjusted Children, 32
International Association of Youth Magistrates, 35
International Bureau for the Elimination of White Slavery, 53
International Catholic Union of Social Services, 53
International Center for Comparative Criminology, Montreal, 43, 189-90, 202
International Chiefs of Police, 35
International Commission of Criminal Police, 53
International Commission of Jurists, 35
International Conference of Catholic Charities, 53
International Conference of Societies for Encouragement of Mental Health, 53
International conferences, 31, 32, 33, 34, 50, 253
International congresses, 8, 37-38, 41-42, 45, 49-50, 51, 52, 66, 74, 78, 83, 84, 165, 220
International Council of Women, 53
International courses, 32, 44-45
International Court of Justice, United Nations, 67
International crime, 52, 70-74, 100-106
International criminal court, 67, 68
International Criminal Police Organizational (INTERPOL), 35, 52, 79, 102, 258
International Federation of High Police Officials, 53
International Federation of Senior Police Officers and Youth Magistrates, 32
International Labor Organization, 49, 50
International Penal and Penitentiary Foundation, 35, 51-52, 66
International Prisoners Aid Association, 35, 80
International Society for Criminology, 32, 37-49, 80; history, 37-39; and United Nations, 38, 49
International Society for Social Defense, 32, 35, 51, 52, 80
International Society of Criminal Prophylaxis, 37
International Sociological Association, 32, 34
International Union for Protection of Children, 52
Irini, Styllianoss, 208
Irurzun, Victor, 167, 170, 171
Irwin, John, 293
Izabuirre, Fray Alberto, 242

Jackson, George, 147
Jacobs, James B., 287
Jansson, Carl Gunnar, 193
Jaramillo, Gloria, 229, 230
Jayewardene, Cleobis, 191, 192
Jeffery, C. Ray, 289
Jilek, Wolfgang, 194, 205
Jiménez de Asúa, Luis, 167, 168, 170, 265
Jinesta, Ricardo, 241, 246, 248
Johansen, Eva, 181
Johnson, Elmer H., 25, 26, 274, 285
Johnson, John M., 288
Johnson, Stuart, 192
Journals, criminological, 41, 47-49, 50, 51, 52, 53, 80, 83, 93, 120-21, 160, 161, 165, 201, 270, 282
Juárez, Benito, 253
Judicial technicality, 178-80
Juvenile courts, 154, 194, 214, 258
Juvenile delinquency, 42, 43, 44, 46, 47, 51, 68, 94, 100, 101, 102, 182, 188, 189, 193, 219, 244

Kahn, Jacob, 181
Kaiser, Günther, 181
Karadima, Oscar, 229

Karah, Mustafa Abdul Majid, 64
Kassebaum, Gene, 287
Kautsky, Karl, 122
Kent, Jorge, 266
Kent, Victoria, 266
Khalifa, Ahmad M., 44, 64
Kibuka, Eric Paula, 89, 95
Kidnapping, 70, 151
Kinberg, Olof, 44, 57
King, Joan, 29
Kirchheimer, Otto, 134-35, 143, 147
Kitsuse, John T., 275, 286
Klare, J. J., 54
Klein, Doris, 108, 115
Klein, John F., 188, 202, 203, 204, 207
Klockars, Carl, 290, 293
Koenig, Daniel, 188, 203, 204
Kornhauser, Ruth Rosner, 294
Kos-Rabcewicz-Zubkowski, Ludwik, 191
Kranz, Heinrich, 157
Kress, June, 108, 115
Kretschmer, Ernst, 224, 262
Krohn, Marvin D., 289, 290, 294

Labeling theory, 14, 33, 100, 275, 276, 277
Lacassagne, Alejandro, 253
Lackner, Luis, 242, 244, 246
LaFare, Wayne R., 286
LaForest, L., 202, 206
Laignel-Lauastine, M., 265
Lambert, Leah R., 206
Lamers, M. E., 42
Landreville, P., 188, 204
LaPlante, Jacques, 191
Larceny, 100, 105, 108, 129, 216-17, 234, 236
Larsen, Donald, 205
Larson, Otto, 288
Lascoumes, P., 47, 59
Latin American Institute of United Nations for the Prevention of Crime and Treatment of Offenders (ILANUD), 240, 244
Latin American Society of Criminology, 44
Lauderdale, Pat, 289, 294
Lautt, Melanie, 192
Lavados, Ivan, 227
Law, 7, 11, 22, 23, 33, 40, 51, 86, 89, 90, 119, 123, 128, 130, 136, 139, 158, 160, 161, 162, 164, 166, 167, 173, 178, 178-80, 190, 195, 196, 202, 213, 252, 253-54, 270, 272, 276, 277, 281; reform, 179; schools, 151, 158, 159, 173, 174, 177, 178, 179, 180, 190, 221-22, 225; and social control, 7
Leal, Aureliano, 174
Learning disabilities, 188
LeBlanc, Marc, 188, 204, 207
Lee, John, 208
Lefton, Mark, 26
Legal perspective, 154, 158, 173, 174-77, 178-80, 190, 209, 241
Legal positivism, 158
Legal reform, 196, 219, 238-39, 242
Legal rights, 31, 46, 52, 77, 152, 255
Lejins, Peter, 39, 46, 56, 59, 181
Lemaine, Gerald, 25
Lenin, V. I., 122
Leon, Jeffrey S., 188, 203, 286
Letkeman, Peter, 203, 206, 207
Levene, Ricardo, 152, 167, 168, 169, 170
Levesque, René, 189
Lewin, Kurt, 221
Liazos, Alexander, 116
Lima, André Teixeira, 178
Linebaugh, Peter, 142
Lipton, Douglas, 290, 294
Llorente, Alberca, 157
Lomas, Roberto A. Teran, 167
Lombroso, Cesare, 40, 86, 165, 173, 174, 175, 209, 226, 253
Longitudinal studies, 278-79
López-Rey y Arroyo, Manuel, 64, 81, 169, 178, 181, 183, 228, 258
Loudet, Osvaldo, 164
Loureiro, Osman, 185
Lowenthal, Max, 142
Lowinson, Joyce, 181
Lukács, George, 122, 141
Lumpenproletariat, 125
Lundman, Richard L., 288
Lussier, Jean-Pierre, 189

Lynch, Jennifer, 205
Lyra, Roberta, 177, 178, 184, 185, 186

McCaghy, Charles H., 26
McCartney, James L., 284, 286
McCord, Joan, 157
McCord, William, 157
McDonald, Lynn, 193, 205, 287
Macedo, Sergio Rego, 178
McGrath, W. T., 204
Machado, José Alcantara, 174
McIntosh, Mary, 29
MacIver, Luis Cousino, 152
McKay, Henry, 275
Mackellar, M. L., 98
Mackenna, Benjamin Vicuna, 228
MacLeon, Roy, 25
MacNamara, Donal E. J., 58
McNaughton-Smith, Peter, 190, 204
Macro analysis, 8, 9, 10
Madden, Patrick G., 206
Maggiure, S., 179
Magnicide, 259-60, 264
Magulis, Mario, 170
Magundkar, M. S., 206
Mahony, Francis Joseph, 64
Mailloux, R. P., 42, 45, 46, 55
Maldonado, Angel Pacheco, 181
Maldonado, Horacio, 152
Malo Comacho, Gustavo, 258
Mann, Edward, 208
Mannheim, Hermann, 9, 18, 24, 26, 39, 44, 180, 228
Manning, Peter K., 181, 286, 290, 294
Manzanera, Luis Rodriquez, 152
Manzi, A., 176
Marabuto, P., 54
Marchiori, Hilda, 258, 265
Marcó Del Pont, Luis, 265
Marcopoulos, Mario, 152
Marcuse, Herbert, 123, 124, 125, 141
Mardones, J., 181
Marin, Encina, 181
Marsh, Robert M., 27
Martin, J. P., 264
Martin, Robert G., Jr., 97
Martindale, Don, 215, 227
Martinez, Victor Rene, 152
Martínez de Castro, Antonio, 265
Martinson, Robert, 290, 294
Marx, Karl, 30, 121-26, 128, 130, 132, 133, 135-36, 140, 141, 142, 143, 144, 145, 146; as humanist, 121-23, 133; as scientist, 121-23, 133
Marxism, 100, 120, 131-32, 281; critique, 121-23
Masculine criminal stereotype, 113-14
Mass media, 79, 85, 88, 153, 219, 235
Mathiesen, Th., 47, 59
Matthews, Catherine, 205
Matza, David, 228, 294, 295
Maurice, A., 188, 203
Mayer, Katia Luce, 205, 208
Maynes Puentes, Samuel, 259-60
Mayorca, J. M., 141
Meadows, A. J., 28
Mediation, 90, 94
Medical model, 166, 274, 275
Medical schools, 177
Medicine, 39, 44, 153, 159, 161, 162, 163, 164, 173, 174, 177, 178, 188, 210, 219, 221, 243, 244, 253, 256, 258
Medina, Gregorio Aramayo D., 181
Mednick, Saarnof, 181, 228, 289
Meier, Robert F., 284, 285, 288, 290, 292, 294, 295
Melossi, Dario, 135, 138, 143
Mendes, Antonio Evaristo, 184, 185
Mendes, Nelson Pizzotti, 152
Mendonca, Yolanda, 185
Menghile, C., 188, 204
Mental abnormality, 51, 52
Mental disorder, 192
Mercader, Ramón, 260
Mercado Villar, Olga, 170
Merkel, Peter H., 28
Merle, Béatrice, 48
Merleau-Ponty, Maurice, 124
Merritt, Richard L., 25, 28
Merton, Robert K., 17, 26, 142, 225, 275, 285
Methodology, 10, 13, 34, 47, 209, 223-24, 225, 277-79
Metzger, Albert, 64

Mexican Academy of Penal Sciences, 257
Mexican Society of Criminology, 257
Mexico, 251-63; history, 251-54
Mezger, Edmund, 179, 224
Migration, 73, 85, 88, 93, 152, 168, 211, 235, 236
Miguel, Jorge V., 164
Mileski, Maureen, 287
Miliband, Ralph, 144, 145
Miller, Walter B., 275, 276, 286, 289, 294, 295
Mills, C. Wright, 26
Milutinovic, M., 42, 44
Minority groups, 85, 203
Miranda Gallino, Rafael, 170
Mizushima, Keüch, 27
Models of criminology, 10-11, 21
Modernization, 10, 11, 19, 86-87, 89, 105, 108, 110, 235
Mohr, Hans, 187, 196, 197, 206
Mohr, J. J., 190, 204
Molina, Manuel Antonio, 247
Money, John, 181
Montague, Arthur, 207
Montenegro, Hernán, 229
Montero, Jorge A., 64, 242, 249
Moore, James J., 181
Moore, Wilbert E., 11, 25
Mora, Louis Castillon, 181
Moreno, Rafael, 258
Morris, Albert, 284, 294
Morton, Mary, 200
Motta, Cândido, 174
Mueller, Gerhard O.W., 12, 25, 81, 152, 169, 181, 226, 231
Muelling, Rudolph, 246
Mugford, Stephen K., 132, 141
Mujica, Dalia Marti, 181
Mulkay, Michael, 25
Mullin, Neil, 140, 145
Multidisciplinary approach, 7, 9, 15, 18, 40, 53, 158-59, 167, 182, 189, 190, 242, 283
Muñoz, Eduardo, 227, 229
Murphy, Brian C., 196, 205
Murphy, Fred J., 287
Naranjo, Claudio, 43, 229, 232
National Deviancy Conference, 120
Naqui, Khaleeg, 84
Náquira, Jaime, 229
Nefzaoui, Chadly M.A., 64
Neiderhoffer, Arthur, 276, 286
Neto, V. V., 116
Nettler, Gwynn, 190-91, 192, 204, 294
Neumann, Franz, 123
Neves, Akaor Metzker Countinho Serrano, 185
New Left, 121-23, 124, 125
Newman, Donald, 287
Newman, Elias, 167, 171
Newman, Graeme, 28, 287, 289, 290, 294
Nieva, Odilon, 152
Nocera, Juan B. Vitale, 160
Nogueira, Paulo Lúcio, 186
Noll, Alfons, 181
Nomothetic discipline, criminology as, 9, 11, 16-17, 19-22
Nordic Association of Criminalists, 32, 53
Nordic Council, 32
Normandeau, André, 189
Noronha, E. Magalhães, 185
Npka, Nwokocha K.U., 97
Núñez Chávez, Francisco, 257

Obando, Victor Manuel, 242
Oberschall, Anthony, 284
Obregon Loria, Rafael, 245
Occupation, criminology as, 15-17, 21-22, 23, 218, 240-41, 272, 273, 277
O'Connor, James, 145
Odekunle, 'Femi, 97
Offee, Claus, 145
Ohlin, Lloyd, 43, 47, 59, 228, 275, 276, 280, 286, 291, 295
Olden, John, 64
Ombudsmen, 188
Open institutions, 46, 254
Opolot, James S.E., 97
Opportunity theory, 115
Ormrod, Roger, 28
Ortiz, Liana, 229

Ortiz, Orlando, 265
Oscar Freire Institute, São Paulo, 55, 181
Ottenberger, Ana, 230
Ottenhof, R., 44, 58

Pablo de Tavira y Noriega, Juan, 257
Pabon, Elvia Velasquez, 181
Pad, E., 44
Pagano, Jose, 169
Palma, Roberta, 181
Panamerican Society of Criminology, 157
Pardon, 155, 213
Parker, Graham, 202, 208
Parlett, T.A.A., 196, 205
Parmelee, Maurice, 284
Parole, 79, 190, 195, 213, 239, 254
Parsons, Talcott, 28
Pashukanis, C. B., 139, 140, 145
Pasmaik, Jacobo, 229, 231
Pearce, Frank, 147
Peco, Jose, 164
Peimbert, Roberto, Jr., 263
Peixoto, Isadora Durval, 184
Peixoto, Julio Afrânio, 177, 184, 186
Penal institutions, 46, 74, 129, 134-35, 137-38, 155-56, 180, 188, 195, 197, 203, 214, 220, 238-39, 240, 241, 253, 254-56, 256, 277; world survey, 75-76
Penal nihilism, 175
Penal reform, 138, 213, 240, 253, 254-57
Peña-Núñez, Julio, 231
Pende, Nicola, 173, 224, 262
Penology, 51, 157, 158, 160, 161, 162, 175-76, 215, 254, 257
Pepin, P., 188, 204
Perceptions of crime, 16, 33, 87, 88, 274, 275
Pérez, Fernández, 258
Perrier, David, 187
Petersen, David M., 287
Pettinato, P., 54
Pimentel, Manuel Pedro, 173, 176, 180, 183
Pinatel, Jean, 39, 44, 46, 54, 55, 56, 57, 59, 60, 181, 228
Pīna y Palacious, Javier, 257, 258, 265
Pinto, Beatriz, 229
Pires, A., 204
Pirs, Susan, 206
Pitman, Ruth, 206
Piven, Francis S., 137, 144
Planning, 46, 66, 76-77, 152-53, 168, 195, 212, 220, 244
Platt, Anthony, 120, 125-25, 141, 142, 145, 147, 286
Polanyi, Karl, 136, 143
Police, 94, 154, 188, 189, 192, 193, 195, 196, 197, 203, 214, 215, 237, 238, 240, 253, 258, 272, 277; professionalism, 78; research, 43, 218
Policy, 69, 154, 160, 161, 163, 194-95, 197-98, 212, 213, 235, 244, 245, 253-54, 257, 282; and criminology, 18, 19, 32, 33, 34, 51, 73, 76-77; and research, 69, 194-95
Political economy, 122, 124
Political repression, 91, 119-20, 121, 127
Political science, 7, 272
Political systems, 7, 12, 16, 31, 34, 91-92, 102, 240
Porchat, Reynaldo, 174
Porterfield, Austin L., 287
Positive school, 165, 209, 215, 253
Positivism, 99, 121, 125-26, 175-76, 215, 253, 274, 275, 277
Poulantzas, Nicos, 138, 139, 144, 145
Povina, Alfredo, 163
Power, 85, 86, 100, 237
Prediction, 40, 47
Preston, W., 142
Prevention, 13, 18, 42, 46, 47, 49, 50, 57, 65, 66, 67, 70, 76-77, 79, 84, 89, 90-91, 152-53, 154-55, 158, 163, 168, 188, 196, 202, 209, 213, 242, 254, 257, 259, 261
Prieto, Maria Luisa, 152
Prins, A., 51
Prison Discipline Society, 138
Prisons, Standard Minimum Rules, 74-78, 254
Probation, 79, 155, 214, 221, 239, 242, 272
Problete, Manuel, 229
Professional crime, 85, 113-14

Professionalism, 15, 17, 18, 19-20, 21, 269, 276
Pronovost, L., 204
Prostitution, 79, 101, 102, 114, 129, 251, 276
Protest movements, 119, 124-25, 127-28
Prus, Robert, 208
Przeworski, Adam, 10, 24
Psychiatry, 22, 40, 42, 120, 156-57, 160, 174, 175, 176, 178, 190, 210, 213, 224, 256, 269, 277
Psychoanalysis, 40, 42
Psychology, 22, 32, 40, 42, 46, 79, 160, 161, 163, 167, 178, 188, 209, 210, 218, 221, 222, 224, 243, 256, 257, 269, 272, 275, 282
Psychopathy, 152, 156-57, 165, 213-14, 219
Puente, Samuel Maynes, 264, 265
Punishment, 215, 251, 277, 279

Quinney, Richard, 26, 125, 126, 127, 133-34, 141, 142, 144, 147, 290, 295
Quintessential criminal, 113-14
Quiroz Cuarón, Alfonso, 254, 257, 258, 263, 264, 265
Quiroz Cuarón, Rául, 261, 265
Quiros, Shanti, 242

Race, 194, 203, 211, 278, 279
Radical criminology, 6, 34, 119-41, 221, 227, 281; critical version, 123-30, 140; definition, 119-20, 125; materialist version, 130-39; structural version, 123, 139-41
Radzinowicz, Leon, 23, 26, 29, 223, 228
Rajagopal, P. R., 64
Raymondis, Louis-Marie, 55
Receiving stolen property, 100, 102
Recidivism, 214, 215, 218, 221
Reckless, Walter C., 26, 225, 228
Reform, 11, 13, 16, 19, 31, 125-26, 162, 215, 234, 268, 270-71, 275, 280
Regions of world, 73
Reid, Sue Titus, 285
Reimer, David J., 287
Reimer, Joan, 230
Reintegration of prisoners, 155-56
Reiss, Albert J., Jr., 286, 288
Release from prison, 155, 156
Research, criminological, 14, 18-20, 21-22, 35, 42, 44, 151, 157-58, 178-79, 181, 187-88, 189, 190, 191, 192, 195-202, 209, 222, 223-25, 242, 244-45, 257, 269, 283; barriers to, 244-45; and development, 78-79; and policy, 69, 194-95
Research Committee for Sociology of Deviance and Social Control, 34
Resocialization of criminals, 13
Restitution, 225
Revolutionary potential of crime, 131, 132
Rezende, Astolpho, 184
Ribeiro, Fernando Bastos, 177
Ribeiro, Leonído, 38, 184
Richard, Patricia, 229
Richardson, James F., 286
Richman, Alex, 202, 206
Riera, Argenis, 141
Rizkalla, Samir, 205
Robbery, 70, 72, 73, 84, 91, 100, 102, 111, 115, 129, 216-17, 251, 253, 259, 263
Robert, Philippe, 47, 49, 59
Roberts, C. Clifton, 29
Robertson, Roland, 29
Robinson, Ronald W., 29
Roby, Pamela A., 286
Rocco, Arturo, 176, 177, 179
Rock, Paul, 29
Rodd, David J., 288
Rodrigues, Raimundo Nina, 174, 184, 185, 186
Rodríguez Cabo, Matilde, 257
Rodríguez Manzanera, Luis, 253, 258, 263, 264
Roesch, Ronald, 188, 204
Rojas, F., 141
Rokkan, Stein, 14, 25, 28
Roles of criminologists, 5, 15-18, 21-22, 46
Roman, Miguel Figueroa, 167, 168
Romero, Leo M., 152
Rootman, Irving, 202, 206

Rosenberg, Gertrude, 205, 208
Rosett, Arthur, 287
Ross, Robert, 188, 202, 204
Rossi, Peter K., 289
Roth, Guenther, 29
Roth, Loren H., 289
Rothman, David, 129, 143
Roumagnac, Carlos, 253
Roy, Chunilal, 194, 205
Roy, Prodipto, 29
Rozes, Simone Andrée, 64
Rubenstein, Jonathan, 286
Rubin, Robert, 181
Ruiz Funes, Mariano, 265
Ruiz Harrell, Rafael, 258
Rusche, George, 130, 134-35, 143, 147
Ruzuela, Vicente Louis Alberto, 152

Sáez, Felipe, 230
Sagarin, Edward, 26, 30, 284
Salhadar, Saladh El-Din, 64
Salles, Romeu De Aleida, Jr., 185
Salvation Army, 53
Samenow, Stanton E., 285
Sánchez Galindo, Antonio, 258, 265
Sanctions, 152, 155-56, 251, 275
Sandoval, Luis, 228, 231
San Martín, Germán, 230
Santos, Ary, 185
Santos, J.W. Seixas, 184
Santos, Theophilo De Azeredo, 180
Sartre, Jean-Paul, 124
Saveland, Walter, 206
Scandinavian criminology, 32-33
Scandinavian Research Council for Criminology, 33
Scheerer, Sebastian, 24-25
Scheff, Thomas J., 286
Schuessler, Karl, 288
Schur, Edwin M., 275, 295
Schweitzer Speisky, Miguel, 64
Schwendinger, Herman, 145, 148
Schwendinger, Julia, 145, 148
Science and criminology, 14-24, 86-87, 125-26, 131, 158, 242, 271-72
Scormaiendri, Disnei Francisco, 152
Scott, Joseph W., 170
Security Council, United States, 63
Seelig, Ernst, 228
Seidman, Robert B., 291
Sellin, Thorsten, 16, 22, 24, 26, 39, 40, 210, 228, 288, 289, 296
Sentencing, 46, 47, 52, 77, 155-56, 163, 202, 213, 221, 225, 242, 254
Sex offenses, 70, 190, 216-17, 220, 251, 253, 263
Sex status: and crime, 262-63, 278; change in roles, 102, 110-11
Shah, Saleem A., 181, 289
Shannon, Lyle W., 288
Sharma, N., 106, 116, 117
Shaw, Clifford, 275
Shearing, Clifford D., 188, 203, 205
Sheldon, W. H., 262
Shim Han, Young-Hee, 144
Shirley, Mary M., 287
Shoham, Shlomo, 181, 228
Short, James F., Jr., 276, 286, 289, 292, 295
Shover, Neal, 286, 295
Silberman, Charles E., 289
Silva, Juary C., 185
Silverman, Robert, 194, 202, 205
Simon, Frances H., 47, 59
Simon, Rita J., 102, 103-4, 106, 107, 115, 116, 117, 288
Simon, William, 289
Simondi, Mario, 36
Singh, Ramananda, 64
Sinoir, G., 54
Skipper, James K., Jr., 26
Skolnick, Jerome H., 29, 286
Skyjacking, 57
Small, Shirley, 202, 206
Smart, Carol, 108, 116, 118
Smart, Reginald G., 181, 202, 206
Smelser, Neil J., 30
Smith, Douglas A., 288
Smuggling, 88, 89, 93-94, 128, 237
Soares, F., 185
Soares, Macedo, 173
Soares, Orlando, 186
Sobera De La Flor, Higinio, 260
Social change, 6, 11, 72, 89, 93, 110, 125, 234-35, 240

Social class, 113, 120, 122, 123, 126-27, 130, 132, 133, 234, 235, 269, 276, 278, 279
Social control, 7-8, 31, 34, 35, 47, 73, 85, 87, 93, 131, 134-35, 202, 277; and criminology, 7-8, 16-17, 31-32
Social defense, 46, 63, 242
Social Defense Research Institute, United Nations, 69
Social Development Commission, United Nations, 63, 78
Socialism, 122, 212; and criminology, 11, 13, 33
Social Sciences and Humanities Research Council, Canada, 197-98, 200
Social work, 120, 160, 161, 209, 221, 241, 243, 256, 257, 267, 269
Society of Comparative Legislation, 53
Society of Criminal Anthropology, Psychiatry, Medicine, and Legal Medicine, Brazil, 174
Society of Criminalistics, Legal Medicine, and Criminology, Chile, 219, 220
Society of Criminal Science and Legal Medicine, Argentina, 163-64
Society of Forensic Medicine and Criminology, Brazil, 174
Sociocultural perspective, 195-196
Sociocultural systems, 7, 10, 11-13, 15, 16
Sociology, 7, 9, 13-14, 19-20, 21, 22, 32, 33, 34, 40, 42, 139, 160, 161, 163, 164, 167, 174, 175, 176, 178, 179, 190, 191, 195, 209, 210, 218, 219, 221, 222, 243, 244, 268, 272, 273, 275, 277, 281, 282, 283
Soler, Sebastian, 170
Sophocles, 92
Sorhegui Mato, Silvino Julián, 64
Soueif, M., 181
Souza Lima, Agostinho José, 173
Sparks, Richard F., 288
Speisky, Miguel Schweitzer, 228
Spencer, Robert F., 25
Spitzer, Steven, 131, 132, 143, 144
Spouse abuse, 90, 220
Srole, Leo, 225
Stalin, Joseph, 122, 124
Stampa Braun, José Maria, 179, 183
Stanciu, V. V., 265
Standard Minimum Rules, United Nations, 74-78, 254
Stanley, Paul R.A., 205
State, the, 122-23, 133-35, 281
Staub, Hugo, 224
Stead, Philip J., 58
Steffensmeier, Darrell, 107, 116
Stolzman, James, 143
Storer, Norman W., 20, 26
Stradtbeck, Fred L., 276, 286, 295
Strasburg, Paul A., 289
Strecker, Margaret, 206
Structural variables, 100, 107, 108, 111
Strumpf, Friedrick, 157
Stürup, G., 44
Subculture, 101, 114, 203, 277; of masculinity, 114; of violence, 101, 114, 220
Sudnow, David, 287
Summary justice, 252
Susini, Jean, 48, 49
Susrata, 92
Sutherland, Edwin H., 114, 115, 116, 117, 228, 275, 285, 295
Suzuki, Yoshio, 64
Swanson, Guy E., 13, 25
Swigert, V., 113, 116
Sykes, Gresham M., 26, 228, 290, 295
Sylvester, Sawyer F., Jr., 29, 30
Szabo, Denis, 13, 25, 39, 43, 44, 46, 57, 181, 189, 228

Tabler, Carlos Hugo, 152
Tacia, Odette, 211, 226
Takagi, Paul, 145, 147
Tarde, Gabriel, 173
Tardif, Guy, 189, 204
Taylor, Ian, 36, 120, 130, 131, 132, 133, 134, 141, 143, 147, 148
Taylor, Laurie, 29, 120, 141, 285
Technical assistance, 65, 69, 74
Technology, 103, 105, 108
Teeters, Negley K., 214-15, 226, 227, 232
Teevan, James, 202, 205

Tena Ramírez, Felippe, 265
Tepperman, Lorne, 193, 202, 205
Terrorism, 43, 57, 68, 151, 156, 216-17
Teune, Henry, 10, 24
Theft, 70, 72, 89-90, 253
Thelin, H., 44
Theory, criminology, 18, 99-100, 113-15, 269, 275-77, 279-83
Therborn, Göran, 126, 142
Thernstrom, Stephen, 143
Thieghi, Osvaldo N., 152, 167
Thomas, Charles W., 286
Thomas, J., 229
Thompson, Augusto, 186
Thompson, E. P., 128, 142
Thornberg, Terence, 282, 285, 290, 291, 296
Tittle, Charles R., 275, 288
Toch, Hans, 295
Tolerance, 88
Tongue, Archer, 181
Topinard, Paul, 14
Torres, Dionísio, G., 181
Tourism, 94, 168
Traffic offenses, 217, 218, 237
Training of personnel, 46, 69, 77, 154, 159, 160, 163, 214, 223, 244, 255, 256, 257, 259
Transnational criminology, 6, 9-11, 15, 17-18, 20-21, 22, 23-24
Treatment, 46, 47, 50-51, 65, 79, 154, 163, 166, 188, 196, 202, 239, 254, 255, 281
Trepanier, Jean, 189
Troncoso, Alvaro, 230
Trotsky, Leon, 260
Trusteeship Council, United Nations, 63
Tubenchiek, G., 185
Turk, Austin T., 143, 295
Turner, R. E., 190, 204
Tushnet, Mark, 145
Typologies, 127, 215, 261-62

Unemployment, 88, 91, 108, 152, 212, 218
UNESCO, 44, 49, 50, 68
UNICEF, 68, 211
Union of Radical Criminologists, 120
United Nations, 6, 12-13, 32, 38, 44, 49-51, 63-80, 83-84, 181, 225, 240, 242, 244
United Nations congresses, 66, 68, 76, 83-84, 168, 220, 244
United States of America, 267-83
Universities, 43, 45-46, 87, 89, 90, 120, 151, 158-60, 162-63, 165, 167, 178, 179, 189-93, 196, 198, 200, 202, 209, 210, 214, 215, 220-22, 224, 225, 241, 242-44
Urbanization, 11, 72, 73, 84, 87, 88, 93, 152, 211, 217, 235, 236, 244
Urrutia, Manuel, 230

Vagrancy, 136-38, 213
Valenzuela, Manuel D., 226
Valier, Ivan, 25, 29, 30
Values, 47, 162, 167, 271-72, 275
Van Bemmelen, J. M., 55
Van den Haag, Ernest, 275, 290
Van Hamel, G. A., 51
Van Nieuwenhuijze, C.A.O., 10-11, 25
Vargas, Eduard, 247
Vargas, Heber Scares, 180
Vargas Gene, Joaquin, 242
Vásquez De Coronado, Juan, 233
Vassali, G., 44
Vaughan, Diane, 289
Veiga De Carvallo, Hilario, 265
Vengeance, crimes of, 85
Vente, Juan Carlos Garcia, 164
Verde, Ved P., 81
Verdun-Jones, Simon, 192, 202
Verin, Jacques, 39
Vernet, R. P., 54
Versele, Severin Carlos, 181
Vervaeck, L., 54
Vicarious experience and criminology, 5-6
Victimization, 42, 70, 72, 73, 120, 132, 193, 202, 211, 220, 254, 259-60, 278
Vila, Carolos, 230
Vilanova, Antonio Carlos, 177
Villarreal, Homero, 258
Villemez, Wayne L., 288
Vincent, Claude L., 208

Viola, G., 262
Violence, 100, 101, 102, 105, 111, 114, 157, 180, 182, 194, 201, 202, 253, 259, 278, 279
Viveros, Ana, 229
Vold, George B., 228
Volunteers, 197
Von Hirsch, Andrew, 290
Von Liszt, Franz, 51
Voss, Harwin L., 288

Waite, Emily, 289
Waldo, Gordon P., 275, 287
Walker, William, 234
Waller, Irvin, 190, 204, 208
Waller, Willard, 264
Walton, Paul, 130, 131, 132, 133, 134, 141, 143, 147, 148
War, 84, 86, 91, 234-35
Ward, David A., 287
Warner, R. Stephen, 30
Wasson, David K., 205
Webb, Jim R., 204
Webb, Vincent J., 285
Weber, Max, 29, 139
Weinberg, S. Kirson, 97
Weingart, Peter, 25
Weinstein, Graciela, 230
Weinstein, Luis, 229
Weiss, J. G., 108, 115, 116
Weiss, Robert, 144
Wellford, Charles, 288
Werkentin, Falco, 145
West, D. J., 47, 59
West, Gordon, 200
Wetzel, Hans, 157
Wheeler, Stanton, 26, 194, 205, 269-70, 284
White, W. J., 206
White collar offenses, 68, 83, 84, 85, 105, 180, 278, 279
Whitehead, Paul, 195, 202, 205, 206
Wickwar, Hardy, 80, 81
Wilkins, James L., 200, 206
Wilkins, Leslie T., 192, 228
Wilks, Judith, 290, 294
Willett, T., 47, 59
Wilner, Daniel, 287
Wilson, James Q., 275, 290, 295
Wilson, Nanci Koser, 116, 117
Wines, Enoch C., 253, 263
Wise, Edward M., 81
Witmer, Helen L., 287
Wolfgang, Marvin E., 21, 26, 47, 59, 181, 189, 192, 282, 285, 288, 289, 290, 291, 296
Women: consciousness of, 107-8; in labor force, 99, 100-101, 105, 106, 108, 110-12; personality factors, 101; prisoners, 108, 197. *See also* Females and crime
Wood, Arthur L., 97
Woolgar, S. W., 14, 25
Workhouses, 134, 137
World crime survey, United Nations, 69-74, 84
World Health Organization, 49, 50-51
World Mental Health Federation, 53
World regions, 11-13
World Union for Protection of Children and of Adolescents, 52
World War II as bench mark, 6, 11, 18, 19, 32, 274-83
World Youth Assembly, 53
Wormith, Steve, 192
Wright, Eric Olin, 148
Wurtenberger, T., 44

Yanagimot, Masaharu, 97
Yeager, Peter C., 291
Yeudall, Lorne, 188, 203
Yip, Candace, 206
Yip, Yat-Hoong, 64
Yochelson, Samuel, 285
Young, Jock, 129, 130, 131, 132, 133, 134, 141, 143, 147, 148

Zaffaroni, Eugenio Raul, 152
Zamorano, Manuel, 228
Zay, Nicholas, 193, 205
Zerpa, Dora, 152
Zilboorg, Gregory, 39
Zimring, Franklin E., 296

ABOUT THE CONTRIBUTORS

AYUSH MORAD AMAR: As director of the Latin American Office of the International Council on Alcohol and Addictions, Amar's major activity is the promotion of research on drugs and criminality in Latin America. In addition, he serves as professor of forensic medicine at the University of São Paulo, professor at the São Paulo Police Academy, and medical director of the Division of Toxicology and Forensic Medicine of the Oswald Cruz Hospital. His extensive international activities have included service as visiting professor at the universities of Venezuela, Peru, and Paraguay. His publications include several books and more than 250 studies.

WILLIAM CLIFFORD is director of the Australian Institute of Criminology. He was formerly director of the United Nations Crime Prevention and Criminal Justice Programs; executive secretary, Fourth U.N. Congress on the Prevention of Crime and Treatment of Offenders; senior advisor for the United Nations Asia and Far East Institute for the Prevention of Crime and Treatment of Offenders, Japan; United Nations Inter-Regional Advisor of Social Planning, University of Zambia; and director, Social Development, Cyprus.

PEDRO R. DAVID: Doctorate of jurisprudence and social science, National University of Tucuman (1956); Ph.D. in sociology, Indiana University (1962); and doctorate of political science, John F. Kennedy University, Buenos Aires. David is chairman of the Department of Sociology, University of New Mexico; professor of sociology at the Law School of the University of Buenos Aires: and vice-president of the John F. Kennedy University, Buenos Aires. He has lectured extensively in the Americas and Europe. Among his numerous scholarly publications are *The World of the Burglar* (1974) and *Sociologia Juridica* (1980).

PAUL FRIDAY: Ph.D. in sociology, University of Wisconsin (1970); M.A., University of Wisconsin (1966) and University of Stockholm (1968). Now professor at Western Michigan University, Friday has been a visiting fellow at Cambridge University and visiting professor at Wilhelms University, Münster, and the University of Stockholm. Participating in a number of international conferences on criminology, he has published in the areas of comparative criminology, theory, youth crime, and shock probation.

ANTONIO SANCHEZ GALINDO: An attorney-at-law, Sanchez Galindo is the head of the Department of Coordinated Services of Prevention and Social Readaptation, the State of Jalisco. His career experience includes director of prevention and social readaptation, the State of Mexico; director of the North Preventive Jail of Mexico City; head of the Pharmacodendency Program for juveniles in the State of Guerrero; and advisor for the "L" Federal Legislature. He is the author of more than a hundred publications, some of which are included in the bibliography following his chapter on the criminology of Mexico.

MARCO A. GONZÁLEZ-BERENDIQUE: Professor of legal medicine since 1960 and professor of criminology since 1973, School of Law, University of Chile, González-Berendique has served as professor of criminology in the academies for higher police officers, director, Institute of Criminology of the Chilean prison service, and director of the Institute of Criminology, University of Panama, and has been very active in international conferences and United Nations affairs. He was the founder and first president of the Panamerican Association of Criminology (1972-1973) and of the Chilean Society of Criminology, Social Psychiatry and Criminalistics (1979 to date). His publications include the textbook *Psicología Jurídica* and many articles on penology and criminology.

JIM HACKLER: Professor at the University of Alberta, Hackler obtained his Ph.D. in sociology at the University of Washington (1965). Active in the leadership of a number of professional associations, he has been president of the Canadian Association for the Advancement of Research in Criminology and Criminal Justice (1973-1975), the Western Association of Sociology and Anthropology (1973), and the Section on Deviance and Social Control, International Sociological Association (1974-1978). In addition to *The Prevention of Youthful Crime: The Great Stumble Forward* (1978), he has published extensively on criminological research, prevention, delinquency, and theory.

ELMER H. JOHNSON: Ph.D. in sociology, University of Wisconsin (1950). Johnson has served from assistant professor to professor, North Carolina State University at Raleigh (1949-1966); assistant director of the North Carolina Prison Department on academic leave (1958-1960); and professor of sociology and criminal justice, Center for the Study of Crime, Delinquency, and Corrections, Southern Illinois University at Carbondale (1966 to date). Author of *Crime, Correction, and Society*, 4th ed. (1978) and *Social Problems of Urban Man* (1973), he has published considerably on correctional issues, criminological theory, the community and criminal justice, and comparative criminology.

ROBERT F. MEIER: Ph. D., University of Wisconsin. Meier has been assistant professor of social ecology at the University of California at Irvine and is presently associate professor of sociology at Washington State University. His interests include criminological theory, processes of deviance and social control, and white-collar crime. His publications include *White-Collar Crime: Offenses in Business, Politics and the Professions*, co-editor with Gilbert Geis (1977); editor of *Theory in Criminology: Contemporary Views* (1977); and *Sociology of Deviant Behavior*, co-author with Marshall B. Clinard.

JORGE A. MONTERO: Law degree, University of Costa Rica (1949). Professor of civil law, University of Costa Rica (1950); professor of human rights, School of Law, University of Costa Rica; professor of penitentiary law and legislation for minors, University Center of Cartago; advisor to Managerial Council Center for Democratic Studies of Latin America since 1960, deputy to Legislative Assembly of Costa Rica (1962-1966); first secretary of Legislative Assembly (1962) and vice-president (1965); vice-president of First Panamerican Parliament, Lima, Peru (1965); president, Commission of Social Affairs of Legislative Assembly (1966); member of Superior Council of Social Defense of Costa Rica (1971); home secretary of Costa Rica (1973-1974); vice-president of Committee for Prevention and Control of Crime, United Nations (1974-1978); director, Latin American Institute for Prevention of Crime and Treatment, United Nations, since 1975; director of journal *Ilanud al Dia*. He has written numerous journal articles on issues of penitentiary and penal justice affairs.

GERHARD O.W. MUELLER: J.D., University of Chicago (1953), LL.M., Columbia University (1954), Dr. Juris honoris causa, Royal Swedish University at Uppsala (1971). Mueller was professor of Law at West Virginia University (1955-1958) and at City University of New York (1958 to date). While preparing his chapter, he was chief of the Crime Prevention and Criminal Justice Branch, United Nations, in Vienna. Currently, he is with the School of Criminal Justice, Rutgers University, Newark, New Jersey. Among his publications are *International Criminal Law* (1965), *Criminal Law and Procedure* (1965), *Comparative Criminal Procedure* (1969), and *Sentencing Process and Purpose* (1977). Jointly with Dr. Freda Adler, he received the Beccaria Medal in Gold.

JEAN PINATEL: Doctor of laws, University of Paris (1935). Pinatel's career has been varied: magistrate (1937), inspector (1941), and general inspector of administration (1951) in the Ministry of Justice; chair in applied criminology, Institute of Criminology, the Law Faculty of Paris (1952-1973); and visiting professor, University of Montreal (1963 and 1967). He was a member of the Scientific Council, Council of Europe (1962-1970); served as secretary-general (1950-1972) and then as president (1973-1978) of the International Society of Criminology; and has received the Laureate of the Institute of France. His publications include *Elementary Treatise of Penitentiary Science and Social*

Defense (1950); *Criminology*, 3d ed. (1975); a work on Etienne De Greeff (1967); and *The Criminogenic Society* (1971).

ROBERT WEISS is an assistant professor, University of Houston at Clear Lake City, Texas. He was awarded a Ph.D. in sociology (1980) by Southern Illinois University at Carbondale. His research interests are the evaluation of the American private police, the process of defining behaviors as criminal, and crime control, with particular reference to socioeconomic and political systems. He was formerly director of the high school at Ohio State Reformatory, Mansfield.

NANCI KOSER WILSON: Ph.D. in sociology, University of Tennessee (1972). Wilson has taught at Central Missouri State University and, since 1972, at Southern Illinois University at Carbondale where she is now an associate professor at the Center for the Study of Crime, Delinquency, and Corrections. Her publications usually focus on women as offenders, as prisoners, or as criminologists.

FRANCISCO CANESTRI CEDEÑO

While developing the manuscript that would have been the chapter on the criminology of Venezuela, Francisco Canestri Cedeño died on October 31, 1980. Fluent in Spanish, French, English, Italian, and Portuguese, he was active in the affairs of international criminology as a delegate of Venezuela to UNESCO; participated in numerous courses of the International Society of Criminology and the International Society of Social Defense; and served as secretary and member of the executive committee of the International Center of Criminal Biology and Legal Medicine, São Paulo, Brazil.

The bridging of theory and practice—the underlying theme of his professional career—is illustrated by his numerous articles, books, and manuals in penal law, juvenile justice, criminalistics, prison and police administration, and criminological theory. Similarly, he served as a professor in both universities and educational institutes operated by action agencies. He was a professor on the Faculty of Law, Central University of Venezuela (1963-1976); professor of criminology and penology, Catholic University "Andres Bello" (1968-1969 and 1974-1976); and invited professor at the University of Pau, France (1977, 1978, 1979). Professional service in Venezuela also included the School of Penitentiary Studies of the Ministry of Justice, the School for Technical Personnel of the Judicial Police, the School of Officers of the Integrated Armed Forces, and the Academy of the National Police.

The breadth of his career is suggested by some of his professional experiences: member of the Commission on Prevention of Delinquency (1963-1967); director of the Institute of Penal and Criminological Sciences, Central University of Venezuela (1966-1967); chief of the section on criminology and penitentiary science of that institute (1967-1972 and 1974); and director of the School of Law, Central University of Venezuela (1969-1971).

Professor Cedeño obtained his degree in law in 1960 from Central University of Venezuela. Thereafter, he studied criminal law at the Institute of Criminology, University of Paris, where he submitted the thesis, "The Administration of the Protection of Minors in Venezuela and Other Countries of Latin America." At the Institute of Police of the Prefecturate of Paris, he earned a certificate for advanced studies in policing and criminalistics; his thesis was on "Police and Prostitution." In 1966 he participated in courses on correctional administration, jail management, probation, and parole conducted by the U.S. Department of Justice.

Francisco Canestri Cedeño was one of the most well known criminologists of Latin America and will continue to be so regarded.

Elmer H. Johnson